T0339837

How to Write about Economics and Public Policy

How to Write about Economics and Public Policy

Katerina Petchko
National Graduate Institute for Policy Studies, Tokyo, Japan

ACADEMIC PRESS
An imprint of Elsevier

Academic Press is an imprint of Elsevier
125 London Wall, London EC2Y 5AS, United Kingdom
525 B Street, Suite 1650, San Diego, CA 92101, United States
50 Hampshire Street, 5th Floor, Cambridge, MA 02139, United States
The Boulevard, Langford Lane, Kidlington, Oxford OX5 1GB, United Kingdom

Notices

Knowledge and best practice in this field are constantly changing. As new research and experience
broaden our understanding, changes in research methods, professional practices, or medical
treatment may become necessary.

Practitioners and researchers must always rely on their own experience and knowledge in
evaluating and using any information, methods, compounds, or experiments described herein.
In using such information or methods they should be mindful of their own safety and the safety
of others, including parties for whom they have a professional responsibility.

To the fullest extent of the law, neither the Publisher nor the authors, contributors, or editors,
assume any liability for any injury and/or damage to persons or property as a matter of products
liability, negligence or otherwise, or from any use or operation of any methods, products,
instructions, or ideas contained in the material herein.

Library of Congress Cataloging-in-Publication Data
A catalog record for this book is available from the Library of Congress

British Library Cataloguing-in-Publication Data
A catalogue record for this book is available from the British Library

ISBN: 978-0-12-813010-0

For information on all Academic Press publications
visit our website at https://www.elsevier.com/books-and-journals

Working together
to grow libraries in
developing countries

www.elsevier.com • www.bookaid.org

Publisher: Candice Janco
Acquisition Editor: J. Scott Bentley
Editorial Project Manager: Susan Ikeda
Production Project Manager: Anusha Sambamoorthy
Cover Designer: Victoria Pearson

Typeset by SPi Global, India

To Andrew, who gave me so much to think about. Without that, I would have finished this book in half the time.

Contents

Preface

TARGET AUDIENCE FOR THIS BOOK

This book is for graduate students from both English-speaking and non-English-speaking countries, who are studying economics, public policy, public administration, public affairs, public finance, or policy analysis in English and who seek guidance on designing and completing a research study in their chosen area. It is especially relevant for students who are not familiar with professional research writing in economics and public policy.

This book also serves the needs of undergraduate students majoring in economics or public policy, particularly in programs that emphasize research. Students in such programs will find many useful suggestions for conducting research in economics and public policy and preparing a high-quality research paper.

Many issues covered in this book may appeal to a broader audience, including graduate students of management, sociology, and political science, particularly to those who are new to graduate study and who do not have a strong background in disciplinary research. The material covered in this book is also appropriate for novice researchers working in public-policy-related fields who would like to improve their proficiency in disciplinary English.

This book can be used for self-directed learning, as a reference, or as a text in a writing course for graduate students.

PURPOSES OF THIS BOOK

This book has been written for graduate students in public policy and economics with three purposes in mind. The first purpose is to familiarize students who are new to graduate study with the basics of research in public policy and economics. To achieve this purpose, the book describes quantitative and qualitative approaches to research; outlines options for writing a research proposal and a research paper; and makes suggestions for reading, analyzing, and evaluating academic literature.

The second purpose of the book is to familiarize students with the expectations of those who will be evaluating their work—professors, journal editors, and more experienced colleagues. This is achieved by providing an explicit description of the elements, features, and structural arrangement patterns that readers of economics and public policy papers expect to find in a research paper.

The third purpose of the book is to show how professional authors employ a range of rhetorical, linguistic, and organizational devices to meet their readers' expectations. To achieve this purpose, the book provides and analyzes a diverse set of examples from papers in economics and public policy, showing how authors accomplish various communicative goals such as justifying a study, explaining its motivation, or describing its contribution, and how they make their arguments persuasive to their colleagues. By analyzing professional writing in their research field, students can improve their own understanding of disciplinary discourse and their own writing.

HOW THIS BOOK CAME ABOUT

This book has evolved out of my own educational, teaching, and research experience. Initially, I wrote parts of it in response to my nearly decade-long experience as a graduate student in public policy and public administration and, later, in applied linguistics. The initial ideas were further developed and clarified as I researched academic writing to create courses, materials, and programs for my graduate students and as I began to teach.

My earlier experiences as a graduate student in public policy and public administration had been marked by a great deal of frustration at the inability to find a suitable textbook that would help me, a non-native speaker of English unfamiliar with Western-style education, to understand what was required of me as a graduate student writer, and to produce the kind of writing that my supervisors would find acceptable. I learned to write research papers in those programs in an ad hoc manner, by collecting and analyzing samples of professional writing that I found clear and persuasive. It was only later that I was able, as a doctoral student in applied linguistics, to look back at those earlier experiences in a more systematic manner and to find a name for what I had been doing—I was essentially acquiring a metacognitive awareness of the rhetorical strategies, organizational patterns, and discourse markers through which writers in public policy accomplish their communicative purposes.

Later, as I began teaching academic writing to graduate students in economics and public policy and as I engaged in researching it in order to prepare justifiable writing curricula and teaching materials, I became painfully aware of the discrepancies between the discipline-specific language practices of professional writers and the generic writing advice of many English for Academic Purposes courses and textbooks. Many ideas reflected in this book grew out of the discrepancies that I had observed.

During the preparation of this book, I drew heavily on my dual specialization in public policy and applied linguistics, which enabled me to take a unique perspective on academic writing as both research and discourse practices. My education in public policy and public administration gave me an understanding of the research methods and approaches that are used in public policy and, to some extent, economics research; this knowledge was very useful as I tried to clarify the connections between content and writing. My training in applied linguistics equipped me with the tools I needed to analyze written text as well as with an awareness of the differences in how genres are implemented in different disciplines and social contexts. These tools enabled me to extract the features of various texts in economics and public policy that I believe are essential to understanding how those texts work.

And yet, my own educational and research experiences are just that—my own. To make this book useful, I needed to base my advice on something more objective than individual experiences. This was particularly important because I wanted to make this book useful for writers not only of public policy but also of economics, a discipline of which I have a limited grasp. My solution was to construct a representative corpus of over 400 research articles, which I obtained from more than 50 journals in public policy and economics and to analyze those articles for structure, organization, rhetorical strategies, and linguistic markers in order to understand how professional authors engage in dialogue with their readers and persuade them to accept their knowledge claims. This book is in large part a distillation of my analysis.

SPECIAL FEATURES

The following features make this book unique among books that teach academic writing.

- The book focuses on disciplinary writing in public policy and economics.

- The book covers writing on a wide range of issues in public policy and economics.

- The book focuses on, and provides suggestions for, three areas that are important for the successful completion of an academic paper—research, reading, and writing.

- The book presents over 300 writing samples—including whole papers and proposals—taken from the work of international researchers and graduate students.

- The concepts taught in this book apply to students from both English-speaking and non-English-speaking backgrounds.

A FOCUS ON DISCIPLINARY WRITING

Academic discourse refers to the ways in which language is used in the academy. Until recently—and in many writing programs even today—academic discourse has been treated as a homogeneous set of skills and steps, which, once mastered, would transfer across disciplines and genres. Yet, recent research in disciplinary writing has shown that disciplines differ greatly in how they approach knowledge construction and in how they represent the constructed knowledge in writing. Contrary to what many students and teachers believe, the ideas we put down on paper when we write are not entirely "ours"—they are influenced greatly, and to a large extent implicitly, by the expectations, assumptions, and beliefs of our readers. Discourse in an academic discipline, therefore, can best be understood as a collection of specific rhetorical and linguistic practices that members of that discipline use to formulate problems, frame questions, and present knowledge claims in ways that colleagues find persuasive.

Disciplines differ considerably on what their members see as persuasive writing. One way to understand what makes writing persuasive in a particular discipline is to engage in rhetorical and linguistic analysis of academic texts and to relate their features—their structure, organization, and the specific language forms used—to both the logic behind the research approach used by the authors and the authors' communicative purposes. This is what I have done in the preparation of this book. My intention here is to show what makes writing in economics and public policy persuasive by demystifying the relationship between academic language and scientific content and by showing how texts in economics and public policy are constructed and how they work.

To achieve this goal, I present academic discourse in economics and public policy in three different ways: as an outgrowth of the process of scientific inquiry, with its own favored methods, approaches, and tools; as a product of knowledge construction, with its own preferred modes of argumentation; and as a dialogue in which writers engage with their readers as they attempt to persuade them to accept their knowledge claims. Using a genre-based approach to writing—an approach that relates the communicative purposes of the writer, the existing conventions of the discipline, and the language, structure, and organization of the text—I also show how texts can be analyzed for organizational patterns, rhetorical strategies, and language use and how that analysis can help novice writers improve their writing.

Acknowledgments

First and foremost, I would like to thank my students, who kindly agreed to my request to include their work in this book. I chose your papers because I admire what you did during your study at GRIPS. Your achievements as academic writers are a constant inspiration to me and a source of professional pride.

I would like to thank Yasmin Adam for her outstanding job completing the million small tasks that this project has entailed. Yasmin, you have been wonderful, and I am so lucky to work with you. I also gratefully acknowledge the generous help of Olimjon Djumabaev, Hristina Gaydarska, and Hoang Ngan in preparing a corpus on which the suggestions outlined in this book are largely based. Your careful work reviewing journals and articles in public policy and economics has been extremely helpful.

I would also like to thank Lawrie Hunter for his help editing some of the examples included in this book, and the administrative staff of my institute, who have been supportive of my work throughout this project.

This book would not exist without the generous contribution of my dear friend and colleague Gavin O'Neill. Thank you, Gavin, for your hard work and for your invaluable feedback. Your contribution is truly beyond measure.

Finally, I thank my parents and my family for their encouragement and never-ending patience and support and my sister for the very helpful comments on an earlier draft.

DISCLAIMER

Some of the examples included in this book contain minor errors in grammar, wording, or punctuation. These examples are from published articles and I leave them as they are. I believe that they represent an achievable, if somewhat imperfect, model for students to emulate. All other errors are my responsibility. Examples from student papers have been edited for clarity.

Chapter 1

What Is Academic Writing?

ACADEMIC WRITING AS A UNIVERSAL SET OF SKILLS

Academic writing is often defined as a form of argumentative writing that is directed toward an academic audience and that is characterized by certain writing conventions (such as the use of references) and language use (such as the use of the passive voice or the third person).

This definition underlies many *English for Academic Purposes* courses, where students are taught linguistic and rhetorical forms that are said to be characteristic of all academic writing and where they learn various composing strategies such as outlining, summarizing, and proofreading. Students practice these forms and strategies by writing essays about personal experiences and opinions, which are evaluated by language teachers who often do not have any discipline-specific expertise in the students' discipline.

The implicit assumptions behind this definition are that good writing is good writing regardless of the context, and that writing can be learned as a series of context-independent skills and strategies, which, once mastered, will transfer across genres and disciplines. Yet, research in writing shows that there are no abstract, context-free standards of writing quality because different contexts and reader expectations impose different constraints on writers: What is good writing in one context and for one type of audience may not be as successful in other contexts and for other audiences (Diederich, 1974). Good writing is really "a matter of achieving [the] desired effect upon an intended audience" (Irvin, 2010, p. 5). Achieving this effect requires, above all, understanding the rules and conventions of the particular research area the writer is working in.

There are enormous disciplinary and genre variations in writing, and these variations determine how writers go about completing and presenting their work. Ultimately, it is the conventions of the discipline and research area that will dictate not only what writers can write about but also how they should write about it—how they should frame their study, describe their contribution, present their results, and support their claims. As Hyland (2005, 2009) reminds us, even such "obvious" and universal academic practices as using and citing sources appear to be guided by disciplinary conventions, which dictate whether the writer should quote or summarize, cite or assume common knowledge, or place citations at the beginning of a sentence or at the end. Becoming a good academic writer, therefore, is not just a matter of acquiring generic skills and

How to Write about Economics and Public Policy. https://doi.org/10.1016/B978-0-12-813010-0.00001-6

strategies for summarizing, describing, or citing sources; it is a matter of mastering "a repertoire of linguistic [and rhetorical—we might add] practices" (Paltridge, 2004, p. 90) that members of the writer's discipline or research area find persuasive.

ACADEMIC WRITING VS. GENERAL-PURPOSE WRITING

Perhaps a better way to define academic writing is to look at its features and how it differs from other types of writing. Below are some features that distinguish academic writing from general-purpose writing in English. If English is not your native language, as you read, consider to what extent the features of academic writing that are described below would apply to academic writing in your native language.

- **Purpose.** The main purpose of academic writing is to persuade the reader to accept the writer's claims to knowledge. This requires that the writer display subject-matter knowledge as well as present arguments in ways that members of the discipline find appropriate. In general-purpose writing, the purpose is to inform or to entertain, and no display of subject-matter knowledge is usually required.

- **Audience.** In academic writing, the audience is experts, people with expertise in their field and knowledge of what counts as acceptable writing in that field. In general-purpose writing, the audience is nonexperts.

- **Use of evidence.** In academic writing, claims to knowledge are supported with evidence, which usually comes in the form of scholarly literature or data. General-purpose writing, in contrast, does not require presentation of evidence beyond personal opinions or experiences.

- **Intellectual engagement.** General-purpose writing does not require a great deal of intellectual engagement and has been compared to impromptu speaking (Bereiter & Scardamalia, 1987); it requires only that the writer be familiar with the topic and have a grasp of the linguistic system including grammar and vocabulary. Academic writing, in contrast, requires a significant amount of intellectual engagement, as writers are expected to analyze, synthesize, and interpret academic literature and data.

- **Style of argumentation.** Academic writing is explicit in argumentation. Ideas are developed clearly, reasons behind claims are explained, and arguments are supported. The reader should not have to ask, "Where does this come from? What does this mean? What is the basis for this assertion?" There is often a clearly formulated central argument, which is developed without departures from the main point. In general-purpose writing, writers usually present personal opinions and support them with personal experiences.

- **Tentativeness**. Academic writing tends to be cautious in making claims. Hedges are used to make claims sound more tentative. General-purpose writing is usually more direct.

- **Predictability in structure**. Academic writing has a predictable organizational structure, with an introduction, a conclusion, and a body that is often broken into sections and subsections. In each of these sections, information is organized in a predictable manner. For example, in an Introduction, there is usually a statement of the problem, a review of relevant literature, and a statement of purpose.

- **Strict conventions**. Academic writing follows strict conventions for citations, references, use of rhetorical devices, and format including headings and subheadings. There are virtually no strict conventions beyond the conventions of grammar in general-purpose writing.

A focus on the features of academic writing may be useful for learning the similarities that many academic texts share across disciplines. However, such a list of distinguishing features obscures one crucial fact: that the specific realization of these features—the specific things that make academic writing logical, explicit, predictable in structure, and so on—differs among disciplines and genres. Successful academic writing, therefore, depends not only on the writer's understanding of how academic writing differs from general-purpose writing but also, crucially, on the writer's understanding of the specific rules and conventions that exist in his or her discipline and in the target genre (Hyland, 2005). These two concepts—discipline and genre—are at the heart of becoming a successful academic writer.

THE NOTION OF GENRE IN ACADEMIC WRITING

The term *genre* may refer to two things—a type of text such as a description, comparison, or problem-solution, or a category of communicative events that share certain characteristics, such as a research article, a book review, a university lecture, or an academic textbook (Paltridge, 2001). It is in this latter sense that the word *genre* is used in this book.

Genres exist in a particular social, cultural, and institutional context; this context reflects the goals, values, and expectations of the members of a discipline, and at the same time it determines the specific features that characterize a particular genre in a particular discipline (Paltridge, 2004). Because of their inseparability from the context, genres cannot be learned in a decontextualized manner. This is especially true of the genre *research article* because this genre is strongly influenced by disciplinary ways of thinking, researching, and writing. Not only the content but also the structure, style, and features of this genre will depend on the discipline, subdiscipline, and even on whether the article is qualitative or quantitative; they will also depend on the institutional and cultural contexts and on where exactly the article has been published. As a result, a qualitative research article in public administration written for a discussion paper series will look very different in content, structure, style, and language from a quantitative research article in labor economics written for a major publication of the American Economic Association.

To understand how a particular genre "works," writers need to become aware of the context in which that genre is produced and understand what one can write about in that context and how. Above all, writers need to understand what sort of writing members of their discipline find acceptable and what sort of arguments they find persuasive. This is how Ken Hyland (2004) puts it:

> The persuasiveness of academic discourse ... does not depend upon the demonstration of absolute fact, empirical evidence or impeccable logic, it is the result of effective rhetorical practices, accepted by community members. Texts are... persuasive only when they employ social and linguistic conventions that colleagues find convincing. ... Notions of what counts as convincing argument, appropriate theory, sound methodology, impressive logic and compelling evidence are community-specific. (p. 8)

Learning to write in a discipline, it seems, involves developing competence in at least three areas: the discipline's subject matter, its methodology, and the appropriate use of language—the way in which members of the discipline use words to make their writing persuasive to their colleagues.

DISCIPLINARY DIFFERENCES IN ACADEMIC WRITING

Disciplines differ by what they write. There can be no academic writing without competence in the subject matter. Developing this competence involves acquiring a body of knowledge that exists in the discipline—its topics, beliefs, approaches, controversies, theories, models, and assumptions. Equally important, it involves developing discipline-appropriate ways of thinking and asking questions, learning the discipline's preferred approaches to knowledge construction, and acquiring the associated methodologies and analytic techniques.

What topics do economists study today? What topics are appropriate for research in your particular context? What topics are of interest to faculty members at your particular institution? How do researchers in your area approach these topics? What theories do they find convincing? What methodologies do they use for data collection, and what statistical techniques do they use for data analysis? Would a qualitative study, for example, be convincing to an economist working in this area? To design a study that would be acceptable to members of your discipline, you need to know the answers to these questions.

Disciplines also differ by how they write. Developing competence in discipline-appropriate use of language is particularly crucial because claims to knowledge are made through language (Backhouse et al., 1993). To be accepted by readers, knowledge claims must reflect the modes of argumentation and ways of persuading that are favored by the particular discipline.

How should a problem be presented in a paper? Should you stress the novelty of your approach or the functionality of your solution? Or should you present your study as an attempt to resolve a controversy? How, and how often, should you cite others to support your claims? What writing style should you use? How should you present your model or theory—visually, mathematically, or in narrative form? The answers to these and similar questions depend on the conventions of the particular discipline or research area, and to be successful as an academic writer, you need to learn these conventions.

To summarize, in order to write an acceptable paper in a particular discipline, writers need to acquire the appropriate body of knowledge and the preferred methodologies as well as learn what particular textual features make it persuasive to members of their discipline. The problem is that in contrast to the subject matter, which forms a course of study in a discipline, language use is rarely taught explicitly. The purpose of this book is to fill this gap.

ACADEMIC WRITING: A DEFINITION

In this book, academic writing is defined as research-based writing done for an academic audience in response to scholarly literature or data. To narrow down the scope of this book, I focus on the research paper as the target genre and public policy and economics as the target disciplines.

The approach to academic writing taken in this book is based on a view of writing as a collective social practice embedded in cultural, historical, and institutional contexts: The writing takes place within a specific context and for a specific audience (Hyland, 2004). The context and the audience dictate not only what problems are investigated and what methods and techniques are used but also, crucially, how knowledge claims are presented, how research papers are organized, and how the writer goes about using language to persuade readers to accept his or her claims.

My view of academic writing as a collective social practice has been strongly influenced by the works of Ken Hyland; I borrow heavily from his writings about disciplinary discourses and language variation in academic writing across disciplines, especially from *Academic Discourse: English in a Global Context* (Hyland, 2009), *Metadiscourse* (Hyland, 2005), and *Academic Discourse Across Disciplines* (Hyland & Bondi, 2006). I encourage students who are interested in understanding how and why writers in specific disciplines write the way they do to read these highly informative works.

ACADEMIC WRITING AS RESEARCH

Academic writing is inquiry based. It relies on research to produce answers to questions. It is, therefore, important for any writer of academic papers to understand how research is done. Where do you start? What exactly do you do? Here is a common, step-by-step presentation of what a student may need to do in order to write an academic paper.

1. Select a topic.
2. Review relevant literature.
3. Design the study.
4. Collect data.
5. Analyze the data.
6. Interpret the data.
7. Write the report.
8. Revise and proofread as needed.

This presentation of research and writing as a generic, step-by-step process is somewhat misleading, however. This is because academic writing in a particular discipline cannot be separated from how research is done in that discipline because the writing must fit "the philosophical and methodological assumptions" (Shih, 1986, p. 619) of the discipline. Rather than learning generic steps in research, what you need is to understand how research is done in *your* particular discipline or area of inquiry. Below are some questions that might help you assess your own understanding of how research is done in your discipline. See if you can answer them.

- What topics are appropriate for study in your area? What constitutes a "good" research question? How many research questions is it appropriate to have in an academic paper in your area?

- What constitutes "literature" in your area? Do authors of research papers in your area limit their review to journals and scholarly books or do they also include policy literature or even popular literature? How much literature is usually included in a review?

- What designs are considered appropriate for your topic in your area? Are they usually quantitative or qualitative?

- What constitutes "data" in your area? What kinds of data are considered appropriate for your research topic? What limitations do different kinds of data have? How are data collected in your area? Do researchers commonly collect data themselves, or do they obtain them from somewhere? Which data sources are considered appropriate?

- How are data analyzed in your area? In a quantitative study, what statistical techniques are commonly used? How are they interpreted? What coefficients and other statistics are commonly included in a paper? In a qualitative study, what type of analysis is appropriate? What data collection strategies and coding schemes are commonly used?

You also need to learn how research is presented in your area of inquiry. Below are some questions that may help you assess your own understanding of how research is commonly presented in your area. See if you can answer them.

- Do researchers usually present a research question, a hypothesis, or a purpose in their papers? In formulating research questions, do they use directional words such as "effect," "impact," or "influence," or do they avoid these words?

- How much background do they usually provide, and how do they frame the problem? Do they frame it as a way to test a new or existing theory, as a way to resolve a controversy, or as a way to provide a deeper, more holistic explanation for a phenomenon?

- When describing previous research, do writers place the authors of previous research in the subject position (e.g., *Smith argued*), in parentheses at the end of a sentence or paragraph, or in footnotes? Which arguments are supported with references and which ones are presented without attribution, as common knowledge in the field? How much space is generally devoted to a literature review? Is the literature reviewed in a separate section or in the Introduction?

- How much detail do writers include in describing the design of their study? Do they put definitions of concepts and variables in the main text or in a table in an appendix? Do they devote more space to the description of case selection or to the measurement of variables? Do they acknowledge the limitations of their data or variable definitions? How? In which part of the paper? How, specifically, do they convince the reader to accept their design as valid?

- How do writers present their results? When do they appear definitive and when, tentative? Do they present results in visual or narrative form? What expressions do they use to discuss their results and explain their implications?

- What specific language forms and expressions do writers use when presenting problems, describing background, and making arguments?

The generic description of the research and writing process is also misleading because of its linear nature. In fact, the process is never linear as writers go back and forth between literature, data, analysis, and results, looking for ways to frame the problem, explain their motivations, and present their arguments. The process may not even begin with topic selection; it may start with the analysis of available data, which you come across or collect as part of your job as a policy analyst, and then the entire paper—the specific research question, the literature review, the interpretation, and the arguments—is written to support that analysis.

It is also misleading to present writing as a final step in the research process—just "writing up" your results—although this view of writing is inadvertently supported by the neatly organized, linear presentation of research in published articles. As many graduate students who have completed a research project can probably attest, no part of the research process can be completed without writing: Research questions, definitions, measurement procedures, assumptions, and arguments can only be developed and refined after they have been written down, thought over, and revised—often multiple times. As McCloskey (2000) has pointed out, writing helps us understand what exactly we want to say; clarify vague notions; and make explicit our hunches, beliefs, and assumptions.

It is perhaps useful to think of writing as one of several cognitive tools that we use when working on a research project. The other tools are reading, thinking, and researching, and they are just as important. These four processes—reading, thinking, researching, and writing—occur throughout the entire process of working on an academic paper: You read, you think, you read some more, you write, you research, you read again, and write again—and so on and on. Academic writing is never about just writing.

Because research and academic writing are so inseparably connected, I devote considerable space in this book to a discussion of research in public policy and economics. In Chapters 2 and 3, I explain what academic research is, what options exist for graduate students, how a topic can be selected, and what distinguishes good topics from those that are not good. However, the discussion of research in this book is rather basic and limited, and it may not be sufficient for many students, especially for those who have had limited experience with research. If this is your case, I suggest that you obtain a textbook on doing research in your discipline or area. The following textbooks are excellent sources of information on how to do research in a particular discipline.

- If you are interested in **research in economics**, read Steven A. Greenlaw's *Doing Economics: A Guide to Understanding and Carrying out Economic Research*.

- If you are interested in **political research**, read Alan D. Monroe's *Essentials of Political Research*.

- If you are interested in **social science research methods** in general, read Earl Babbie's *The Practice of Social Research*.

- If you are interested in **public policy research**, read Allen D. Putt and J. Fred Springer's *Policy Research*: *Concepts, Methods, and Applications*.

ACADEMIC WRITING AS A DIALOG

Academic writing has sometimes been described as a dialog, a conversation that the writer of the text has with the reader. The writer's goal is to persuade the reader to accept his or her claims to knowledge. This is not an easy task, as the reader in this dialog is "all-powerful" (Johns, 1990, p. 31), an expert who "has the power to accept or reject writing as coherent, as consistent with the conventions of the target discourse community" (p. 31). Engaging in this dialog is especially challenging when the writer is an outsider, a novice researcher who is just trying to gain acceptance in the disciplinary community.

So how do writers persuade readers to accept their claims? They do that, first of all, by making sure that their content meets the discipline's conventions for producing knowledge—that they have used an appropriate methodology, collected appropriate data, and performed appropriate analyses. Equally important, writers persuade readers by creating a flow of text that readers find coherent and by engaging with them in ways that help readers understand and accept the writer's argument. Writers accomplish this engagement in several ways including

- By following the discipline's preferred patterns for text organization. For example, empirical articles in economics typically have an introduction, a methodology section, and a results and discussion section, whereas nonempirical articles and some qualitative articles may be organized into thematically titled sections. Writers also use headings, subheadings, section numbering, periodic reviews, and previews to guide the reader throughout the text.

- By making judgments about the readers' knowledge. Every discipline has a body of knowledge that is assumed to be common knowledge; writing an academic paper, therefore, requires making predictions about what the reader is likely to know and what needs more detailed elaboration.

- By anticipating possible questions or criticisms and addressing them. Expert readers read academic papers with a critical eye; anticipating their questions or objections helps the writer understand what should be included as well as how arguments should be structured and worded. For example, anticipating readers' questions, the writer may choose to explain the limitations of the data, describe in greater detail the paper's methodology and analysis, include an alternative interpretation, or present the findings as more tentative.

- By showing proper respect for the reader and the reader's opinions. This is accomplished by using citations to give credit to others' words and ideas, by describing alternative interpretations, and by presenting one's own claims as tentative rather than definitive.

- By presenting themselves as an authority. This is accomplished by demonstrating knowledge of the discipline's terminology, key concepts, and relevant vocabulary—in addition to the knowledge of the discipline's subject matter and methodology.

In interacting with readers, writers also use specific linguistic markers—words and phrases that help them guide the reader to the appropriate interpretation of the text. These markers are sometimes called sentence connectors because they help authors connect ideas in a text and create a flow. Below, I describe several groups of such markers and their purpose. They have been adopted from Hyland (2005, pp. 50–53). As you go over the examples, think about the specific function these markers play in each sentence.

- **Transition markers**. These are phrases that help show logical connection between steps in an argument. For example: *thus, therefore, consequently, likewise, in the same way, furthermore, moreover.*

It is, **therefore**, interesting to note that our estimated promotion rates are, in general, much larger than the error rates, which suggests that, even though we had to impute these rates from matched data sources with multiple measurements, there is reason to believe that we have correct magnitudes. **Thus**, employment is growing in our highest-skill category exclusively because promotions outnumber the lo[s]ses from excess exits by about ten to one. (Abowd et al., 1999, p. 180)

Consequently, any differences between industrialising societies should eventually disappear as economic development continues. (Arts et al., 1999, p. 63)

The benefit from training minority groups may arise as much from raising the average quality of the group as from raising the quality of the individual trainee; and, **likewise**, the returns may be distributed over the whole group rather than to the individual. (Akerlof, 1970, p. 495)

An exception was gambling. Gambling, unlike the other sensitive behaviors, is not a defining characteristic of the counterculture to which study participants belong. **Furthermore**, after receiving a cash handout, it's possible that men were reluctant to admit they'd gambled some of it away. (Blattman et al., 2016, p. 111)

Somewhat reduced public subsidies for the strategic industries of the war-torn provinces would not likely have changed the overall pattern of trade protection. **By the same token, though,** the threat perceived from Germany was sufficient to deliver protection for the coal and steel, machinery, chemical and auto sectors — even without the support of protectionist agriculture and textiles. (Horowitz, 2004, p. 48)

- **Frame markers**. These are phrases that help sequence and order parts of the text. For example: *to summarize, to begin, there are several reasons/ possible explanations for.*

In summary, the facts suggest that it is not just supply-side conditions or foreign-loans/government intervention that are important. (Brinton et al., 1995, p. 1112)

Let me summarize what we know and what we do not know about the costs and benefits of inflation. First, we know that very high inflation is very bad, not only for economic growth, but also more generally for social and political stability. (de Grauwe, 2002, p. 701)

We begin by discussing the results from the unrestricted specification, that is, we define self-employed households as households in which at least one member was self-employed in year *t*. (Engström & Hagen, 2017, p. 99)

The arguments that the Olympics bring long-term benefits **fall into several categories**. First, the Games might leave a legacy of sporting facilities that can be used by future generations. (Baade & Matheson, 2016, p. 211)

There are several possible explanations for these surprising results. Rose and Spiegel (2011) suggest that it is not the event itself or the resulting tourism or advertising that increases exports, but rather that the very act of bidding serves as a credible signal that a country is committing itself to trade liberalization that will permanently increase trade flows. (Baade & Matheson, 2016, p. 213)

There are several reasons why parent and child wealth would be similar. First, wealth, unlike income, is directly transferred between generations. (Charles & Hurst, 2003, p. 1163)

- **Endophoric markers**. These are phrases that refer the reader to other parts of the text. For example: *see Table 2, refer to the next section, as noted above.*

A second point we want to discuss in this section pertains to the question of why the predicted increase of disagreement on perceived and preferred inequality has been so much higher in Poland than in Hungary **(see Figures 4 and 5)**. (Arts et al., 1999, p. 75)

As noted above, our parent and child *Z* controls include measures of parent and child income, education, and asset choice, as well as direct transfers such as gifts and expected bequests. (Charles & Hurst, 2003, p. 1167)

The next section describes the data sources and our methods for sampling, matching, and verifying the various elements of the flows. (Abowd et al., 1999, p. 171)

- **Evidentials**. These are phrases that show the source of an idea. For example: *according to Smith, Brown argued.*

According to Babcock and Marks (2011), time devoted to academics by the average full-time student has fallen from forty hours per week in 1961 to twenty-seven hours in 2004. (Allgood et al., 2015, p. 305)

As **Hirschman** (1981) **has argued**, Keynesian thought opened the intellectual space within which these heterodox, developmentalist ideas could flourish. (Babb, 2012, p. 273)

- **Code glosses**. These are phrases that provide additional information by rephrasing or explaining. For example: *in other words, this means that, this can be defined as.*

However, other papers have stressed the role of migration as one of the mechanisms for price adjustments (Jones et al., 2003, 2004, 2005; Jones and Leishman, 2006). **In other words**, these papers address the role of migration in the spatial house arbitrage process between different regions. (Chen et al., 2011, p. 318)

In one direction, development alone can play a major role in driving down inequality between men and women; in the other direction, continuing discrimination against women can, as Sen has forcefully argued, hinder development. Empowerment can, **in other words**, accelerate development. (Duflo, 2012, p. 1053)

At the same time **this means that** medical insurance is least available to those who need it most, for the insurance companies do their own "adverse selection." (Akerlof, 1970, p. 494)

- **Hedges**. These are phrases that help writers present their views in tentative ways. For example: *a possible interpretation, perhaps, the data suggest.*

The results from Table 4 show that the house price indices appear to have different integration orders across cities. **Possible explanations could be** the presence of structure breaks (Chen et al., 2007; Chien, 2010), non-linearity implied by the nature of the data (Cook, 2003; Cook and Speight, 2007), new real estate policies, or the financial crisis that generated structural change to housing prices. (Chen et al., 2011, p. 320)

The audio/video **data suggested** that economic factors that determined the relation of players with the dilemma (i.e. with the resources for which there is joint access, and with the rest of users who have access to them) **might explain** the degrees of cooperation and social efficiency achieved by the different groups. (Cardenas, 2003, p. 272)

Opinion surveys further confirm this analysis. **Table 2 suggests** that economists have in general less regard for interdisciplinarity than their social scientific and even business school brethren. (Fourcade et al., 2015, pp. 94–95)

More important, the constant aside, every common coefficient and its t-value in these equations is increased in absolute value, and the coefficient of the synchronous real stock price is positive, as the substitution effect would imply, and statistically significant. Hence, **these regressions suggest** that there is both a wealth effect and a substitution effect, with the wealth effect the stronger. (Friedman, 1988, pp. 232–234)

These two examples suggest that just reducing the grip of poverty on these households or helping them to deal with crises **could improve** the welfare of women of all ages. (Duflo, 2012, p. 1055)

- **Boosters**. These are phrases that help writers to express certainty. For example: *clearly, obviously, the data demonstrate.*

Table 12 indicates that house prices in LTC, the capital, are **clearly** the most exogenous in Taiwan. (Chen et al., 2011, p. 327)

Meanwhile, the favoured country will gain as regional industry relocates to its soil and real wages rise as a result. **Clearly** these effects would generate substantial political tensions over time, which in turn would undermine integration processes. (Draper, 2010, p. 18)

These different measures demonstrate the intensity of accessions, separations, and employment movements for those plants that increase employment in a given year. (Abowd et al., 1999, p. 176)

For example, J. K. Rowling was a welfare mother when she wrote her first *Harry Potter* manuscript. **The result demonstrates** the potential of small, seemingly inconsequential efforts (Bell, 2012). It took Rowling 12 attempts to find a willing publisher. (Feldman et al., 2016, p. 16)

- **Attitude markers.** These are phrases that show the author's attitude toward propositions. For example: *unfortunately, more important, appropriate, remarkable.*

Therefore, many believe that a special effort is needed to educate girls, and that educating girls would have tremendous spillover effects. **Unfortunately**, the evidence for this is not as strong as is commonly believed. (Duflo, 2012, p. 1065)

The inclusion of the synchronous real stock price raises the correlation and reduces the standard error, though only modestly, for both equations B and C. **More important**, the constant aside, every common coefficient and its *t*-value in these equations is increased in absolute value, and the coefficient of the synchronous real stock price is positive, as the substitution effect would imply, and statistically significant. (Friedman, 1988, pp. 232–234)

The two **most remarkable** trends of recent financial history have their origin in Chimerica: rapid advances in the globalization of production, and the emergence of massive foreign currency reserves in the vaults of (mostly Asian) central banks. (Ferguson & Schularick, 2007, p. 228)

For those establishments at which employment decreases, these ratios are reversed. **Surprisingly**, those establishments with stable employment in a given year are also very active. (Abowd et al., 1999, p. 176)

- **Self-mention.** This refers to the use of first person pronouns in the text. For example: *I, me, we, our.*

The theoretical research on religious strictness and religious networks has widened the scope of theoretical models in the economics of religion, but in **my** view, this still remains a comparatively less-researched area in the microeconomics of religion. (Iyer, 2016, p. 416)

We focus **our** attention on Mexico because it represents a unique case among developing nations. (Enamorado et al., 2016, p. 128)

- **Engagement markers**. These are phrases that address readers. For example: *notice that, you may notice, consider [the following example]*.

Consider the following neoclassical textbook model. We assume an economy in which markets are complete, there [are] no externalities and competition is perfect. (Ferguson & Schularick, 2007, p. 223)

Notice that we have data concerning only the average seniority of these workers and not the individual seniority of the short-term contract workers who leave. (Abowd et al., 1999, p. 175)

THE DEMANDS OF GRADUATE WRITING

Because of its strong basis in disciplinary discourse, graduate academic writing is a foreign language to all students who are new to graduate study. Essentially, students need to learn a new way of looking at the world—not just as scientists but also as members of their particular disciplinary community. This new way of looking at the world brings with it a new way of talking about the world, with its own vocabulary, grammatical structures, organizational patterns, and rhetorical strategies.

Research has identified significant differences in the types of writing that undergraduate and graduate students are required to do, as well as in the skills that students need in order to succeed in their programs (Reid, 2001). At the undergraduate level, writing tasks tend to emphasize transactional orientations toward learning—that is, students are expected to demonstrate the knowledge that they have acquired in their classes and display their mastery of content. Assignments are often descriptive and include essays, summaries, and reviews.

In contrast, writing tasks at the graduate level emphasize transformational orientations toward learning—that is, graduate students are expected to demonstrate their ability to contribute to the field. Writing tasks are often research-based and analytical and require mastery of the research process, the ability to read, critically evaluate, and synthesize a large amount of research, and an understanding of the writing requirements and conventions of the discipline in order to engage with readers in ways that are discipline-appropriate.

What do faculty members expect from graduate students' writing? Research that has looked into this question (e.g., Ballard & Clanchy, 1991) has identified at least four areas that appear to be important to faculty members across academic disciplines. What many advisors want to see, it turns out, is

- **A clear focus on the topic**. Everything you include in a paper should be relevant to the main argument and the relevance should be explained rather than assumed. Irrelevant material is a particular problem in literature reviews as students often include material that is unrelated to the main topic "just to give some background information," in the words of one student.

Keep in mind as you write that the connections between what you include in your paper—your country's background, its laws and regulations, the details of your country's policies and reforms—and your main argument must be made explicit.

- **Wide and critical reading**. The paper should demonstrate that you have read widely, that you have thought carefully about the topic, and that you have assessed the credibility of previous authors' arguments. Show your advisor that you have read key texts in your area, that you are familiar with the main controversies, approaches, or beliefs, that you know how to evaluate the validity of other authors' claims, and that you do not take anything for granted.

- **A reasoned argument**. "Reasoned" means supported by credible evidence. Different disciplines have different standards for what counts as credible evidence and you need to make sure that the evidence you present conforms to the standards of your discipline. Generally, evidence in academic writing refers to research findings—either your own or other researchers'—and it does not refer to other people's unsupported claims (even if those people have the right credentials), your own opinions (even if they are supported with your personal experiences), or general beliefs (even if those beliefs seem commonsense).

- **Clear presentation**. Again, there may be large variations between disciplines, subdisciplines, and even individual faculty members regarding what constitutes "clear presentation." Often, it is equated with error-free writing; however, clear presentation is also a matter of appropriate organization of the text, appropriate development of ideas, and the use of appropriate writing conventions such as citation styles or headings. Perhaps even more important, it is a matter of the writer's understanding and evaluation of how much the reader knows and how much needs to be explained.

SPECIAL PROBLEMS OF NON-ENGLISH WRITERS

English academic writing may be particularly difficult for students with non-English educational, cultural, and linguistic backgrounds. Many misconceptions may lie at the root of the problem of poor writing of non-English students. Chief among them are misconceptions about what knowledge is and how it is produced. This may be particularly a problem for students from non-Western countries, whose educational experience has emphasized mastery of facts, equating knowledge production with the description of facts and opinions. Students who are new to Western educational practices may lack the intellectual training that is necessary to evaluate others' ideas or make their own arguments and may find themselves facing a whole new approach to knowledge, which stresses critical thinking, synthesis, analysis, appropriate use of sources, and reader orientation.

There may also be cultural differences in what students see as coherent writing. As Hyland (2005) reminds us, writers may be writing from one cultural background, whereas readers may be reading from a different cultural background. This mismatch between cultural expectations may make it difficult for native English readers to comprehend the writing of students from other cultures. The situation is even more complex when both the writer and the reader are nonnative speakers of English coming from two different cultural and educational backgrounds, yet writing and reading in English. This is the case, for example, of thousands of international students studying in English in graduate schools throughout Europe and Asia. It is for this reason that I have attempted to include in this book writing examples from international scholars writing in English.

Finally, students for whom English is an additional language may have a range of linguistic problems including insufficient vocabulary, inaccurate grammar, and poor writing mechanics. It is interesting to note that faculty members' perceptions of, and attitudes toward, nonnative English writers' linguistic problems vary tremendously. Some faculty members may be quite forgiving of errors unless these errors interfere with comprehension, whereas others may insist that writing be error-free. Regardless of individual faculty members' preferences and attitudes toward error, it is important to keep in mind that in professional settings, grammar problems are often unacceptable.

LEARNING TO WRITE LIKE AN EXPERT

Academic writing skills are neither universal nor transferrable between disciplines or genres. Entering a new discipline means developing a new way of looking at, and talking about, problems and solutions. To become successful academic writers, students need to understand the requirements of their discipline—they need to find out what is expected of them and try to approximate their writing to the writing in their research area. Many experts, therefore, see the process of academic writing development as a process of socialization through which students come to understand the notions of the discourse community, academic culture, university rules, and writing conventions—a kind of apprenticeship. In this sense, learning to write in an academic setting is about acquiring the linguistic and rhetorical practices that are used in a particular discipline and that are based on that discipline's preferred approach to building knowledge. Students need to understand who their audience is, what this audience knows and what it does not know, and what criteria are used in their research area to assess knowledge claims.

Below I give four suggestions for learning to write like an expert.

- **Learn by understanding the requirements, preferences, and conventions of your discipline**. I cannot emphasize this enough. Perfectly grammatical and clearly written sentences mean nothing if your writing does not follow the preferences and requirements of your discipline. Learn what topics and questions researchers in your area study and what methodologies they use; learn the key theories, schools of thought, concepts, and controversies that exist; learn the standards for what counts as appropriate evidence and convincing argument; finally, learn your discipline's writing conventions such as citation styles or the appropriate use of headings and subheadings.

- **Learn by analyzing the language of research papers.** Graduate study requires that students read widely in their area. This almost always means reading for content, or to extract the author's main ideas. What I suggest here is that in addition to reading for content, you also read for language. This means that you should analyze text in order to understand the following elements:

  - **Textual organization**: How is the text organized? What is the structure of the whole paper? Of individual sections? Where do authors put concept definitions, descriptions of variables, details about analyses, and other important elements of the text?

  - **Purpose of paragraphs**: What is the specific purpose of each paragraph in each of the sections of the paper? What is the author doing in these paragraphs (e.g., summarizing findings, explaining analyses, describing visuals, drawing implications, and so on)?

  - **Idea development**: How do authors develop ideas in a paragraph? What connecting words and phrases do they use and for what purpose?

  - **Presentation of results**: How do authors present their results? What words and phrases do they use to highlight importance? How do they guide readers between the text and the visuals?

  - **Argument structure**: How do authors present their arguments? What linguistic markers do they use to connect ideas? What words and phrases do they use to guide their readers? How do they present themselves? How do they address their readers? What words and phrases do they use to soften or strengthen their claims?

  - **Use of citations**: How do writers acknowledge other authors? What reporting verbs (e.g., *argue*, *claim*, *explain*) do they use when presenting the work of other authors?

- **Learn by doing.** Writing cannot be learned by reading or talking about it; writing can only be learned by writing: by practicing it regularly, by reviewing it critically, and by revising it thoroughly. And it is not so much the amount of writing as it is the kind of writing that matters. Writing emails, for example, would not be helpful, and neither would writing about personal experiences. To learn to write in economics, political science, or public policy, you need to practice writing as a specialist in those fields. Analyzing accomplished authors' ways of expressing ideas and trying to emulate them will also help.

- **Learn from feedback**. Show your work to a colleague, a classmate, or anyone whose judgment you trust and ask for their feedback. Although specialists would be preferable, even people without a strong background in your area can often give you valuable feedback on your writing, even if only on its surface features.

Emulating published articles, especially articles in your area, can be very helpful for improving your writing ability. However, for students in master's programs including professional programs in public policy, published papers may often represent a difficult, even an impossible goal to achieve. Perhaps a better model would be papers written by students in similar programs. This book contains a selection of papers written by master's students in various public policy programs. All but two of those students were nonnative English speakers and only two had had some background in economics before beginning their studies. They wrote those papers in the space of just a few months while attending classes full-time. They wrote them well, and so can you.

Chapter 2

Research in Public Policy and Economics

WHAT IS RESEARCH?

Suppose you wanted to find an answer to this question: *Do graphs promote the learning of economics?* This question has important implications for both students and teachers because if the use of graphs results in better learning of economics (a difficult subject), then teachers should be encouraged to use more graphs in their lectures, textbooks, and study materials, and students should be taught to rely more on graphs in their learning. How can you make an informed decision about the effect of graphs on learning? Consider these possibilities.

Decision-making by personal experience. One way to answer this question is to think of your own experiences. Do you learn better when text is supplemented with visual information? Do graphs help you remember difficult concepts and theories? The danger with "going by experience," however, is that your individual experiences may not be generalizable, or applicable to others.

Decision-making by anecdote. Perhaps you could ask your friends who have taken courses in economics what they think. Do graphs help them better remember information? But what if some say yes, and others, no? And even if all of your friends agree on a particular answer, would the same answer apply to other people? How can you be sure?

Decision-making by expert opinion. Perhaps it's time to turn to an expert. The expert may explain that visual cues help us process and remember information, which in turn results in better retrieval. Thus, graphs do appear to be useful for learning. But who says that the opinion of an expert is always correct? Why should you trust expert opinion? Actually, you should not. In fact, there is compelling evidence in psychology showing that an expert is less likely to provide an objective review of all the evidence on a particular problem than is a nonexpert (Kahneman, 2011).

The problem with these approaches to answering a question is that they are unsystematic and, as such, are prone to *bias*. Bias is a systematic difference between what we actually observe and what is real in the outside world. There are

How to Write about Economics and Public Policy. https://doi.org/10.1016/B978-0-12-813010-0.00002-8

many sources of bias in everyday reasoning. Our beliefs or expectations may influence our interpretations of information; our observations may be based on a sample that is too small or unrepresentative, or we may neglect to incorporate prior known probabilities when evaluating the possibility of an outcome. When we reason informally, we make no attempt to eliminate bias.

Science is different from informal reasoning in that it incorporates mechanisms that are designed to eliminate or minimize bias. It does so by following explicit procedures that have been specified in advance to help us produce knowledge in a systematic way. This production of knowledge in a systematic way by following explicit procedures is called *research*. The procedures that researchers follow involve formulating a research question, clarifying the meaning of concepts under investigation, collecting data, analyzing the data, and drawing conclusions. Understanding how your discipline or research area goes about following these procedures will help you design and complete a research project.

It is important to note, however, that science is not the same as truth, and that the goal of research is not to uncover truth or show how things "really" are. Rather, science is a system of beliefs—just one among many other systems—that helps us understand the reality around us. And as with any system of beliefs, science has its own limits and limitations. Rather than producing indisputable facts, what researchers do, essentially, is make propositions in an attempt to explain an observed phenomenon and persuade their peers, other researchers working in the same area, to accept their explanations. This is not an easy task, because researchers are a skeptical bunch. The spirit of challenging the work of others—as well as one's own—is perhaps one of the distinguishing features of modern science. So how do researchers go about persuading each other? They do that by following the rules of their discipline or research area. These rules concern both how researchers conduct their studies (e.g., how they formulate questions, build a theoretical framework, and collect and analyze data) and how they write their reports. And as Hyland (2004, 2005, 2009), among others, points out, different disciplines and areas of research have different rules for what counts as a persuasive argument, compelling evidence, and logical discussion.

RESEARCH IN PUBLIC POLICY AND ECONOMICS

Social science produces knowledge about people, their behavior, their beliefs, and their interactions. Yet, research in the social sciences is extremely diverse, and each field, discipline, subdiscipline, or research area has its own standards and conventions for producing knowledge and conducting research projects. As an area of inquiry, public policy is a subfield of social science; yet, it is hardly a distinct discipline. Rather, public policy is a broad and interdisciplinary area of research that draws on such diverse disciplines as economics, political science, sociology, education, public administration, law, psychology, and the behavioral sciences. Designing research projects that address problems in such diverse areas requires not only subject-matter knowledge but also an understanding of how research is done in those areas.

For students in public policy programs, such diversity may present significant problems, as they will often have to face the rules and conventions of very different disciplines, which at times may be contradictory. Sometimes, there may not even be clear rules to follow, or the rules may differ from school to school and even from advisor to advisor. As a result, theses and final papers produced even in the same program may look very different, both in content and in form. Ultimately, you will need to learn and follow the rules and requirements that pertain to your specific area of research as well as to your school and your program.

Many areas of public policy research rely on quantitative analysis and the tools and approaches of economic research for data collection and analysis. For example, a recent study of public policy programs in the United States (Morçöl & Ivanova, 2010) found that the top three methods taught to public policy students in American universities were surveys, regression analysis, and cost-benefit analysis—the three methods of data collection and analysis that are strongly associated with economic research and quantitative analysis. A review of journals addressing public policy problems (see Appendix D) also reveals that such problems are often analyzed using quantitative tools.

Quantitative economic research, however, is not the only option for a public policy student. Some areas of public policy—for example, security studies, international relations, law, and public administration—call for qualitative approaches to data collection and analysis. This chapter briefly reviews the nature and assumptions of the two types of research—qualitative and quantitative—and describes how these two types of research are used to study problems in public policy and economics.

EMPIRICAL VS. NONEMPIRICAL RESEARCH

Research in public policy and economics can be broadly categorized as empirical and nonempirical. **Empirical** research involves collecting data, or *empirical observations*, and analyzing the data to answer a specific research question; it can be quantitative or qualitative. These two types of research—quantitative and qualitative—are explained later in this chapter.

Nonempirical research does not rely on data collection; it can be theoretical or literature-based. Theoretical research in public policy and economics develops a theoretical model to predict what would happen under certain conditions. Theoretical papers are based on assumptions about relevant agents and their behavior, and they use mathematics to show what would happen or how agents would behave in a particular situation. An example of a theoretical paper is George A. Akerlof's "The Market for 'Lemons': Quality Uncertainty and the Market Mechanism" published in 1970 in the *Quarterly Journal of Economics*.

Because theoretical papers focus on theoretical rather than applied problems, they are rarely an option for students in professional public policy programs, particularly at the master's level.

The other type of nonempirical research is essentially a literature review. In this type of paper, the author formulates a set of questions and reviews a large body of existing literature in order to answer these questions. The goal is not only to provide an overview of what is known about a topic but also to structure and organize that knowledge in ways that clarify relationships between relevant concepts, theories, approaches, and findings. The focus of review-based papers, therefore, is on the problem rather than on a particular country, organization, or setting. An example of a review-based paper is Allgood et al.'s "Research on Teaching Economics to Undergraduates" published in 2015 in the *Journal of Economic Literature*.

Writing a nonempirical paper based entirely on a literature review is usually not an acceptable option for a thesis for students in public policy and economics programs, even at the master's level. It is never an option for doctoral students. Students in these programs are expected to write an empirical—and often quantitative—paper.

PURPOSES OF EMPIRICAL RESEARCH

The following presentation of the purposes of empirical research is based on Earl Babbie's (1998) description. Other authors (e.g., Putt & Springer, 1989) have suggested additional purposes such as estimation and choice analysis.

Exploration

Exploratory research addresses problems that we know little about. The goal of exploratory research is to formulate more precise questions for descriptive and explanatory research, so it is often conducted as a first step toward designing a more systematic study. For example, researchers may want to know if a particular problem (e.g., drug use, domestic violence, or alcohol abuse) exists in a particular community, and if it does, how big it is, and what it is really about.

Exploratory research in public policy often relies on qualitative methods and may use multiple sources of information including in-depth interviews, records, review of existing literature, and focus group discussions. Because of the nature of qualitative research, it cannot yield definitive answers, and it is usually followed by more rigorous studies.

An example of a qualitative exploratory study is Dorey et al.'s "Children and Television Watching: A Qualitative Study of New Zealand Parents' Perceptions and Views" published in 2009 in the journal *Child: Care, Health, and Development*. In that study, the researchers used focus groups to examine New Zealand parents' attitudes toward their children's TV watching, strategies to reduce TV viewing, and opinions about ways to restrict TV watching among children.

It should be noted that a study may have the word "exploratory" in its title or description and yet be descriptive or even explanatory in its purpose. For example, studies in economics are sometimes called exploratory but are, in fact, quantitative studies conducted to assess a policy. An example of such a study is McKenzie's "An Exploratory Study of the Economic Understanding of Elementary School Teachers" published in 1971 in the *Journal of Economic Education*. In that article, McKenzie assessed the impact of training in economics on elementary teachers' understanding of this subject and compared elementary teachers' understanding of economics with that of other groups.

Description

Descriptive research addresses problems for which a detailed picture of a population, setting, or phenomenon is needed. A descriptive study may examine what percentage of people hold a particular view or engage in a particular form of behavior, how certain people act in certain situations, or who is involved in a particular process. For example, researchers may want to know how people make voting decisions, or what kinds of children are at risk for reading failure, or they may want to describe health risk behavior of a particular population in a particular setting (e.g., low-income young women living in rural areas of Russia). Descriptive studies often use surveys to collect data, which are then analyzed quantitatively; they may, however, rely on other methods including qualitative methods.

An example of a descriptive study is Rossi et al.'s "The Urban Homeless: Estimating Composition and Size" published in 1987 in *Science*. In that study, the researchers used a novel approach to estimate the size and composition of a homeless population in a large American city. The ultimate goal was to describe the characteristics—or paint a portrait—of a typical homeless person.

Explanation

Explanatory research seeks to explain social phenomena. Some explanatory studies develop a novel explanation and then test it. Others outline two competing explanations and test them to compare. Still others take an existing explanation, often derived from previous research, and extend it to explain a new issue, phenomenon, or the behavior of a group of people. For example, a researcher may want to know which variables explain why some children fail to finish high school, why some cities have high unemployment rates, or why some companies are more productive than others.

Explanatory research relies on experimental and correlational methods. In **experimental designs**, the researcher manipulates a variable and observes its effect on another variable or variables while keeping everything else constant *by design* (i.e., using a control group). In **correlational designs**, the researcher cannot manipulate variables; instead, statistical controls are used, for example, by including control variables in the model and statistically "neutralizing" their effect on the outcome variable in order to observe the effect of the variables of interest on the outcome.

Explanatory research can also use qualitative methods, especially in comparative designs, where pairs of cases are compared to identify possible causes of an outcome. However, explanations provided by qualitative research are always tentative because there is no way to test them: The data obtained in a qualitative study cannot be simultaneously a source and a test of a hypothesis. The only way to test propositions obtained in a qualitative study is to use quantitative methods and an independent set of data.

Explanation is closely related to prediction: Understanding what factors shape particular behaviors or phenomena may help the researcher make accurate predictions. However, explanation and prediction are not the same. Understanding why things happen requires establishing cause-and-effect relationships, whereas making predictions requires only that the variables of interest correlate with one another.

In public policy and economics, both explanatory and predictive models rely heavily on the use of causal theories, because these models are usually based on correlation (i.e., regression). Theory, therefore, becomes crucially important as it justifies the inclusion or exclusion of variables in a model and the expectations of a causal or predictive relationship.

QUANTITATIVE VS. QUALITATIVE RESEARCH

One way to define qualitative and quantitative research is to focus on the technical distinctions between these approaches. Quantitative research uses numeric data and large N-sizes, whereas qualitative research uses nonnumeric data and small N-sizes. In fact, the distinctions between quantitative and qualitative research go much deeper, to the 19th-century arguments that contrasted the study of natural-science phenomena and the study of human beings and their actions (Firestone, 1987). Today, authors writing about research methods (Creswell, 2003; Neuman, 2004) generally agree that there is a philosophical, epistemological, and methodological divide between the two approaches, as they are based on different views of reality and assumptions about the nature of the world, have different purposes, use different methodologies, and rely on different strategies for persuasion.

View of reality and assumptions about the nature of the world. Quantitative research is based on positivism, a philosophical position that emphasizes observation, measurement, and logic. A fundamental assumption in the positivist view of the world is that social reality is objective, that social phenomena can be studied and measured just like natural phenomena, and that statistics can be used to test theories. The reference point is in the outside world, and it is independent of the researcher, who should be detached from the object of the study in order to minimize bias. This approach emphasizes standardized measures and hard data in the form of numbers; its main purpose is to test theories.

Qualitative research, in contrast, is based on interpretivism, a view of the world that emphasizes subjective and socially constructed reality as well as the perceptions of individual people. A fundamental assumption of the interpretive approach is that human social life is qualitatively different from natural-science phenomena because it is too complex, too varied, and too culturally diverse. Qualitative researchers assume that our experiences and interests shape how we see reality (Smith, 1983), and therefore, human social life can be understood only by observing people in their social and cultural contexts. This approach emphasizes beliefs, ideas, and perceptions of individual people in their unique environments, rather than objective reality; its main purpose is to develop a theory explaining a particular social phenomenon or aspect of human behavior. This theory can then be tested using the quantitative approach.

Purpose. Quantitative research attempts to describe and explain the causes of social phenomena as well as to predict changes in human social life. Qualitative research, in contrast, attempts to explore a social phenomenon or social process through the perceptions and beliefs of the people involved in order to obtain an in-depth understanding of a case or to develop, strengthen, or challenge a theory.

Research questions. Quantitative research questions are narrow and specific and they usually focus on the following:

- **Estimating the effect** of one variable on another (e.g., what are the effects of free trade on the economy?).

- **Assessing the effectiveness** of a particular action or policy for some outcome (e.g., does a minimum wage increase unemployment among unskilled workers?).

- **Determining the strength and/or magnitude of the relationship** between two or more variables (e.g., how does a government budget deficit affect the economy?).

- **Comparing** populations, countries, or policies on some outcomes (e.g., do graduates of private schools earn higher incomes than graduates of public schools?).

Quantitative research questions are often restated as hypotheses, which are then tested.

Qualitative research questions are usually broad and descriptive and they focus on exploring the following:

- **Processes** by which a particular phenomenon happens (e.g., how do Japanese electronics firms make decisions to invest overseas?).

- **The meaning of a phenomenon** for the people experiencing it (e.g., what does it mean for young women living in urban settings to be unemployed?).

- **Trends and changes** governing particular institutions or groups (e.g., how has federal involvement in educational policy changed over the last decade as a result of emerging institutional arrangements in contemporary US school systems?).

- **Characteristics** of a phenomenon or process and underlying factors that shape it (e.g., what approaches do educational agencies use to disseminate research information and what factors shape their choice of approach?).

Methodologies. Quantitative research uses standardized instruments for data collection and statistical methods for data analysis. It is concerned with variables (e.g., *age*, *gender*, or *GDP*), and it involves a large number of observations and unbiased sampling. The goal is to test a hypothesis with collected data in order to explain or predict a phenomenon. Data are often collected through surveys, tests, or direct observation; the most common statistical tool used for data analysis in public policy and economics research is multiple regression analysis.

In contrast, qualitative research involves the study of a small number of cases, which are examined as complex wholes. Methods of data collection include in-depth interviews and participant observation, and data analysis is systematic, but nonstatistical. Box 1 summarizes some of the main differences between quantitative and qualitative approaches.

BOX 1 Quantitative and Qualitative Approaches to Research

	Quantitative research	Qualitative research
Purpose	To describe, explain, or predict a phenomenon.	To explore and produce an in-depth understanding of a phenomenon.
Research questions	What is the effect of X on Y? What is the effectiveness of X for Y? How much does X contribute to Y? To what extent does X affect Y? What are the determinants of X? Does X produce a better outcome than Y?	How does X occur? Who is involved? Why does X occur? What is the process by which X originates or develops? What does it mean to be X? What are recent trends/changes in X?
Use of theory	A specific theory is used to guide the selection of variables that are included in the model and to make specific predictions, which are then tested. Results may confirm or challenge the theory.	A theory may be used to provide a framework for the design, but often, no specific theory is used. Qualitative researchers often attempt to develop their own theory to explain observations. No predictions are usually made about the relationship between concepts.

BOX 1 Quantitative and Qualitative Approaches to Research—cont'd.

Sample size	A large number of cases is required; the specific number will depend on the purpose, preferred statistical technique, and the number of variables included in the model. For regression analysis with several predictors, a sample size of more than 100 cases may be required.	Sample size can be as small as one.
Sample selection	Ideally, sample selection should be unbiased, using sampling techniques to produce representative samples.	Sample selection is purposive—cases are selected because they are similar, different, or unique in some way.
Data	Responses to standardized questionnaires with mostly close-ended questions collected through large household surveys; Responses to a testing instrument hypothesized to measure a particular ability or behavior; Existing statistics, often collected by large bureaucratic organizations.	Responses to in-depth, semistructured interviews with many open-ended questions; Detailed qualitative observations of participants' behavior in a given setting; Historical and other records, documents, news accounts, photographs, videos, and other cultural artifacts.
Data analysis	Statistical; a common technique in public policy and economics is multiple regression analysis.	Nonstatistical; the goal is to reduce a large amount of data to several patterns or themes that will help describe or explain the observed phenomena.
Results reporting	Results are often reported in table form and often include regression coefficients, p-values, percentages of explained variance, and other statistics.	Patterns and themes are described in a narrative and supported with multiple quotations from participants. Tables and graphs are not often used.

WHICH APPROACH IS PREVALENT IN PUBLIC POLICY PROGRAMS?

Since the 1970s, public policy literature has been characterized by the pervasive use of quantitative methods of data collection and analysis including survey research, quasiexperimental research, multiple regression analysis, cost-benefit analysis, and economic modeling. Although public policy research became more diversified in the 1990s (Radin, 2000) and began to include qualitative studies, quantitative research remains prevalent in public policy and, especially, policy analysis, both in journal publications and in educational curricula. For example, in a review of educational curricula of 44 programs in public policy and policy analysis taught at leading public policy schools in the United States, Morçöl and Ivanova (2010) found that quantitative courses constituted an overwhelming majority of courses taught at both the master's (88%) and doctoral (79%) levels. They also found that the most frequently taught method of data collection was survey and the most frequently taught method of data analysis was multiple regression analysis. This emphasis on quantitative methods is also reflected in the predominantly quantitative types of papers that students in public policy programs are often required to write.

THE RHETORIC OF QUANTITATIVE AND QUALITATIVE RESEARCH

The distinctions between quantitative and qualitative research have important implications for writing, because these approaches lend themselves to different ways of presenting information, different styles of argumentation, and different strategies for persuading readers. We can easily see this if we compare a quantitative and a qualitative study on the same topic. Firestone (1987) describes just one comparison of a quantitative and a qualitative study on the role of leadership and environment in organizational outcomes.

In the quantitative study (Firestone & Wilson, 1986), the authors tested a theory to determine the extent to which student learning was influenced by four predictor variables: teaching, support, centralization of decision-making, and socioeconomic status. Data were collected using a survey of a national sample of more than 100 elementary and secondary schools, and analyses involved statistical testing to determine the precise effect of the predictor variables on the outcomes. The end product was a statistical report in which argumentation was based on a detailed description of procedures for data collection and analysis, and the use of precise numbers, statistical tests, and visuals (e.g., tables) in the presentation of results.

In the qualitative study (Firestone & Rossman, 1986), the authors looked at the role of regional educational service agencies in research dissemination and training. Two overarching research questions were formulated: what characteristic approaches do regional educational service agencies use in their work, and what factors shape those approaches? The study used pairs of agencies (i.e., cases) selected purposively because they were known to differ in their approaches. Data collection involved semistructured interviews with multiple stakeholders and data analyses focused on examining each case, identifying patterns, and comparing pairs of cases to identify the preferred approaches used by each agency and to explain these preferences.

The authors of these two studies used very different strategies to persuade readers in the validity of their claims. The differences were in the kinds of information they chose to present, in the ways they presented that information, in how they structured the paper, and in how they used rhetorical devices to support their arguments. Box 2 summarizes these differences.

BOX 2   Persuasion Strategies: A Comparison of Two Studies

Firestone & Wilson (quantitative)	Firestone & Rossman (qualitative)
The study has a very detailed description of the methodology, devoting almost as much space to this section as to the description of results. The focus of the methodology is on procedures used to measure variables, which are described in great detail in order to persuade the reader that they were appropriate for the research purpose.	The study has a very detailed description of results, devoting ten times more space to this section than to the methodology section. The methodology section, in turn, emphasizes case selection, rather than measurement procedures in order to convince the reader that the cases were appropriate for the purpose of the study.
The study is guided by a clear theoretical framework and is presented as an attempt to test it.	The study is presented as exploratory and is not guided by a particular theory.
Past research is reviewed early in the study to justify the inclusion of variables and the choice of measurement procedures.	Past research is incorporated in the description of results to provide more credibility to the authors' arguments.
Arguments are based on deductive reasoning (applying a general principle to specific cases).	Arguments are based on inductive reasoning (inferring a general principle from specific cases).
The emphasis in the description of results is on statistical analyses, tables, and regression coefficients, which are used to quantify the precise effect of each variable on the outcomes.	The emphasis in the description of results is on quotations from participants and "thick" description including the description of concrete details, history, and specific practices of each case.
The language focuses on variables, coefficients, and percentages of variance; effects are quantified in precise numbers.	The language focuses on people and their actions, describing them in great detail, often by using the participants' own words.
The title uses the words *outcomes* and *effects*, underscoring the precise, theory-testing nature of the research.	The title uses the word *exploring* to underscore the exploratory nature of research.

Note. This table was created by the author using information in Firestone (1987) and Firestone and Rossman (1986).

RESEARCH DESIGNS IN PUBLIC POLICY AND ECONOMICS

Research design refers to the overall logical framework used in a study to answer the research question. It is, therefore, the research question that dictates the type of research design that should be used. In other words, once you decide on a particular research question, you will often no longer be free to choose any research design you want; rather, your research question will bind you to a particular design.

Research design is different from method of data collection and data analysis, although it often influences decisions about what type of data should be used and how the data should be collected and analyzed.

The central questions in research design are

- How should the researcher go about answering the research question?
- What kind of data should be used?
- How should the data be collected and analyzed?

This section briefly explains research designs commonly used in public policy and economics.

Quantitative Designs

Two quantitative designs, experimental and correlational, are common in public policy and economic research.

The purpose of experimental research is to test causal relationships, or relationships in which one variable causes another. This is done by isolating a variable of interest (called an *independent* variable) and manipulating it to observe the effect of this manipulation on another variable (called a *dependent* variable).

For a causal relationship to exist, the following conditions must be met.

- Temporal order: The cause must precede the effect.
- Statistical correlation: The cause must be related to the effect.
- Absence of alternative explanations: There should be no plausible alternative explanations for the effect other than the cause.

We can observe the first two conditions—temporal order and statistical correlation—directly, but we cannot observe the third one. Yet, elimination of plausible alternatives is crucial for establishing cause-and-effect relationships, because the hypothesized relationship may be due to a third variable, called a *confound*. Such a false relationship between variables is called *spurious*. Spurious relationships occur when there is another, unseen, variable that affects both variables, making them show a correlation. An often-cited example of a spurious relationship is the relationship between a child's shoe size and the child's math score. As the shoe size increases, so does the math score, but this does not mean that shoe size causes math scores to go up; rather, as the child grows and receives more education, the shoe size increases, and so does the child's math ability.

In experimental research, we eliminate alternative explanations by design: by using a control group, by randomly assigning participants to the treatment and control groups, and by measuring the target variables before and after the treatment. As a result, we can often be fairly confident that the results we obtain come from the experimental manipulation rather than from extraneous factors.

Some experiments in public policy and economics are conducted in a laboratory; others, in a natural environment—in the field. Laboratory experiments are often conducted with students as subjects, and their purpose is to examine in a "pure" environment how manipulating a certain variable or variables may affect an outcome. An example of a laboratory experiment with important policy implications is Sigall and Ostrove's study "Beautiful but Dangerous: Effects of Offender Attractiveness and Nature of the Crime on Juridic Judgment" published in 1975 in the *Journal of Personality and Social Psychology*, in which the authors examined the effects of physical attractiveness of a criminal defendant on sentencing decisions. In the study, students were randomly assigned to examine cases with attractive or unattractive defendants involved in attractiveness-related or -unrelated crimes (i.e., swindle vs. burglary) and were asked to sentence the defendants to a term of imprisonment. A control group was also used with no information about the defendant's attractiveness. The researchers found that attractiveness did in fact influence sentencing decisions.

An example of a field experiment is Altmann and Traxler's study "Nudges at the Dentist" published in 2014 in the *European Economic Review.* The researchers wanted to know if reminders for medical check-ups influenced patient behavior. The dependent variable was whether a patient contacted the dentist within a certain period to arrange a check-up appointment. Patients who were due to schedule a check-up were sent a neutral reminder, a reminder with additional information on the benefits of prevention, or no reminder. The researchers found that sending reminders had strong positive effects on patients' decision to make a check-up appointment.

Another example is Bloom's "Lessons from the Delaware Dislocated Worker Pilot Program" published in 1987 in the *Evaluation Review*, in which the author reports a field experiment to examine whether a job-training program helped dislocated workers reenter the job market. A pool of potential participants was identified, and participants were randomly assigned to a training program and a control group. The treatment group received job-search workshops, counseling, and retraining, while the control group did not receive any of those services. After a year, the groups were compared on earnings and receipt of unemployment benefits. Bloom found that the program had a negative effect on the participants—those who participated in the training program earned less and received more benefits than the nonparticipants.

In policy research, however, where the emphasis is on applied problems, experiments with random assignment to groups, or randomization, (the so-called *classical experiments*) are rare, and experimental research usually takes the form of **quasiexperiments**—experiments without randomization. Such experiments are appropriate when we are interested in conditions that cannot be randomly assigned because events have already occurred, or because they cannot be manipulated. For example, a researcher may want to know how natural disasters affect people's psychological and economic well-being by comparing a group of people who have been exposed to a natural disaster with a group of people who have not had such exposure.

The limitation of quasiexperimental research is that it precludes strong causal inferences, which are possible in classical experiments. Essentially, quasiexperimental designs are correlational and require statistical controls. Two things can strengthen quasiexperimental designs: having a good theoretical model that predicts relationships between the variables, and equating the groups on baseline characteristics that may be related to the dependent variable.

Correlational designs are much more common in public policy and economic research than experimental ones. In these designs, the researcher builds a model that hypothesizes how certain variables (called *predictor* variables) affect other variables (called *outcome* variables). Data are collected on both predictor and outcome variables, and the model is tested using regression analysis to explain sources of variance in the data. How much variance can be attributed to this or that variable in the model? Often, different statistical models, based on different assumptions, are tested to see which one provides the best fit for the data.

To eliminate plausible alternative explanations, researchers also include control variables—sometimes more than a dozen such variables—in the model. These are variables that may have independent effects on the outcome variables, and omitting them may result in biased estimates of the effect of the predictors on the outcome. These variables are used as statistical controls. For example, a researcher may want to know how drinking water quality affects child health in a developing country. He or she collects statistical data on drinking water quality and child health as well as on a large number of control variables—other variables that may be linked to both drinking water quality and child health and that may provide an alternative explanation for the relationship. Where do these control variables come from? They come from a theory that the researcher uses to explain how drinking water quality affects child health. The theory would guide the researcher in the selection of variables that should be included in the model. In our example, control variables may include type of housing, water supply sources, seasonal changes, water storage, sanitation (e.g., solid waste management), hygiene behavior, household's health status, knowledge about hygiene, and nutrition. The researcher then runs a regression (or several regressions) with these variables and observes the effects of drinking water quality on child health by statistically controlling (keeping constant) all the other variables.

Statistical controls are not as strong as experimental controls, which are built into the design and make it possible to keep everything except the treatment constant. Thus, correlational designs may suffer from **omitted variable bias**—bias resulting from failure to include an unobserved variable or variables that correlate with both a predictor and an outcome variable. To see why, suppose that you want to know if free-trade agreements (FTA) between countries result in more trade. If you simply correlate an FTA dummy variable (i.e., trade before and after an FTA) with trade, your estimation results may be biased—they may not accurately reflect this relationship—because there may be other, unobserved variables that correlate with both a country's decision to sign an FTA and the decision to trade. These variables may include trade barriers, specific policies, or the environment.

Economists have created special tools and approaches to avoid or minimize omitted variable bias. One approach, for example, is to use panel, rather than cross-sectional, data and estimate a fixed-effects regression model. Such models are important with group-level data, for example, households, countries, or organizations, because groups may have unobservable characteristics that correlate with the outcome variables. If these characteristics are time-invariant (if they do not vary with time within the groups), then fixed effect models will eliminate omitted variable bias. Researchers also often perform robustness checks to check for, and eliminate, alternative explanations.

Results of both experimental and correlational studies are often interpreted by looking at

- Whether the relationship is statistically significant (which is shown, for example, by the p-value),

- The strength of the relationship (which is shown, for example, by the correlation coefficients),

- The direction of the relationship (which is shown by the sign of the coefficients),

- The percentage of explained variance in the model (which is shown, for example, by the coefficient of determination, or R^2), and

- The contribution of each variable (which is shown by the size of the regression coefficients).

These statistical concepts are explained in greater detail in Chapter 14, along with suggestions for how to present these statistics in a quantitative paper.

Qualitative Designs

Qualitative research is not intended to test a hypothesis or a theory. Rather, it begins with observation and attempts to propose a tentative theory that explains the themes and patterns that have been observed. Although qualitative research includes a constellation of methods and approaches, its designs can often be described as case study or comparative case study. Case-study designs are characterized by the following:

- A focus on in-depth and holistic exploration: Researchers try to understand phenomena as complex wholes, from different perspectives, often without attempting to control for any factors.

- Use of multiple sources of information: Researchers collect data through semistructured interviews with multiple stakeholders, a review of various official and unofficial documents and scholarly literature, direct or indirect observation, or examination of various artifacts, and then search for common patterns and themes in the collected data.

- Inductive reasoning: Researchers move from specific observations to specific themes, and from those themes, they may propose a more general theory.

The end product in a case study is a narrative report, usually containing multiple quotations from participants. Interpretation often involves three levels:

- Describing the point of view of the participants, using direct quotations or citing relevant places from the collected documents.

- Interpreting and explaining the underlying meaning of these quotations, from the researcher's point of view.

- Explaining what these observations and interpretations suggest for the overall understanding of the phenomenon under study or proposing a theory that explains these observations.

For example, in the article "Successfully Exiting Homelessness: Experiences of Formerly Homeless Mentally Ill Individuals" published in *Evaluation and Program Planning*, Thompson et al. (2004) describe an exploratory study they conducted to examine the processes through which homeless people achieved positive outcomes (e.g., stable housing). They recruited a small sample of participants (12 people) and conducted semistructured interviews with them on experiences of being homeless, processes of exiting homelessness, and the role of significant relationships in this process. The interviews were transcribed and coded by three independent raters to identify important "content categories" (p. 425)—themes into which participants' statements could be classified. The authors identified eight such categories after analyzing 224 statements from the participants. They organized the categories according to the "frequency and proportion of statements" (p. 426) to highlight the relative importance of each category. In presenting the results of the study, the authors offered three levels of interpretation:

- **Participants' views**: What do they say about their experiences and beliefs?

- **The researchers' explanation**: What do these views mean?

- **Connection to theory**: How do these explanations advance our understanding of how homeless individuals exit homelessness?

Three data collection methods are common in qualitative research. Perhaps the most common method is semistructured (or unstructured) interviews, which are in-depth, open-ended, and informal interviews conducted to obtain as much detail from the participants as possible in order to create a comprehensive picture of the phenomenon under study. Another method is direct observation, and it involves the researcher visiting the site to observe what is happening, who is involved, and how things develop. The final method of data collection that is often used in case-study research involves collecting various documents, records, and artifacts. Qualitative researchers often use all three data collection methods in the same study to provide more detail and strengthen their arguments.

Case-study research is common in public policy, particularly in such areas as international relations, security studies, comparative politics, law, and public administration. It is much less common in economics, although some researchers argue that it does have a place in economic research. For example, Piore (2006) describes how case-study research based on qualitative, in-depth interviews with "economic actors" (p. 17) can help economists create or refine theories. He argues that although evidence obtained from qualitative interviews cannot be used in economic research directly as empirical evidence, it can be used to build better theoretical models, which can then be tested empirically.

Qualitative research in public policy often relies on comparative designs. In the simplest design, comparable data are compiled on several countries or settings, and a list of alternative explanations is assembled to explain the trends observed in the cross-country data. The researcher then examines the alternative explanations one by one to see how well they fit the data until he finds one that is most consistent with the data.

For example, in the study "International Trends in Economics Degrees During the 1990s" published in the *Journal of Economic Education*, Siegfried and Round (2001) tried to explain a downward trend in the number of undergraduate degrees in economics in the 1990s. They collected comparable data from four developed countries and assembled several alternative explanations for the observation including changing interest in business education, rising costs, changes in labor market returns to an economics degree, and changes in teaching methods and grading standards. They then checked how consistent each explanation was with the data to identify the one that had the most promise for further investigation. It should be noted that explanations obtained in this way are always tentative and should be described only as possibilities—just as Siegfried and Round did in their study.

Comparative designs can also be used to strengthen theoretical explanation (Lim, 2006). In this case, the researcher examines a range of cases in a step-by-step manner and uses each case to strengthen or modify an existing theory. The goal is to fit the selected cases into a bigger theoretical perspective and modify it where needed. For example, a researcher may be interested in modernization theory and its effects on economic development in Asia. He would examine a series of countries in the Asian region and use each country "as a stepping stone" (Lim, 2006, p. 23) to develop or modify the original theory.

Lim (2006) describes more sophisticated comparative designs, in which the researcher attempts to "control" for other factors by choosing cases (e.g., countries, regions, organizations) that are either very similar or very different. These designs are called the most similar systems (MSS) design and the most different systems (MDS) design. In these designs, cases are selected strategically to enable explanation of outcome variables.

In the MSS design, two or more cases (e.g., countries) are selected such that they share many political, social, cultural, economic, and other relevant characteristics, but also differ on some. The differences must be on at least two variables: the outcome variable and one (or more) of the explanatory variables. In other words, both the outcome variable and one of the explanatory variables must vary between the selected cases. Lim (2006) explains that the similar characteristics can then be held constant, which allows the researcher to look for the explanatory variable on which the cases differ. This variable is then used to explain the differences in the outcome. The choice of specific countries depends on the research question, but MSS designs are often based on the use of similar neighboring countries or regions such as Scandinavian countries, the United States and Canada, or Taiwan and South Korea.

In the MSD design, cases are selected such that they are different in almost every respect except for the outcome variable. The researcher then looks for a key similarity or similarities between the cases, which can explain the same outcome. In contrast to the MSS design, in this design, the outcome variable should be the same across all the cases, so cases are selected based on that variable.

Case selection is crucial in comparative designs, and it is always purposive and strategic—guided by the research purpose and research question. To be comparable, the cases that are being compared must share some characteristics that are theoretically relevant to the research question and differ on others. Thus, we can compare cases whose attributes are in part shared and in part nonshared. If cases are selected such that they are similar on the outcome AND similar on all potentially explanatory variables, then a comparison would not be possible; comparing cases that are different in all respects is equally meaningless.

Another important point to keep in mind with qualitative designs is that even the most sophisticated comparative designs cannot control for extraneous variables in the same way as experiments do, where the researcher can manipulate one variable and keep constant all the other variables. In comparative research, variables cannot be manipulated directly and must be analyzed retrospectively and indirectly (Lim, 2006). And because there are many more differences between "similar" cases (or similarities between "different" cases) than we can potentially identify, we cannot assume that the characteristics we have identified are the ones responsible for explaining the outcome. Conclusions drawn from qualitative comparisons should, therefore, be small, tentative, and nondefinitive.

Combining Quantitative and Qualitative Approaches

It is often difficult to combine quantitative and qualitative approaches because they are based on fundamentally different assumptions and have different purposes. Specific research questions are usually amenable to either one or the other type of approach, but not to both.

It is, however, possible, and in some research areas even advisable, to complement a quantitative research project with a qualitative component. For example, your main research question may ask about the effectiveness of a policy and may call for developing and testing a model that specifies the effects of the policy on some outcome. To that question, you may add another question to clarify participants' opinions about the policy. You will then conduct in-depth interviews with some of those affected by the policy to obtain a fuller picture of the policy's effects.

EXAMPLES OF QUALITATIVE AND QUANTITATIVE APPROACHES

Below are two examples of how you, as a researcher, may proceed with a research project focusing on microfinance programs for farmers in a developing country. The first example is of a project based on a qualitative approach, and the second example is of a project based on a quantitative approach.

Qualitative Approach

- Search relevant literature to find out what is known about the topic and what is not known. Formulate a broad research question. The question may focus on farmers' personal experiences with microfinance programs (i.e., case study) or on how different agencies make lending decisions (i.e., comparative case study).

- Select a small sample of participants who you think would be appropriate for your purposes. They need not be representative of a larger population. Rather, they should be selected purposively, for reasons that would help you answer your research question. For example, you may choose to focus on young women, people with particular skills, or participants from certain income groups. Having a general theory about participants' experiences with microfinance or about factors that influence lending decisions may help you make an appropriate selection.

- Decide what kind of data you need to answer your research question. Often, qualitative researchers collect several kinds of data from many sources in order to examine the issue from different perspectives. Data may be collected through in-depth, open-ended interviews with stakeholders, by examining—and comparing—the official documents and records of several lending institutions, or by directly observing the process of applying for and receiving a microfinance loan. Keep in mind that the strength of qualitative research comes from the diversity of sources, so the more sources you include, the better. It may also be a good idea to interview participants several times over a period of time and compare their answers.

- Take notes on the material you have collected and record your own thoughts during or immediately after the interviews, while impressions are still fresh. Transcribe responses and put them into categories reflecting the themes and patterns that emerge from the data. What are some of the main themes? What do all or many of the participants say?

- Examine the documents and other information you have collected and try to sort the data into the categories you have created—or create new ones.

- Try to reduce the categories by grouping ideas and discarding those that cannot be sufficiently developed or supported.

- Determine how the categories logically relate to one another. This will help you determine the best structure for your paper and highlight your main findings.

- Compare your findings with those of previous research or with predictions from a relevant theory. Do your findings confirm previous research or theory or diverge from it?

- Think about theoretical and practical implications of your findings.

- The result of your analysis will be a narrative that should construct a larger meaning from your analysis of individual responses and other information. Use quotations from your participants and documents to support your arguments.

Quantitative Approach

- Search relevant literature to find out what is known about the topic and what is not known. Try to narrow down the topic to something very specific. You may want to focus on the determinants of lending decisions or microfinance delinquency among farmers or on the effectiveness of microfinance programs for poverty reduction.

- Formulate a specific, narrow question. What are the main determinants of lending decisions in microfinance programs in Country X? What are the determinants of microfinance delinquency among farmers in Country X?

To what extent have microfinance programs reduced poverty among the participants?

- Decide on the meanings of your main concepts. Your definitions should come from the literature. Decide how your concepts will be measured. Support your decisions by appealing to previous research.

- Develop a theoretical framework that explains the relationship(s) among the variables you are interested in. From the theory, derive a specific model that you will test.

- Obtain data on all the variables. *Data* in quantitative research means numeric data. Such data are often created from responses collected through surveys or obtained in the form of existing statistics from large government organizations.

- If you decide to collect data by yourself, you would need to select a sample that is representative of the target population. Representativeness is important in surveys as the ultimate goal is to generalize to a wider population. Response rate is also important and should ideally be above 50%.

- Data are often subject to various transformations before analyses. The specific transformation will depend on the purpose of your research and the original form of the data you have collected or obtained.

- Enter your data into a statistical program such as SPSS or STATA, select a statistical procedure that is appropriate for your analyses, and perform the analyses.

- Examine the output of the statistical program. Do your results confirm or disconfirm your hypothesis? What is the answer to your research question(s)? Think about theoretical and practical implications of your findings.

Chapter 3

Research Topics and Paper Options

POSSIBLE TOPICS

The research topic is the general area that a research project is about. It is usually rather broad and can cover a local issue, a national issue, or an international issue; it may be about a specific sector of the economy (e.g., agriculture), a specific organization, or a specific geographical area.

The range of topics that can be studied in public policy and economics is virtually endless. In fact, any kind of human behavior, individual or social activity, or social phenomenon is amenable to economic or policy analysis as long as the focus is on the following:

- Decisions, choices, and trade-offs that individuals, organizations, or governments make in order to allocate limited resources;

- Needs, wants, and demands of individuals, organizations, or governments and how these needs, wants, and demands affect decisions;

- Availability and distribution of resources;

- Goods or assets, including immaterial ones such as beliefs, confidence, self-esteem, or hope, which can be produced, consumed, or invested in; or

- Historical, cultural, institutional, or social contexts or processes and how they affect individual or collective behavior.

Professional researchers usually specialize in a particular area of research and are well aware of what is known in their area, what research has been done, and what issues or problems have not yet been explored or remain controversial. In contrast, students who are new to graduate study may not have a clear idea about an appropriate research area or topic. Box 3 lists some examples of broad topics for research in public policy and economics.

NARROWING DOWN A TOPIC

The topics shown in Box 3 are extremely general, and they would be difficult or impossible to research: Just imagine researching immigration or public

How to Write about Economics and Public Policy. https://doi.org/10.1016/B978-0-12-813010-0.00003-X

41

BOX 3 Sample Research Topics in Public Policy and Economics

Politics	Good governance, democracy, elections, transparency, corruption, public/community participation in local decision-making, female participation in local decision-making, decentralization, rural development, rural depopulation, mergers of municipalities
Sustainable Development	Climate change, water pollution, waste management, disaster management planning, natural disasters, energy security
Economic Policies and Development	Budgeting, budget administration, fiscal deficit, privatization, land use, real estate markets, asset management, agrarian reforms, forestry policies, taxes, tax reforms, inflation, effects of exchange rates on different aspects of the economy, foreign direct investment, economic growth, monetary policies, microfinance, remittances, stock markets, corporate governance, industrial policies, competitiveness of industries, competition policies, trade policies, trade liberalization, trade facilitation, free-trade agreements, investment and investment treaties, foreign aid effectiveness, oil price shocks, unemployment
Foreign Policy and Security Studies	Peacebuilding, civil conflicts, terrorism/war on terror, regional cooperation, free-trade zones, bilateral and multilateral agreements, membership in regional organizations
Public Management	Public debt, public procurement, public expenditure, public service, public housing
Social Policies	Educational policies, public health, pension reforms, gender equality, women empowerment, social safety, poverty, anticorruption policies, human capital, immigration, tourism, religion, mass media, language policies, energy policy, labor policy, transportation policy, environmental policy

housing! Where would you even begin? These topics need to be narrowed down. One way to narrow down a topic is to specify a geographical setting and/or a time frame. For example, you can focus on educational policies in China in the 1990s, peace and democracy building in Myanmar in the 1990s, or trade liberalization in developing countries in the past decade.

Adding a geographical area or a time frame to a topic does help make it a little less general, but it does not help make it less descriptive. Take educational policies in China in the 1990s, for example. You can describe them in detail but what exactly are you going to research? Their effectiveness for something? Their origin? The factors that have influenced them? How can you decide what should be the focus of your research?

What you need to do, ultimately, is formulate your topic as a relationship between two or more phenomena or concepts. Below are some examples.

- Unemployment and crime rates
- Institutional reforms and educational attainment
- Trade facilitation and economic growth
- International trade and foreign direct investment
- Foreign direct investment and technology transfer
- Globalization and inequality
- Housing policy and home ownership

For example, the topic focusing on educational policies in China in the 1990s could be reformulated as a study of the relationship between educational policies and student outcomes. Educational policies can then be narrowed down even further—to policies in mathematics or language education. The topic focusing on peace and democracy building in Myanmar can be reformulated as a relationship between peacebuilding and economic development, whereas the topic focusing on trade liberalization can be restated as a relationship between trade liberalization and economic growth in developing countries.

But how do you come up with this other relevant concept or variable so that you can reformulate your topic as a relationship? Where should it come from? The best way to come up with a researchable relationship is to read, read, and read.

If you do have a general area in mind but are not very familiar with that area, start reading around to understand what issues are important, what is known, what controversies exist, and what ideas might be worth exploring further. Try to choose a topic that elicits different opinions, feelings, or positions, that is related to many issues, and that can generate many questions. The best way to start is to look for review articles in academic journals—articles that summarize research in a particular topic. In addition to providing a summary of research in an area, such articles usually outline areas for future research and may even contain research questions that may be of interest to you.

If you do not have a specific research area in mind, here are a few suggestions for finding a good topic.

1. Check the websites of economics departments of major universities, institutes, or research centers. One useful directory of such institutions is called EDIRC. It lists nearly 14,000 economics institutions in more than 200 countries and territories and can be searched by country or research field. It can be accessed at https://edirc.repec.org/goodies.html.

2. You may also want to check the websites of major schools of public policy such as the Kennedy School of Government at Harvard University, the Goldman School of Public Policy at the University of California at Berkley, or the Ford School of Public Policy at the University of Michigan. The

websites of these schools provide links to faculty research projects, publications, and working paper series, which can be accessed for free.

3. Visit the website of the Center for Economic and Policy Research (http://cepr.net/) and browse through their Publications and Issues sections. Try to identify topics that might be of interest to you.

4. For ideas beyond economics, check the Almanac of Policy Issues, which is a directory of general public policy resources and links to major public policy organizations (http://www.policyalmanac.org/).

5. Check theses written by past students in your program. Do any of the topics look interesting to you?

6. Check your school faculty members' profiles. What are their current research interests? What are they working on? Are any of their topics interesting to you? This strategy may be particularly useful for doctoral students as there are clear benefits to finding an advisor who is an expert on the topic you would like to pursue.

7. Talk to your advisor (if you have one) or a professor who is teaching a course that you like. Ask them for advice for a good topic to pursue.

8. Another suggestion might be to turn to current events. Periodicals—newspapers, magazines, and various business publications—may be a good source of ideas for research. However, keep in mind that the way news sources present information is very, very different from the way academics present their arguments, and that articles written for popular consumption can hardly serve as a model for academic writing. I explain further the differences between academic and mass media discourse in Chapter 4.

SUGGESTIONS FOR A GOOD TOPIC

A Good Topic Is Limited

- It focuses on a relationship.
- It specifies a geographical setting and/or time frame for the research.
- It is doable within the time frame of your degree program.

A Good Topic Is Researchable and It Is Researchable by You

A topic is researchable when you can obtain the necessary data to research it. Perhaps one of the main difficulties that graduate students encounter in master's programs is obtaining data. There are three ways to obtain data:

- Collect by yourself.
- Purchase from an organization that sells data.

- Obtain (usually for free) from a national or international organization such as the World Bank, which compiles various statistical data.

Each of these options has its advantages and disadvantages; the choice depends on the specific goals of your project, data availability, and many other things including the time frame for your research.

Another thing to consider when choosing a topic is whether you have—or will be able to acquire—the necessary analytic skills for your research. Many interesting topics in economics and public policy focus on multiple relationships and require the use of sophisticated multivariate statistical techniques for analysis.

A Good Topic Focuses on a Debatable Issue

Your topic should be policy-related—it should have clear implications for policy formulation, implementation, or evaluation. Most topics in applied economics and public policy do have policy implications, so this criterion is not difficult to satisfy. What is important is that the issue you choose to research be debatable. An issue is debatable when it can be looked at from different perspectives, each one leading to a different conclusion. For example, the topic "institutional reforms in Kenya" is not debatable, at least not in the way it is formulated, but a topic focusing on the effects of institutional reforms in Kenya on private sector development is debatable because different researchers might have different opinions about these effects.

A Good Topic Allows You to Make an Original Contribution

Students sometimes justify their choice of a topic by saying that "it has never been done or studied before." But this justification is often insufficient. There are many things in the world that have never been done or studied before but this does not mean that we should do or study them. Rather than choosing a topic just because it has never been studied before, think about its importance for advancing the field or for improving policy. What does your research add to the field that is not already there? Why should members of the academic or policy community care about your research? These questions are especially important for doctoral students, whose work has to make an original contribution to the field to be accepted.

A good way to add to the field is to try to resolve an existing controversy. Try to choose a topic that has generated different results, with some studies, for example, finding a positive relationship, and others, finding a negative relationship or no relationship. Then think of a way to improve on the existing research to resolve the controversy.

For master's students, especially students in professional degree programs, who are often described as consumers rather than producers of knowledge, making an original contribution may not be as important as for doctoral students. Such students can often "get away" with a replication or a "replication plus"—for example, a study testing an existing model with a slightly different set of variables. For more suggestions on how to develop a research topic, see Chapter 6.

A Good Topic Is Grounded in Theory and Previous Research

In any research project, you will have to make many important decisions including decisions about

- How to design the study in order to answer your research question,
- What variables to include in the model,
- What data to use and how to collect these data, and
- What analytical techniques to use to analyze the data.

The decisions you will make will need to be justified, often on both theoretical and empirical grounds, by referring to theory and past empirical research. Thus, there should be at least some literature, including theoretical literature, on the topic to guide you in your decisions. Some of the literature may even come from a different field. For example, many problems that have traditionally been investigated by psychologists—such as child rearing, student achievement, or mental health—have now become topics for economics and public policy research. It is not uncommon in economics and public policy studies on these topics to draw on psychological or medical research findings when building a theoretical framework for the study.

COMMON PROBLEMS WITH TOPIC SELECTION

There are several mistakes that students who are new to graduate study— especially students with work-related policy background—often make when selecting a topic. Below I explain some of the most common ones.

"The Current Situation..."

A common mistake is the desire to focus on "the current situation." Topics that fall into this category include

- The current situation in country X/policy Y,
- Existing policies of government X in area Y,
- Strengths and weaknesses of policy X or organization Y, or
- Benefits or drawbacks of policy X.

These topics are too broad and too vague to be researchable. Students who choose such topics often find themselves in a difficult position, not knowing what to include in their paper or how to select relevant information and end up writing descriptive or opinion-based papers about everything they can find on their topic.

"What Can Be Done…?"

Another mistake is to try to formulate a topic as "what can be done" to achieve something good or prevent something bad. For example, a student may formulate a topic as "what can be done to alleviate poverty," "what can be done to achieve sustainable growth," or "what can be done to prevent corruption." The problem with such topics is that there are numerous ways in which a goal could be achieved or a negative impact, mitigated, each with its own costs and consequences. In order to determine what can be done in a given situation or for a given outcome, you need, at a minimum, to specify the outcome and the available options and compare them using a set of predetermined, specified criteria. The problem here is that the number of options is usually very large or even limitless; simply listing them as something that "can be done" in theory to solve a given problem does not amount to doing research.

"Research as Advocacy"

Another mistake is to choose a topic about which you have a strong personal opinion. Students choosing such topics often want to "prove" something rather than engage in dispassionate inquiry. Avoid topics on which you have a strong position, or you may end up doing policy advocacy rather than research. Instead, choose a topic in which you have a scholarly interest and which generates questions to which you do not yet have answers.

Research on "My Country"

Many international students, especially students from developing countries, want to focus their research on their country. In a way, this is understandable—if your country faces many problems, it may be tempting to focus on one of them. In some cases this may be a good idea, especially if you have already done some work in this area or have access to relevant data.

However, choosing to do a research project on a particular country just because you happen to come from that country is not sufficient justification. If you do want to focus on your country, you need to justify your choice based on your research question and the potential contribution of your research to the field. Why does it make sense to answer your research question using data from that particular country? In what way can research on your country contribute to our knowledge about the topic? This is particularly important for doctoral students.

Economic research on "my country" may also be problematic on methodological grounds. For example, there may not be enough data on your country to provide the necessary number of observations, or the data may be of low quality. Many interesting questions in public policy also call for the use of international, or cross-country, data.

However, if you do have a good reason for doing research on your country, and if you are confident that you can obtain good-quality data, then go for it! Country-specific research can be particularly useful in advancing our knowledge about economic, political, and social processes in developing countries and other contexts that we do not know much about.

RESEARCH PAPER OPTIONS

Your options with respect to what kind of paper you can write will depend on several things including the requirements of your program, whether you are a master's or a doctoral student, as well as your topic and area of research.

Generally, master's students in professional public policy programs have two options. They can write an empirical quantitative paper or an empirical qualitative paper. These types of paper are described below.

- **An empirical quantitative paper.** Students who are new to graduate study, especially students from non-Western cultures who have never conducted research often misunderstand what quantitative research is, believing that if they include numbers in their paper, the paper will be quantitative. In fact, what distinguishes empirical quantitative papers from all other papers is the logic they follow to show how things are. Empirical quantitative papers follow the logic of hypothesis testing. Researchers formulate a hypothesis, collect (or obtain) numeric data, and then run statistical analyses to confirm or disconfirm the hypothesis. An example of an empirical quantitative paper is shown in Appendix B.

- **An empirical qualitative paper.** Empirical qualitative papers may take many forms, but unlike quantitative papers, they do not have hypotheses or statistical tests and are not based on an analysis of numeric data. Data in qualitative papers come from interviews or an examination of external or internal documents or artifacts and take the form of quotations from participants or extracts from documents. Data in a qualitative study may also come from direct or indirect observation. Many qualitative studies in public policy are based on data collected through multiple methods including documentary research and qualitative interviews. An example of an empirical qualitative paper is shown in Appendix B.

In economics programs, students are often encouraged—or even required—to do an empirical quantitative paper.

In shorter programs, especially 1-year programs in public policy, master's students may sometimes have the option of doing a nonempirical paper. Nonempirical papers can be broadly divided into two kinds: pure literature reviews and what could be called *argumentative papers.* **Literature reviews** are essentially reviews of research on a particular topic that have been organized in some way to show where the field currently is and what questions remain unanswered.

Argumentative papers, in contrast, present an argument and try to support or refute it by drawing on previous research. The argument may be about a political, social, or economic phenomenon, an existing or new policy or policies, a historical event, or current trends. These papers are often supplemented with some qualitative data, such as data from relevant documents.

Argumentative papers differ from pure literature reviews in that they make a specific argument and use both literature and some data to support it. They also differ from traditional empirical qualitative papers because the data are often limited and come primarily from available documents rather than from interviews or observation. An argumentative paper that is based primarily on the existing literature and that is supplemented with limited documentary research is often a good option for master's students in public policy programs who wish to do qualitative work, but who do not have much time for data collection. Pure literature reviews, in contrast, are often not an option.

Doctoral students in public policy and economics programs also have three options. They can write an empirical quantitative paper, an empirical qualitative paper, or a theoretical paper. Empirical papers in doctoral programs differ from those in master's programs in substance as well as in length; students in doctoral programs are expected to collect their own data and perform more comprehensive analyses. Additionally, doctoral students in economics often write several loosely connected papers (called *essays*) instead of one big dissertation. **Theoretical papers** at this level often take the form of mathematical proofs of a concept or theory.

The following types of paper would be largely inappropriate in public policy and economics programs for both master's and doctoral students.

- **A descriptive paper**: a paper that gives a factual account of a particular phenomenon or that merely describes the current situation in a particular country.

- **An advocacy paper**: a paper that is based on the author's personal opinion and that advocates a particular policy based on the author's subjective judgment, even if the judgment is supported by quotations from policy-makers.

- **A literature review**: a paper that merely reviews literature on a particular topic.

Chapter 4

Identifying Literature to Review

WHAT IS ACADEMIC LITERATURE?

Academic literature is a body of published and unpublished written works that are related by subject matter. Generally, there are three kinds of literature that students consult for a research project in public policy and economics: scholarly literature, policy literature, and popular literature. Understanding the features of each kind of literature and its applicability for research will help you make informed decisions about what literature to look for in your project.

SCHOLARLY LITERATURE

Scholarly literature includes articles in scholarly journals, scholarly books and textbooks, doctoral dissertations, and academic conference reports. Each of these types of literature is described below.

Scholarly Journals

Articles in scholarly journals are one of the most important sources of information on any academic issue for two reasons. First, most articles that are published in scholarly journals have undergone peer review—a review by fellow academics, who have found those article to be of sufficient quality to be published. Second, only articles in scholarly journals provide all the necessary details about a particular piece of research to allow you to understand how it was done and what its strengths and limitations are.

Four types of articles can commonly be found in scholarly journals in public policy and economics. Each type of article is briefly described below.

- **Review articles.** These are articles reviewing scholarly works on a particular issue or problem. Such articles can be very useful for students especially at the beginning of research as they can provide an overview of important conceptual and methodological issues related to the topic. An example of an article of this type is Esther Duflo's "Women Empowerment and Economic Development" published in 2012 in the *Journal of Economic Literature*. This article reviews the literature on the empowerment-development debate and makes suggestions for policy.

How to Write about Economics and Public Policy. https://doi.org/10.1016/B978-0-12-813010-0.00004-1

51

- **Theoretical articles**. Theoretical articles in economics develop a model of economic behavior that occurs under certain assumptions and that is subject to well-defined constraints. The author may construct a theoretical model from scratch, modify an existing model, or develop a novel application for an existing theoretical model. The goal is to derive theoretical implications about the actions and decisions of economic agents. Some theoretical articles in economics are highly mathematical and the goal is to derive proofs for a solution. An example of a theoretical article is George A. Akerlof's "The Market for 'Lemons': Quality Uncertainty and the Market Mechanism" published in 1970 in the *Quarterly Journal of Economics* or Marcelo de C. Griebeler's "Friendship and In-class Academic Dishonesty" published in 2017 in the journal *Economic Letters*.

  Theoretical papers in economics may also rely on graphs to show how changes in economic conditions or behavior will affect variables of interest. An example of an article of this type is Paul de Grauwe's "Challenges for Monetary Policy in Euroland" published in 2002 in the *Journal of Common Market Studies*, in which the author analyzes the effects of the monetary policy of the European Central Bank and the implications of the growth of the European monetary union.

- **Empirical articles**. These are articles that are based on data analysis. Empirical articles in economics are almost exclusively quantitative and often correlational; empirical articles in public policy may be quantitative or qualitative, depending on the specific area and research question. An example of an empirical quantitative article in economics is Bharadwaj, Loken, and Neilson's study "Early Life Health Interventions and Academic Achievement" published in 2013 in the *American Economic Review*. An example of an empirical qualitative article is Andrew Roberts' study "The Politics of Healthcare Reform in Postcommunist Europe: The Importance of Access" published in 2009 in the *Journal of Public Policy*.

- **Methodological articles**. These articles describe new approaches to data collection or data analysis, modifications to existing approaches, or discussions of existing data analytic techniques. They may offer a theoretical discussion of a research approach or technique or illustrate the use of a particular approach with examples or data. An example of an interesting—if somewhat unconventional—methodological article in economics is Michael J. Piore's "Qualitative Research Techniques in Economics" published in 1979 in the journal *Administrative Science Quarterly*.

It is important to keep in mind that there is significant variation in the quality of published research among journals. Learn early on which journals are at the top of your field and try to rely on them more than on other journals in your research. One way to make sure that the journals you choose are good quality is to check the publisher. Good-quality journals are published by well-known, academic publishers such as Elsevier, Cambridge University Press, Willey, Oxford University Press, Sage, and others. For journals in economics, it might be a good idea to start with the journals published by the American Economic Association (https://www.aeaweb.org/journals/). These are reputable, high-quality journals covering a very wide range of topics in economics.

It may also be a good idea to check the **impact factor** of the journals you have found. This is a measure of the frequency with which the average article in a journal was cited in a particular year; the higher the impact factor, the more prestigious the journal. Many journals in economics and public policy have an impact factor, which can be a good indicator of a journal's quality; however, not all journals have an impact factor, especially outside the field of economics. Not having an impact factor does not necessarily mean that the journal is low-quality.

A special difficulty for students and novice researchers is presented by so-called **Open-Access Journals,** journals that provide their articles to readers on the Internet free of charge. As of January 2017, the Directory of Open Access Journals (DOAJ) listed nearly 10,000 titles; there are also many open-access journals that are not listed in this directory. How good are open-access journals? It is probably fair to say that a small number of these journals are near the top of their field but many are not particularly reputable and some are downright predatory, publishing anything for a fee.

So how can you distinguish between reputable and less reputable open-access journals? This is not an easy task. Some librarians have made these suggestions.

- Check if the journal is included in the DOAJ. Journals that are included in this directory must meet a number of quality-assurance criteria.

- Check if the journal's publisher is an academic publisher; if not, check if the publisher is a member of the Open Access Scholarly Publisher's Association (ASPA). Academic publishers and publishers who are members of the ASPA are a safer option.

- Check if the journal is indexed in a major indexing and abstracting service such as Scopus or Web of Science.

For more information about scholarly journals in public policy and economics, see Appendix D, which lists many reputable journals along with their impact factor and other important information.

Textbooks and Scholarly Books

University textbooks are an important source of disciplinary knowledge, conveying "the values and ideological assumptions of a particular academic culture" (Hyland, 2004, p. 105). Students often see textbooks as one of the most important and authoritative sources of academic knowledge and tend to rely on them for their research projects. However, the extent to which textbooks are seen by the academic community as "central to the disciplinary construction of new knowledge" (Hyland, 2004, p. 105) depends on the discipline.

In economics and public policy, for example, textbooks are generally considered to be less important for advancing knowledge than are scholarly articles.

For one, textbooks are directed toward students, rather than experts, and they present a carefully ordered, "established" (Hyland, 2005, p. 101) version of the discipline. Individual research studies may not be mentioned at all or may be presented very briefly, with an emphasis on the findings rather than on how those findings were obtained. More important, their purpose differs markedly from the purpose of the research article: Whereas the purpose of the latter is to persuade the reader, an expert, to accept the author's claims to knowledge, the purpose of the former is to present established facts to an audience of novices.

Because of their difference in purpose, textbooks and research articles differ significantly in their use of rhetorical and linguistic devices to present information. As Hyland explains (2005, p. 102), in research articles, language is used to assist persuasion whereas in textbooks, it is used to assist comprehension. Compared to research articles, textbooks are characterized by more transitions, fewer references to past studies, more unmodified and unsupported assertions, and a greater level of certainty with which claims are presented. Furthermore, knowledge is presented in textbooks as objective and uncontroversial, existing outside the knowledge-making process—a finished product, for students to absorb (Hyland, 2005). For these reasons, textbooks may not be a good source of original research or a good model for students to emulate and to learn how to write persuasively in their discipline.

Scholarly books may be a better choice for learning about current research as well as for mastering persuasive writing, as many such books are written for experts and their purpose is to advance an academic argument. This is particularly the case of edited books, which are collections of research reports written by different experts on the same topic. Such books can provide useful reviews of past research and suggestions for research ideas. However, even edited books seldom provide enough information to determine the validity or applicability of the studies they discuss. If a study described in a scholarly book looks promising, you should obtain it and read it, rather than rely on its description in the book.

Doctoral Dissertations

Many doctoral dissertations are eventually published as articles or books; however, most dissertations are probably never published. Unpublished doctoral dissertations represent the so-called *gray literature*. There are different opinions on whether such dissertations should be included in systematic literature reviews. Some argue that dissertations are inherently of inferior quality compared to journal articles; others believe that doctoral dissertations merit inclusion in literature reviews because they are thoroughly reported and can be evaluated for potential bias. If you decide to include a doctoral dissertation in your review, make sure that the dissertation comes from a reputable university or program and that it provides sufficient information to make it possible to evaluate the quality of the research.

Academic Conference Reports

Researchers working in economics and public policy often present their research at professional conferences before publishing it. Papers presented at conferences may later be published in conference proceedings and/or in scholarly journals.

The main advantage of conference reports is that they provide the most up-to-date information about the research. However, the quality of conference reports depends crucially on the quality of the conference. There are many reputable, well-established conferences for economists and public policy researchers; unfortunately, there are even more borderline or pure junk conferences.

Before deciding whether to include a conference report in your literature review, try to find answers to these questions.

- Who organized the conference? Is the conference affiliated with a reputable university or research institution? Conferences affiliated with reputable academic institutions (i.e., universities, associations) are generally better in quality than conferences organized by commercial companies.

- Is the conference local, regional, national, or international? Conferences that are bigger in scope, especially *annual conferences*, are often—but not always—more reputable than smaller, local conferences.

- Does the conference cover a very diverse range of subjects, from business and economics to education and psychology? If it does, this may be a sign that the conference is not very good.

If you cannot answer these questions, ask your adviser. If this is difficult, it would probably be safer not to use the report.

Do not take the fact that the conference submissions have gone through a peer review as an indication of high quality of the conference. All conferences require submission of at least an abstract; whether the abstract did in fact go through a legitimate peer review is often impossible to determine.

POLICY LITERATURE

Policy literature includes government reports, working papers, discussion papers, and similar publications. These publications may report on original, empirical research but may also focus on description of best practices, recommendations, or proposals.

Policy literature is usually published by institutions such as government agencies, think tanks, or universities. For example, many universities publish working papers or discussion papers as work in progress, making these reports available to the general public. Such reports are usually written by the university's faculty members and they describe research completed as part of funded projects. Government agencies and international organizations may also publish results of research that they have commissioned or conducted themselves.

The quality of policy literature varies depending on the specific goals and standards of the particular institution. For example, working papers published by universities may be written by experts in their field, but they generally do not undergo peer review and are published in the form in which they are submitted. Reports published by think tanks or international organizations such as the World Bank or the International Monetary Fund are not peer-reviewed either and may be written to promote a particular view or idea.

Policy literature is another example of the so-called gray literature because it is published outside the regular publishing process and often does not undergo peer review for quality control. Nevertheless, policy literature is often used in economics and public policy research and it can be a useful source of research ideas and information about specific policy areas. It may be particularly useful in the initial stages of research because many working papers provide summaries of the current economic and policy thinking on a diverse range of topics.

Below are some sources of high-quality policy literature that includes working papers, discussion papers, and research and policy briefs and reports.

- National Bureau of Economic Research (NBER): nber.org
- Center for Social Development, Washington University of St. Louis: csd. wustl.edu
- Center for Economic and Policy Research: cepr.net
- Center for Global Development, Washington, DC: cgdev.org
- European Centre for Development Policy Management: ecdpm.org
- European Bank for Reconstruction and Development: ebrd.com/home
- Freeman Spogli Institute for International Studies, Stanford University: fsi. stanford.edu
- German Institute for Economic Research: diw.de/de
- John F. Kennedy School of Government, Harvard University: hks.harvard.edu
- Inter-American Development Bank: iadb.org
- International Bank for Reconstruction and Development, World Bank: worldbank.org/en/about/what-we-do/brief/ibrd
- International Monetary Fund: imf.org/external/index.htm
- United Nations Research Institute for Social Development: unrisd.org
- World Bank Group: worldbank.org

- Institute for the Study of Societal Issues, University of California Berkley: issi.berkeley.edu

- Institute for New Economic Thinking, University of Cambridge: inet.econ. cam.ac.uk

- Centre for Competitive Advantage in the Global Economy, University of Warwick: warwick.ac.uk/fac/soc/economics/research/centres/cage

POPULAR LITERATURE

Students who are new to graduate study sometimes prefer as their literature popular, or mass media sources such as *The Economist, Time, Business Week*, or *The Wall Street Journal* because these sources often provide summaries of long and complicated research articles in a succinct and readily understandable form. It is important to realize, however, that although popular literature may be useful for understanding current affairs, trends, and questions, its purpose, audience, structure, and language are very different from the purpose, audience, structure, and language of scholarly literature.

To see that, compare the following two articles that are written on the same topic. The first one is a research article written by George J. Borjas, Kirk B. Doran, and Ying Shen and published in *The Journal of Human Resources*, a scholarly journal specializing in economics research. It is titled "Ethnic Complementarities after the Opening of China: How Chinese Graduate Students Affected the Productivity of Their Advisors" and it is freely available at this site: https://www.hks.harvard.edu/fs/gborjas/publications/journal/JHR2018.pdf.

The second one is a summary of this article and it appeared in *The Economist*, a popular magazine, under the title "Mediocre Academic Researchers Should Be Wary of Globalisation"; it can be accessed through this site: http://www.economist.com/news/science-and-technology/21715639-
effects-foreign-competition-professors-mathematics-mediocre-academic.

First, look at the titles of the two articles. In what way are they different? Next, look through both articles briefly and compare them on the following dimensions:

- Author
- Purpose
- Audience
- Structure and focus
- Writing tone
- Vocabulary
- Style of argumentation

Then compare your answers with those shown in Box 4.

Because of significant differences in style and language between scholarly and popular literature, it is not a good idea to use popular literature as a research source

BOX 4 Differences between Academic and Mass Media Sources

Dimension	Academic Sources	Mass Media Sources
Author	An expert in the subject matter.	A nonexpert; often a journalist with little or no subject-matter expertise.
Purpose	To persuade a community of experts of the appropriacy of the author's methodology and the validity of the author's claims.	To celebrate the novelty of a research study and its results; the validity of arguments is taken for granted.
Audience	A relatively small number of experts, many of whom will assume a critical stance toward the author's arguments.	A lay audience; the bigger, the better. The audience is unlikely to question the validity of the author's claims.
Structure and focus	Main arguments are presented toward the end of the article; the focus is on the process of knowledge construction (i.e., how the findings were obtained).	Main arguments are presented at the beginning, often following a sensationalized statement; the focus is on the topic rather than the process of knowledge creation.
Writing tone	Cautious and tentative, with hedges used as often as every 2–3 sentences.	Sensationalized and enthusiastic; claims are "boosted" to emphasize their importance and general utility.
Vocabulary	Highly specialized and technical.	General, nonspecialized; terms and "difficult" parts are clarified for the general audience (i.e., which means that…).
Style of argumentation	Arguments are presented as possibilities.	Arguments are presented as unalterable truths or facts.
Accuracy of information	Information is presented as accurately and in as much detail as possible to enable replication.	Articles often overstate the importance of findings and may lack important information to allow readers to make informed judgments.
Prominence	Authors give prominence to methodology and results to provide evidence for their claims.	Authors give prominence to the topic of research rather than to scientific activity and the process of discovery.

Note. This table was constructed by the author based on the analysis of popular discourses described in Hyland (1998, 2008, 2009).

or as a writing guide. If you come across a summary of a research study that appears interesting in a popular literature source, get the original study and read it.

HIERARCHY OF ACADEMIC LITERATURE

Academic sources are not equal in their credibility. Some are traditionally considered more credible than others. Partly, this is determined by the conventions of the discipline as some disciplines may traditionally rely more on one type of source than others. There are also many cross-disciplinary similarities especially among related disciplines in what types of sources are considered credible.

What counts as credible sources in public policy and economics? Below is a common hierarchy of sources.

1. At the top of the hierarchy are articles published in scholarly journals. These publications report on empirical and theoretical research and are written for a professional audience. This is where academics exchange research findings, debate, and "accumulate professional credit" (Hyland, 2004, p. 105), and this is where knowledge is constructed. In most academic papers in public policy and economics, journal articles would comprise an overwhelming majority of sources.

2. At the next level are scholarly books (authored or edited), monographs, and high-quality policy literature (working papers, discussion papers, research reports, and so on). These sources can generally be trusted but the extent to which they are used depends on the specific area of research.

3. At the bottom of the hierarchy are government-commissioned reports, unpublished dissertations, papers presented at academic conferences (and published in conference proceedings), and similar gray literature. These sources should be carefully evaluated for credibility and used judiciously.

You should generally avoid the following sources when working on your research project.

- **Popular literature**: Newspapers; magazines; books written for the general readership, especially books written by journalists; and commercial websites. These sources can be used as sources of ideas and, sometimes, of data if your research question calls for it (e.g., if your research question asks about bias in newspaper coverage of a recent election). However, they should not be used as evidence to support your arguments.

- **Reports of unknown origin**: Papers and drafts found on the web whose origin is not clear. Students sometimes forget that the Internet is not a source—it is a place, just like a library, only without the gatekeepers, so whatever you find there may not necessarily be credible even if it looks usable.

- **Sources that are difficult or impossible to verify**: Papers that have not been published, course papers, and similar sources. An exception is personal communications, which include such sources as private email messages, personal interviews, conversations (e.g., with an expert), and the like. Personal communications can, in principle, be used to support arguments but because personal communications do not provide recoverable data and cannot be verified, they are not considered strong evidence.

How can you quickly understand if a source you have found is an acceptable academic source? I suggest using the following three steps.

- **Check the publisher**. Credible sources are published by academic publishers or professional societies. If you are not familiar with the publisher, google it and try to find out more information about it to determine how reputable it is. If you cannot find any information about the publisher on the web, avoid using the source.

- **Check the structure and other elements of the paper**. Does the paper look like an academic paper? Does it have an introduction, a review of the literature, a methodology, and results? Does it have in-text citations and references? Check the authors' affiliation—are they affiliated with a university or research institute?

- **Look at the language**. It is possible to distinguish an academic paper from a nonacademic one by the language used. The language of academic papers is dry and dispassionate, whereas the language of sources intended for the general public including mass media sources is often emotionally laden, exaggerated, and flowery. Do not waste your time with reports written in such language.

LOOKING FOR RELEVANT LITERATURE: WHERE TO START

Searching for literature in the initial stages of research—before you have clearly identified a research idea that you will explore—is different from the more focused survey of the literature you will need to do once you have formulated your research question. In the early stages, your search should be guided by these questions.

- What literature exists in the area and where should you look for the most important information? Which journals are most reputable? Besides journals, what other publications publish research in your area? Are there government reports, working papers, or other types of policy literature on your topic?

- Which issues are appropriate for study in this area?

- Which issues are especially important and what is known about them (so that you can infer what is not known)?

- What approaches and methods are commonly used in your area?

- What controversies exist in your area? What do researchers disagree about?

- Which researchers are especially active in your area? What names keep popping up again and again?

- What are the most important or influential pieces of research—the so-called seminal studies—in your area?

A good way to start is to look for review articles in scholarly journals that are related to your area of interest. Even if you don't have a specific interest yet, browsing through articles summarizing research in a particular area can help you identify areas that may be worth exploring further.

There are several clear advantages to starting with review articles, especially when you do not have a clear idea about what you want to do. First, you can familiarize yourself with the current research in a particular area and see if it interests you. Second, review articles not only summarize research but also organize it, neatly breaking a large body of work into thematically and sometimes methodologically distinct chunks, showing what relationships and trends exist in a particular area and how questions can be approached. Third, review articles often include more comprehensive reference lists than do empirical articles and these references can be used to locate more studies in that area. Finally, review articles often provide directions for future research and sometimes outline questions that have not so far been answered.

Below is a brief description of journals that publish literature reviews on a wide range of topics in economics and public policy. They may be a good place for you to start your quest for research ideas.

The Journal of Economic Literature (JEL)

This journal publishes excellent peer-reviewed literature surveys on a wide range of topics in economics. These surveys can help you understand the current state of knowledge in various areas of economics and generate ideas for your own research. Besides literature reviews, JEL also provides annotated bibliographies of new books classified by subject, a list of dissertations in economics, and reviews of scholarly books. The journal can be accessed free of charge at https://www.aeaweb.org/journals/jel/issues and it can be browsed or searched with keywords.

Below is an abstract from a JEL article on economics education. As you read the abstract, notice the phrases that indicate that this article is a literature review. These phrases have been highlighted.

Allgood, S., Walstad, W. B., & Siegfried, J. J. (2015). Research on teaching economics to undergraduates. *Journal of Economic Literature, 53*(2), 285–325.

This survey summarizes the main research findings about teaching economics to undergraduates. After **briefly reviewing the history of research** on undergraduate economic education, it **discusses the status** of the economics major—numbers and trends, goals, coursework, outcomes, and the principles courses. Some economic theory is used to explain the likely effects of pedagogical decisions of faculty and the learning choices that students make. **Major results from empirical research**

are reviewed from the professor perspective **on such topics as** teaching methods, online technology, class size, and textbooks. **Studies** of student learning **are discussed in relation to** study time, grades, attendance, math aptitude, and cheating. The last **section discusses changes in** the composition of faculty who teach undergraduate economics and effects from changes in instructional technology and then **presents findings from the research about** measuring teaching effectiveness and the value of teacher training. (p. 285)

The Journal of Economic Perspectives (JEP)

This is an excellent source of review articles on a diverse range of topics in the social sciences, from public policy, politics, and economics to education, psychology, and the arts. According to the journal's website, JEP aims, among other things, to

- Synthesize and integrate lessons learned from economic research.
- Provide economic analysis of public policy issues.
- Offer readers an accessible source for state-of-the-art economic thinking.
- Suggest directions for future research.

Articles appearing in the journal are usually solicited by the editors and are of very high quality. According to the journal's website, all issues of the *Journal of Economic Perspectives* (1987–present) are accessible online free-of-charge at https://www.aeaweb.org/journals/jep/about-jep.

Below is an abstract from a JEP article on the insights from genetic research into social policy. As you read, notice the phrases that the author uses to organize existing research on the subject, summarize the distinguishing features of each type of literature, and make an argument in support of one of the types. These phrases have been highlighted. Notice also that the author uses two rhetorically different phrases to make his argument—a definitive one (i.e., "I will argue that") and a tentative one (i.e., "make a cautious argument that"). Why do you think he does that?

Manski, C. F. (2011). Genes, eyeglasses, and social policy. *Journal of Economic Perspectives, 25*(4), 83–94.

Someone reading empirical research relating human genetics to personal outcomes **must be careful to distinguish two types of work. An old literature on** heritability attempts to decompose cross-sectional variation in observed outcomes into unobservable genetic and environmental components. **A new literature measures** specific genes **and uses** them as observed covariates when predicting outcomes. **I will discuss these two types of work in terms of how they may inform** social policy. **I will argue that** research on heritability is fundamentally uninformative for policy analysis, but **make a cautious argument that** research using genes as covariates is potentially informative. (p. 83)

Policy Studies Journal (PSJ)

This journal is the main outlet of the Public Policy Section of the American Political Science Association. It publishes reviews, empirical and theoretical articles, as well as thematically organized bibliographies on a wide range of public policy issues.

Below are two abstracts from the journal—from a review article and from an empirical article. Read them, paying special attention to how the authors describe what they did and how they present their arguments. Notice the words and phrases in each abstract and in the title of each article that give the reader a clue about what type of article this is. These words and phrases have been highlighted.

Conner, T. W., & Rabovsky, T. M. (2011). Accountability, affordability, access: **A review of the recent trends** in higher education policy research. *Policy Studies Journal, 39*(S1), 93–112.

The following research note **surveys the most recent literature** published in the past two years on higher education policy and politics in the United States. **We identify three prominent themes in the literature** including research on accountability, affordability, and issues concerning access and equity. **We observe that there has been increased attention** paid to theories of politics by those who study higher education, which has played a vital role in pushing the boundaries of education research to help begin answering many of the field's most complex and multi-dimensional questions. **This theoretical development has allowed** education policy scholars **to better understand** why various policies are adopted, how they change over time, which groups benefit, and how institutions are affected by changes in the economic and political landscape. (p. 93)

Rodgers, H. R. Jr., & Payne, L. (2007). Child poverty in the American states: **The impact** of welfare reform, economics, and demographics. *Policy Studies Journal, 35*(1), 1–21.

This article identifies the predictors of child poverty rates at the state level **before and after** the adoption and implementation of the Personal Responsibility and Work Opportunity Reconciliation Act of 1996. **The analysis shows that** the most important state-level **factors** that influence child poverty rates are demographics, the health and viability of the state economy, and often the generosity, inclusiveness, and quality of state welfare programs. States with large numbers of black citizens, and those that score highest on infant mortality, teen births, births to unmarried women, children living with a parent without a high school degree, and children living with a single parent **have the highest rates** of child poverty. Child poverty rates are lowest in states that suffer less unemployment, and in wealthier states. States that **score higher** on per capita personal income, tax revenues, and taxable resources **have lower** child poverty rates. While specific "tough" welfare policies adopted by some states **seem to have no impact on** child poverty rates, **we tested for the first time** a **sophisticated measure of the overall quality of** state welfare programs. **The analysis reveals** that the global quality of a state's welfare programs **is often an independent predictor of** child poverty. States with the most generous, inclusive, and supportive welfare programs **have done the best job of** lowering and containing child poverty. (p. 1)

HOW TO READ LITERATURE REVIEWS

1. **Begin with the title**. What is the topic that the literature review covers? Could it be of interest to you? If you are not sure what the title refers to, consider skipping the article for the time being.

2. **Read the abstract**. What is the purpose of the article? What kind of studies are included (e.g., theoretical, empirical, methodological)? What is the author's main argument? Does it sound interesting to you? If yes, download the article and look at it more closely.

3. **Look at section headings and subheadings**. Literature reviews are usually organized thematically, focusing on one issue or a set of related issues at a time. Section headings in such articles are often worded as a question or as a relationship between variables. Box 5 shows an example of headings and subheadings taken from a JEL article on economics education. Notice how specific the headings are and how many headings are worded as a relationship between two or more variables.

BOX 5 Headings and Subheadings from a Review Article in JEL

Allgood, S., Walstad, W. B., & Siegfried, J. J. (2015). Research on teaching economics to undergraduates. *Journal of Economic Literature, 53*(2), 285–325.

1. Introduction
2. A Brief Research History
3. The Economics Major
   3.1. Numbers and Trends
   3.2. Goals and Objectives of the Major
   3.3. Economics Coursework for the Major
   3.4. Factors Affecting the Number of Majors
   3.5. Outcomes from the Major
   3.6. Principles Courses and the Major
4. Faculty and Student Decisions: Some Theory
   4.1. Professorial Choice
   4.2. Student Choice
5. Alternative Teaching Methods and Practices
   5.1. Classroom Experiments
   5.2. Cooperative Learning and Peer Effects
   5.3. Online Instruction
   5.4. Class Size
   5.5. Textbooks
   5.6. Benefits and Costs of Alternative Pedagogies
6. Course Requirements and Student Behavior
   6.1. Study Time and Grades
   6.2. Attendance
   6.3. Mathematics Aptitude
   6.4. Cheating

BOX 5 Headings and Subheadings from a Review Article in JEL—cont'd.
7. Teacher Change and Teaching Effectiveness
  7.1. Teacher Composition and Change
  7.2. Student Evaluations of Teaching
  7.3. Effective Teachers and Grades
  7.4. Alternative Assessment of Faculty Teaching
  7.5. The Value of Teacher Training
8. Conclusion

---

4. **If you find an idea that looks interesting or promising, it's time to read the whole article**. Read it, paying special attention to the works the author cites.

5. **Check the references**. What types of literature are being cited most often (e.g., journal articles, working/discussions papers, books)? Which journals are cited most often? Try to obtain some of the studies the author cites and read them to get a better understanding of the issue.

6. **Pay attention to the conclusion**. This is the section where authors often describe directions for future research. What areas appear to be underexplored? What questions remain unanswered?

Box 6 shows an excerpt from a JEL article reviewing literature on the economics of religion. In this article, the author traces the origins of the field, describes

---

BOX 6 An Excerpt with Suggestions for Future Research
Iyer, S. (2016). The new economics of religion. *Journal of Economic Literature, 54(2),* 395–441.

Unanswered Questions for Future Research
Although much research is being conducted on the economics of religion, **there are a number of unanswered questions for future research that remain. First**, what does it really mean to be religious? Is it intrinsic or more socially driven? **Second,** at a macro level, we have seen a great deal of economic development across a range of countries, and yet religion seems both very pervasive and persistent. Why is religion still so pervasive and persistent even as countries are becoming richer? If it is the case that richer countries are becoming more secular, but the world is becoming more religious, then more work on the secularization hypothesis, and how it interacts with factors like income inequality, is needed. **Third,** especially in non-Christian and non-Western societies, such as for example in India or China, what might make the nature of religion there similar to or different from the United States or northwestern Europe? **We need to further our understanding** of the economics of Islam, Hinduism, Buddhism, Jainism, Sikhism, and tribal religions, especially in Africa, the Middle East, and South Asia. **In this context, there are four areas of research that I argue are still relatively underresearched** by economists of religion: (1) religion and demography; (2) religion, political processes, and their interactions with economic processes; (3) the marketing, management, and communication aspects of religion; and (4) how the economics of religion can contribute to broader debates about science and religion. (pp. 430–431)

several groups of factors that have influenced the economics of religion, and identifies broad research themes that economists have investigated globally. The excerpt comes from the section called *Unanswered Questions*, which appears at the end of the article. As you read the excerpt, note the phrases that the author uses to help the reader quickly understand what the section is about (they have been highlighted). What is the purpose of using transition markers (i.e., first, second, third)? What is the purpose of using numbers in this section?

SUGGESTIONS FOR SEARCHING FOR EMPIRICAL LITERATURE

Whether you are writing an empirical paper or a paper based on a review of the literature, the bulk of your sources will be empirical studies. Every research area has journals that publish predominantly empirical reports. Appendix D lists many such journals in public policy and economics.

Start with the most recent issues and work backward. How far back you should go will depend on your area and the specific research question. Research in many areas moves fast and definitions, models, and measurement procedures may become outdated; even terminology may change. Unless you are writing a historical paper, it is perhaps a good idea to limit the time period of your search to the past 10 years or so.

Try to identify landmark or seminal studies in your field. Such studies may outline a new theory or propose a model that later becomes widely used in the area. These studies will help you better grasp the context of your research.

When searching for empirical literature, use different keywords to broaden your search. For example, if your topic focuses on the relationship between *globalization* and *economic growth*, first search for articles using these keywords. Then think about additional keywords that might describe this relationship, for example: foreign investment and economic growth, globalization and inequality, international dependence and growth, and so on.

WHERE TO LOOK FOR LITERATURE

Every discipline has its own databases and portals of resources. Below is a list of portals and databases that provide access to papers in economics and public policy.

RePEc (Research Papers in Economics, repec.org) is a comprehensive portal for the dissemination of research in economics and related fields. It provides links to databases containing close to two million research reports in economics from 2300 journals and 4300 working paper series. Some of the most useful links on this site are

- **IDEAS**: a bibliographic database in economics with many full-text articles, and

- **EconPapers**: a directory of RePec bibliographic data, providing access to a large collection of working papers and journal articles in economics.

EconLit (Economic Literature, aeaweb.org/econlit) is a comprehensive resource of the American Economic Association, a major association for economists, which publishes some of the most reputable journals in economics including the *American Economic Review*, the *Journal of Economic Literature*, and the *Journal of Economic Perspectives*. EconLit indexes journals, books, dissertations, articles in collective volumes, working papers, and book reviews from the *Journal of Economic Literature*.

SSRN (Social Science Research Network, ssrn.com/en) is a collection of specialized research networks directed by leading scholars; these networks disseminate full-text papers and abstracts from scholars around the world. Papers include articles from specialized e-journals, papers from research centers, and papers from relevant university departments. The SSRN eLibrary contains more than 600,000 full-text articles and over 700,000 abstracts. The majority of papers can be downloaded for free. Some of the most relevant networks for economics and public policy research are shown below.

- Economics Research Network (ERN)
- Financial Economics Network (FEN)
- Health Economics Network (HEN)
- Innovation Research & Policy Network (IRPN)
- International Business & Management Network (INTL)
- Organizational Behavior Research Network (ORG)
- Political Science Network (PSN)
- Sustainability Research & Policy Network (SRPN)

NBER (National Bureau of Economic Research, nber.org/papers.html) is a leading economic research organization that indexes and provides access to a large collection of working papers written by some of the leading scholars in their field. Many NBER-affiliated researchers are tenured professors at their institutions, and many NBER research projects are supported by grants from government agencies and private foundations.

CEPR (Center for Economic and Policy Research, cepr.net) is a research organization that disseminates research on important economic and social problems and policies aimed at improving people's lives.

PAI (Public Affairs Index) is a bibliographic database covering a diverse array of national and global contemporary public policy issues, from public health and the environment to human and civil rights and international commerce. PAI contains abstracts of journal articles, books, statistical yearbooks, conference proceedings, research reports, and government documents on issues in economics, public affairs, political science, public administration, politics, and international relations. PAI is accessed through EBSCO and requires institutional subscription.

EconStor (econstor.eu) is a collection of more than 130,000 full-text open-access documents—working papers, conference proceedings, and journal articles—from more than 400 research institutions.

PSO (Policy Studies Organization, ipsonet.org) is an outgrowth of the American Political Science Association, a publisher of academic journals and book series; it disseminates scholarship for policy-making and offers access to many journals in public policy including open-access journals.

ScienceDirect (sciencedirect.com) is the world's leading database of scientific and technical research, providing access to academic journals, articles, and books. Access requires institutional subscription.

JSTOR (jstor.org) is a digital library of academic journals, books, and primary sources. It provides access to more than a dozen top economics journals. Access requires institutional subscription.

Chapter 5

Reading and Analyzing Literature

UNDERSTANDING THE STRUCTURE AND ORGANIZATION OF RESEARCH PAPERS

Understanding how research papers are organized can help you quickly locate the information you need. This section shows some common elements of research papers in public policy and economics and explains what information can be found where. The suggestions and examples I give here can also be used as a resource for writing—for learning what information to include in different sections of a paper and how to structure those sections.

You should also keep in mind that the specific organization of a paper and its elements often depend, among other things, on the specific field or area of research, on whether the paper describes quantitative, qualitative, or nonempirical research, and on the requirements of the journal where the paper has appeared.

Title

The title of a research paper usually states the topic of the research and delimits it in some way, for example, by adding a geographical area, a specific focus, a question, or a detail about the topic. The following types of title are common in economics and public policy.

Two-part titles where the first part announces the topic and the second part provides a detail about it (sometimes in the form of a question)

In quantitative studies, the detail in the second part of the title often gives a clue as to what was done in the study, what approach was used, or what results were obtained. In quantitative studies focusing on a particular country or group of countries, the second part often has the words *the case of [name of country]* or *evidence from [name of country]*. In qualitative studies and in papers reviewing research, the detail in the second part often shows the focus of the study and may be worded as a question. In review papers, the second part may contain the

How to Write about Economics and Public Policy. https://doi.org/10.1016/B978-0-12-813010-0.00005-3

words *review*, *literature*, *trends*, *implications*, or *lessons* or a policy-related question (i.e., What should we do…?).

Box 7 shows examples of two-part titles. Can you tell which ones come from quantitative studies and which ones come from qualitative or review studies? Explain why.

BOX 7 Examples of Two-Part Titles

1. The gender gap in mathematics: Evidence from Chile (Bharadwaj et al., 2016)

2. China-US trade: A global outlier (Thorbecke, 2015)

3. Three decades of money demand studies: Differences and similarities (Knell & Stix, 2006)

4. The determinants of tax morale in comparative perspective: Evidence from European countries (Lago-Peñas & Lago-Peñas, 2010)

5. The caloric costs of culture: Evidence from Indian migrants (Atkin, 2016)

6. Trade liberalization, intermediate inputs, and productivity: Evidence from Indonesia (Amiti & Konings, 2007)

7. The double challenge of market and social incorporation: Progress and bottlenecks in Latin America (Franzoni & Sánchez-Ancochea, 2014)

8. Leadership, hegemony, and the international economy: Naked emperor or tattered monarch with potential? (Lake, 1993)

9. Reversing globalization: Trade policy consequences of World War I (Horowitz, 2004)

10. Stroke in developing countries: Epidemiology, impact and policy implications (Lloyd-Sherlock, 2010)

11. Drugs policy: What should we do about cannabis? (Pudney, 2010)

Titles stating the topic or the main argument

A title can simply state the topic of the research. Such titles are especially common in qualitative studies and studies based on a review of literature. Sometimes the topic may be formulated as a relationship between concepts or variables. Alternatively, a title may announce the author's main argument or main conclusion. Box 8 shows examples of titles of this type.

BOX 8 Examples of Titles Stating Topic or Argument

1. Private investment in Latin America (Cardoso, 1993)

2. China's exchange rate policy dilemma (Goldstein & Lardy, 2006)

3. 'Chimerica' and the global asset market boom (Ferguson & Schularick, 2007)

4. Macroeconomic performance and adjustment under policies commonly supported by the International Monetary Fund (Doroodian, 1993)

5. Why the United Kingdom should not join the Eurozone (Minford, 2008)

6. Why China should abandon its dollar peg (Roubini, 2007)

7. Climate change, human well-being and insecurity (Adger, 2010)

Titles showing what was done

Titles may also emphasize what the researchers did in the study. This is often done by using an *-ing* verb such as *investigating, modeling, determining,* or *assessing* or a noun derived from such a verb (i.e., *assessment, investigation, determinants*) in the title. The title may also name the analytic technique that was used in the study. Box 9 shows examples of titles of this type.

BOX 9 Examples of Titles Showing What Was Done

1. Measuring economic policy uncertainty (Baker et al., 2016)

2. Measuring the sorting effect of migration on spatial wage disparities (Nakajima & Okamoto, 2014)

3. Estimating the effects of pronatal policies on residential choice and fertility (Nakajima & Tanaka, 2012)

4. Dissecting anomalies (Fama & French, 2008)

5. Long-run determinants of economic growth in South America (Vedia-Jerez & Chasco, 2016)

6. New estimates on the relationship between IQ, economic growth and welfare (Hafer, 2017)

7. Cost-benefit analysis in monopolistic competition models of urban agglomeration (Kanemoto, 2012)

Abstract

The abstract is a summary of the main features of the research. Its length usually ranges from 100 to 300 words, depending on the publication or university requirements. Not all publications require an abstract but many do, especially journal articles.

The abstract is a very useful guide for understanding what the study is about and determining its relevance to one's research. Abstracts also contain clues about whether the study is empirical or nonempirical and whether it is quantitative or qualitative.

Abstracts of empirical studies usually contain the following elements:

1. The topic of the research (what was studied)
2. The purpose (what was done)
3. The methodology (how the research was done)
4. Main findings (what was found)
5. Main argument (what the researchers argue)
6. Policy and other implications (significance of the findings)

Abstracts of quantitative papers often contain a very specific description of the methodology (e.g., survey, field experiment), data, and findings. The language of such abstracts includes words related to quantitative analysis such as *data, significant, magnitude, test, statistical results, analysis,* and *hypothesis,* as well as directional words such as *impact, effect,* and *increase/decrease.*

Abstracts of qualitative papers put less emphasis on the methodology and focus instead on the main arguments, which are often introduced with the phrase *we/I/this paper argues.* The language of a qualitative abstract often includes nondirectional words such as *explore, consider, discuss,* and *perspective.*

Abstracts of nonempirical review papers often describe the topic and purpose of the study and indicate that the study is a review of some sort by using phrases with the words *review* and/or *literature,* for example: *this paper reviews the existing literature, we describe recent research, we provide a detailed review, we review evidence,* or *the paper sets out arguments for... .*

As in abstracts of qualitative papers, the focus is often on the main argument, which may be introduced with such phrases as *we argue, we suggest, this paper discusses arguments for,* and *we highlight central issues/important questions.* Often, abstracts of review papers contain phrases showing how the author has categorized and organized the literature and what themes and patterns he or she has identified. This may be indicated by such words as *four themes, three types, several directions,* or *two perspectives.*

Box 10 shows three abstracts, an abstract from a quantitative study, an abstract from a qualitative study, and an abstract from a review. All three articles are on the same topic, homelessness. Read the abstracts and try to determine which one comes from which type of study. Underline the words and phrases that have helped you make your decision.

BOX 10 Abstracts from Three Types of Study

Abstract 1

Zlotnick, C., Robertson, M. J., & Lahiff, M. (1999). Getting off the streets: Economic resources and residential exits from homelessness. *Journal of Community Psychology, 27*(2), 209–224.

Based on a 15-month prospective study, the following variables demonstrated an association with residential stability in a countywide probability sample of 397 homeless adults: female gender, a history of less than 1-year homelessness, absence of a health problem that limited work ability, entitlement-benefit income, and use of subsidized housing. Multivariate analyses show that two forms of public support—entitlement income and subsidized housing—were the most important variables associated with exits from homelessness into stable housing. Homeless adults with substance use disorders were more likely than other homeless adults to obtain unstable, but not stable housing. Homeless adults with mental disorders were no less likely than other homeless adults to report stable housing. Stable housing is necessary to break the cycle of homelessness, and economic resources such as entitlement income and subsidized housing are associated with stable housing for homeless adults. (p. 209)

Abstract 2

Thompson, S. J., Pollio, D. E., Eyrich, K., Bradbury, E., & North, C. S. (2004). Successfully exiting homelessness: Experiences of formerly homeless mentally ill individuals. *Evaluation and Program Planning, 27,* 423–431.

This study aims to identify and describe processes of change enabling achievement of stable housing among homeless individuals. Twelve previously homeless individuals who had maintained stable housing for a period of at least 24 consecutive months provided information through semi-structured interviews on the following topics: (1) the personal experience of homelessness, (2) the process of becoming housed, and (3) the role of significant life relationships. Only the second and third topic areas were included in this discussion. Eight categories were developed and analyzed from the qualitative interviews, including: work/employment difficulties, substance use and/or mental illness, cyclical nature of homelessness, personal motivation, housing-related issues, lessons learned, relationships with family/friends and relationships with service providers. The participants highlighted relationships with family, friends and service providers as central in the processes of achieving stable housing. (p. 423)

Abstract 3

Fischer, P. J., & Breakey, W. R. (1991). The epidemiology of alcohol, drug, and mental disorders among homeless persons. *American Psychologist, 46*(11), 1115–28.

This article describes recent research on the prevalence of alcohol, drug, and mental (ADM) disorders and the characteristics of homeless substance abusers and persons with mental illness. Methodological problems in homelessness research are reviewed, particularly in relation to definitions of homelessness and sampling- and case-ascertainment methods. Prevalence rates of ADM disorders are much higher in homeless groups than in the general population. As is true of homeless people in general, homeless substance abusers and mentally ill persons are characterized by extreme poverty; underutilization of public entitlements; isolation from family, friends, and other support networks; frequent contact with correctional agencies; and poor general health. Knowledge of these disadvantages should be used to advocate for better services to prevent homelessness and support homeless people. (p. 1115)

Introduction

The Introduction describes the topic and its importance, provides a very brief overview of what is known about the topic, referencing most important or relevant studies. It then highlights what is still unknown (the so-called *research gap*) and explains why knowing it is worthwhile. This is followed by the purpose of the study and sometimes, by the specific research questions that were examined.

Additionally, the Introduction may provide a more or less detailed review of relevant literature on the topic (especially if there is no separate Literature Review section), define key terms, describe the paper's methodology or approach, highlight its results, and explain the contribution of the research to the field.

In empirical economics papers, the Introduction may have a somewhat different structure, which reflects economists' preference for seeing the contribution of a paper and its main highlights early on. Below is a common structure of the Introduction section in economics articles.

- A brief description of the problem and its importance
- Statement of purpose or what was done
- A brief description of main results
- Description of the methodology, main challenges, and solutions
- Description of the paper's contribution in relation to previous research
- Organization of the paper

In such papers, literature is often reviewed, and a research gap described, toward the end of the Introduction, in relation to the contribution of the study to the field.

Box 11 shows an example of an introduction from the paper "Foreign versus domestic education: Does place of education matter for Australian immigrants?" written by Jessica Montgomery, a graduate student in Public Policy. Read it and highlight the parts where the author

- Describes the importance of the topic,
- Highlights what is known about it,
- Indicates a research gap,
- Describes the purpose,
- Indicates the study's methodology, and
- Describes the study's contribution.

Notice the structure of the Introduction and how it narrows down from general to specific. What words and phrases does Jessica use to narrow down the problem?

BOX 11 Example of an Introduction

The labour market adjustment of immigrants is an important consideration for policy makers. In particular, the extent to which an immigrant's skills are recognized in the local labour market has implications for the level of skill utilization in an economy and is a determinant of the living standards of immigrants (Chapman & Iredale, 1993; McDonald & Worswick, 1999). This is particularly true in large recipient countries such as Australia, the host of the world's third largest migrant population and where approximately 28 percent of the population are born overseas (Australian Bureau of Statistics, 2017; Organisation for Economic Cooperation and Development [OECD], 2017a).

Since Chiswick (1978), the literature on immigrant labour market assimilation has focused on quantifying the magnitude of the immigrant-native earnings differential and the rate of wage convergence, which is considered a proxy for the assimilation rate (Friedberg, 2000). A principal determinant of wage outcomes is an individual's human capital (Borjas, 2014), of which education is one element. The role of education in determining income is two-fold: it can enhance an individual's skills and thereby their productivity, and it can signal to employers a person's potential productivity (Patrinos, 2016). A key issue for immigrants is the extent to which the human capital obtained in their home country is "transferable" to their destination country.

To assess the transferability of immigrants' educational credentials and better discern the drivers of potential native-immigrant differences in wage outcomes, the returns to foreign and domestic education must be allowed to vary. However, there is limited analysis in an Australian context of the impact of source country on the returns to education. Further, the minority of studies that have distinguished between foreign and domestic education tend to be dated and have used limited cross-sectional data. This study addresses this gap.

Drawing on the methodology of Friedberg (2000), this study builds on the conventional approach by allowing: (i) the returns to foreign and domestic education to vary for immigrants, and (ii) the returns to domestic education to vary between natives and immigrants. This analysis is undertaken separately for immigrants from English-speaking backgrounds (ESB) and non-English speaking backgrounds (NESB). As explained in detail later, there are several reasons to suggest that the human capital held by these cohorts is likely to be valued differently in the labour market.

A further innovation of this study is the use of longitudinal data from the Household, Income and Labour Dynamics in Australia (HILDA) survey. This rich data source helps to address some of the shortcomings of Australian studies that use cross-sectional data.

This paper begins with a brief overview of the literature regarding immigrant assimilation in the labour market and the role of education in determining earnings outcomes. The next section provides a summary of the empirical strategy, followed by a more detailed description of the HILDA data used and descriptive statistics. Finally, regression estimates and a discussion of the results are provided ahead of concluding remarks, including potential policy implications.

For the remainder of this paper, the term ESB immigrants refers to individuals born in the "main English speaking countries," as specified by HILDA. These countries include the US, UK, Canada, New Zealand, Ireland and South Africa. NESB immigrants are individuals born in all other countries. (Montgomery, 2017, pp. 1–2)

Body of the Paper

The organization of this part largely depends on the type of paper, especially on whether it is empirical or nonempirical; the research area; and the requirements of the publication where the paper appears.

Empirical papers, especially quantitative papers appearing in economics journals, will have a relatively rigid, predictable structure containing very specific elements that roughly correspond to the steps in a linear research process (e.g., Introduction, Literature Review, Methodology, Results, and Discussion). Empirical qualitative papers, or papers based on qualitative data collection (i.e., interviews) will often have a similar structure; however, they may also be organized around themes. The headings of the specific sections in such papers will depend on the content of the paper. Nonempirical papers, or papers that are largely based on a review of previous research, are organized thematically.

Below is a description of a common organization of the body of an empirical quantitative paper and that of a nonempirical qualitative paper.

Common Organization of the Body of an Empirical Paper

- **Literature Review**. In this section, authors present a big-picture view of the relevant literature. Studies are often grouped and organized into several strands or themes according to a specific criterion, making it easy for the reader to grasp the distinctive features of each strand. In published research, this section is often combined with the Introduction, or it may have a different name such as *Empirical Studies on [Topic]* or *Review of Relevant Research*. In some publications, the literature review can be very short—less than a page.

- **Theoretical Framework**. This section outlines the basic theory used for analyses and explains, on theoretical grounds, why the authors' expectations make sense. In econometric studies, this section may include a mathematical description of the theoretical model used in the study and the assumptions on which it is based. More often, however, and especially in noneconometric studies, this section is a narrative explanation of how the study's key concepts and variables are related and why.

  Not all studies have this section. In fact, in many cases, especially in noneconometric studies, a theoretical framework is described in the Literature Review or in the Introduction rather than in a separate section. Or it may be described in a separate section under such headings as *Conceptual Framework*, *Framework for Analysis*, or *Theoretical Perspective*. For more about Theoretical Framework, see Chapter 10.

- **Data and Methodology**. This section describes the data used in the study and how they were collected or obtained as well as the empirical model, variables, and analytical approach used. This section may also be called *Research*

Design or there may be separate sections called *Data*, *Variables*, *Empirical Model (or Empirics)*, *Sample*, *Methodology*, and *Estimation Strategy*.

- **Results**. This section describes the main results of the study. It will usually contain visuals—graphs and tables showing correlations among variables and estimation results. It may also include a subsection called robustness checks (or this could be a separate section), in which the author modifies the regression equation by adding or removing variables to see how regression coefficients would behave. The purpose of robustness checks is to disprove alternative explanations for the results: Results that remain robust support the validity of the findings. This section is sometimes combined with Discussion.

- **Discussion**. The purpose of this section is to compare the study's results with those presented in the Literature Review or Introduction. If the results confirm previous findings, the author will usually proceed to outline their implications; if they contradict previous findings, the author will try to explain the contradictions.

  This section also describes policy implications and recommendations, limitations of the study, and suggestions for future research. In economics and public policy studies, this section is often combined with the Results section.

Common Organization of the Body of a Nonempirical Paper

Nonempirical papers in public policy and economics are often organized thematically, around several related subtopics. For example, a paper reviewing a particular policy may have a section called *Relevant Policy Issues* and several subsections in which these issues are explained and discussed. It may also have several sections discussing the specific effects of this policy on relevant outcomes.

Another common way to organize such papers is to present section headings as questions and then answer the questions in each section. This may also be a good way to write such papers because a question at the beginning of a section may help you critically review your own writing to make sure that the question you posed at the beginning has actually been answered.

Box 12 shows the organization of two nonempirical review papers. The first one is a review of evidence on the scope and nature of climate change and its challenges. In this paper, the author describes how climate change has come to be framed as a security and foreign policy issue and highlights the dangers of underemphasizing the equity and individual human security dimensions of climate change. The second paper is a report on chronic poverty prepared by the Chronic Poverty Research Centre, an international partnership of universities, research centers, and nongovernmental organizations. As you look at the organization of these two papers, notice the use of questions in the headings of some of the sections. Why do you think the authors chose questions as headings? Notice also the use of many subheadings in the second paper. Why do you think the authors decided to divide some of the sections into subsections?

BOX 12 Organization of Nonempirical Papers: Examples

Adger, W. N. (2010). Climate change, human well-being and insecurity. *New Political Economy, 15*(2), 275–292.

Introduction

Climate change: reality bites

Reframing climate change and security

Who is vulnerable and why?

How adaptation affects climate security

Justice and equity dimensions of human security

Conclusions

Shepherd, A. (2011). *Tackling chronic poverty: The policy implications of research on chronic poverty and poverty dynamics.* Manchester: Chronic Poverty Research Centre.

Summary

Chapter 1: The big idea: chronic poverty, the MDGs and the CPRC

1. What is chronic poverty?
2. The CPRC
3. Chronic and severe poverty: no shortcuts on data
4. Why is chronic poverty important?
5. Selection of key issues in this paper

Chapter 2: Chronic poverty: unpacking the poverty 'black box'

1. The four 'ds'
2. Intergenerational poverty

Chapter 3: Chronic poverty: key findings

1. The statistics on chronic poverty and poverty dynamics
2. The significance of context: the nature and causes of chronic poverty compared
3. Assets and markets
4. Vulnerability and protection
    4.1 Labour markets
    4.2 Changing household demography
    4.3 Assets-markets-protection synergies
5. Social, economic, and political relations: adverse incorporation and social exclusion
    5.1 The worst forms of adverse incorporation
    5.2 Measures against discrimination

BOX 12 Organization of Nonempirical Papers: Examples—cont'd.

6. Location
    6.1 Landlocked countries
    6.2 Conflict

Chapter 4: Chronic poverty: the policy implications

1. Social protection

2. Economic growth
    2.1 Growth, labour markets and labour relations
    2.2 Assets, markets and protection
    2.3 Integration of chronically deprived countries and regions
    2.4 Focus on youth and young adults
    2.5 New, focused social contracts in postconflict recovery

3. Progressive social change – addressing discrimination and deep-rooted inequalities

4. A commitment to improving the data

5. Answering the 'how?' question

Chapter 5: Future research and action

Conclusion

In an empirical paper, this section will contain a summary of the analysis that the author presented in the paper, a summary of the main results, and a brief discussion of what these results mean for theory or policy. Sometimes, the author will conclude by restating the main argument. The language of this section will depend on the type of paper: Quantitative papers will often contain directional words such as *effect*, *influence*, or *causality*, whereas qualitative papers will often use more tentative expressions such as *there appears to be*, *may indicate*, or *tentative findings*.

In a nonempirical paper, this section will often contain a restatement of the topic and its importance, a summary of what the author did, an evaluation of the presented evidence, and a (re)statement of the main argument. The language of this section will often be very tentative.

In both quantitative and qualitative reports as well as in nonempirical papers, the conclusion may contain a paragraph with suggestions for future research.

References

This section will contain a list of works cited in the paper. It is sometimes called *Bibliography* or *Works Cited*. This section will be organized alphabetically by the author's last name and will follow the conventions of a particular citation style such as the Chicago style. This section may be especially useful in the initial stages of research when you are trying to locate relevant literature. Use it to get more information about relevant studies. It may also be a good idea to check this section to see what exactly authors cite when they mention a particular name in their article. This will help you evaluate the credibility of the authors' claims.

Appendices

In empirical papers, this section contains information about the instruments of data collection (e.g., questionnaires), variables, or data used as well as technical details related to the analyses. This information may be useful when you plan your own research. In economics studies, in particular, an appendix will often contain a table of variables used in the study and an explanation of where they come from. This information can be used to decide how a particular variable can be measured or where to obtain data on a particular variable. Nonempirical papers do not usually have appendices.

READING EMPIRICAL STUDIES

Reading research studies from cover to cover is unproductive and often unrealistic. Of course, research studies that are closely related to your own research area should be read carefully, probably even several times. However, when reading research studies as part of a review of existing literature, you should be guided by the following purposes.

1. **Read to understand the state of current knowledge in your area.**
   What is known about your topic? How much research has been conducted on your topic? What gaps in knowledge still exist? Try to identify a gap in research that your study can fill. This will be the justification for your study.

   What to check: Sections called *Introduction* and *Literature Review*.

2. **Read to find an appropriate theoretical framework.**
   In your study, you will need to articulate a theory to justify your expectations. Why do you expect your variables to be related? How do you expect them to be related? Ultimately, the purpose of an empirical study is to test a theory, so it is important that you place your study within an appropriate theoretical framework.

   What to check: Sections called *Theory*, *Theoretical Framework*, *Conceptual Framework*, and/or *Literature Review*.

3. **Read to understand your own methodological options.**
   What methodological approaches have been used to answer your type of question? What models are commonly used? What variables are included

in these models? How are they defined? How are they measured? What kinds of data are used to answer your type of question? Where could the data be obtained?

What to check: Sections called *Methodology, Data, Research Design,* and/or *Data and Variables.*

4. **Read to evaluate the validity of knowledge claims**.
Claims to knowledge that authors make in an empirical paper are only as good as the methodology and analysis on which these claims are based. To evaluate the validity and strength of knowledge claims, look how the study was designed, what model and data were used, and how the data were analyzed. Virtually all research studies have weaknesses, but the real question is whether those weaknesses are serious enough to invalidate the conclusions.

What to check: Sections called *Methodology, Data, Research Design,* and *Analyses.* Check also tables of results to see if the authors' arguments are supported by the actual results.

5. **Read to learn the organization and rhetorical devices.**
Every discipline has its own conventions for structuring and organizing empirical reports as well as preferences for the use of specific vocabulary in reporting previous research, describing results, or making knowledge claims. Understanding and learning these conventions can go a long way to helping you not only quickly locate necessary information in a study but also organize your own literature review.

What to check: Headings and subheadings of papers that are similar to the one you will be writing and the language (i.e., the specific words and expressions) that authors use to describe, present, outline, argue, explain, and guide the reader throughout the text.

HOW MANY STUDIES TO READ?

In the early stages of research, students often worry that they would have to read too much. In the later stages, they worry that they haven't read enough. So how much should you prepare yourself to read?

A lot will depend on your area, topic, and the specific question you are trying to answer. Generally, you should keep reading until you feel more or less confident that you can situate your own research within the body of existing literature. This means that you should have a more or less good idea about what is and what is not known in your area, the theories and models that have been used, the ways that variables are commonly defined and measured, and the ways that reports in your area are organized. It is hard to imagine that an understanding of a research area could be gained after reading fewer than at least a dozen research studies.

To give you a very rough idea of how many papers you may need to read, here is an estimate that is based on a review of the references taken from a large number of empirical papers written by graduate students in a wide variety of policy areas.

- For a final paper in a 1-year master's program, the goal should probably be anywhere between 15 and 30 studies.

- For a master's thesis in a 2-year program, somewhere between 30 and 40 studies would be common.

- In a doctoral dissertation, the number of references would often exceed 100; because not all studies that the student has read will be included, the actual number of studies that the student would read would be even bigger.

ANALYZING EMPIRICAL STUDIES

This section explains how to read empirical studies and how to organize them in preparation for your own writing.

Step 1: Determine Relevance

Determine the study's relevance to your needs. The simplest way to do that is to read the abstract. A good abstract summarizes critical information about a study including its purpose, method(s), and major findings.

When you begin looking for relevant literature, look for studies that have focused on your topic and do not limit your search to a particular geographical area, theory, or model. For example, if your topic is *foreign direct investment* in a particular Asian country, do not limit your search to studies of that country or area. Look for studies that have examined this topic in a variety of contexts, over a period of time, and using different theoretical or methodological approaches. Your goal should be to understand what is known about your topic, rather than your specific setting, and what your theoretical and methodological options are in studying your topic.

Step 2: Assess Basic Quality

Assess the basic quality of the study. Is it of sufficient quality to be potentially included in your literature review? To do that, scan the whole study to see if it has these basic elements:

- An explicitly stated purpose or research question,

- An explanation of why the study was done and why it was needed,

- A review of the literature, which can be quite brief,

- A description of the methodology and analysis, which should make it clear how the main concepts were defined and measured, how the data were collected, and how the data were analyzed,

- An answer to the research question, and

- References.

If some of these elements are missing, this may not be a high-quality study.

Step 3: Group Studies into Categories

One of the most important tasks in reviewing the literature is to impose some sort of order on the material. In order to do that, you need to sort the studies you have found into groups or categories according to a particular criterion. Doing this will help you later make an argument about what the literature really shows. This criterion could be

- Different settings (e.g., developed vs. developing countries),

- Different results (e.g., positive vs. negative effect or no effect),

- Different methodologies (e.g., experimental vs. correlational; quantitative vs. qualitative),

- Different theoretical frameworks (e.g., modernization vs. dependency theory),

- Different types of data (cross-sectional vs. panel data), or

- Different dependent, independent, or control variables included in the model.

Do not cherry-pick studies that support a particular view. If you find that different studies have produced different—even contradictory—results, include both groups of studies in your literature review. Later, when you look at these studies more closely, try to understand *why* they have produced different results. Was it because of the differences in the methodology, time period, or type of data? Was there a flaw in the design of the studies producing a particular result? Try to relate differences in one area (e.g., results) to differences in another area (e.g., geographical setting, time period, specific variables included in the model). This will help you make an argument about the differences among the studies.

Step 4: Identify Main Arguments

The concept of an **argument** is central to all academic writing because the goal of an academic paper is to make an argument and persuade the reader to accept it. An academic argument can be defined as a claim to knowledge that is supported with research evidence—the stronger the evidence, the stronger the argument.

Arguments should not be confused with **facts**. Students who are new to graduate study often mistake academic arguments for facts and treat authors' statements as objectively proven "truths." Yet, it is important to remember that scientific knowledge is conjectural and that arguments in research articles are evaluated on the basis of the research evidence that authors present; they can be either accepted or rejected by readers.

Arguments should also be separated from **claims and opinions**. Arguments are based on research evidence; claims and opinions are not. Always check if a statement making a claim to knowledge is supported with research evidence. Question, rather than rely on, textual authority. Ask yourself, "Why does the author say this?" "What is the basis for this claim?"

Claims and arguments look similar. For example, consider the following statement:

> Two forms of support—income support and subsidized housing—are most closely associated with improved outcomes for homeless individuals.

Is this a claim or an argument? In order to tell, you need to check what it is based on. How is it supported in the paper? In the space below, I describe two types of argument that are commonly used in academic papers and show how they can be supported.

Two Types of Argument

There are two types of argument that authors make in academic papers. The first one is arguments about the state of current knowledge. These arguments are common in the Introduction and Literature Review sections, and their function is to justify the study and the author's particular expectations. These arguments are supported in two ways: by including citations to relevant studies or by providing a more detailed explanation that supports the author's claim, which is then followed by citations to relevant studies. Box 13 shows examples from a paper by Lai See Sue, a graduate student in Public Finance.

The second type of argument is the actual claim to knowledge that the author makes based on the results of his or her study. These arguments are central to a research study. They are usually located in the Abstract, at the end of the Introduction, and in the Results and Conclusion sections. These arguments may be directly preceded or followed by the evidence; alternatively, evidence may be presented in one particular place (e.g., Results) and in other places, it may be implied by such phrases as *we find that, our findings indicate that,* or *our analyses demonstrate/suggest that…*

Box 14 shows some examples of arguments that are based on the authors' own results. The arguments are underlined; the part that presents, or implies the presence of, evidence is shown in italics.

BOX 13 Arguments about the State of Current Knowledge

Previous research has generally identified a positive relationship between trade liberalization and economic growth (Dollar, 1992; Edwards, 1998; Harrison, 1996; Sachs & Warner, 1996; Wacziarg, 2001; Yanikkaya, 2003). It has been argued that trade liberalization has many benefits. For example, according to Dornbusch (1992), trade liberalization increases the variety of goods in a country and raises productivity by providing less expensive or higher quality intermediate goods.

Several studies have demonstrated a positive relationship between trade liberalization and economic growth. For instance, Dollar (1992) investigated the effect of outward orientation of an economy on economic growth using cross-sectional regression analysis across 95 developing countries covering the period from 1976 to 1985. He constructed two indices to capture the outward orientation of an economy: an index of real exchange rate distortion and an index of real exchange rate variability. He found that exchange rate was overvalued by 33 percent in Latin America and by 86 percent in Africa during the study period. Dollar then estimated growth equations across countries using each country's measure of exchange rate distortion and controlling for differences in the level of investment and the variability of the exchange rate. He found that, on average, trade distortions in Africa and Latin America reduced the growth of Gross Domestic Product (GDP) per capita by between 1.5 and 2.1 percent per annum. (Lai See Sue, 2011, p. 2)

BOX 14 Examples of Arguments

In this paper, we find that the age-adjusted elasticity of child wealth with respect to parental wealth is 0.37 before the transfer of bequests. *Our results imply that* while parents do pass on human capital and saving propensities to their children, the level of intergenerational fluidity is much greater than that suggested by recent accounts in the popular press. (Charles & Hurst, 2003, p. 1155)

Using detailed administrative data on schooling and birth records from Chile and Norway, we establish that children who receive extra medical care at birth have lower mortality rates and higher test scores and grades in school. *These gains are in the order of* 0.15–0.22 standard deviations. (Bharadwaj et al., 2013, p. 1862)

Population growth, inequality and economic development are among the most pressing social issues confronting us today. This research argues that these national problems are embedded within the context of increasingly complex multi-dimensional international networks, commonly referred to as globalization. *Using cross-national comparisons among 88 less developed countries, I construct a series of structural equation models to estimate the effects of* two aspects of globalization, foreign capital dependence and trade openness, on these three domestic concerns between 1980 and 1997. *I find that* foreign capital dependence has a positive effect on income inequality, raises fertility rates, accelerates population growth and retards economic development. Trade openness, in contrast, has long-term positive effects on economic development. (Kentor, 2001, p. 435)

We find strong evidence that firms with employee-friendly workplaces achieve greater innovative success, particularly in industries where innovation is more difficult to achieve. These findings are consistent with the view that an employee-friendly workplace helps to develop tolerance for failure, which encourages engagement in innovation. (Chen et al., 2016, p. 61)

Step 5: Assess the Validity of Arguments

To assess the validity of an author's arguments, you need to examine and evaluate the evidence on which these arguments are based. This evaluation is often referred to as *critical reading*.

Recall that to be valid, an argument must have some sort of evidence to support it. In academic papers, *evidence* comes in two forms: scholarly literature or the author's own data.

Scholarly literature is often used to support arguments about the state of current knowledge including arguments about

- The importance or timeliness of a topic,
- Difficulties or challenges in researching a topic,
- The appropriateness of a particular approach to analyzing a topic,
- Expectations of a particular outcome or relationship, or
- Existing controversies.

Such arguments are always followed by citations or a description of previous research, with citations. To assess the strength of these arguments, you need to assess the strength of the evidence (i.e., research studies) on which they are based.

Go to the reference section and check what type of study is being cited in support of the argument. Distinguish between empirical results and opinions. Arguments should be supported by empirical literature—by results of empirical studies, rather than by other authors' opinions. Do the studies cited as evidence look like empirical studies? Do they come from reputable journals? If you are not sure, consider obtaining and reading the studies, especially those that are used to support some of the more important claims. This is particularly important for doctoral students, as their arguments will only be as good as the sources on which they are based.

In contrast to arguments about the state of current knowledge, which are supported by scholarly literature, authors' own claims to knowledge must be supported by the authors' actual research—by the results that they obtained and by the methodology that they used. To evaluate an author's claim to knowledge, you need to check the methodology and analysis sections to understand how the study was designed and conducted.

Box 15 shows some questions to keep in mind when evaluating an author's claims in an empirical study. If you cannot answer any of these questions because there is not enough information in the study or if the answers reveal flaws in the study, consider if this lack of information or if those flaws only weaken the author's arguments or if they invalidate them. There is no such thing as a perfect study in the social sciences; what is important to understand is that some flaws are more detrimental to the author's arguments than others. The next section briefly explains some of these flaws.

It is also important to keep in mind that critical reading and argument analysis at this stage require subject-matter knowledge and an understanding of how

BOX 15 Questions for Determining the Validity of Empirical Studies

1. What was the purpose of the study? What was the research question?
2. What were the names of the concepts under study? How were they measured? Does the measurement appear to be appropriate?
3. What was the design of the study? Was it appropriate for the research question?
4. How were the data collected? If existing statistics were used, did the author's definitions match the definitions of the data collector?
5. How were the data analyzed? Does the analysis match the purpose of the study? Does the unit of analysis match the level of aggregation?
6. What is the answer to the research question? Is it warranted by the methodology and analysis?

research is done in your particular discipline or area. Researchers working in different areas have their own preferred research strategies and their own standards for what counts as acceptable evidence. These strategies concern both data collection and data analysis. Understanding what research strategies are commonly used in your area will help you evaluate the strength of arguments presented in a research paper.

For example, research in many areas of economics relies on correlational designs and regression analysis, often with robustness checks to minimize bias. Qualitative research is uncommon and evidence obtained from a qualitative study would not be considered convincing by economists. Research on public opinion relies on data collected through public opinion surveys, which are analyzed quantitatively. Here too, qualitative analysis would not be considered strong evidence. Studies of program effectiveness in education, health, and other social areas often use experimental or quasiexperimental designs and conduct quantitative group comparisons; arguments about program effectiveness that are based on survey methods would not be convincing. In international relations, researchers often base their arguments on data collected through in-depth interviews or through examination of documents, which are analyzed qualitatively. Historical research relies on archival data collection and may involve both quantitative and qualitative analyses.

COMMON FLAWS IN EMPIRICAL STUDIES

Perhaps the single most important criterion in evaluating claims to knowledge is whether the particular research design is appropriate for the research question. To put it differently, does the design allow the author to answer the research question? A design that is not appropriate for the research question not just weakens the author's arguments—it invalidates them. The following example shows why. Consider the following research question:

How effective are police patrols in reducing crime?

Now imagine that an author claims that his or her study has found police patrols to be highly effective for reducing crime. However, when you examine the design of the study more closely, you discover that the study is based on a survey of local residents, many of whom claimed that police patrols were effective. Is the researcher's claim warranted by the study's design?

No. Surveys are tools for studying what people *think* or *do*, not for determining if a policy or a program *works*. A more appropriate design in this case would be experimental or quasiexperimental and it would call for dividing the neighborhood into sectors and assigning some of the sectors to have police patrols while using the remaining sectors as controls.

Consider another example. A government agency conducted a study to examine the relationship between illegal drugs and violence. The agency used a correlational design and found a strong and statistically significant correlation between the two variables. The authors of the study argue that ending drug use will greatly reduce acts of violence. Does this argument make sense given the design of the study?

No. This argument assumes that drug use *causes* violence but this assumption is not warranted by the design of the study because correlation is not causation. Finding that two variables correlate—even strongly and statistically significantly—should not be taken to mean that one causes the other. The strong correlation may be due to a third variable, which the researchers have failed to measure in their study. In this case, the third variable could be emotional disorders: People with such disorders are more likely to use drugs and also commit acts of violence.

Thus, when evaluating a study, you need to consider to what extent the design of the study is appropriate to the research question. In the remainder of this section, I show four very broad groups of questions that are often addressed by studies in public policy and economics and discuss common problems associated with the design of such studies or their data. Keep these problems in mind when evaluating others' research studies or when designing your own.

Questions about program or policy effectiveness and policy outcomes often call for an experimental or quasiexperimental design, in which an experimental group (a group that has been subjected to the program or policy under study) is compared to a control group (a group that has not been subjected to the program/policy). Sometimes, a study may involve more than one group. In such designs, the most important factor in evaluating the validity of claims is whether the groups were equivalent at baseline (before the beginning of the program/policy). If they were not (or if there was no control group), then the arguments would not be valid. Baseline equivalence can be ensured through random assignment of participants to groups or, when this is not possible, by equating the groups statistically on key characteristics that are relevant to the research question.

Often, researchers in public policy and economics use correlational designs to answer questions about program or policy effectiveness or the effect of one variable on another. However, simple correlational designs preclude arguments about cause and effect for two reasons. First, correlations may be attributable to unobserved factors, or variables that have not been included in the model. For example, we may find a strong and statistically significant correlation between income and obesity, but this does not necessarily mean that programs aimed at increasing incomes would automatically reduce obesity. There may be a third, unseen, variable, such as personal or family characteristics or economic variables such as parental education which cause both low income and obesity. Failure to include these variables in the model would invalidate the author's conclusions about the relationship between the variables. This problem is called **omitted variable bias**.

The second problem is **reverse causality**—or incorrect interpretation of the direction of causality in the relationship between two variables. For instance, in the earlier example with obesity, low income could lead to obesity because low-income families may not be able to buy high-quality food and rely on junk food instead; it is also plausible that obesity lowers income by making it difficult for people to work and earn high incomes. Reverse causality is a particularly serious problem when we correlate endogenous variables. For example, you may find a correlation between alcohol use and depression but is it the alcohol that causes depression or is it depression that makes people turn to alcohol? In this case, it could be both.

To minimize reverse causality bias, it is important to have a theory predicting the relationship of interest. It is also important to use research designs that make causal inferences about the effects of independent variables possible. Such inferences should be derived from exogenous, rather than endogenous sources of variation.

Questions involving cross-country, cross-region, or international comparisons may rely on quantitative or qualitative designs. In economics and public policy, comparative research often involves quantitative analysis of secondary data, or existing statistics, collected by large government organizations. Common problems in research involving existing statistics may include the following.

- **Mismatch** between the units of analysis required to answer a research questions (i.e., individual people) and the level of aggregation in the data obtained from a government agency (i.e., groups, regions, schools). For example, the research question may be asking about math performance of individual students in different geographical areas, but the data are at the level of the classroom or school.

- **Mismatch** between the author's definition of a concept and the definition used by the agency collecting the data. For example, the author may have defined drug use to include the use of prescription drugs, but the official definition in government reports may include only the use of illicit drugs.

- **Use of a proxy** that does not fully represent the theoretical concept. For example, the author may be interested in comparing crime rates in different cities and, therefore, uses police records on arrests as a proxy for crime rate. However, in some situations, crimes may go unreported or may not result in an arrest.

- **Noncomparable definitions**. Different countries and regions may use different official definitions and methods of data collection, which may also change over time. For example, there may be big differences in how different countries calculate unemployment rate and these differences result in numbers that will not be comparable. Or a country may change its definition of unemployment at a certain point, making direct comparisons without adjustment difficult. The quality of data collected by national governments in different countries may also vary substantially.

Qualitative comparisons are also common in public policy research, especially when the goal is an in-depth exploration of a phenomenon. In qualitative comparisons, the most important criterion in assessing the validity of the research design is whether the cases (e.g., countries, regions, groups, or organizations) are comparable. Thus, case selection is of paramount importance. As I explained in Chapter 2, qualitative researchers often use the following two designs in comparative research:

- **Most similar systems design**, in which cases sharing many relevant characteristics are selected and then matched on the independent variables so that a key difference can be identified, which can then be used to explain the differences in the outcome variable.

- **Most different systems design**, in which cases are selected so that the outcome variable is the same, and most of the other variables are different; the goal is to identify a common factor that may explain the same outcome variable in each case. This design looks for different cases in which there are key similarities on the outcome variable and on one or a few independent variables.

Inappropriate case selection is one of the main problems with qualitative comparisons. If cases are selected such that they are similar on the outcome and on all potentially explanatory variables, then a comparison would not be possible. To be comparable, the cases must share some characteristics that are theoretically relevant to the research question and differ on others.

It is also important to keep in mind that qualitative designs do not involve hypothesis testing, and therefore, cannot provide definitive answers to research questions. Instead, they provide tentative directions for future, more rigorous research. Check that the author's conclusions are in line with the qualitative design of the study—that the arguments are tentative.

Questions about how a social or organizational process or a phenomenon occurs rely on case study and qualitative methods. Data collection is often based on in-depth interviews and longitudinal observation, and data analysis involves looking for patterns and common themes in the data. Case selection is especially important in such designs, and it should be purposive—guided by the purpose of the research and by the research question. Check what criteria the author used for case selection. A common problem here is selecting cases simply because they are available. Such cases are called **samples of convenience**. Arguments derived from the analysis of samples of convenience should be interpreted with great caution because such arguments may not be applicable to other cases.

Questions about public opinion rely on survey research. Studies of public opinion collect information not only on people's opinions but also on people's behavior (e.g., How often do you ride a bus?), attitudes (e.g., What is your attitude toward immigration?), demographic characteristics (e.g., Are you married?), and knowledge (e.g., How many people in the United States live with HIV?). Depending on the research question, studies of public opinion may correlate people's opinions with their demographic characteristics or behavior to find out to what extent the latter are associated with the former.

Several sources of bias can weaken and potentially invalidate arguments derived from public opinion surveys. They include the following:

- A small sample size. The size of the sample needed for a survey depends on several things including confidence intervals (how precise we want to be when we generalize to the target population) and confidence level (how confident we want to be of sample results when we generalize to the target population). A well-designed survey would usually have at least several hundred participants.
- An inappropriate sampling method, resulting in a nonrepresentative sample. Check how the sample was selected and whether it was representative of the target population.
- Unclear questions or the respondents' inability or unwillingness to answer the questions.
- A low (i.e., less than 50%) response rate.

Chapter 6

Research Questions, Hypotheses, and Purpose Statements

WHAT IS A RESEARCH QUESTION?

A **research question** is the main question a research study aims to answer. A good research question does the following:

- It provides a summary of the study: It should be possible to understand, by looking at the question, what the study is about.

- It establishes parameters of the research: It should be possible to understand, by looking at the question, what the context (e.g., population, country, time period) of the study is.

- It provides clues about the methodology: It should be possible to understand, by looking at the question, how the study was conducted.

A research question is different from a topic: It is much narrower and more specific than a topic, and it usually specifies the context for the research (e.g., country, region, population). A research question is different from a hypothesis: It summarizes the idea that will be examined in the study, whereas a hypothesis summarizes a proposed answer. A research question is also different from a research objective or purpose: It is usually formulated as a relationship between variables, especially in quantitative studies, whereas a research purpose may only describe what the study intends to do—for example, test a model, advance a definition, or identify the driving factors behind a phenomenon. It should, generally, be possible to reformulate a clearly stated purpose into a research question, but doing so may require reading beyond the description of the purpose to understand what the researchers did in the study.

WHERE DO RESEARCH QUESTIONS COME FROM?

Although research in public policy and economics can address both theoretical and applied, or practical, problems, most research projects that students do in public policy schools are devoted to applied problems, especially those that

How to Write about Economics and Public Policy. https://doi.org/10.1016/B978-0-12-813010-0.00006-5

address the human condition such as lack of access to health care, food safety, or environmental pollution. The purpose of examining these problems is to suggest ways to improve the human condition. Thus, the most appropriate research question for a project in a public policy program would be one that helps solve a practical problem. Where can you find such a research question? Below are three suggestions.

Literature. Perhaps the most common source of research questions is academic literature. There are two strategies for finding research questions in the literature. The first one is to look for a gap in research, something that has not yet been studied. A gap could be a variable that has not yet been included in a model, a specific relationship that has not yet been examined, or a country setting or a population that has not yet been studied. Another strategy is to critically appraise the literature looking for something that does not quite make sense. This could be flaws in the research strategy, research design, or measurement. You can then try to devise a way to improve on these flaws, for example, by using data that are richer or less biased; by measuring variables in a different, more precise, way; or by using a bigger sample.

Here is an example of a project that grew out of critical appraisal of a best-selling book. In *Research Confidential: Solutions to Problems Most Social Scientists Pretend They Never Have,* Freese (2009) describes reading a book written by a prominent researcher, Frank Sulloway, on the effects of birth order (i.e., being firstborn vs. being later-born) on political and social attitudes and personality. In that book, Sulloway argued, using historical data, that birth order had a significant effect on personality and political and social attitudes and that firstborns tended to be more conservative than later-borns. Freese found these arguments unconvincing and the research approach used by Sulloway, flawed, and he decided to test Sulloway's predictions on a more unbiased data set. In a way, this project grew out of Freese's dissatisfaction with the original author's arguments.

Policy practice. Another source of research questions is policy practice. Students with work experience in the public or private sector often use that experience to come up with interesting research questions that are related to their work. This question could be related to a problem that they may have observed in the course of their work or a policy that they have been wondering about. For example, one of my students had spent a few years working for the Ministry of Transportation in a European country and wanted to know what effect transportation infrastructure projects had on regional development. Another student from the Central Bank of Maldives wanted to do a study on the determinants of inflation in her country because such research had direct relevance for the bank's policy on inflation. Another student, who had worked as a chief investment officer at a holdings company in Japan, was interested in learning why countries hold foreign exchange reserves. After surveying the literature, he narrowed down his topic to this question: What are the costs of holding foreign currency reserves for Japan?

Personal interest. Research questions may also be motivated by personal interest—a desire to learn something that is relevant to your life, work, or personal relationships. For example, if you are a university instructor, you may want to know if humor helps students learn difficult subjects such as economics or statistics, or if you work in a local government, you may want to find out how you can promote tourism in your area.

DO ALL STUDIES HAVE A RESEARCH QUESTION?

Every empirical study has a research question, but not all studies have research questions that are stated explicitly in the paper. In fact, in economics and public policy papers, research questions are often implied in the objective, or purpose, of the study or in the description of what the researchers did. It is especially rare to see an explicitly stated research question in economic studies.

Yet, it is important to understand that even though a research question may or may not be stated explicitly in a paper, it plays a crucial role in the research process. In the early stages of research, the research question guides the researcher through the literature, helping to clarify what exactly is to be studied. In the later stages, it shapes the direction of inquiry and helps the researcher decide on an appropriate research design, population, and data.

For example, in a quantitative study, the research question will help determine what variables should be included, what hypotheses should be postulated, what data should be collected, and how the data should be analyzed. In a qualitative study, the research question will help focus the investigation and decide what is, and what is not, relevant; what should be included; and what should be excluded.

Regardless of whether your program, advisor, or journal you are submitting your manuscript to requires that you state your research question explicitly in the paper, you will need to formulate one in order to engage in research. No study can be done without a clearly formulated research question.

CLOSED-ENDED VS. OPEN-ENDED QUESTIONS

Closed-ended questions are yes/no questions; open-ended questions are questions that start with a question word (e.g., *what, why, how*). Although research questions can be both closed- and open-ended, in public policy and economics, research questions are often open-ended, both in quantitative and in qualitative studies. In quantitative studies, this is because the goal of statistical testing is not just to test if the variables are related but also to see how strongly they are related—to estimate parameters (or coefficients) for the variables in the model. When you are testing if X and Y are related, you are simultaneously determining the strength of that relationship.

In qualitative studies, open-ended questions are also much more common than closed-ended ones because the focus in qualitative research is on processes

BOX 16 Closed-Ended and Open-Ended Questions

Closed-Ended Questions	Open-Ended Questions
Is X related to Y?	To what extent is X related to Y?
Does X have an effect on Y?	What is the effect of X on Y?
Is X associated with Y?	How is X associated with Y?
Is there any relationship between X and Y?	What is the relationship between X and Y?
Does X have an impact on Y?	What is the impact of X on Y?
Does X contribute to Y?	How does X contribute to Y?

(i.e., how something happens), causes (why it happens), and details (what it really is or what it is like).

Box 16 shows examples of closed-ended and open-ended questions.

EMPIRICAL VS. NORMATIVE QUESTIONS

Not every question we may wish to ask can be answered through research. There are many interesting questions that cannot be settled in this way. Here are some examples.

- Should capital punishment be abolished?

- Should the government raise the minimum wage?

- Would it be right to allow the use of performance-enhancing drugs among athletes?

- Are policies aimed at eradicating inequality more important than policies aimed at increasing economic growth?

- Is it important to empower women?

- How important is it to reduce corruption in government?

- What is the best way to eliminate corruption?

Answers to these questions do not rely on empirical evidence and cannot be tested directly. Rather, they depend on an individual person's system of beliefs and values, on the law, or on a set of criteria used to determine what is more or less important, good, or necessary. Such questions are called **normative** and they deal with how the world *should be*. Research questions, in contrast, are **empirical**—they deal with how the world *is*. The purpose of answering research questions is to describe the world as it is, in an unbiased manner.

OTHER NONEMPIRICAL QUESTIONS

Besides normative questions, there are many other types of questions that cannot be settled through research. Below are some examples. To understand why they cannot be answered through research, just think about what kind of research strategy could be used to answer them. Notice also how vague most of these questions are.

Metaphysical questions: Does God exist? What happens after we die? Was the Chernobyl accident inevitable?

Metaphysical questions cannot be answered through research because there is no research strategy that could be used to answer them. How, for example, can you test God's existence? Or what criteria could you use to measure the inevitability of a past event? Metaphysical questions cannot be converted into researchable questions.

Legal questions: Can the taxpayer deduct bonuses from gross income?

Legal questions can be answered by simply consulting the law, an expert, or existing rules. You do not need to engage in academic research to answer such questions. This is not to say, however, that you cannot do research on legal topics. In fact, there are many interesting questions in this area that can be researched both quantitatively and qualitatively. Here is an example of a quantitative question related to law: How do a defendant's looks and the nature of the crime affect sentencing decisions? And here is an example of a qualitative question: How do Australia and Japan interpret international law on whaling and how do these interpretations affect these countries' policies on whaling?

Fact-oriented questions: How is Policy X conducted by Government Y? What framework regulates public debt management in Country Z?

These questions are too descriptive. Answering them is a matter of describing what the government has done or is doing or what frameworks and mechanisms exist to manage a particular problem. Descriptive questions can be converted into researchable questions by reformulating them as a relationship. For example: How has a recent anticorruption law affected the implementation of Policy X by Government Y? How does the regulatory framework shape strategies used for public debt management in Country A and Country B? What economic factors explain the choice of strategies used by different countries for public debt management?

"What can be done" questions: What can be done to reduce poverty? What can we do to eliminate corruption? How can we reduce environmental pollution?

In a way, these questions can be answered quite simply: "Many, many things can be done." It all depends on the goals, context, resources, and many other things. Without specifying all those things, it is impossible to answer questions about an appropriate course of action. To make such questions researchable, we would need to specify relevant variables such as the outcome and the conditions under which the problem exists. For example: To what extent has microfinance lending reduced poverty in rural Uganda? How do corruption norms affect what is viewed as acceptable and what is viewed as unacceptable behavior? We would also need to identify other variables that may have an effect on the outcome and include them as control variables.

Points of view disguised as questions: Is corruption a serious problem? Does inequality affect people in developing countries?

Essentially, these questions take a problem and ask if it is a (serious) problem. The purpose is usually to explain why the person asking the question thinks that the problem is, indeed, a problem. To make these questions researchable, focus on the factors that are associated with the problem you are interested in, on the differences in the magnitude or manifestations of the problem in different contexts, or on how the problem affects certain populations. For example: What economic and social factors are associated with corruption in local government? What is the impact of institutional factors on foreign direct investment inflows? What is the effect of government decentralization on domestic terrorism?

Assumption-based questions: Why is globalization increasing inequality?

This question is actually two questions, and the answer to one of these questions is assumed. The author assumes that globalization increases inequality and asks, why. But what is the basis for this assumption? How can you be sure that globalization does, in fact, increase inequality? To research the original question, you need to convert it into two: Does globalization increase inequality (OR: To what extent does globalization increase inequality) and if globalization does increase inequality, why is it the case? The "why" question could then be answered by specifying and testing a series of hypotheses about the connection between different characteristics of globalization and inequality.

Questions about the future: Will Afghanistan ever eliminate terrorism?

Future-oriented questions can be answered in two ways—by using a crystal ball or by doing a simulation. The crystal-ball strategy is not scientific, and therefore, is beyond the scope of this book. Simulations, in contrast, are common in many areas of public policy and economics, but they work as a way to test a model or a system—just as you might in a laboratory. To run a simulation, we need to specify, using equations, the behavior of the system and its underlying assumptions—in other words, we need to build a mathematical model of the system and test it. Simulations are a good tool for predicting the behavior of various macroeconomic variables such as unemployment, consumption, investment, or government expenditure; however, they only work if we can identify all the relevant variables and describe how they are related in the model. In the above example with terrorism, there are simply too many unknown variables—variables that cannot be specified in advance and whose relationships to other variables is unknown or unknowable.

Questions without a framework for analysis: What are the strengths and weaknesses of Policy A? What are the advantages and disadvantages of Action B? What are the pros and cons of accepting Plan C? What are the challenges and opportunities of Approach D?

Such questions are quite common in business and policy practice. In fact, some models of decision-making in policy analysis and evaluation incorporate some of these questions. However, answering such questions requires that there be a set of criteria for categorizing strengths and weaknesses and a yardstick by which strengths, weaknesses, advantages, disadvantages, and so on are measured. Taken on their own, these questions cannot be answered because there is no way to decide what would count as a strength and what would count as a weakness. The same thing can be a strength or a weakness, depending on how you look at it and what criteria (e.g., accountability, sustainability, or cost) you use.

RESEARCH QUESTIONS IN A PAPER

There are three common ways to indicate a research question in a paper.

- By stating it explicitly as a question, with a question mark. For example:

What are the determinants of foreign direct investment in Country X?

To what extent does financial training affect firms' performance?

Explicit questions are usually located at the end of the Introduction section and/or at the end of the Literature Review section. Sometimes, they can also be found in the Results section. In some cases, the research question may also be included in the title of a study; this is sometimes the case with qualitative studies. Explicitly stated research questions are rare in economics and public policy.

- By stating it indirectly, often as an objective of a paper. For example:

We examine whether a firm's commitment to providing a high quality workplace for its employees spurs innovation. (Chen et al., 2016, p. 61)

In this paper, we investigate whether and how parental *presence* affects the intergenerational correlation of educational attainment. (Kalil et al., 2016, p. 870)

It is much more common in economics and public policy to embed a research question into the objective, purpose, goal, or aim of the study. Indirect research questions stated as a purpose are almost always found in the Introduction. They can be easily converted into direct questions.

- By implying it in the description of what the researchers did. For example:

This paper presents a model of the human capital investment process of longer-lived spouses over the life cycle and tests its predictions using innovative new data on financial literacy and financial decision-making. (Hsu, 2016, p. 1037)

This paper measures the long-run change in ridership induced by price and service changes using a new location-specific panel data set. (Voith, 1991, p. 360)

This is another common way to present a research question in an economics or public policy paper. Implied questions can often be found in the Introduction section. It may not always be easy to convert such statements into direct questions because doing so requires understanding exactly what the researchers did in the study.

FORMULATING EMPIRICAL QUESTIONS

Quantitative Questions

Quantitative questions are specific. Their main purpose is to **test a specific theory** about a relationship between variables. These relationships can be causal or correlational, and we describe them by showing whether the variables are related, how they are related (e.g., positively or negatively), and how strongly. Here are some common types of quantitative questions.

- What is the relationship between X and Y?
- How does X affect Y?
- What is the impact/effect of X on Y?
- What factors are associated with Y?
- What are the determinants of Y?
- Does X increase/decrease Y?
- How does X contribute to Y?

Another purpose of quantitative questions is **prediction**. However, quantitative research cannot predict a relationship directly because empirical data are not available before the event has happened. So we predict by using two approaches: by investigating the current empirical relationship between variables and then extrapolating the estimates we have obtained for the variables to predict how an increase or a decrease in one variable would affect another, *ceteris paribus* (all other things being equal), or by running a simulation in which we specify certain scenarios and assumptions and use a model to estimate the contribution of some variables to other variables. Both approaches are based on our current knowledge of the precise empirical relationship between the variables of interest. In other words, in order to predict that an increase in X will lead to a decrease in Y, we first need to describe the relationship between X and Y and find out to what extent a change in X is accompanied by a change in Y.

For example, we can investigate an empirical relationship between educational attainment and teenage pregnancy and find that schooling reduces teenage pregnancies by a certain amount. We can then use this information to predict by how much each additional year of schooling would reduce the number of teenage pregnancies. Or we can study determinants of inflation and their relative importance and then use this information to predict what would happen to inflation if there were a certain change in one or more of its determinants.

We can also run experiments to simulate a future impact of some event on a specified variable or variables; these experiments, however, are based on current data and on our current description of the relationship between the variables. For example, after the exit of the United Kingdom from the European Union, researchers did many simulations to assess both the short-run and long-run impact of Brexit on various macroeconomic variables including GDP and net household income. To conduct such experiments, they had to specify various scenarios—for example, in Scenario 1, both the United Kingdom and the EU impose import tariffs on each other; in Scenario 2, in addition to tariff imposition, transportation costs increase by 20%, and so on. They then used different models to simulate how the variables would behave under the conditions described in each scenario. However, because there are many uncertainties with future events, estimates and predictions usually vary widely among studies and often turn out to be wrong.

Predictive questions, therefore, are not really about the future; they are about the present, and they are based on current data. You should therefore formulate your question using present tense rather than future tense (not *What will be the effect of trade liberalization on economic performance?* but *What is the effect of trade liberalization on economic performance?*). You can then use the estimated values to predict what might happen to the dependent variable if there were a certain change in the predictor variable(s).

Some quantitative questions may be formulated as comparative questions, for example: *What is the difference in Y between Group A, which received X, and Group B, which did not receive X?* or *What is the difference in Y between people who have X and those who do not have X?* Yet, the purpose of such comparisons is ultimately to describe the relationship between X and Y rather than describe the presence or absence of a certain attribute in different groups. Essentially, these questions are asking about the effect of X on Y or the association between X and Y in different populations, and comparison is just a means for clarifying this association.

For example, we may want to investigate the effect of banking sector globalization on economic growth and use a panel data set to see how banking sector globalization (measured, for example, as the presence of foreign banks in a country) affects economic growth. To further understand this relationship, we can divide our sample of countries into categories representing different levels of economic growth (e.g., high, medium, and low) and compare the obtained results across the categories while controlling for other macroeconomic variables related to growth. In this case, the comparison becomes a tool that helps us better understand the relationship between banking sector globalization and economic growth.

For specific examples of quantitative research questions from different areas of public policy and economics, see Box 19 at the end of this chapter.

Qualitative Questions

Qualitative questions are broad. They are about a process, a phenomenon, an experience, or an event. There is usually a central question and several associated subquestions that narrow the focus of the study. For example:

Central question: How do Japanese firms make decisions about where to invest?

Subquestions: What factors facilitate the decision-making? What factors hinder it? Who are the key participants in the process? How long does it take?

Qualitative questions may do one of the following:

- **Explore a phenomenon:** What does it mean to be X/live in X/live with X/do X? How does [a group of people] do X? For example:

  What does it mean to live in poverty? How do single mothers in rural areas cope with chronic poverty? How do middle-aged women prepare to re-enter the labor force? How does the local government in Province X promote tourism?

- **Describe a process or a phenomenon:** What is X? How does X happen/develop/occur? What is the current state of X? What strategies have been shown to be successful for X? For example:

  What is economic development? How does corruption occur in local government? What strategies have been found successful for empowering women in developing countries?

- **Explain a phenomenon:** Why does X happen? What accounts for X? What is the role of X in Y? What are the drivers behind X? How can the concept of X help us understand Y? For example:

  Why do revolutions happen? What accounts for a recent resurgence of nationalism in Russia? What role does cyber technology play in international relations? What are the driving forces behind the economic rise of China?

When formulating a qualitative question, avoid using words that suggest a directional orientation such as *impact, effect, influence, determine,* or *cause.* Such questions cannot be answered through qualitative research.

For specific examples of qualitative research questions from different areas of public policy and economics, see Box 19 at the end of this chapter.

CHARACTERISTICS OF A GOOD RESEARCH QUESTION

It Asks about Something that Is Currently Not Known

This may seem obvious—after all, why would you want to do research on something that is already known or established? And yet, one of the most common problems students have when formulating a research question is formulating questions that are essentially points of view in disguise (e.g., *Is pollution a serious problem?*). What you need to do is formulate a question the answer to which is not known—both to you and to your target research community.

It Is Answerable through Empirical Research

To see if your question is answerable through research, think about your research strategy. How will you go about answering your question? What will be the design of your study? What data will you need to answer it? How will you analyze your data?

Avoid normative and other questions that cannot be answered through research. Change *should* questions to questions about the relationship between variables of interest or the effect of one variable on another. Change future-oriented question (e.g., *What will happen...?*) to present-oriented (e.g., *What is the relationship between...?*).

It Is Sufficiently Limited

Avoid global questions such as *How did the 1997–1998 currency crisis affect Asia?* Instead, try to limit the scope of your question to a more specific population or area. For example: *How did the 1997–1998 currency crisis affect the housing market in Indonesia?*

It Is Theoretically Motivated

A research question must be theoretically motivated. It is not enough to just pick a relationship that has never been studied before and "wonder" what it might be. You need to explain

- Why you expect a relationship,
- What kind of relationship you expect, and
- What the implications of this relationship are.

For example, you may be interested in studying the effect of political decentralization on terrorism. But why do you think that decentralization and terrorism may be related? What is the mechanism that relates these two phenomena? And how might decentralization and terrorism be related? Would decentralization increase or decrease terrorist activity? Why do you think so? What would be the implications of this relationship?

It is not enough to answer these questions based on your personal opinion or your own theory; you need to justify your expectations by appealing to established theories, those that have been advanced and tested by other researchers, or to empirical findings of previous research. Your arguments about your expectations should come from the literature and should be supported by it. To have a theoretically motivated question means to be able to justify expectations based on the findings of theoretical and empirical literature.

It Is Significant for Theory or Policy Practice

The answer to your question must be valuable to other people: It must contribute to the existing body of knowledge—theoretical, applied, or both. For professional researchers in economics and public policy, theoretical relevance is often more important than practical significance. For students in public policy programs, however, significant often means relevant to policy, or having important policy implications. To see if your research question has theoretical significance, ask yourself if the answer to your question has the potential to:

- Lend support to an untested theory,
- Extend an existing theory,
- Challenge an existing theory, or
- Clarify or resolve an existing controversy in the literature.

To see if your research question is significant for policy practice, ask yourself if the answer to your question has the potential to:

- Benefit the policy community,
- Help find a solution to a practical problem, or
- Reevaluate and/or improve existing policies or practices.

HYPOTHESES

What Is a Hypothesis?

A hypothesis is a specified, testable **prediction** about a relationship between two or more variables that involves a statistical test. Here is how Babbie (1998) describes the characteristics of a hypothesis.

- It has two or more variables.
- It expresses a relationship between the variables.

- It is testable.
- It is logically linked to a theory and the research question.
- It is stated in a value-neutral form.

Hypotheses are derived from theories and are used to test the strength and direction of a predicted relationship.

Directional and Nondirectional Hypotheses

Hypotheses can be directional (or one-tailed) or nondirectional (or two-tailed). A **directional hypothesis** specifies how the variables are related, whereas a **nondirectional hypothesis** specifies only that there is a relationship between the variables. Whether you should state a directional or a nondirectional hypothesis depends on whether there is research evidence on the issue.

Recall that a hypothesis is a prediction of an expected relationship. If this prediction is made on the basis of some theory or research showing what kind of relationship you can expect, your hypothesis should be directional. If there is no research evidence supporting a particular expectation, or if there are alternative theories predicting different outcomes, you may state a nondirectional hypothesis.

Most hypotheses in economics and public policy are directional—they not only predict the existence of a relationship but also state what kind of relationship should be expected. We may begin with a nondirectional hypothesis but as we read on the topic and learn more about the relationship, we are often able to formulate a more precise, directional hypothesis. For example, we may begin with the following nondirectional hypothesis: *Financial education influences the saving behavior of employees.* After reading the literature, we can often formulate a more precise, directional hypothesis: *Financial education is positively related to the size of employees' contributions to retirement plans.*

Box 17 shows examples of hypotheses from a selection of articles in economics and public policy. Go over them, paying attention to the language they use. For each hypothesis, decide whether it is directional or nondirectional. How can you tell?

BOX 17 Examples of Hypotheses

Topic	Hypotheses
Perceptions and evaluations of the distribution of income in Eastern Europe before and after the "velvet revolutions"	If "mature" industrial societies differ in starting points and/or the modernising routes they followed, then they will show larger differences in the perceived and preferred hierarchy of the occupational incomes and the perceived and preferred degree of occupational income inequality, than societies that do not differ in starting-points and/or modernising routes.

Continued

BOX 17 Examples of Hypotheses—cont'd.

	If a society comes to follow the same modernising route as other societies, then there will be a convergence between this society and the other societies with regard to the perceived and evaluated hierarchy of occupational incomes and the degree of income inequality. (Arts et al., 1999, pp. 64–65)
Relationship between depth and flexibility of preferential trade agreements (PTAs)	The deeper a PTA, the more flexible it is. The positive relationship between depth and flexibility is weaker for democracies than for nondemocracies. (Baccini et al., 2015, p. 767)
Determinants of pay in corporate hierarchies and the relationship between pay and promotion	The gap between CEO pay and mean VP pay should increase with a greater number of vice presidents. (Bognanno, 2001, p. 291) Increasing the number of competitors increases the first prize and the difference between the first prize and the second prize, even after controlling for executive and firm variables. (Bognanno, 2001, p. 305)
Relationship between public revenues and efficiency in public goods production	Higher local government revenue reduces the efficiency in production of public goods. (Borge et al., 2015, p. 101)
Relationship between employee-friendliness of a firm and innovative success	The positive effect of workplace quality on innovation should be more prominent in firms with higher levels of intangible capital embedded in their key employees and in industries with higher labor mobility. (Chen et al., 2016, p. 62)
Relationship between government decentralization and domestic terrorism	Assuming that terrorists are rational decision-makers who weigh the expected costs against the benefits of their terrorist activities…, less terror should occur in countries with stronger local governments and administrations. (Dreher & Fischer, 2011, p. 223) Government decentralization reduces the number of domestic terrorist incidents. (Dreher & Fischer, 2011, p. 224)
Relationship between foreign ownership and employee wages, employment, and worker turnover rates	We hypothesise that the gap in working conditions between foreign-owned and domestic firms will be greater in developing countries because the technological difference is likely to be greatest, and the availability of comparable alternative job opportunities lowest. (Hijzen et al., 2013, p. 173)
Individual-level and context-level determinants of tax morale	Our hypothesis is that tax morale will tend to be weaker in those countries where taxes are higher or when they have significantly increased in recent years. (Lago-Peñas & Lago-Peñas, 2010, p. 446)

BOX 17 Examples of Hypotheses—cont'd.

Effects of population aging on the size and generosity of public pension plans	*Positive size effect:* Societies with a larger share of elderly citizens devote more resources to public pension programs overall (the open-ended statutory 'entitlements' argument).
	Positive benefit effect: The generosity of individual public pensions increases with a larger share of elderly people in society (the 'elderly power' argument).
	Negative benefit effect: The generosity of individual public pensions decreases with a larger share of elderly people in society (the 'fiscal leakage' argument). (Tepe & Vanhuysse, 2009, p. 7)
Determinants of inward FDI flows	Hypothesis 1: An increasing ratio of the host country's GDP relative to the home country's GDP is expected to attract FDI from the home country.
	Hypothesis 2: Inward FDI flows into the host country are expected to be higher, the lower is the ratio of the host country's real wage rate level compared to that of the home country. (Cuyvers et al., 2011, p. 225)
Determinants of a parent bank's decision to close or sell a foreign bank subsidiary	Hypothesis 1: Parent banks close or sell their foreign subsidiaries due to the low profitability and/or the financial distress of their foreign operations.
	Hypothesis 2: Foreign bank subsidiaries are closed or sold as a result of the low profitability and/or the financial problems of the parent bank in the home country.
	Hypothesis 3: Foreign bank exits are motivated by the simultaneous low profitability and/or the financial distress of the subsidiary and its parent bank. (Hryckiewicz & Kowalewski, 2011, pp. 71–72)
Effects of fathers' presence on intergenerational transmission of educational attainment	In sum, the empirical evidence on the role of the environment in children's educational attainment, along with theory about the relevance of parental socialization and economic inputs into children's educational attainment, leads to the central hypotheses of our study:
	Hypothesis 1: an increase in father presence will increase the intergenerational education coefficient between father and child.
	Hypothesis 2: an increase in father presence will decrease the intergenerational education coefficient between mother and child. (Kalil et al., 2016, p. 873)
Relationship between trade openness, capital openness, and government expenditures	Hypothesis 1: Capital openness is associated with a smaller government size.
	Hypothesis 2: Trade openness is *not* associated with a larger government size. (Liberati, 2007, p. 219)

Alternative and Null Hypotheses

Another important distinction that should be made is between an **alternative hypothesis** (also called a *research hypothesis*) and a **null hypothesis** (also called a *statistical hypothesis*). The alternative hypothesis is a statement about the expected relationship, for example: *If X increases, Y will decrease.* The null hypothesis is a hypothesis of no difference: *If X increases, Y will not increase.*

There are two things about hypothesis testing that you need to keep in mind. First, a hypothesis is never tested directly—there is simply no way to test if, for example, X increases when Y decreases. To test a hypothesis, we first need to restate it as a null hypothesis and then test the null hypothesis at a specified level of probability using an appropriate statistical test (e.g., *t*-test, *F*-test), which shows the odds of the null hypothesis being false.

In other words, we can test directly only the null hypothesis. If evidence supports the null hypothesis, we conclude that the tested relationship does not exist. This implies that the alternative hypothesis is false. If evidence does not support the null hypothesis, then the alternative hypothesis remains a possibility.

The second thing to keep in mind is that in hypothesis testing, negative evidence is given more weight than positive evidence because of the logic of hypothesis disconfirmation. That is, negative evidence shows that the prediction is wrong, while positive evidence may not necessarily show that the prediction is correct because there may be alternative explanations for the observations.

A hypothesis, therefore, can never be proven—it can be either confirmed or disconfirmed, at a specified level of probability. For this reason, you should not use the word ***prove*** when talking about a hypothesis.

How to State a Hypothesis

Hypotheses are declarative statements, not questions. Write them as statements of a relationship. Indicate clearly which variables you are relating by naming the variables and state what outcome you expect. Below are some general examples.

Nondirectional hypotheses	A relationship exists between X and Y. There is a relationship between X and Y. X is associated with Y.
Directional hypotheses with continuous variables (variables that range from low to high such as *age, income,* or *productivity*)	The greater/lower/more the X, the greater/lower/more the Y. X is positively/negatively related to Y. As X increases/decreases, Y goes up/down. A greater/smaller X is associated with a greater/smaller Y. Greater X increases/reduces Y.
Directional hypotheses with nominal variables (variables such as *marital status* or *religion*, which do not range from low to high but rather have two or more categories)	X is more/less likely than X_1 to be/do/have Y. X has greater Y than does X_1.

Several linguistic patterns are commonly used to state a hypothesis in economics and public policy. They are shown below, with examples from Box 17. The first two are especially common.

1. *Statements with comparative adjectives: The more X, the more Y*

   The **deeper** a PTA, the **more flexible** it is. (Baccini et al., 2015, p. 767)

   Capital openness is associated with **a smaller** government size. (Liberati, 2007, p. 219)

2. *Statements where the expected result is shown in the verb: X increases/reduces Y*

   Government decentralization **reduces** the number of domestic terrorist incidents. (Dreher & Fischer, 2011, p. 224)

   An increase in father presence **will increase** the intergenerational education coefficient between father and child. (Kalil et al., 2016, p. 873)

   Notice that both Future and Present Tense can be used to state a hypothesis here. The use of Present Tense is somewhat more common in economics and public policy.

3. *Should statements: X should be more/less when there is more/less Y*

   The gap between CEO pay and mean VP pay **should increase** with a **greater** number of vice presidents. (Bognanno, 2001, p. 291)

   The positive effect of workplace quality on innovation **should be more prominent** in firms with **higher** levels of intangible capital embedded in their key employees and in industries with **higher** labor mobility. (Chen et al., 2016, p. 62)

4. *Conditional statements: If X, then Y*

   If "mature" industrial societies differ in starting points and/or the modernising routes they followed, **then** they will show larger differences in the perceived and preferred hierarchy of the occupational incomes and the perceived and preferred degree of occupational income inequality, than societies that do not differ in starting points and/or modernising routes. (Arts et al., 1999, pp. 64–65)

How to Introduce a Hypothesis in a Paper

Hypotheses can be introduced more or less formally. When they are introduced formally, there is usually an introductory sentence followed by the presentation of numbered hypotheses. For example:

In sum, the empirical evidence on the role of the environment in children's educational attainment, along with theory about the relevance of parental socialization and economic inputs into children's educational attainment, leads to the central hypotheses of our study:

> **Hypothesis 1:** an increase in father presence will increase the intergenerational education coefficient between father and child.
>
> **Hypothesis 2:** an increase in father presence will decrease the intergenerational education coefficient between mother and child. (Kalil et al., 2016, p. 873)

A less formal way to introduce a hypothesis is to begin with "we hypothesize that…," "our hypothesis is that," or "we expect that… ." For example:

> **We hypothesize that** the gap in working conditions between foreign-owned and domestic firms will be greater in developing countries because the technological difference is likely to be greatest, and the availability of comparable alternative job opportunities lowest. (Hijzen et al., 2013, p. 173)
>
> **Our hypothesis is that** tax morale will tend to be weaker in those countries where taxes are higher or when they have significantly increased in recent years. (Lago-Peñas & Lago-Peñas, 2010, p. 446)

Where to Put a Hypothesis in a Paper

Just like research questions, hypotheses may or may not be stated explicitly in a study. In fact, in a corpus of more than 400 articles from various journals in economics and public policy that I reviewed in the course of writing this book, less than 20% of the articles had explicitly stated hypotheses. Explicitly stated hypotheses are somewhat more common in micro-economic studies that use experimental methodology. When hypotheses are stated explicitly, it is usually in the Methodology or Results section.

Hypotheses in a Qualitative Paper

Because hypotheses imply an empirical test, they are inherently quantitative. Qualitative research does not involve testing, and for that reason, qualitative studies do not usually talk about hypotheses. When qualitative researchers do, occasionally, use this word, they use it in the sense of *possible explanation* rather than in the sense of a specific, empirical prediction.

PURPOSE STATEMENTS

A research study may or may not have an explicitly stated research question; however, virtually every study will have an explicitly stated purpose statement. This statement may be described in a variety of ways, using the words *purpose, (research) objective, goal, aim,* or *contribution.* The verb (and especially the verb-noun combination) used in the purpose statement often gives a clue about the nature of the study (empirical/quantitative or nonempirical/qualitative). Below are two lists of verbs that are often used in purpose statements in empirical/quantitative and nonempirical/qualitative studies. Notice that some of the verbs (shown in bold) appear in both lists; in this case, it is the noun-verb combination (the combination of the verb with the noun that follows it), and not the verb alone, that gives a clue about the nature of the study.

Empirical/Quantitative	Nonempirical/Qualitative
examine (effects/effectiveness)	review (evidence)
test (a theory)	recount (past experiences)
estimate (effects)	propose (an explanation)
identify (factors/determinants)	**identify** (developments/driving forces)
provide evidence for (a correlation)	suggest an explanation for (the recent trends)
determine (factors)	put (challenges, trends) in perspective
assess (the contribution)	describe (the role)
evaluate (effectiveness/contribution)	**evaluate** (existing evidence)
compare (alterrnative theories)	advance (a definition/an argument)
analyze (predictors/determinants)	**analyze** (challenges)
explore (determinants)	**explore** (issues, development)
study (effects)	offer an overview of (existing evidence)
extend (existing literature)	summarize (existing literature)
investigate (a problem)	highlight (a deficiency)
develop (a model)	outline and delineate (an explanation)
measure (the change)	survey (the evidence)

Box 18 shows examples of purpose statements taken from empirical/quantitative and nonempirical/qualitative studies in public policy and economics. Read them and underline the parts that describe the purpose. Pay attention to the verbs the authors use and to the subject (i.e., *we/I* vs. *this paper* vs. *the aims of this paper*).

BOX 18 Examples of Purpose Statements

Empirical/Quantitative	Nonempirical/Qualitative
We propose to test whether temporary or permanent housing is associated with human capital, dysfunction, disaffiliation, cultural identification or economic resources. (Zlotnick et al., 1999, p. 212)	This paper surveys the evidence to address these questions and offers an overview of the U.S. economic deregulation experience. (Winston, 1993, pp. 1263–1264)
This paper measures the long-run change in ridership induced by price and service changes using a new location-specific panel data set. (Voith, 1991, p. 360)	The euro is now the most visible and practical symbol of the progress towards political union in Europe. And yet despite the magnitude of the success, the challenges ahead are also formidable. In this article I analyse some of these challenges. (de Grauwe, 2002, p. 693)

Continued

BOX 18 Examples of Purpose Statements—cont'd.

This paper studies the effect of improved neonatal and early childhood health care on mortality and long-run academic achievement in school. (Bharadwaj et al., 2013, p. 1862)

The chief aim of this paper is to advance a definition of economic development that has the objective of creating prosperity and increasing citizens' quality of life. (Feldman et al., 2016, p. 6)

This article explores the determinants of pay in corporate hierarchies as well as the relationship between pay and promotion and presents a narrowly focused effort to determine whether the skewed pay structures at the top of large US corporations result from an attempt to manage tournament incentives according to a specific tournament model. (Bognanno, 2001, p. 291)

The aims of this article are to highlight this deficiency, evaluate existing evidence on the impact of public management variables, and argue for the theoretical and practical importance of research on the relationship between management and service performance. (Boyne, 2004, p. 100)

The objective of this paper is to investigate whether market interaction can, by itself, perpetuate a lack of ethnic diversity in business. (Fafchamps, 2000, p. 206)

The burden of stroke and other non-communicable diseases has risen sharply in developing countries in recent years. This article provides a detailed review of this trend and its underlying causes, and discusses the social and economic effects of stroke and the scope for interventions to reduce incidence and mitigate impacts. (Lloyd-Sherlock, 2010, p. 693)

The objectives of this study are to investigate empirically whether high competition is robustly correlated with high investment and to assess the potential impact of ASEAN competition policy on investment. (Sudsawasd, 2010, p. 467)

This article reviews the existing literature to identify five entry points through which water supply and sanitation service delivery might interact, both positively and negatively, with state-building and/or peace-building processes. (Kooy et al., 2015, p. 433)

Common Patterns for a Purpose Statement

There are three common patterns for describing the purpose of a paper in public policy and economics.

- Referring to the purpose: *The aim/purpose/goal of this paper is to….*
- Referring to what the paper does: *This paper examines, compares, describes…*
- Referring to what the authors do: *In this paper, we test, evaluate, propose…*

What Tense to Use for a Purpose Statement

Generally, when describing the purpose of a paper, you can use Present Tense to refer to the paper and either Present Tense or Past Tense to refer to your investigation. In papers in public policy and economics, the purpose is almost always stated using Present Tense. Below are some examples.

> This study **provides** an empirical test of the relationship between electoral success and government spending, using data for three Eastern European countries.

> The aim of this paper **is** to provide empirical evidence for the effect of globalization on inequality.

> This paper **reports** on the results obtained in a quasiexperimental study of the effects of police patrolling on neighborhood safety.

> The primary focus of this paper **is** on the connection between microfinance and poverty alleviation in rural India.

> The aim of this investigation **is** to compare two teaching methods used in elementary schools to teach mathematics.

EXAMPLES OF RESEARCH QUESTIONS

Box 19 shows examples of research questions from different areas of public policy and economics. Go over them, paying attention to how they are worded. Can you tell which questions come from quantitative studies and which ones come from nonempirical or qualitative studies? Which words give you the clues?

BOX 19 Sample Topics and Research Questions in Public Policy and Economics

Topics	Research Questions
Environment and Energy	
Potential effects of climate change on agricultural output, output per capita, mortality, birth rate, income, and human capital; economic consequences of various types of emissions; links between climate change and migration and climate change	• What is the impact of global warming on maize production in the main maize cultivation regions of China? • How does climate change affect agricultural production in Kenya? • How does environmental change affect human migration? • What is environmental sustainability?

Continued

BOX 19 Sample Topics and Research Questions in Public Policy and Economics—cont'd.

and productivity; environmental policies and environmental regulations and their effect on the environment

- To what extent does energy consumption affect economic growth in developing countries?
- How does international trade impact environmental quality?
- What factors are associated with energy intensity in developing countries?
- How do urbanization and industrialization affect energy intensity?
- Does energy consumption lead to economic growth?

Labor Economics

Role of welfare programs in labor supply; minimum wage; role of diversity in the workplace; impact of workplace practices on productivity; links between stress and work productivity; social capital and job search; women's participation in the labor force; determinants of wage rates and wage differentials

- What are the effects of minimum wage on young workers?
- What factors explain wage differentials between men and women in Japan?
- How do welfare programs affect adult labor supply in developing countries?
- How do employee involvement programs affect labor productivity?
- Does the implementation of inclusive workplace practices enhance firm performance?

International Trade and Economics

Economic freedom and its impact on foreign investment; effects of globalization on demographics, economic growth, inequality, and international trade; trade costs and economic growth; foreign direct investment and economic growth

- What is the effect of international trade on birth rates across Asia?
- What is the effect of a reduction in trade costs on the location of manufacturing activities? How does a decline in trade costs affect economic growth?
- What role does trade play in international technology transfer?
- What is the role of government policy in technology absorption from abroad?
- Do preferential trade agreements increase FDI into developing countries?
- Does international trade increase the growth rate of income?

Public Finance

Relationship between public debt and economic growth; role of market structure in growth in financially dependent industries; distributional impact of decentralization in fiscal and governance structures; effects of various taxes on the allocation of

- What was the impact of public debt on the economic growth of Kenya between 1980 and 1990?
- How does decentralization affect public education outcomes?
- Are larger public deficits always associated with higher inflation?
- What are the tradeoffs in financing deficits through money creation?

BOX 19 Sample Topics and Research Questions in Public Policy and Economics—cont'd.

resources; fiscal institutions and their policies

- Do consumers reduce spending when taxes are raised and increase it when taxes are lowered?
- Does a higher level of public capital spending boost or hinder private investment?

Social Policies (e.g., Healthcare, Immigration, Education)

Impact of healthcare reforms or healthcare policies on health expenditures; differences in educational achievement between immigrants and natives; links between education and entrepreneurship, innovation, and regional growth; factors affecting academic performance; relationship between academic performance, neighborhood, and school conditions

- How does immigrants' educational achievement differ from that of natives?
- What is the relationship between academic performance on the one hand, and neighborhood and school conditions on the other for ethnic minority students?
- What is the effect of schooling on drug abuse?
- What factors determine the cost increase of social health insurance plans in China?
- How do chronic diseases affect household healthcare expenditure and consumption?
- What are the determinants of health in major Russian cities?
- How do healthcare systems and access to healthcare impact the health outcomes of people living in rural areas?
- Does education affect health outcomes?

International Relations and International Political Economy

Foreign policy, security issues, foreign investment and dependency of countries or regions on neighbor countries; stability of countries and regions and causes of political instability; globalization and isolationist effects; territorial disputes; cyber security and the role of science and technology in international relations; politics and international relations; regional integration and institutions

- Does foreign dependency affect the stability of the state?
- What is the relationship between political instability and foreign investment?
- What is the role of diplomacy in solving maritime disputes?
- What are the drivers of terrorism in the Middle East?
- What is the role of cyber technology in international relations?
- What is the role of nongovernmental organizations in recent refugee crises?
- Has globalization reduced poverty and inequality?

Public Policy and Public Administration

Effect of public management on organizational performance; indicators of organizational performance in the public sector; policy impact evaluation; management strategies and organizational performance; role

- Do public R&D subsidies affect firms' innovation activities?
- Do low wages in the civil service cause corruption?
- How does corruption affect organizational performance?
- How do perceived levels of corruption affect national development?

Continued

BOX 19 Sample Topics and Research Questions in Public Policy and Economics—cont'd.

of leadership in public organizations; approaches to innovation; corruption and national development; public service delivery; citizen participation in local government decision-making

- What strategies for protecting the environment in developing countries are associated with poverty reduction?
- What is the role of leadership in achieving high-performance workplace practices?

Macroeconomics and Monetary Economics

Determinants of foreign direct investment; human and institutional factors affecting money supply; determinants of inflation; inflation targeting; interest rate; measurement and effects of technology transfer; impacts of various government policies on output

- What factors are associated with foreign direct investment in Asia?
- What is the effect of financial aid on economic growth in small island countries?
- What is the relationship between health and economic growth in Asian countries? How do investment, exports, imports, and research and development contribute to this growth?
- Does exchange rate stability increase trade?
- What is the link between institutions and volatility?
- Does money supply impact growth in energy scarce countries?

Microeconomics

Firm efficiency; cost reduction and productivity; cost of production; competition; consumer behavior; technology transfer and productivity

- What is the effect of job training on job performance?
- How do health risk factors affect work productivity?
- What is the impact of intellectual capital on a firm's financial performance?
- What factors drive environmental behavior in small and medium manufacturing enterprises?
- What determines labor productivity?

Political Economy and Politics

Role of democracy in economic development; voter characteristics and voting patterns; political stability and economic growth; social order and prosperity; national and international institutions and their role in economic development

- Does an increase in economic development result in a decrease in income inequality?
- To what extent can a level of democracy in a country be predicted by its economic development?
- How does manufacturing become concentrated in a few regions, leaving others relatively undeveloped?
- How large is the impact of public spending on health?
- What is the link between economic institutions, political institutions, openness, and income levels?

RESEARCH QUESTION ANALYSIS

The questions shown below are designed to help you analyze your own research question and avoid common mistakes that students make when formulating a research question. Write your research question in the space provided. Then answer the questions that follow.

Your Research Question _____

_____

_____

1. Is my research question a question?

2. Is the answer to my question obvious without research?

3. Can I research this question in the time available?

4. Should my question be answered through a qualitative or a quantitative methodology? How?

5. Do I have a research paper I can emulate?

_____

_____

_____

_____

6. What do I imagine the possible answers to my question will be?

_____

_____

_____

_____

7. What policy recommendations could be made based on these answers?

_____

_____

_____

_____

Chapter 7

Research Proposals

WAYS TO DEVELOP A RESEARCH PROJECT

Options for a Quantitative Study

By far, the most common option for students in economics and public policy is to take an existing theoretical model and apply it to a different dataset—often a richer one or one covering a longer period. It could also be a dataset for a different country or set of countries. For example, one of my students, Ibrahim Zuhuree, took an existing model describing the numeric relationship between foreign aid (predictor variable) and economic growth (dependent variable) and tested it using data for small-island developing countries. The model had several control variables (or *covariates*) including government policy, quality of aid, and economic vulnerability of the recipient country. His analysis involved testing the model using multiple regression analysis, which estimates model parameters for the relationship between the dependent variable and each of the predictor variables. For more on multiple regression analysis, see Chapter 15.

Another approach is to take an existing model and modify it in some way, for example, by adding one or more variables to it. Ibrahim, for example, later decided to modify the existing model by adding aid uncertainty and by creating a dummy variable for different time periods for one of the island countries he was interested in. Sometimes two or more different models can be combined into one and the resulting model tested on a new dataset.

You can also do a quantitative comparison, comparing groups, time periods, or countries on the determinants of some outcome variable. For example, you can do a study of determinants of women's participation in the labor force in countries that are similar in some ways but that differ on the dependent variable (women's participation in the labor force). A study like that is reported in Brinton et al. (1995); the researchers wanted to find an explanation for the divergent outcomes of women's participation in the labor force in two societies with similar initial conditions for industrialization—Taiwan and South Korea. They tested several models using macro- and microdata and found a plausible explanation that took into account both social and economic factors.

Another option is to do a small-scale survey focusing on a narrowly defined problem. This option may be particularly appealing to mid-career professionals

How to Write about Economics and Public Policy. https://doi.org/10.1016/B978-0-12-813010-0.00007-7

who want to do research on their own organization. For example, you may want to know what employees of your organization think about some work-related policy or system or how their background characteristics (e.g., level of education, work experience, type of work they do, or age) are associated with their attitudes toward this policy or system. You can design a survey measuring attitudes as well as relevant background characteristics, collect responses, and correlate the former with the latter to show how certain background characteristics correlate with certain attitudes. Keep in mind, however, that you will need a theory to explain your expectations and the choice of variables. And if you can obtain data on, say, employees' work productivity, you can also test to what extent employees' background characteristics are associated with work productivity.

Other, less common options for quantitative research include

- A cost-benefit analysis of a policy. For example, you may do a cost-benefit analysis of a new environmental policy banning the use of disposable plastic bags.

- An experimental study with two or more groups to determine the effect of some treatment on a dependent variable. For example, you could do an experimental study to examine whether the use of graphs in an economics class has an effect on learning.

Whichever option you choose, your best approach is to find a study that you understand and that you think is doable within the constraints of your program (including the constraints on data collection) and replicate it using a different dataset, a different sample, or a modified set of variables. If you can, ask your advisor for some good papers in your area.

Students who are new to graduate study often shun the idea of replication. Some may misunderstand it or confuse it with plagiarism; others think that replicating someone else's work will not allow them to show their own originality. In fact, **replication** (and especially replication with modifications or improvements) is a time-honored tradition and a very good way for novice researchers to "get into" research. If anything, we need more replication studies, not fewer, because no single study can be taken as conclusive evidence for "how things are." It is only through replication—with different datasets, different samples, and in different settings—that we accumulate evidence to support a particular view of the world.

Replication is not plagiarism, because plagiarism involves copying ideas or words without proper attribution. With replication, you borrow the logic of a study, not the words, and you acknowledge the source of the original idea and use it to do your own study. Replication studies can make a great contribution to the field because they apply the logic of the original study to new—and often richer—settings, furnishing additional evidence to support or refute the original study's conclusions.

Options for a Qualitative Study

Qualitative empirical studies are rare in master's programs in public policy and economics. This is partly because the field is heavily quantitative, focusing, in particular, on economic analysis. The main reason, however, is probably the difficulty of conducting a qualitative study in the space of just 1 or 2 years. Qualitative research is deep; it looks at phenomena in their natural surroundings and focuses on processes, seeking a deeper understanding of what is going on. In its most conventional sense, qualitative empirical research involves exploring people's experiences and the meanings that people attach to these experiences. And to understand people's experiences—and especially how those experiences relate to behavior or various outcomes—you need to observe the people over a period of time, in their natural surroundings, doing things that they normally do. This requires prolonged observation and time "in the field" as well as the use of multiple sources of data. Master's students often simply do not have enough time in their programs for such deep involvement.

Qualitative empirical research focusing on human experiences is more common at the doctoral level. For example, one of my graduate students, Ganesh Pandeya, conducted a study of citizen participation in local governance in Nepal, a developing country. Ganesh wanted to know how citizens participated in local government decision-making, what forms that participation took, what outcomes it brought about, and how the participants viewed the outcomes of their own participation. In his proposal, Ganesh outlined several aspects of citizen participation on which he wanted to focus and wrote a subquestion for each aspect. He was especially interested in institutional and organizational frameworks that facilitated and hindered participation, in participation mechanisms, and in how citizens' competence impacted citizens' willingness to participate in local planning.

For master's students in public policy and economics, it is more common to do qualitative research that does not involve prolonged observation in the field but instead, combines a review of literature with documentary research, or an examination of various documents containing information the student is interested in. These documents may be historical or contemporary, official or unofficial, internal or external, and published or unpublished. The extent to which a study would rely on academic literature versus documentary data obtained from documents varies greatly. At one end, there are studies that draw primarily on existing scholarship and only supplement it with some data obtained from documents; at the other, there are studies that rely primarily on the analysis of relevant documents and use literature to build a framework for analysis. Box 20 shows three qualitative studies taken from economics journals that combine a review of literature with the use of documentary data. If you check the references of these papers, you will see that each one uses a different mix of academic literature and documentary data.

BOX 20 Examples of Studies Combining Academic Literature and Documentary Data

Study	Focus	Mix of Literature and Documentary Data
Waldron et al. (2014)	Chinese cashmere industry, its impacts on rural development, and policies to increase its competitiveness	38 academic and 22 other references
Pudney (2010)	Policy interventions in the cannabis market and proposed drugs policies	48 academic and 17 other references
Swinnen (2011)	Arguments about the price of food and their implications for developing countries	58 academic and 6 other references

Unlike quantitative research, which begins with an intention to measure variables in order to test a hypothesis, qualitative research begins with an intention to explore an idea, which at the beginning can be rather vague. You may not even know what kind of data you should look for, but as you read about the topic, you should develop a better idea for where to look for data. For example, you may read somewhere about a growing trend of cardiovascular disease (CVD) in developing countries, and you may decide to explore it further. You may start with a review of existing literature to find out what is known about CVD and how this topic has been approached by researchers in your field. As you read the literature, try to formulate relevant subquestions that will help you focus your study. These may be questions about the underlying causes of CVD, its social and economic consequences, and the effectiveness of public health campaigns aimed at CVD prevention. Then, think about the most appropriate sources of data to answer these questions. In many cases, a study like this one will rely heavily on a review of academic literature, which may be supplemented with data from relevant policy documents.

Or you may decide to look at a recent bank crisis in your country and try to determine what processes had led to it and whether it could have been predicted. You may obtain and examine bank annual reports and financial statements, official speeches, credit rating reports, editorials, and published studies on the topic. In this case, your study will rely more on primary documents that on a review of academic literature.

You can also use documentary research to do a comparative case study of different countries' approaches to some important problem. For example, one of my students, Louise Butler, was interested in researching the differences in Japanese and Australian approaches to whaling and the role of international law and diplomacy in providing a resolution to these differences. Data for her study came from relevant policy and legal documents including government statements, parliamentary reports, discussions in international forums, and published scholarship. You can read Louise's proposal later in this chapter.

Documentary research can be supplemented with interviews with relevant stakeholders, which would often improve the study's reliability. For example, one of my students, Asako Sawada, was interested in Japanese ODA (official development assistance) and the role of ODA in Japanese foreign policy and external economic strategies. As she researched the topic, she decided to narrow it down and focus on three aspects: the relationship between Japan's ODA and Japanese FDI (foreign direct investment), the role of Japan's ODA in Japanese foreign policy, and the role of Japan's private sector in ODA. She further decided to limit her research to Southeast Asia. After spending some time researching and reading the literature, she framed her study as one conducted from the perspectives of the developmental state model and neo-liberalism and formulated the following set of subquestions to focus her research:

1. What is the process by which decisions are made about ODA?

2. What are Japan's most salient external economic strategies toward Southeast Asia? How are they connected to ODA?

3. What is the role of ODA in Japan's external economic strategies? To what extent could ODA be viewed as economic leverage in Japan's foreign policy?

4. What is the role of Japan's private sector in ODA?

5. What are the linkages between Japan's ODA and Japanese FDI in specific countries in Southeast Asia? Are there any patterns that characterize this relationship?

These subquestions also provided clues to the appropriate methodology, indicating what kind of data she needed: interviews with policymakers responsible for ODA decisions for Questions 1 and 4, policy and other documents for Questions 2 and 3, and academic and policy literature for Question 5. Data for her study came from various policy documents related to ODA and FDI and interviews with several Japanese policymakers from the Japan International Cooperation Agency and the Japan External Trade Organization.

These examples show that it is quite realistic for students in public policy and even in economics programs to engage in qualitative research, including research that requires primary data collection. I would strongly recommend that students interested in qualitative research read Denzin and Lincoln's *Handbook of Qualitative Research* and Creswell's *Research Design: Qualitative, Quantitative, and Mixed Methods Approaches*. Students interested in comparative qualitative research would benefit greatly from reading Lim's *Doing Comparative Politics: An Introduction to Approaches and Issues*. And if you plan to write a qualitative doctoral dissertation, read Meloy's *Writing the Qualitative Dissertation: Understanding by Doing*.

WHAT IF I JUST HAVE A POINT TO PROVE?

Students without much experience in academic research often misunderstand its purpose, believing that the purpose of research is to prove something—a position, a point of view, a certain "truth." They would often state a belief—sometimes disguised as a "research question"—and then proceed to collect support for it from the literature or policy documents. Here is an example. I recently had a student who wanted to do research on the benefits of financial aid for students from developing countries. His statement of the problem talked about the various benefits of financial aid and the importance of providing it to students from developing countries and his research question then asked: "Is financial aid important for students?"

There are several problems with this student's approach. First, the student *assumes*, even before doing any research, that financial aid is important, and proceeds to look for support for his opinion. And because it is always possible to find at least some support for virtually any opinion, he soon finds what he is looking for. His research strategy involves cherry-picking studies showing positive effects of financial aid on various outcomes and looking for statements made by politicians and academics about the benefits of financial support.

The second problem is that the student chooses a very general topic— financial aid—and does not specify what outcomes he is interested in or what settings he wants to explore. Financial aid and university attendance? Financial aid and academic performance? Financial aid and outcomes beyond university? Financial aid at the graduate level? Undergraduate level? For domestic students? For international students? Surely we should not just assume similar results for all groups of students, in all settings, and for all outcomes.

The biggest problem, however, is that the student's research question is not a question formulated for research; it is a question formulated to prove a point. In effect, it is an opinion disguised as a question, which the student answers in the statement of the problem, even before doing research, when he states that financial aid is important. But if the importance of financial aid is assumed, what is there to research? It really does not make sense to assume that something is true and then pose a question asking if it were true. Unless, of course, the point is to prove a point.

Experiments in psychology show that our beliefs affect the way we look at information. They affect the kind of information we consider, the amount of information we consider, and the criteria we use to evaluate information (Gilovich, 1991). When we believe something, we only ask that there be *some* evidence to support our belief, and when we find it, we stop looking. And if we come across evidence that contradicts our belief, we subject it to much more stringent evaluation, and we usually dig deeper, until we find evidence favoring our position.

This tendency to cherry-pick evidence and use arbitrary criteria in evaluation characterizes much of our casual, nonscientific thinking, and it is the reason why we do science in the first place. In a way, science is the opposite of casual thinking. It requires that we do not assume an answer, that we follow explicit procedures, and that we follow them systematically. We formulate research questions without presuming an answer, we test hypotheses on independent sets of data, and we evaluate scientific evidence by assessing how it was obtained, not by checking whether we agree or disagree with what it shows.

HOW TO PREPARE A RESEARCH PROPOSAL

Below are some suggestions for how to prepare a research proposal, particularly if you are in a master's program or working under time constraints.

Proposal for a Quantitative Study

- Read relevant literature, find a topic that interests you, and narrow it down to a specific research question that focuses on a relationship between two or more variables.

- Find a quantitative study with a similar question. Check its methodology and data. Can you use the same model as in that study? Should you modify it somehow? If yes, how? Can you obtain similar data? If you need to transform the data into a different form, would you be able to do that?

- Write down your research question first. Restate it as a hypothesis.

- Next, write your methodology. Describe the model and variables you will use and the sources of data.

- Finally, write a statement of the problem. It should justify your research question and support your research approach.

- Prepare a list of references, following the format prescribed by your school or program. If there is no prescribed format, use a style that you are familiar with or one that is commonly used in your research area.

Proposal for a Qualitative Study

- Read relevant literature, find a topic that interests you, and narrow it down to a research question. Your research question can be rather broad.

- Decide on the focus of your study. Will you focus on a description of a phenomenon? On a process by which something happens? On people's experiences?

- As you read around, try to generate specific subquestions. They will help you focus the study and provide direction for data collection and analysis (Rudestam & Newton, 2001, p. 70).

- Try to find a qualitative study with a similar focus. How was it designed? How were the data collected and analyzed? Can you use the logic of that study for your own research? Keep in mind, however, that unlike quantitative studies, which can be replicated or emulated rather closely, a qualitative study may be difficult to emulate because qualitative research often focuses on unique cases, people, or circumstances. As a result, the extent to which you will be able to borrow the logic of a qualitative study for your own research may be quite limited. Still, it is useful to check how previous researchers have approached similar problems.

- Write your broad research question first. Then write your subquestions.

- Next, write your methodology. Because there is no model to test in a qualitative study, this section can be rather general, especially at the master's level. Master's students may only need to describe tentative sources of data; doctoral students or researchers should also include an explanation for case selection and a description of their approach to data collection and analysis.

- Finally, write a statement of the problem. Your statement of the problem should justify your research question and support your research approach.

- Prepare a list of references, making sure that they follow the prescribed format. If there is no prescribed format, use a style that you are familiar with or one that is commonly used in your research area.

THE RESEARCH PROPOSAL: WHAT TO INCLUDE

Statement of the Problem

Describe the specific problem you are interested in and explain why it is important. Briefly review relevant literature to show what is known about your problem and to demonstrate why your research is worthwhile or timely. Relevant here means incorporating all the major concepts or variables that you intend to study. This section may also include definitions, a description of relevant policies, and a discussion of measurement approaches used to measure key concepts and variables. Show a limitation—a gap in the existing body of knowledge. This part can be as short as one sentence, and it often starts with the word "however." In some studies, especially in economics, the gap is often implied rather than stated explicitly. Next describe the purpose of your research and explain its policy implications and/or contribution to the field. Box 21 shows a template with alternative expressions that can be used for a statement of the problem.

Research Question(s)

What is (are) the specific research question(s) you will answer? Your questions should be

- Sufficiently limited to be examined within the time of your program,
- Answerable through research,
- Theoretically grounded, and
- Related to policy.

BOX 21 A Template for a Statement of the Problem

Importance and Review of Previous Research

Over the past few decades, one of the most important topics in [your area] has been [your topic].

Much has been written about [your topic]. [Summarize relevant studies.]

Several studies have looked at [your topic]. [Summarize what is known about the topic.]

A number of studies in the [your topic] literature have argued/shown [something about your topic]. For example, [give details of some of these studies].

Several theories have been put forward to explain [something important about your topic]. For example, [summarize relevant studies or theories].

The empirical literature has examined [your topic] using different methods and data obtained from different countries. For example, [summarize relevant studies].

Gap and Purpose

However, despite the growing role of/interest in [your topic], little research has been devoted to this topic in [specific area or setting].

With very few exceptions, previous studies have focused on [some aspect of your topic]. As a result, the arguments made in these studies have often been too narrowly focused, making it difficult for researchers to grasp the overall picture of [the topic]. Using [your proposed method], I attempt to provide an overview of [your topic]. To achieve this goal, I pose three specific questions.

Although the literature has expanded our knowledge and understanding of [your topic], only recently has attention focused on [your specific problem]. There is still no consensus regarding whether/how/why [name the specific problem]. Building on the earlier work that has identified [something important], I use [your proposed method] to explore [your problem]. The focus of my analysis is on [specific part of the problem you will focus on].

Past studies have emphasized the effects of [something about your topic], rather than [something else about your topic]. For example, [review 1-2 studies]. In this paper, I deviate from this tradition by focusing on the question of [your question]. Specifically, I test a model ... and show evidence that ....

Implications and Contribution

In this paper, I extend the existing literature/the existing evidence to show how/why [your study's purpose and/or results]. The findings of this research have important implications for [a particular policy]. [Name and briefly discuss one or two implications.]

The question(s) must be directly related to the problem described in the Statement of the Problem and to the purpose of your research. In a quantitative study, it is common to have just one or two questions, especially at the master's level; in a qualitative study, it is common to have one main question and several related subquestions.

In a qualitative proposal, you may sometimes state **research objectives** rather than research questions. However, questions work better for clarifying what exactly a study will do because they are usually more focused than objectives.

Methodology

A quantitative paper states a hypothesis and tests it using statistical tools (e.g., multiple regression analysis) to produce generalizable results. If you are writing a quantitative proposal, explain what kind of data you will use and where the data will come from. Explain your empirical methodology, also what model you will use, what variables you will include, and how you will measure them.

A qualitative empirical paper explores a phenomenon or a process using multiple sources of information including in-depth interviews, documents, and observation. If you are writing a proposal for a qualitative study, explain why and/or how you selected your case(s), what data you plan to use, and how you will collect the data.

References or Bibliography

List all sources cited in the proposal. Do not list any that are not cited. Do not include sources that you have not read. For each reference, include the name of the author(s) or editor(s), date of publication, title of the work, and publication details. Alphabetize the references by the author's last name, following the format prescribed by your school or program. Do not number the references. See Appendix A for details about two citation styles that are commonly used in public policy and economics.

COMMON PROBLEMS

Title

Students who are new to graduate study sometimes start writing their proposal—and in fact, their final paper—with the title. But this approach is unproductive and rather illogical because the most appropriate title can be determined only after you have completed your research. This is because a good title of a paper in economics and public policy should give clues not only about the topic of the paper but also about its methodological approach and, often, its findings. For common types of titles in public policy and economics, see Chapter 5.

Statement of the Problem

What is the problem? Students often misunderstand what the word *problem* means in the Statement of the Problem, thinking that it refers to the overall topic of their study. As a result, they write about everything they know about their topic including its importance for some outcome, the benefits of a particular policy that is related to the topic, or the need for government action to improve a particular situation (e.g., importance of financial assistance to developing countries, benefits of women's empowerment, or the need for government policy to reduce poverty). Their research question often comes as a surprise to the reader because their Statement of the Problem is too general and fails to prepare the reader for the upcoming research question.

In fact, what students need to focus on in the Statement of the Problem is the specific relationship they intend to study and what is known about that relationship. For example, if the research question asks about the effect of women's empowerment on women's participation in the labor force, the Statement of the Problem should focus on explaining how women's empowerment affects women's participation in the labor force and on discussing relevant variables. If the focus of the study is on the role of governmental and nongovernmental organizations in poverty alleviation, the Statement of the Problem should explain what is known about this role rather than discuss the importance of poverty alleviation in general.

Another common mistake is to focus too much in the Statement of the Problem on the country or region the student has chosen for research rather than on the research problem. For example, a student interested in doing research on the relationship between inflation and economic growth in Bangladesh might focus in the Statement of the Problem on Bangladesh, its policies, challenges, achievements, and government plans. In fact, the focus of this section should be on the problem rather than on the country—on showing the connection between inflation and economic growth and what we know about it.

What is affecting what in your study? Another common problem is flipping the dependent and independent variables in the research question. For example, the Statement of the Problem may focus on how foreign direct investment affects economic growth, but the research question asks about the effect of economic growth on foreign direct investment. Or the Statement of the Problem may describe the effect of stock market development on economic growth, but the research question asks about the effects of economic growth on the stock market.

Economic and public policy phenomena have multiple causes and many relationships among variables are reciprocal—that is, they go in both directions. It is, therefore, important to clarify, based on theory and previous research, your expectations about the direction of the hypothesized relationship—what is affecting what in your study? Make sure that both the research question and the Statement of the Problem describe your relationship in the same hypothesized direction.

Why are you doing this study? A common reply to this question is, "Because it has never been done before." This justification, however, is often insufficient. Proposals should be justified on the basis of their potential contribution to the field, to its theoretical or empirical knowledge, and not just because "it has never been done before."

It is also common for students to fall into the following trap when trying to justify their study: "Policy X has been successful in Country Y, but it has not been implemented in my country; therefore, my country should consider implementing it." This logic, however, is fundamentally flawed. What you need is a critical analysis of why certain policies may or may not have been successful in certain countries and an explanation of why the implementation of such policies in another country would or might be successful.

Why do you expect a relationship? An important part of your proposal is an explanation of your expectations. Why do you expect a particular relationship, effect, or contribution? What evidence is there to justify your expectations? Students sometimes believe that expectations can be justified based on personal experience (e.g., I live there!) or expert opinion (e.g., I heard this expert on TV saying so). In fact, in a research proposal, expectations are justified on two grounds—on theoretical grounds, by outlining the economic, political, social, or psychological theory behind the expectations, or on empirical grounds, by showing previous research studies that support those expectations. Often, both theoretical and empirical justification need to be provided.

What is the relevance? Another common problem is including a lot of irrelevant material in a proposal. Students often justify this practice by saying, "I just want to give the reader some additional background." Yet, material that is not directly relevant to the research question will often confuse the reader rather than help. Of course, understanding what is, and what is not, relevant is not easy, because what matters here is relevance from the reader's perspective, not from the writer's. The writer needs to look at his or her work as a reader would, stepping into the reader's shoes, and assessing the logic from the reader's perspective. And this is not easy to do. One suggestion is to read a proposal paragraph by paragraph, asking yourself what exactly each paragraph does and how it is connected to the research question. Try to summarize each paragraph in one sentence; then write down the sentences and see if they lead up to the research question. Students are often surprised to see that even when all of their paragraphs talk about the topic of their research, they often do not add up to the research question.

Research Questions

Common problems here include questions that are too broad, questions that cannot be answered through research, questions that are purely descriptive, and questions that are not formulated as questions. Below are examples.

- **Too broad**. *What is the current economic situation in Pakistan?*
- **Unanswerable through research**. *What should be done to empower women?*
- **Purely descriptive**. *What is the tax structure of Bhutan?*
- **Nonquestions**. *To examine poverty alleviation policies.*

Methodology

Perhaps one of the most common problems that I see in research proposals is a mismatch between the proposed methodology and the research question. The research question simply cannot be answered through the proposed methodology. For example, a student may be interested in assessing the effects of a policy, but the proposed methodology is a survey of public opinion, or a student may want to investigate the determinants of a phenomenon, but the proposed methodology is qualitative interviews with stakeholders. Make sure that your methodology is appropriate for your research question. If you are not sure, ask your advisor or check the literature to see how a question like yours has been approached. I explain more about methodology in Chapter 13.

Another common problem is not including sufficient information about the model or the variables, their measurement, and sources of data. Providing such information is especially important in quantitative proposals, because this information helps your advisor understand what you are planning to do.

References and Citations

There are three common problems in this section: missing references and citations, incomplete references and citations, and incorrectly formatted references and citations.

Make sure that there is a complete overlap between citations shown in the text and references included at the end of the proposal. All citations must be referenced, and all references must be cited.

The specific elements that should be included in the references and the format of citations and references will depend on the specific citation system being used. Different disciplines and research areas have their own preferences for a citation system; you should learn the system used in your area early on and use it consistently. Appendix A shows how to cite and reference sources using two common citation systems, APA and Chicago.

MAKING AND SUPPORTING CLAIMS IN A PROPOSAL

Statements that are not part of common knowledge in your research area should be supported with research evidence (i.e., literature). Two things are important here: understanding which statements are not part of common knowledge and, therefore, require support, and learning what constitutes acceptable support in your particular area.

Understanding which statements are, and which statements are not part of common knowledge is a result of disciplinary learning and wide reading in the target discipline. It is impossible to tell just by looking at a claim whether it is accepted as common knowledge in a particular research area unless you have a certain degree of competence in that area. More important, the same claim may be accepted as common knowledge in one research area and may require support in another.

Students who have not had a lot of disciplinary exposure before starting on a research proposal often feel unsure about which claims need to be supported. Perhaps the best strategy in this case would be to support all claims of which you are unsure. Once you have developed a degree of competence in your area, you will have a better feel for which claims are part of common knowledge and which ones require support.

It is also important to learn what constitutes acceptable support in your research area. Students who are new to graduate study often think that any kind of support will do if it comes from an academic work and they often support claims with other people's claims or expert opinion. In fact, in many areas of economics and public policy, acceptable support is evidence obtained in a well-designed empirical study, which has been published in a professional journal or reputable working paper series.

Virtually all claims that you will be making in a research proposal are claims about what the research shows. Such claims are supported with citations to relevant previous studies, and these citations are placed immediately after the claim. Different claims may require citations to different kinds of literature. Below are some examples.

- **Claims about relationships, effects, or contribution** of one variable to another are supported with citations to empirical quantitative studies.

- **Claims about the importance of a topic** are supported with citations to empirical studies, both quantitative and qualitative, or reviews of empirical studies.

- **Claims about the state of current knowledge** are often supported with citations to empirical work, which has been organized in some way, or with citations to reviews of empirical studies.

- **Claims about the features or characteristics of a particular research setting** (e.g., country, region, population) are often supported with citations to nonempirical sources including policy-related documents.

SAMPLE PROPOSALS

This section shows examples of research proposals written by students in various master's programs in economics and public policy. Most proposals are for quantitative research because this type of research is more common in such programs.

The students wrote these proposals after only one semester of graduate study. None of the students was a native speaker of English and none had had any background in economics before coming to graduate school. These proposals represent a substantial achievement on the part of the students, showing what graduate students can produce even after a very short period of study.

These proposals are very short; depending on your program, you may be required to write a more substantial proposal. This is especially the case for doctoral students, who often need to provide many details about their proposed methodology.

As you read these proposals, focus on these questions:

1. What is the specific problem under study?

2. What are the main concepts?

3. What gap does the author identify?

4. What is the proposed methodology?

5. What data will most likely be collected for the study?

Anna Liese Roque

Research Proposal 1
Increasing Deposit Insurance: Increasing Bank Moral Hazard?
Statement of the Problem

The banking industry in most countries of the world tends to be subject to government regulation due largely to the important role that banks play as a financial intermediary in the economy (Flannery, 1998). As a financial intermediary, banks serve as a conduit for savers with money to spare and for investors looking for funds to support business operations or expansion. Banks' role as a financial intermediary is especially important in countries where the capital market is not yet fully developed. Governments also establish financial safety nets as a means of minimizing the negative effects of bank closures. The components of financial safety nets include deposit insurance systems, bank failure resolution, and lender-of-last-resort functions (Powell & Majnoni, 2006). However, banks may be encouraged to engage in excessive risk-taking when granting loans, secure in the knowledge that it is the deposit insurer who will shoulder the bulk of the losses should their risks not pay off (Demirgüc-Kunt & Kane, 2002). This is called *the problem of moral hazard*, where the provision of insurance actually encourages risky behavior on the part of the insured.

Empirical evidence on whether deposit insurance increases moral hazard on the part of banks is mixed. Grossman (1992), for example, found a link between deposit insurance and historical bank failures in the United States. On the other hand, Gropp and Vesala (2001) found no such link for European banks and neither did Gueyie and Lai (2003) in their study on the adoption of deposit insurance and risk-taking behavior of banks in Canada. Whether Philippine banks engage in more risk-taking in the presence of increased deposit insurance is the subject of my research. This research has policy implications for the provision of additional deposit insurance in the future. If moral hazard does exist and banks increase their risk-taking behavior in response to an increase in deposit insurance, policies should be crafted to minimize the possibility of increased risk-taking.

Research Questions
1. Is an increase in deposit insurance associated with an increase in banks' risk-taking?
2. Do banks show risk-shifting behavior after an increase in deposit insurance?

Methodology
The research methodology used in this study is modeled after Gueyie and Lai (2003), who employed a regression analysis on bank-level data to see if there was a change in the risk measures after the introduction of official deposit insurance in Canada. To test for an increase in banks' risk-taking, the authors ran a regression on a risk measure against a dummy variable used to represent the predeposit insurance and the postdeposit insurance periods, as well as other variables used to control for other types of risks that banks face. The authors used select ratios from bank financial statements to represent credit risk, liquidity risk, leverage risk, size effects, charter effects, and off-balance-sheet risk. The study also controlled for the effects of macroeconomic variables by including a variable for GNP growth.

In my paper, because of the lack of Philippine bank-level data prior to the introduction of official deposit insurance, I will focus on a comparison of two 5-year periods: 1988–92, which was a period that was characterized by a PHP40,000 limit on deposit coverage, and 1993–98, which was a period that was characterized by an increase in coverage to PHP100,000. I will use quarterly bank-level data for five Philippine banks that account for a big share of the banking industry's total assets listed with the stock market. The data, spanning a 10-year period from 1988 to 1998, are taken from the database of the Philippine Deposit Insurance Corporation. Stock-related information will be requested from the Philippine Stock Exchange.

References

Demirgüç-Kunt, A., & Kane, E. J. (2002). Deposit insurance around the globe: Where does it work? *Journal of Economic Perspectives, 16*(2), 175–195.

Flannery, M. J. (1998). Using market information in prudential bank supervision: A review of the U.S. empirical evidence. *Journal of Money, Credit and Banking, 30*(3), 273–305.

Gropp, R., & Vesala, J. (2001, March). *Deposit insurance and moral hazard: Does the counterfactual matter?* (ECB Working Paper No. 47). Retrieved from https://www.ecb.europa.eu/pub/pdf/scpwps.

Grossman, R. S. (1992). Deposit insurance, regulation, and moral hazard in the thrift industry: Evidence from the 1930s. *American Economic Review, 82*(4), 800–821.

Gueyie, J., & Lai, V. S. (2003). Bank moral hazard, and the introduction of official deposit insurance in Canada. *International Review of Economics & Finance, 12*(2), 247–273.

Powell, A. P., & Majnoni, G. (2006, October). *Intercountry conflicts.* Paper presented at the International Financial Instability: Cross-Border Banking & National Regulation. Conference sponsored by the Federal Reserve Bank of Chicago and the International Association of Deposit Insurers,Chicago, US. Retrieved from http://www.iadi.org/html.

S.M. Susanthi Medha Kumari

Research Proposal 2

Determinants of Interest Margins of Banks in Sri Lanka

Statement of the Problem

Bank credit plays a vital role in economic growth by channeling funds for investment, working capital of businesses, and consumption. In recent years, Sri Lanka has experienced a substantial level of financial deepening, with high credit growth, and it envisages doubling its credit stock between 2008 and 2014 to foster economic growth. Despite the increasing financial deepening, however, the interest margins of banks in Sri Lanka have been high and stood at 4.7% in December of 2009. By comparison, the net interest margin (NIM) in the United Kingdom in 2008 was 1.9% (Bank of England, 2009), whereas in India in 2005, it was 3% (Central Bank of Sri Lanka [CBSL], 2006). High NIMs have persisted in Sri Lanka despite policy actions including moral suasion (CBSL, 2006). This is a problem because high NIMs and high lending rates affect the amount of borrowings by the private sector and can hinder economic growth (Aboagye, Akoena, Antwi-Asare, & Gockel, 2008; Brock & Suarez, 2000).

Past researchers have identified various bank-specific industry and macroeconomic factors that influence the level of NIMs in various countries. Ho and Saunders (as cited in Aboagye et al., 2008) contend that interest rates are set by banks relative to the money market rates, taking into account the risk of excessive loan demand or withdrawal of deposits. The determinants identified by other researchers include market power (Valverde & Fernandez, 2007), treasury bill rates and institutional deficiencies (Beck & Hesse, 2008), operating costs, reserve requirements, and uncertainty in the macroeconomic environment (Brock & Suarez, 2000), and the extent of bank risk aversion and inflation rate (Aboagye et al., 2008). These determinants vary significantly among countries.

Although several analyses of the determinants of interest margins have been undertaken for Sri Lanka (CBSL, 2006), there have not been any studies that included both bank-specific and macroeconomic factors and that have used econometric techniques. The present study attempts to fill this gap in the existing body of research. By revealing the determinants of interest margins of Sri Lankan banks, the findings will provide the direction for policy makers regarding which factors to target through regulatory and policy action.

Research Questions

1. Does Ho and Saunders' model explain the determinants of interest rates in Sri Lanka?
2. Which factors affect the interest margins of banks in Sri Lanka most strongly?

Methodology

This research will employ a quantitative methodology. The model proposed by Ho and Saunders (as described in Aboagye et al., 2008) has been used and extended by many researchers. My research will also be based on Ho and Saunders' model, but will incorporate extensions proposed by Aboagye et al. (2008), Saunders and Schumacher (2000), Brock and Suarez (2000), and Valverde and Fernandez

(2007). The determinants of interest margins that will be tested here will be identified from the works of Aboagye et al. (2008), Beck and Hesse (2009), Saunders and Schumacher (2000), Brock and Suarez (2000), and Valverde and Fernandez (2007) and will include factors found to affect interest margins in other countries/regions as well as factors that are specific to Sri Lanka. As is the case with many previous studies using Ho and Saunders' model, this study will also be based on panel data.

Interest margin will be defined as the difference between interest income and interest cost in terms of average assets. Quarterly data spanning a period from 1998 to 2010 will be obtained for the largest (in terms of assets) seven licensed commercial banks in Sri Lanka. Other macroeconomic data such as interest rates and inflation rates will be obtained from various publications of the Central Bank of Sri Lanka.

References

Aboagye, A. Q. Q., Akoena S. K., Antwi-Asare, T. O., & Gockel, A. F. (2008). Explaining interest rate spreads in Ghana. *African Development Review, 20*(3), 378–399.

Bank of England. (2009, June). *Financial stability report* (Issue No. 25). London: Bank of England.

Beck, T., & Hesse, H. (2009). Why are interest spreads so high in Uganda? *Journal of Development Economics, 88*(2), 192–204.

Brock, P. L., & Suarez, L. R. (2000). Understanding the behavior of bank spreads in Latin America. *Journal of Development Economics, 63*, 113–134.

Central Bank of Sri Lanka. (2006). Annual report. Colombo: Central Bank of Sri Lanka.

Saunders, A., & Schumacher, L. (2000). The determinants of bank interest rate margins: An international study. *Journal of International Money and Finance, 19*, 813–832.

Valverde, S. C., & Fernández, F. R. (2007). The determinants of bank margins in European banking. *Journal of Banking and Finance, 31*, 2040–2063.

Louise Butler

Research Proposal 3
Finding a Compromise: Law, Diplomacy, and Whaling in the Southern Ocean
Statement of the Problem

Australia opposes commercial and scientific whaling, while Japan considers scientific whaling a right rather than a "loophole" under the International Convention for the Regulation of Whaling (ICRW). Policy commentary on whaling generally highlights differences in the positions of Japan and other nations on the usefulness of scientific whaling and the continuation of the moratorium on whaling. Morishita (2006), for example, reviews the whaling issue from the Japanese perspective, discussing resource management and political, economic, and cultural perspectives and suggesting options for progress. Clapham et al. (2007) respond to Morishita's paper, arguing in favor of regulation of the whaling industry.

Australia has found that it must balance the risks posed to bilateral relations with Japan if judicial resolutions are pursued in response to significant public pressure (including from nongovernmental organizations) to take action. Recent Australian legal commentary has focused on proceedings brought in Australia by the Humane Society International against the Japanese company Kyodo Senpaku Kaisha Ltd. for whaling in the Australian Whale Sanctuary. McGrath (2005, 2006) reviews the international and domestic legal issues raised by these proceedings, including their significance for environmental law and domestic law, and argues that a focus on domestic law is insufficient for resolving the whaling issue. Blay and Bubna-Litic (2006) review international law relevant to Australia's domestic legislation and examine the relationship between international and domestic law to consider the merits of applying domestic law to international issues in the context of these proceedings. They advance the view that efforts to stop commercial whaling should have an international focus rather than a domestic law focus.

There is little research specifically targeting the differences in domestic law between Australia and Japan. In order to fill this gap, this paper will examine the positions of Japan and Australia on whaling conducted under Article VIII of the ICRW (scientific whaling) to identify policy and legal issues relevant to resolving the differences of view over the conduct of scientific whaling in the Southern Ocean.

Research Questions
1. What are the differences between Australia's and Japan's domestic law regarding whaling?
2. How can international law accommodate both the Australian and Japanese positions?

Methodology
This paper will ask whether international law can provide a resolution to the differences in view between Japan and Australia over whaling in the Southern Ocean through an examination of the relevant policy and legal issues. I will review sources such as government statements, parliamentary reports, and discussions in

international forums to clarify the policy objectives and concerns of both parties. I will attempt to explain, to the extent possible, why there are differences of view that have so far not been resolved. I will review and summarize the relevant international and Australian domestic law (legislation and case law), academic literature, and commentary to assess the scope for effective unilateral action through domestic law, summarize the existing legal situation in light of this analysis, and comment on the policy options available to both parties, including the role of diplomacy in finding a compromise.

References

Blay, S., & Bubna-Litic, K. (2006). The interplay of international law and domestic law: The case of Australia's efforts to protect whales. *Environmental and Planning Law Journal, 23,* 465–489.

Clapham, P. J., Childerhouse, S., Gales, N. J., Rojas-Bracho, L., Tillman, M. F., & Brownell, R. L. Jr. (2007). The whaling issue: Conservation, confusion, and casuistry. *Marine Policy, 31,* 314–319.

McGrath, C. (2005). The Japanese whaling case. *Environmental and Planning Law Journal, 22,* 250–257.

McGrath, C. (2006). Japanese whaling case appeal succeeds. *Environmental and Planning Law Journal, 23,* 333–336.

Morishita, J. (2006). Multiple analysis of the whaling issue: Understanding the dispute by a matrix. *Marine Policy, 30,* 802–808.

Ibrahim Zuhuree

Research Proposal 4
The Impact of Foreign Aid on Economic Growth in Small Island Developing States: Relevance of Economic Policy and Aid Uncertainty

Statement of the Problem

Although recently there has been a substantial increase in foreign aid, the results of studies on the effectiveness of foreign aid in promoting economic growth in developing countries are inconclusive (Dalgaard, Hansen, & Tarp, 2004; Easterly, 2003). Consequently, recent studies have sought to identify the conditions that enhance aid effectiveness. One study, which has influenced foreign aid commitments by donors, argues that aid is effective in the presence of appropriate economic policy in the recipient government (Burnside & Dollar, 2000). However, an investigation of that argument using an extended dataset found the results to be statistically insignificant (Easterly, Levine, & Roodman, 2004). Prompted by the findings of Burnside and Dollar (2000), several researchers have studied economic growth and aid effectiveness in relation to a wide range of variables, including governance (Feeny, 2005; Feeny & McGillivray, 2010), investment (Easterly, 2003), geographical location (Dalgaard et al., 2004), and quality of aid (Rajan & Subramanian, 2008). However, only a few studies (e.g., Lensink & Morrissey, 2000; Neanidis & Varvarigos, 2009) have examined the impact of uncertainty on foreign aid transfer, and even fewer have investigated the implications of aid uncertainty for economic growth of small island developing states (SIDS).

This lack of attention to uncertainty issues is surprising for several reasons. First, the per capita aid flow to SIDS is vastly greater than that to other developing countries, yet the living standards in some SIDS have fallen significantly in recent years (Feeny, 2005; Feeny & McGillivray, 2010). Second, despite the use of initiatives to strengthen donor coordination, recent empirical studies have consistently shown that aid uncertainty has persisted in many developing countries, including SIDS (Neanidis & Varvarigos, 2009). Third, although the defining characteristics of SIDS—particularly small size, vulnerability to natural disasters and economic shocks, and a history of state formation—make them a distinct group of developing countries, the existing literature on aid effectiveness says little about how SIDS may differ from other developing countries (Feeny & McGillivray, 2010).

Given the near absence of SIDS from the aid effectiveness literature, this paper's replication of an earlier study, Feeny and McGillivray (2010), which examined the impact of foreign aid on economic growth in SIDS, makes an important contribution. Feeny and McGillivray (2010) concluded that foreign aid is a stimulus for economic growth in SIDS, but that aid effectiveness decreases with increased aid relative to GDP. The purpose of this study, then, is to test the conclusions of Feeny and McGillivray (2010) using a more recent dataset, and then to extend the theoretical model of Feeny and McGillivray's study to determine if aid uncertainty has a significant impact on the success of foreign aid as a stimulus to economic growth in SIDS. The results of this study will have policy implications for the effective allocation and utilization of foreign aid in SIDS.

Research Questions

1. What is the impact of foreign aid on the economic growth of SIDS?
2. What are the relative contributions of policy and aid uncertainty to economic growth?

Methodology

In this study, *foreign aid* is taken to mean official development assistance (ODA) as defined by the Organization for Economic Cooperation and Development (OECD). Analysis will use the pooled panel regression model used by Feeny and McGillivray (2010), which is based on the findings of recent quantitative empirical studies of aid effectiveness. The model specifies the relationship between gross domestic product (GDP) and foreign aid, subject to control variables including government policy, quality of aid, and country vulnerability. This study will augment the Feeny and McGillivray model to include an additional variable by using regression methods developed by Lensink and Morrissey (2000) to estimate the impact of aid uncertainty on the economic growth of SIDS. A separate dummy variable for the Maldives will also be used to estimate changes in the coefficients of the regression model over time.

Scarcity of data on SIDS presents a challenge; therefore, a number of data sources will be utilized to obtain objective data for the control variables and to extend the dataset used by Feeny and McGillivray (2010) to 29 additional SIDS for the periods 1980–2004 and 1971–2010. Data sources include the aid portal of the OECD, development indicators from the World Bank, country statistics from the United Nations, and the searchable data portal AidData, which was released in 2010. Data will be grouped into four 10-year time intervals: 1971–80, 1981–90, 1991–2000, and 2001–10. Both cross-country and time-series analyses will be performed to allow comparison with earlier empirical results.

References

Burnside, C., & Dollar, D. (2000). Aid, policies, and growth. *American Economic Review, 90*(4), 847–868.

Dalgaard, C., Hansen, H., & Tarp, F. (2004). On the empirics of foreign aid and growth. *The Economic Journal, 114*(496), 191–216.

Easterly, W. (2003). Can foreign aid buy growth? *Journal of Economic Perspectives, 17*(3), 23–48.

Easterly, W., Levine, R., & Roodman, D. (2004). Aid, policies, and growth: comment. *American Economic Review, 94*(3), 774–780.

Feeny, S. (2005). The impact of foreign aid on economic growth in Papua New Guinea. *The Journal of Development Studies, 41*(6) 1092–1117.

Feeny, S., & McGillivray, M. (2010). Aid and growth in small island developing states. *The Journal of Development Studies, 46*(5), 897–917.

Lensink, R., & Morrissey, O. (2000). Aid instability as a measure of uncertainty and the positive impact of aid on growth. *The Journal of Development Studies, 36*(3), 31–49.

Neanidis, K. C., & Varvarigos, D. (2009). The allocation of volatile aid and economic growth: theory and evidence. *European Journal of Political Economy, 25*(4), 447–462.

Rajan, R. G., & Subramanian, A. (2008). Aid and growth: What does the cross-country evidence really show? *The Review of Economics and Statistics, 90*(4), 643–665.

AM I READY TO WRITE A PROPOSAL?

To check if you are ready to write a proposal, answer these questions. If you are ready, you should be able to answer all of these questions.

1. What journals specialize in your area?

_____

_____

_____

_____

2. What are the most influential studies in your area?

_____

_____

_____

_____

3. Who are the current leading experts in your area?

_____

_____

_____

_____

4. What are the most important debates or controversies in your area?

_____

_____

_____

_____

5. What is the specific problem that your study will address?

_____

_____

_____

_____

6. Why is it important?

_____

_____

_____

_____

7. What is your research question?

_____

_____

_____

_____

8. What are the most common methodologies used in your area?

_____

_____

_____

_____

9. What methodology do you propose to use to answer your research question?

_____

_____

_____

_____

10. What other studies have used the same methodology to answer a similar question?

_____

_____

_____

_____

11. What data will you use to answer your question? How will you obtain the data?

_____

_____

_____

_____

12. Have you talked to your academic advisor about your proposed research? What does he or she think?

_____

_____

_____

_____

Chapter 8

Structure of a Research Paper

COMMON STRUCTURE OF A RESEARCH PAPER

When students learn academic writing—in writing classes, from writing textbooks, or from their advisors—they are usually told that they need to have certain sections in a research paper. A common list includes Introduction, Literature Review, Theoretical Framework, Methodology, Results, Discussion, and Conclusion. Box 22, for example, shows some common sections that are included in a research paper and what those sections may contain.

It is important to realize, however, that the specific sections that will be included in a research paper and the specific content of those sections depend on many things including

- Requirements of your discipline or research area,

- Requirements of the publication (e.g., the journal you are submitting your paper to),

- Requirements of your educational program or university, or the wishes and preferences of your advisor,

- Type of paper (whether you are writing a dissertation, a thesis, a journal article, a working paper, and so on),

- Type of research (whether the paper is empirical or nonempirical, quantitative or qualitative), and

- The specific content of your paper (what it is about).

As a result, even papers written in the same discipline, published in the same journal, or submitted to the same university program may look very different. To understand how diverse in structure academic papers can be, take a look at Box 23. It shows the headings of main sections (from the Introduction to the Conclusion) taken from a large collection of empirical papers published in various journals in public policy and economics. The references for these papers are given in the Corpus Details at the end of the book.

Several things should be noted about the structure of the papers shown in Box 23.

How to Write about Economics and Public Policy. https://doi.org/10.1016/B978-0-12-813010-0.00008-9

- First, there are clear differences between quantitative and qualitative papers. Quantitative papers have section headings that roughly reflect the research process; qualitative papers have section headings that are thematic, reflecting the specific topics that are covered in these sections.

- Second, although there is a large diversity in the specific names of sections that are included in the papers, conceptually, the main structure (excluding the abstract, references, and appendices) of all quantitative papers can be divided into three distinct parts—research background, methodology, and results and main arguments. Qualitative papers show more diversity, but they, too, usually proceed from a description of some general research background to a specific examination of one or more aspects of the topic, to a description of results or conclusions of some sort.

- Third, the papers differ greatly in the length of their sections, which reflects differences in disciplinary research as well as publication preferences and requirements.

Because there is such a large diversity in the kinds of sections that are included in empirical papers, perhaps the best way to describe the structure of an empirical paper is to describe its parts conceptually, on the basis of their content and purpose. I do that in the following section.

CONCEPTUAL PARTS OF AN EMPIRICAL PAPER

Regardless of what specific sections an empirical paper may consist of, conceptually, it will have several distinct parts. Each of these parts may be described in one or more different sections.

Research Background

This part has three purposes: to justify the study and its predictions and expectations, to situate the study within the existing body of theoretical and empirical research, and to highlight the study's importance and contribution. This part often contains the following elements:

- Description of the problem and its importance,

- Motivation for the study, or the description of a specific gap in knowledge that the study fills,

- The specific contribution of the study to the field,

- Description of the country, policy, historical, or other context of the research, and

- Theoretical predictions and empirical findings of previous research.

Every paper will have at least some background, described at the beginning, before the methodology. In quantitative papers, this part can be as short as a few paragraphs or as long as a third of the paper, with an average length somewhere between one and three pages in a 20-page paper. In qualitative papers, this part is usually longer. Sections that are associated with this part are the Introduction, Literature Review, and Theoretical or Conceptual Framework.

The background part of a paper should be the last part you write. Write it after completing all the analyses and obtaining results because only then will you have a clear idea about how best to frame your study, present your arguments, and describe your contribution.

Methodology

The purpose of this part is to explain how the research was done. This part is really the heart of an empirical study: It describes how the study was designed and how the data were obtained, and it allows readers to judge the validity and credibility of the author's arguments. In quantitative papers in economics and public policy, this part often describes the following elements:

- Data and how the data were collected,
- Variables and measurement-related issues,
- Model and any modifications that have been made, and
- Estimation strategy and other related empirical issues.

In empirical qualitative papers, this part usually describes the rationale behind case selection and explains why the cases selected for the study are appropriate. In studies based on interviews, this part will also describe interview procedures; in studies based on documentary research, this part will describe sources of data.

In quantitative papers and in qualitative papers that are based on extensive data collection (e.g., interviews), the methodology part can be quite substantial and may constitute between a quarter and a third of the paper. In qualitative papers that are largely based on a review of academic literature, this part can be as short as a few paragraphs, and it can be described in the Introduction rather than in a separate section.

In quantitative papers, the methodology is usually described in the middle of the paper, after the Introduction, in sections titled Data and Method, Empirical Model, and Empirical Specification. However, because of the importance of the methodology in an empirical study, many papers in public policy and economics—especially quantitative papers in economics—also include a brief explanation (a preview) of the data and methodology in the Introduction. This is because in order to persuade the reader to accept their arguments, authors need to show early on that the data, measures, and models that they have used are appropriate for their specific purpose. Thus, Introduction sections in economics papers often include a rather detailed description of the data the authors used, their methodology, and the specific challenges they may have encountered (e.g., establishing causality), as well as an explanation of how the data and/or empirical strategy the authors used helped them overcome those challenges.

The methodology part of a paper is usually the first part we write. You can write it even before completing your analyses. Starting a paper with this part makes a lot of sense because this part is rather straightforward and relatively easy to write compared to the other parts of the paper. Unlike the background part of a research paper, for example, which requires synthesizing previous research, the methodology part is descriptive and requires only that you describe your data, model, and variables. In quantitative papers, some of this description could be done in the form of graphs, tables, or mathematical formulas.

Results and Main Arguments

The purpose of this part is to describe results and make claims to knowledge on the basis of the obtained results. It often includes the following elements:

- A description of analytic procedures (how the data were analyzed),
- A description of results,
- An interpretation of results,
- A discussion of results and how they compare with those of previous research,
- Policy and other relevant implications,
- Limitations of the study, and
- Conclusions.

This part is the most substantial part of an empirical paper: It usually constitutes at least half of the paper, and often, more. In quantitative papers, this part will contain a large number of tables and figures showing results of the study in numeric or graphic form. In qualitative papers based on interviews, this part will contain a large number of quotations to support the author's arguments. In qualitative papers based on documentary research, this part may contain extracts from relevant documents.

It is also common for authors of quantitative economics papers to include a description and a brief discussion of main results in the Introduction. Qualitative papers often include main arguments in the Introduction, which are announced with the words "I/we argue that..." or "This paper argues that."

The part describing results and main arguments should be written after the methodology but before the research background. In quantitative papers, much of this writing will involve describing and interpreting the visuals (i.e., tables and figures).

SECTIONS IN AN EMPIRICAL PAPER: EXAMPLES

Box 22 shows common sections in an empirical paper, with alternative section headings, and what these sections may contain. Keep in mind that these are only suggestions and that the specific elements that you will need to include in your study and the way that you will need to describe them will depend on your discipline, program requirements, and other factors. Ask your advisor for specific suggestions or consult papers in your area to find out what is expected.

BOX 22   Structure of Empirical Papers

Section	Alternative Names	Comments
Abstract	Summary	This is a 100–200-word summary of the research. It usually starts with the purpose and then describes, in 3–4 sentences, the methodology, results, and main argument(s) of the study.
Introduction		In quantitative studies, this section describes the problem under study, explains its importance, summarizes what is known about it, states a research gap, and describes the purpose of the study. In quantitative economics studies, it also often briefly explains • the methodology, various methodological challenges that the authors encountered, and how those challenges were overcome; • obtained results and how they compare to those of previous research; • the author's main argument(s); and • the study's contribution to the field. Literature in such studies is often summarized in relation to the study's contribution and appears toward the end of the Introduction. In published articles, this section can be fairly short—less than a page. The last paragraph usually describes the structure of the paper. In qualitative studies, this section often outlines main argument(s).
Literature Review	Review of Literature Conceptual Framework	In quantitative studies, this section is often absent in published studies, where literature is reviewed in the Introduction. Alternatively, this section may be divided into two subsections—Theoretical Literature and Empirical Literature. This section shows what is known about the topic, explains how previous studies are related to the current research and to one another, and tries to justify the author's expectations. Definitions may also

Continued

BOX 22 Structure of Empirical Papers—cont'd.

		be discussed and relevant studies may be summarized in table form in this section.
		In qualitative studies, this section often describes the overall conceptual framework for the study.
Theory	Theoretical Framework	In quantitative studies, this section describes the theory behind the research, the theoretical model, and may also describe relevant definitions. The description of theory can be mathematical (using equations), visual (using a graphic depiction of how variables are related), or narrative.
		In studies that are more closely related to sociology, psychology, educational research, or public administration than to economics, and in qualitative studies, this section is often absent and theoretical issues are addressed in the Literature Review or in the Introduction.
Methodology	Data and Model Empirical Specification Model Specification Empirics Econometric Approach Estimation Strategy Analytical Framework	In quantitative studies, this section provides details about the dataset, variables, instruments, and measurement procedures used in the study. If the data were collected by the authors, this section will describe how the sample was selected and how the data were collected. If specific instruments were constructed to collect data, they will be described here and included in an appendix. Procedures used to measure variables are often described in sufficient detail to permit replication. In economics papers, this section describes the empirical model and estimation strategy used by the authors. In qualitative studies, much of the focus in the methodology is on describing and justifying case selection. For example, if only one case is used in the study, justification for the selection often focuses on the uniqueness of the case or its special appropriateness to the research purpose. In a comparative case study, where two or more cases are compared, the focus is on demonstrating comparability. If a qualitative study is based on interviews, this section will often describe how the interviews were conducted, how the data were coded into themes, and how the authors ensured the reliability of the coding procedures.

BOX 22 Structure of Empirical Papers—cont'd.

Results	Results and Discussion	In quantitative studies, this section presents results in table form and then describes and interprets them. Results are often described in terms of statistical significance, size and sign of the estimated coefficients, and the amount of variance that is attributable to the variation in the independent variable(s). Sometimes regressions are presented and sometimes, they are shown in an appendix. This section may also include robustness checks or these checks can be described in a separate section.
		In qualitative studies, this section is often organized thematically, according to the themes uncovered in the data. It often consists of quotations from participants or extracts from documents, followed by the authors' interpretation of what these quotations or extracts mean.
Discussion		In quantitative studies, in this section, authors compare their study's results with those of previous research. If the results confirm previous findings, no further explanation is usually needed; if they do not confirm previous findings, authors would usually discuss possible reasons for the discrepancy. This section often outlines policy and other implications of the research and may provide recommendations. It may also describe the study's limitations and outline suggestions for future research.
		In qualitative studies, this section usually relates results to a wider theory and explains what they mean for the theoretical understanding of the problem under investigation. For example, an author may argue that the results strengthen an existing theory or that they show that an existing theory should be modified, discarded, or replaced with a new one.
Conclusion	Concluding Remarks	This section summarizes what was done, what was found, and what the findings mean for policy, theory, or practice.
		This section can be very short—as short as a paragraph—and it is often absent altogether, especially in economics papers.
Acknowledgements		In this section authors acknowledge the people or organizations that have helped in the research. It is also common to acknowledge financial assistance received for the research here.

Continued

BOX 22 Structure of Empirical Papers—cont'd.

References	Bibliography	The format of this section depends on the citation
	Works Cited	system used. Two common systems used in the
	References	social sciences are APA and Chicago. These systems
	Cited	are different in style and format. Students should
		find out early what the preferred citation system is in
		their research area and use it consistently.

Box 23 shows section headings taken from a selection of empirical articles, both quantitative and qualitative. The pie charts next to the first four quantitative articles show the amount of space that is devoted in each article to the research background, methodology, and results. Go over the headings of the quantitative articles first and try to group the headings into the three conceptual parts that I described earlier. Then check the pie charts to see what percentage of the article is devoted to the research background, what percentage is devoted to the methodology, and what percentage, to results. What conclusions can you draw from this analysis? Then go through the headings of the qualitative articles. In what way are they different from those of the quantitative articles?

BOX 23 Examples of Sections from Papers in Public Policy and Economics

Paper and Topic	Structure

Quantitative Studies

Paper and Topic	Structure	

Determinants of spending on public pensions
 	
Authors: Tepe & Vanhuysse (2009)
	Introduction
	
	Population aging and public pensions: theory and evidence
	
	Refined hypotheses
	
	Data and method
	    – Dependent variables
	    – Independent variables
	    – Estimation strategy
	
	Empirical analysis: baseline effects of population aging
	
	The role of politics and institutions
	
	Discussion
		Background 21%
		
		Methodology 26%
		
		Findings and main argument 53%

BOX 23 Examples of Sections from Papers in Public Policy and Economics—cont'd.

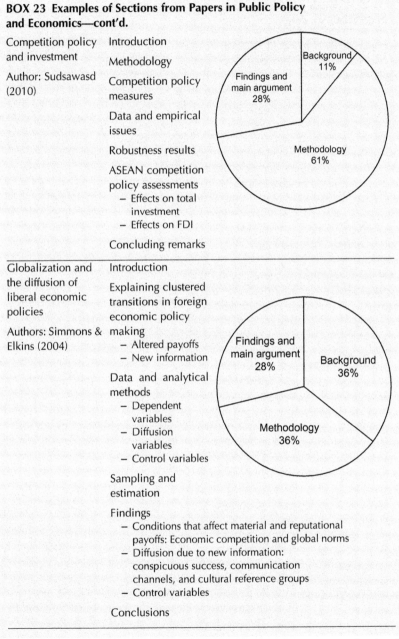

Competition policy and investment	Introduction
Author: Sudsawasd (2010)	Methodology
	Competition policy measures
	Data and empirical issues
	Robustness results
	ASEAN competition policy assessments
	— Effects on total investment
	— Effects on FDI
	Concluding remarks

Globalization and the diffusion of liberal economic policies	Introduction
Authors: Simmons & Elkins (2004)	Explaining clustered transitions in foreign economic policy making
	— Altered payoffs
	— New information
	Data and analytical methods
	— Dependent variables
	— Diffusion variables
	— Control variables
	Sampling and estimation
	Findings
	— Conditions that affect material and reputational payoffs: Economic competition and global norms
	— Diffusion due to new information: conspicuous success, communication channels, and cultural reference groups
	— Control variables
	Conclusions

Continued

BOX 23 Examples of Sections from Papers in Public Policy and Economics—cont'd.

Institutional factors and FDI flows	Introduction
Author: Kurul (2017)	Foreign direct investment flows to developing countries
	Econometric methodology
	Data
	Empirical results
	Conclusion

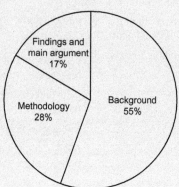

Effects of lead exposure on antisocial behavior	Introduction
Author: Reyes (2015)	Behavior and lead
	– Behavior
	– Lead
	– Lead and behavior
	Data
	– NLSY79 Child and Young Adult
	– NLSY97
	– Lead
	– Other Data
	Empirical approach
	Results: Predicting blood lead
	Results: Behavior
	– Preliminary results
	– Childhood behavior problems
	– Teen risky behavior
	– Aggression, violence, and criminal behavior
	– Robustness
	Interpretation
	Conclusion

Determinants of parental saving for postsecondary education	Introduction
Authors: Hossler & Vesper (1993)	Purpose
	A perspective on parental saving for postsecondary education
	Family background characteristics
	Student and parental aspirations and activities
	Information and incentives

BOX 23 Examples of Sections from Papers in Public Policy and Economics—cont'd.

Method
- Sample
- Surveys and interviews
- Discussion and measurement of variables

Analysis

Limitations

Results
- Survey analysis
- Discussion
- Qualitative data analysis

Discussion of survey and interview results

Implications

Recommendations for research

Effects of foreign ownership of firms on wages, employment, and worker turnover rates
 	
Authors:
Hijzen et al. (2013)
	Introduction
	
	Theory
	
	Empirical Literature
	  – Firm-level evidence
	  – Evidence from linked employer-employee data
	
	Data sources and cross-country comparability
	  – Data sources
	  – Cross-country comparability
	  – Descriptive statistics
	
	Methodology
	
	Results
	  – The effect of foreign ownership at the firm level
	  – The effect of foreign ownership at the worker level
	
	Concluding remarks

Perceptions of income distribution in Eastern Europe
 	
Authors: Arts et al. (1999)
	Introduction
	
	Modernization, division of labor, and occupational hierarchy
	
	Hypotheses
	
	Data set and operationalisation
	  – Data set
	  – Operationalisation
	
	Analysis
	
	Elaboration
	
	Conclusion

Continued

BOX 23 Examples of Sections from Papers in Public Policy and Economics—cont'd.

Effects of banking sector openness on economic growth	Introduction
	Trends and patterns in banking-sector globalization and economic growth
Author: Ghosh (2017)	— Measuring banking-sector globalization
	— Economic growth patterns
	Estimation framework, data and methodology
	Results and robustness checks
	— Results across levels of economic development
	— Does the extent of foreign bank penetration matter?
	— Addressing model uncertainty
	— Results using yearly data
	Foreign banks and private credit flows
	Conclusion
Estimation of income underreporting among the self-employed	Introduction
	Estimating underreporting of income of the self-employed
	— The basic model
	— Key assumptions and institutional setting
	— Accounting for transitory income
Authors: Engström & Hagen (2017)	Data
	— Consumption survey
	— Income data
	— Key variables and sample restrictions
	— Tax treatment
	— Differences between wage earners and the self-employed
	Estimation results
	— Persistence in self-employment status
	— IV results
	— Evaluating the instruments
	Robustness
	Conclusions
Income inequality and violent crime in Mexico	Introduction
	The literature on the links between income inequality and crime
	— Violent crime and inequality in Mexico
Authors: Enamorado et al. (2016)	Income inequality and crime in Mexico: some stylized facts
	— Trends in income inequality
	— Trends in crime and violence in Mexico
	— Law enforcement
	Data
	— Data on income, poverty, and inequality in municipalities
	— Crime indicators
	— Other sources of municipal data
	— Summary statistics
	Estimation strategy

BOX 23 Examples of Sections from Papers in Public Policy and Economics—cont'd.

	Results
	   – Robustness checks
	   – Effects in urban and rural areas
	   – Interaction with police spending
	   – Results disaggregated by type of crimes
	   – Results by demographic characteristics
	
	Concluding remarks

Relationship between public revenues and efficiency in the production of local public goods
 	
Authors:
Borge et al. (2015)
	Introduction
	
	The Norwegian local governments
	   – Financing and responsibilities
	   – Revenues from hydropower
	
	Measuring local government efficiency
	
	Testing the Paradox of Plenty hypothesis
	   – The instrument
	   – Empirical results: The Paradox of Plenty hypothesis
	   – Robustness checks: The Paradox of Plenty hypothesis
	
	The Rentier State hypothesis
	
	Concluding remarks

Correlation of wealth across generations Authors: Charles & Hurst (2003)	Introduction Data Elasticity of child wealth with respect to parental wealth Decomposing the intergenerational wealth elasticity The role of preferences Conclusion

Married women's employment in South Korea and Taiwan
 	
Authors: Brinton et al. (1995)
	Introduction
	
	Possible explanatory models
	
	Methodological approach
	
	What needs to be explained
	
	Macrolevel analysis
	   – Labor supply conditions
	   – Patriarchal values
	   – Labor demand conditions
	Microlevel analysis
	   – Work before and after marriage
	   – Current work
	
	Discussion

Continued

BOX 23 Examples of Sections from Papers in Public Policy and Economics—cont'd.

Relationship between trade liberalization and productivity Authors: Amiti & Konings (2007)	Introduction Model and estimation strategy Trade policy in Indonesia Data Results Conclusions

Qualitative Studies

Trends in economics degrees
Authors: Siegfried & Round (2001)
	Introduction
	Trends in economics degrees in four counties
	Possible explanations for the fluctuations
	  – Trends in the overall number of degrees
	  – Changing gender mix in university students
	  – Changing interests of male and female students
	  – Changing interest in business education
	  – Changes in other competing degree programs
	  – Fluctuations in the academic price of an economics degree
	  – Changing teaching methods
	  – Changing relative labor market returns to an economics degree
	Conclusion

Drivers of economic reform in four provinces in Vietnam Authors: Schmitz et al. (2015)	Introduction The starting point: what do we know and not know? Methods and sources Similarities and differences across four provinces Role of the private sector in enhancing reform Learning in provincial government The role of the Party Lessons for other countries

Healthcare reform in postcommunist Europe
Author: Roberts (2009)
	Introduction
	The reform menu
	Theories of health politics
	The importance of access
	Evidence
	  – The Czech Republic
	  – Poland
	  – Hungary
	Conclusion

BOX 23 Examples of Sections from Papers in Public Policy and Economics—cont'd.

Effects of China's one-child policy on family outcomes
 	
Author: Zhang (2017)
	Introduction
	
	Evolution of family planning policy in China
	
	Trends in total fertility rates in China and selected countries: 1950–2010
	
	Empirical approaches to identifying the effect of the one-child policy
	
	Micro evidence
	  – Effect of the one-child policy on fertility
	  – Effect of the one-child policy on child education
	  – Effect of the one-child policy on other family outcomes
	
	Concluding remarks

Internationalization of Korean higher education
 	
Authors: Byun & Kim (2011)
	Introduction
	
	Driving forces behind the internationalization of Korean higher education—a historical overview
	
	National policies and implementation strategies for the internationalization of Korean higher education
	  – Student mobility
	  – Internationalizing research and academic staff
	  – Institutional mobility: education exports and the recruitment of foreign branch campuses
	  – Internationalization and the "Englishization" of university curricula
	  – Challenges confronting the internationalization of future Korean higher education
	
	Concluding remarks: Shifting rationales for the internationalization of Korean higher education

Political economy of international monetary relations
 	
Authors: Broz & Frieden (2001)
	Introduction
	  – National exchange rate policy
	  – International monetary systems
	
	The domestic political economy of exchange rate policy
	  – To fix or to float?
	  – Interest groups and regime choice
	  – Class-based (partisan) approaches to regime choice
	  – Political institutions and regime choice
	  – To appreciate or depreciate?
	  – Interest groups and the level of the exchange rate
	  – Political institutions and the level of the exchange rate
	
	The international political economy of exchange rate policy
	  – Coordination in international monetary relations
	  – Cooperation in international monetary relations
	
	Conclusions

Continued

BOX 23 Examples of Sections from Papers in Public Policy and Economics—cont'd.

Role of Chinese cashmere global value chains in rural development Authors: Waldron et al. (2014)	Introduction Global and agricultural value chains The international cashmere trade Branding and retailing The processing sector Input supplies Product upgrading and mislabelling International and policy implications

Women empowerment and economic development
 	
Author: Duflo (2012)
	Introduction
	
	Can economic development cause women's empowerment?
	  – Relaxing the grip of poverty through economic development
	  – Economic development, fertility, and maternal mortality
	  – Giving women hope by expanding their opportunities
	  – Freeing up women's time
	  – Economic development and women's rights
	  – But will economic development be enough?
	
	Can women's empowerment cause economic development?
	  – Women empowerment and changes in family outcomes
	  – Women as decision-makers
	  – Empowering women: what policy instruments?
	  – Empowering women: is it free lunch for development policy?
	
	Conclusion

Welfare effects of changes in food price and changes in the views of relevant organizations on the matter
 	
Author: Swinnen (2011)
	Introduction
	
	Food-price effects: some basic principles
	
	180° turnaround in food-policy analysis and communication
	  – Analyses from NGOs
	  – Analyses from international organizations
	  – Out of context?
	  – Do poor farmers benefit from high food prices?
	
	Policy implications
	  – Export restrictions and the WTO
	  – Back to the future or forward to the past? The old CAP as a model for global food security?
	  – Land grabbing and headline grabbing
	
	Conclusion
	  The political economy of (food) policy analysis and communication
	  – Scientific progress (analysis vs. communication)
	  – Urban bias and relative incomes
	  – Fundraising and legitimacy
	  – Raising attention with (semi-)consistent policy advice
	
	Mass media and policy communication
	
	Some concluding comments

Chapter 9

Justifying a Study: The Introduction

All research must be justified on theoretical, empirical, or practical grounds. Recall that an author's goal in an academic paper is to persuade the reader to accept his or her study as legitimate and valid—and that includes persuading the reader to accept the fact that the study was needed in the first place. Essentially, you need to convince the reader that your research is worthwhile and that reading your paper is not a waste of time. To do that, authors often try to demonstrate the following three elements:

- Importance of the problem under study;
- Insufficient knowledge about the problem, or a research gap; and
- Contribution of their research to academic or policy debate.

These elements are often referred to by economists as **motivation** for a study. In this book, I draw a slight distinction between motivation and contribution—the former is about the importance of the problem and, especially, the gap, whereas the latter is about the importance, significance, or timeliness of your own research. I explain this distinction later in this chapter.

Justification is always presented at the beginning of a study and usually in the Introduction section, where these three elements can be described quite succinctly, in just a few short sentences. Here is an example from de Coulon and Wolff (2010).

There is a growing literature on the main determinants of the decision for immigrants to return to their origin country (Dustmann, 2001, for a survey), **but the literature has primarily investigated** the return of working-age immigrants. **This article brings some fresh findings** on the location intentions of immigrants at the time of their retirement. (de Coulon and Wolff, 2010, p. 3319)

Here, the phrase "there is a growing literature" shows the importance of the topic, "determinants of the decision for immigrants to return to their origin country," and the phrase "but the literature has primarily investigated" describes the motivation for the study by indicating a research gap—lack of research on a particular aspect of the topic. The second sentence describes the contribution of the study: "fresh findings on the location intentions of immigrants at the time of their retirement."

How to Write about Economics and Public Policy. https://doi.org/10.1016/B978-0-12-813010-0.00009-0

161

It is important to stress that the specific elements that are included in a paper as justification, the way these elements are described in a paper, and the amount of space that is devoted to the description of each element depend on many things including the requirements of the publication to which the paper is being submitted. Primarily, however, decisions about what elements to include, how to describe them, and in how much detail will be dictated by the conventions of the particular discipline or research area that the writer is working in.

Different research areas have different conventions for which elements should be included and how those elements should be described. These conventions reflect readers' expectations, preferences, and what readers find convincing. For example, it is often expected that authors of empirical papers in economics will discuss their contribution and the appropriateness of their data and methodology as part of the justification for their study. Such discussions are not as common in qualitative papers and papers in areas outside economics. Studies in public policy relating to sociology, psychology, education, and public administration, for example, often focus more on describing a gap for the study rather than on describing the contribution.

Authors writing for policymaking, rather than academic, audiences may devote more space to explaining the importance of the problem and describing the practical usefulness of their research for policymaking and may only imply, rather than explicitly describe, a research gap. Here is an example from a policy proposal written by Mariyam Rashfa, a graduate student in Macroeconomic Policy.

Given that the Maldivian economy is very much dependent on imports, inflation in the Maldives is largely import-driven and thus is mostly explained by price developments in major trading partners (Maldives Monitary Authority, [MMA], 2009). However, recent increases in government expenditure, combined with high levels of modernization of the fiscal deficit in the period from 2006 to 2008 have resulted in a rapid expansion in money supply and thus intensified inflationary pressures in the economy (MMA, 2009). **As Maldives is gradually moving from a fixed exchange rate regime towards a more flexible exchange rate regime—which would require a monetary policy framework with an alternative nominal anchor—a better understanding of the causes of inflation has become important in order to guide the formulation of monetary policy.** In this regard, this paper will attempt to identify the main determinants of inflation in the Maldives, which will help in gaining a better insight into the causes of inflation and thus contribute to the formulation of effective monetary policy. (Rashfa, 2012, p. 1)

Mariyam justifies her research by appealing to the need to solve a practical policy problem rather than by describing a gap in existing scholarship. Notice how much space she devotes to the description of the relevant aspects of the Maldivian economy as part of the justification for her study.

Disciplinary conventions also change. For example, two decades or so ago, economists seldom talked about the contribution of their study to the field. Now, however, describing a study's contribution is considered by many to be an important part of justifying research and persuading the reader to accept it. It is, therefore, important to find out the current, existing conventions of your field or research area and follow them. You can do that by examining published studies in your area to see how, exactly, authors justify their research and which elements they tend to emphasize—problem importance, research gap, or their study's contribution. The following technique may be helpful. Keep in mind that because conventions change over time, you should focus on more recent studies—those that have been published in the past five years or so.

1. Find at least 8–10 papers that are close to your research topic. Ideally, the papers should focus on the same—or a similar—relationship as the one you intend to study.

2. Go over the background parts of each paper (i.e., Introduction, Conceptual Framework, and other parts before the Methodology), focusing on the purpose of each paragraph. Try to determine what the authors are doing in each paragraph. Are they describing the problem and its significance? Outlining a gap? Explaining their contribution? For each paragraph, write the author's purpose in the margins. Then underline the specific words and phrases that the authors use to achieve those purposes.

3. Look at the linguistic markers that the authors use to interact with the readers. What is the purpose of these markers? Which markers are used most commonly? (See Chapter 1 for various examples of linguistic markers.)

4. After you have analyzed all the papers in this fashion, try to create a skeletal structure for the introductory part of each paper. Are there any common elements? Is there a particular order in which the authors present these elements? The common elements that you have identified will most likely reflect the conventions of your research area and the readers' preferences and expectations.

5. Finally, create a structure for your own paper, which should follow, as much as possible, the conventions of your field.

The sections below give some general guidelines on how to describe the problem, gap, and contribution in a paper related to public policy or economics. These guidelines are based on my review of a large corpus of both published and unpublished papers written in various areas of public policy and economics. Some of these papers were written by professional researchers and others, by graduate students. You can find references for these papers in the appendix Corpus Details at the end of this book.

PROBLEM AND ITS IMPORTANCE

In describing the problem under study, it is important to distinguish between three things—**problem, topic, and fact**. Compare these three sentences:

1. Maintaining a reasonable degree of price stability has been a primary goal of monetary policies in many transition economies.

2. Kazakhstan gained independence in 1991.

3. This paper focuses on the value-added tax.

The first sentence describes a problem—the importance of maintaining price stability. We can imagine that after this sentence, the author will probably describe why this is important, whether transition economies have been successful in achieving this goal, or what approaches exist for maintaining price stability. The second sentence, however, is a statement of fact. It is difficult to imagine what the author may talk about here because the idea that Kazakhstan gained independence in 1991 is difficult to develop further. The third sentence describes the topic and although it gives us some idea about what the author will be talking about in the paper, it is still rather vague and it does not describe a problem.

Good papers describe a problem rather than stating a fact or announcing the topic of research. A problem is something that needs to be addressed, dealt with, researched, and/or overcome. Unlike problems we face in real life, which are often synonymous with something difficult or unpleasant, a research problem is not necessarily something bad. It may simply refer to the emergence of a new phenomenon, the establishment of a new policy or rule, or the beginning of a new trend. It can, of course, also refer to something difficult or unexpected.

In academic writing, a research problem is often indicated by words showing that something is challenging or that there has been a change in the status quo. For example:

There has been an increase/decrease in [something].
[Something] has become a challenge for [something].
[Something] has become [something else].

Below are some examples.

Europe is an aging continent where the demand for long-term care **will undoubtedly increase** during the next decades. (Bonsang, 2007, p. 172)

Parents have **the difficult job** of guiding and regulating children's behavior while also allowing them the freedom to explore their world—exploration necessary for proper socialization and development. (Vandewater et al., 2005, p. 609)

One effect of the financial crisis of 2007-09 was that public debt in industrial countries **reached levels not recorded since** the end of World War II. (De Bonis & Stacchini, 2013, p. 290)

The dominant academic and policy-oriented discourse on economic development **has been progressively adopting** concepts that had been originally introduced in different arenas or academic fields. Fragility is one of these concepts... (Bertoli & Ticci, 2012, p. 211)

The last two decades have seen **a rapid increase** in the process of banking sector globalization. (Ghosh, 2017, p. 83)

The description of a problem is usually followed by a statement of its importance. In research papers in public policy and economics, importance is commonly demonstrated by showing a growing interest in the problem from the academic community or by indicating the importance of the problem to public policy or policymaking. Importance is often indicated with these and similar expressions:

There has been increasing interest in/an ongoing investigation of [your problem].

Research on [your problem] has intensified in the last few years.

[Your problem] has been growing in importance in [your setting].

[Your problem] is one of the most pressing social issues confronting governments around the world today.

Policymakers have recently attempted to [achieve a solution to your problem].

Below are some examples. The last two examples are more detailed, showing not only that the problem is important but also why it is important and why we should care about solving it.

As jail and prison populations in the United States have reached levels that are both historically and comparatively unprecedented, **there has been increasing interest in better understanding** the determinants of incarceration. (Arum & LaFree, 2008, p. 397)

Changing demographic conditions **are playing havoc** on the public pension systems of countries both rich and poor. (Pfau, 2008, p. 2)

Remittances **are growing in importance in our globalizing world and are consequently receiving greater attention from researchers.** (Pfau & Long, 2008, p. 2)

Managerial capital, or the ability to manage a business, **has received attention in recent years as one of the major determinants** of enterprise productivity, growth, and longevity. (Suzuki et al., 2013, p. 1)

The success of the launch of the euro is not only technical and economic, it is also and foremost political. The euro is now the most visible and practical symbol of the progress towards political union in Europe. And yet **despite the magnitude of the success, the challenges ahead are also formidable.** In this article I analyse some of these challenges. (de Grauwe, 2002, p. 693)

This paper studies the effect of improved neonatal and early childhood health care on mortality and long-run academic achievement in school.... The question of whether such interventions affect outcomes later in life **is of immense importance for policy not only due to the significant efforts currently being made** to improve early childhood health world wide, **but also due to large disparities** in neonatal and infant health care that remain between (and within) countries. While the stated goal of many such interventions is to improve childhood health and reduce mortality, **understanding spillovers and other long-run effects** such as better academic achievement **is key to estimating their efficacy.** (Bharadwaj et al., 2013, p. 1862)

The credit scheme in Ethiopia, however, **raises some concerns,** as many other top-down credit schemes in developing countries do. First, the input distribution tied to credit may limit the emergence of private sector retailers, as pointed out by Jayne et al. (2003). Second, the public input distribution tends to deliver inputs, which are of low-quality and arrive, too late. Spielman et al. (2010), for instance, quote a study which finds that half of the surveyed Ethiopian smallholders reported that their fertilizer arrived after planting, and 25 percent complained of the poor quality of the fertilizer they received. Third, the application of standard packages to very diverse environments in Ethiopia may lead to a low efficiency of fertilizer use. **Thus, it is very important to evaluate the impact** of the fertilizer credit scheme on the farm productivity and welfare of the farmers. Fortunately, there are large variations in the use of credit access across regions and over time, and **such variations provide an opportunity to evaluate the effects** of the credit scheme on crop production and income using panel data. (Matsumoto & Yamano, 2010, pp. 2–3)

Using Statistics to Demonstrate Importance

Authors often use statistics to demonstrate the importance of their problem. This is often a good strategy; however, in order to be understandable and effective, statistics must be put in context so that readers can interpret them. Consider, for example, the following two sentences.

1. Public education expenditures have increased in Ghana to 20% of the total expenditures.

2. The interest margins of banks in Sri Lanka stood at nearly 5% in 2009.

How can we interpret these statistics? Are these numbers high? Low? How high or low? Just by looking at these sentences, it may be difficult to understand what the author is trying to show here. To help the reader interpret these numbers, we need to contextualize them—to provide a reference point or something to compare these numbers to. Below is an example of how these numbers can be contextualized.

1. Public education expenditures have increased in Ghana to 20% of the total expenditures and now constitute approximately 5% of GDP and 74% of all social spending in the country.

2. The net interest margins of banks in Sri Lanka stood at 4.7% in 2009. For comparison, the net interest margins in the UK in 2008 were 1.9%, and in India, 3%.

In the new versions, the numbers can be easily interpreted because there is a clear reference point—percentage of GDP and a share of social spending in the first example and similar data for other countries in the second example.

How Much Background to Include?

In describing the problem under study, authors often want to provide some background about their research context. The key questions here are what kind of background to include and how much of it to include. Students who are new to graduate study often interpret the word *background* in the broadest sense, as all the background of the country or policy they are researching, and try to include everything that they can find. As a result, they often write long passages describing their countries' geography, history, political and economic systems, related laws and regulations, policy efforts, and the current situation—"just in case my advisor wants more information," as students often put it. Well, we usually don't.

In fact, indiscriminate inclusion of background information is often more confusing than helpful to the reader. The key idea that should guide your selection of the specific information to include in the background is **relevance**—and not so much to your country as to the problem under study. The information you include in the background should help you make an argument about the importance of your problem, and not simply sit there "just in case." Every sentence should help you advance your argument, so that after reading the background part of your study, the reader could see why the problem is important and why a study like yours is indeed needed.

The idea of relevance is not a simple one because it is important to look at it from the reader's point of view. In fact, decisions about the amount of detail that should be included and the amount of space that should be devoted to the description of the problem should be guided by the author's estimation of what the reader is likely to know and what information the reader is likely to need in order to understand the author's research. These are the key things that you, as an author, need to decide in order to include the right kind and amount of information in the background of your paper.

Consider the problem from the point of view of the reader. What aspects of the problem is the reader likely to be familiar with? What aspects does he or she need to know more about in order to understand your research? If the context of your research is well-known to your readers, you may not need to provide a lot of background. On the other hand, if you are researching a new area that has not been well-researched, you may need to provide more background information. For example, if you are writing a paper on women empowerment in the United States for an audience that is familiar with the topic and context of the research, you will likely need less background than if you were writing about women empowerment in Pakistan or Bangladesh for an audience that is not familiar with those contexts.

Interdisciplinary research may also require more background. For example, if you are writing a paper that combines both economics and health for an audience of economists, you may need to include some additional background from epidemiology or other relevant health-related areas. Or if you describe a global security problem from a theoretical perspective of social psychology for an audience of international relations experts, you may need to provide additional background on relevant psychological theories.

Below are some examples of how authors describe the background of their research in their studies. Notice how the description of the relevant background quickly narrows down to the description of the problem under study. Notice also the use of sentence connectors to show logical relations between the sentences describing the background of the problem and those describing the motivation for the study.

In the 1970s and early 1980s, many African countries adopted state-led fertilizer distribution policies where governments were heavily involved in fertilizer supply schemes via public agencies. During this period, the fertilizer use increased significantly, along with increased adoption of improved seeds, thereby raising hopes for some countries to follow the Asian Green Revolution (Eicher, 1995; Byerlee and Eicher, 1997). However, because of heavy financial burdens to support state-led policies, such as through subsidies or credit that was written off, many public agencies accumulated debts over years. As a result, during the following structural adjustment period in the late 1980s and 1990s, many governments adopted market reform policies, although the degree of how thoroughly these have been implemented varies from country to country (Jayne et al., 2003). (Yamano & Arai, 2010a, p. 2)

Another motivation is provided by the state of the school system in Uganda. Despite the introduction of universal primary and secondary education in Uganda the rate of continuation to the 5th year remains low at 56%. One factor among many affecting the low performance may be the preference of the parents and the adolescents themselves towards education, since education entails long-term investment with uncertain outcomes. Such investment does not only include opportunity cost of schooling for adolescents but also direct cost of education such as uniforms, meals and scholastic materials. Past studies have acknowledged the role of risk attitude and discount rate in household decision on schooling, but have typically focused on the preferences of one actor such as the parent (e.g., Wölfel and Heineck, 2012) or the elicited risk attitude of the individual as an adult (e.g., Belzil and Leonardi, 2007). However it may be that for adolescents of secondary school age, not only the parents' preferences but their own preferences affect the schooling decision. In this context we conduct an experiment targeting adolescents aged 12 to 18 to investigate the impact of adolescents' preferences on their own schooling decision. (Munro & Tanaka, 2014, pp. 2–3)

Despite occasional fluctuations, Maldives enjoyed stable rates of inflation averaging 5% from 1986 until mid-2006, supported by the exchange rate peg to the US dollar and favorable external conditions. However, in recent years, the rate of inflation has become more volatile, rising from 3% in 2006 to 12% in 2008, then falling again to 4% in 2009 before rising again to 11% in 2011. Given that the economy is very much dependent on imports, much of this increase in inflation has been attributed to external factors, particularly the increase in global commodity prices. However, expansionary fiscal policy and monetary accommodation of the fiscal deficit from 2006 to 2009 resulted in a rapid expansion in the domestic money supply, which also intensified inflationary pressures in the economy. (Rashfa, 2012, p. 3)

RESEARCH GAP

Although it is possible to justify a study simply on the basis of the importance of the problem, especially in papers that are related more to policy than to academic scholarship, readers may find such a justification unconvincing. To convince the reader of the importance of your research, you need to show that there is something missing from existing scholarship—that there is a gap in our current knowledge.

A research gap is a question for which we do not yet have an answer or a problem for which we do not yet have a solution. The notion of a *research gap* is central to all research because a research gap provides a strong **motivation**—a reason—for conducting research. Although not all studies will describe a research gap explicitly, many published studies will do so. Those that do not describe an explicit research gap often imply that there is one by claiming that there is a need for more research, further clarification, or a better understanding of something.

Three research gaps are commonly used to justify empirical studies in public policy and economics: (1) lack or scarcity of research on a given topic or in a given setting; (2) ambiguous, mixed, or controversial findings; and (3) limitations in the existing body of research. These gaps are briefly explained below. Keep in mind as you read that a justification for the same study can be framed differently depending on what the author wants to emphasize. For example, if previous research has examined an issue using only a particular approach, method, or type of data, the study can be framed as an attempt to resolve a limitation in previous research; it can also be framed as an attempt to add to the existing or proposed theories that lack supporting studies conducted using a particular method or type of data. It is also common for authors to describe more than one gap as a justification for their study.

Qualitative studies, especially nonempirical ones, are often justified by the need to reframe a particular policy issue, summarize disparate research efforts on a topic, or examine a phenomenon more deeply or holistically. These justifications are further explained in the subsections below.

Lack or Scarcity of Research

Lack of research can take several forms. First, there may be entirely unexplored geographical settings—settings where the topic you are interested in has not yet been explored. These could be individual countries, regions, or groups of countries such as developing countries, or least developed countries. Second, there may be unexplored populations—or groups of people in which a particular topic has not yet been researched. These could be groups defined by gender, age, or any social characteristic. Third, previous research on a particular topic may have been confined to the use of only certain approaches, methodologies, or data sets, which may not have been ideal.

For example, a problem may have been examined previously only by using qualitative approaches or by using aggregate-level rather than individual-level data. This gap is also often framed as a limitation in previous research. Finally, there may have been only a small number of studies on a topic or a predominant focus on one aspect of the topic and less attention to some other important aspects.

Below are some examples showing how researchers describe lack of research as a motivation for their study. Go over them and underline the parts where the authors describe the motivation for their studies. What specific words and phrases do they use?

In our view, however, studies on employment process in developing economies are still scarce (e.g., Frijiters, 1999; Collier and Garg, 1999), and more importantly, the development process of labor markets beyond the reliance on these personal networks has not been sufficiently examined since its importance was first raised by Marshall (1920). (Mano et al., 2010, pp. 2–3)

Remittances are growing in importance in our globalizing world and are consequently receiving greater attention from researchers. At the microeconomic level, researchers tend to use household surveys to examine why people send remittances, how the characteristics of remittance recipients compare to non-recipients, how remittances impact poverty and the income distribution, how remittances are spent for consumption or investment purposes, and the role of remittances as an insurance mechanism. However, an issue that has received less focus is the role of gender in remittance decisions, from the perspective of both sending and receiving. (Pfau & Long, 2008, p. 2)

Most studies investigating the motives for conversion to organic farming have focused on large-scale farmers, particularly in countries where organic farming has developed well. Few studies have looked into the motives of small-scale organic farmers whose characteristics and farming conditions are different from those of large-scale farmers. Accounting for this difference is important as previous research (e.g., Koesling et al., 2008) has found that the motives for conversion to organic farming are influenced by characteristics of farmers and their farming system. In Indonesia, organic farming was first introduced in the 1990s and it has continued to expand. As a result there was an increase to more than 50,000 hectares of organic farm land in 2009 (Willer et al., 2011). The adoption of organic farming has been seen by small-scale farmers as a solution to problems they face in conventional farming, such as soil degradation, high production costs, and negative effects of chemical fertilizers and pesticides (Macrae, 2011; Martawijaya & Montgomery, 2004). With more and more farmers adopting organic farming practices in Indonesia, the government has begun to promote and develop this sector. If conversion is an important factor for organic farming to develop, as has been found in previous studies, understanding these motives would be a prerequisite to developing agricultural policy. However, no study has yet investigated motives for conversion to organic farming in Indonesia; this study aims to fill this gap. (Yuniarti, 2012, p. 8)

The literature on foreign exchange reserves is extensive for developing countries but not so for developed countries because there appears to be no apparent reason for hard currency economies to hold a large amount of reserves (Williams, 2005). And, indeed, developed countries hold small reserves. However, this is not the case for Japan. (Takeda, 2012, p. 1)

There are only a few studies, however, that have estimated the impacts of school quality on school choice between public and private primary schools in developing countries (Alderman et al., 2001; Carnoy and McEwan, 2001; Glick and Sahn, 2006). Furthermore, there are no studies, as far as we know, that estimate the impacts of the school quality on school progress and transfers by using individual level panel data in developing countries. (Nishimura & Yamano, 2008, p. 2)

Controversies

Controversies may refer to several things. First, there may be **mixed, inconclusive, or contradictory results** of previous research. For example, some studies may have found a positive effect of a dependent variable on an outcome and others, a negative effect or no effect. This kind of controversy is very common in papers in public policy and economics. Second, there may be continuing **theoretical debates** on an issue or alternative hypotheses, which may reflect the existence of different schools of thought, views, or perspectives. Controversy may also arise from an author's arguments or a certain interpretation of results. For example, an author may propose one explanation for the obtained results, but other authors may propose alternative explanations.

Below are some examples showing how authors describe controversies in previous research as a motivation for their study. Go over them and underline the parts where the authors describe the motivation for their studies. Which words and phrases do they use?

To integrate markets and enable the markets, not government agencies, allocate resources, structural adjustment programs were implemented in the 1980s and 1990s in many countries in SSA. To examine the impacts of the structural adjustment programs on market integration, there have been many studies that have tested market integration internationally and domestically by using time series data. Some studies find improved market integration after the liberalization (Badiane and Shively, 1998), while others find that markets remain poorly integrated even after the introduction of the structural programs (Lutz et al., 2006; Negassa et al., 2004; Fafchamps, 2004; Poulton et al., 1998). (Yamano & Arai, 2010b, p. 2–3)

Overall, the recent evidence based on worker-level data provides a somewhat mixed message with respect to the impact of foreign ownership on wages. While most studies indicate that foreign ownership has a positive impact on wages, a number of studies indicate small negative effects. It is not clear what drives these differences in estimated wage premia across studies. (Hijzen et al., 2013, p. 174)

Later studies extend the argument to point out that economic activities could respond asymmetrically to changes in oil price (Hamilton, 1996; Lee, Ni, & Ratti, 1995; Mork, 1989). The effect of the same change in price does not have the same magnitude when the change is positive as compared to when the change is negative. This finding is important because it can capture the impact of both upward and downward changes in oil prices. However, the empirical evidence of such asymmetry is mixed. Huntington (1998) found that increasing oil prices positively affected consumer prices and negatively impacted output growth in developed countries such as the U.S., whereas a decline in oil prices did not significantly impact the U.S. economy. The asymmetric effects of oil price shocks increase inflation regardless of the direction of price change (negative or positive) in developing countries such as Iran (Farzanegan & Markwardt, 2009). Brown and Yücel (2002) suggested that the asymmetric effect could result from the implementation of monetary policy and imbalances in the industrial structure of a country. (Artami, 2017, p. 1–2)

Limitations in Existing Scholarship

Limitations are weaknesses, or shortcomings of research, which limit the applicability or generalizability of its results. In quantitative research, limitations can be conceptual or methodological and may include

- Definitions that are too broad, too narrow, or that fail in some way to capture the nature of the concept under study;

- Samples that are too small for the statistical technique being used;

- Problems with data or a predominant use of one type of data rather than another (e.g., a predominant use of cross-sectional rather than panel data);

- Problems with the model or estimation strategy;

- Overlooked variables; or

- Use of designs that do not preclude alternative explanations.

Keep in mind, however, that it is rather uncommon for authors in public policy and economics to openly criticize individual studies or authors. It is more common to focus on the overall state of previous research and describe limitations in the whole body of that research or some of its parts. In this sense, the word *limitations* may not necessarily indicate weaknesses; rather, it may simply refer to the fact that previous research has not yet considered something—such as a recent fiscal crisis, a group of countries, or certain variables. Seen from this angle, this gap is similar to the one I described earlier—a lack or scarcity of research.

Below are some examples showing how researchers describe limitations in the existing body of research as a motivation for their study. Go over them and underline the parts where the authors describe the motivation for their studies. Which words and phrases do they use?

The earlier studies on those real-side factors, however, do not consider the crop failure of wheat in Australia and/or Ukraine in the latter half of the 2000s. The rice sector has not been analyzed in the context of the recent food crisis or petroleum price hikes. Rosegrant's (2008) analysis of the biofuels' impact does not reach 2008, when the grain prices rose most severely. The partial equilibrium models used by Rosegrant (2008) and Charlesbois (2008) do not describe any linkages among crop and food markets through intermediate input demand and their substitution in consumption.... We need further and more detailed examinations of the impacts of the crop market turbulence with a comprehensive framework of the world trade CGE model that enables us to capture the interaction among markets by alternatively assuming such factors and situations that the earlier studies do not consider. (Tanaka & Hosoe, 2011, p. 4)

A number of empirical studies have examined the relationship between institutions and FDI.... Going through aforementioned studies, it becomes apparent that the majority of the studies assume a linear relationship between institutional quality and FDI flows and employ static or dynamic panel methodologies. This may not be a plausible assumption because.... In this paper, we attempt to contribute to the literature by analyzing the nonlinear impact of institutional factors on foreign direct investment flows using a dynamic panel threshold methodology recently developed by Kremer et al. (2013). To the best of our knowledge, none of the studies in the literature have applied this method to examine the relation between FDI and institutional quality. (Kurul, 2017, p. 149)

Two general approaches have been widely used to assess the welfare impact of public spending: (1) benefit incidence studies, and (2) behavioural approaches. Previous benefit incidence studies (Canagarajah and Ye, 2001; Demery et al., 1995) suggest that, in Ghana, the poorest quintile received about 16 percent of total education subsidies in 1992. Relevant as these studies may still be, their data is nearly 20 years old, suggesting the value of some updated estimates. Besides, by assigning the same unit costs to all users of public services, the benefit incidence approach assumes that all users benefit equally from public services. Again, the benefits incidence method does not have behavioural foundations and therefore cannot be used for policy simulations. On the other hand, the behavioural approach—also called the willingness-to-pay (WTP) method—has often tended to gloss over the distributional implications of the demand estimates (Younger 1999) and the expenditures financing those public services. Thus, we use a combination of benefit incidence and behavioural (willingness-to-pay) approaches to analyse the welfare impact of public education expenditures (Younger 1999). (Gaddah & Munro, 2011, p. 2)

The very few studies that have distinguished between the foreign and domestic education of immigrants took place in the late 1980s and early 1990s and used limited cross-sectional data, mostly from the Census. For example, a 1985 study by Chiswick and Miller used a single year of 1981 Census data and found that immigrants' foreign education was associated with the lowest returns, especially for NESB immigrants. Chapman and Iredale (1993), using cross-sectional data collected in 1988 by the former Office of Multicultural Affairs and a random sample of native-born individuals, assessed the prevalence and impact of non-recognition of overseas qualifications. Their sample, however, allowed conclusions to be drawn only regarding NESB immigrants. They found that Australian education received significantly greater returns than foreign education, and that NESB immigrants with only foreign education were treated relatively homogenously in the labour market regardless of the formal qualifications they had attained in their origin country. This study continues in the same vein as these earlier papers and it contributes to the Australian literature by using a much richer and more recent source of data that spans the last fifteen years. Notably, this paper allows for both:

(i)   differential returns to foreign and domestic education for ESB and NESB immigrants; and

(ii) differential returns to domestic education between natives, and ESB and NESB immigrants. (Montgomery, 2017, p. 6–7)

Justifying Qualitative Research

Qualitative studies are often justified by appealing to the need to reframe an important issue. An author may claim that the existing view of an issue is outdated, too narrow, ignores an important aspect of the existing condition, or is somehow inappropriate and may propose a new framing of the issue, one that takes into account something that previous research has not. For example, previous research may have framed corruption as a moral issue, but you may want to frame it as a security issue and examine its effects on national security, or previous research may have used a fuzzy definition of organizational success and you may want to use one that better reflects the existing situation in organizations that are relevant to your research.

Another motivation for a qualitative study may be the need to summarize existing research or ongoing policy efforts. For example, a recent focus on a particular topic may have generated a large number of quantitative and/or qualitative studies, but they are rather disparate and represent attempts to look at the topic from different perspectives. You may feel that the time has come to summarize this research as a whole to show how individual studies relate to one another, to previous research, to theory, and/or to policy; what agreements and disagreements exist; and in what direction the entire area may be going. Such a study would require working with existing literature and, possibly, policy-related documents.

Finally, a qualitative study may be justified on the basis of the need for more in-depth, holistic examination of a phenomenon. This may be especially appropriate when the focus of previous research has been on outcomes rather than on processes and when you wish to focus on the processes. Such qualitative studies, however, would require extensive data collection in the form of interviews with participants.

Below are some examples showing how researchers justify qualitative research. Go over them and underline the parts where the authors describe the motivation for their studies. Which words do they use?

Climate change is therefore rightly regarded as one of the most significant threats to global security of the incoming century. But the framing of climate change as a threat to the operation of states and the relationship between states (the normal politics of international relations), privileges certain types of impacts and particular aspects of the climate change challenge. I argue that such framing distorts decision making about climate change. (Adger, 2010, p. 276)

Cammack et al. (2006: 16) observe that, besides the fuzziness that surrounds the definition of fragility, a large–and still growing–number of terms often replace the word fragile 'without a precise change in meaning'….The loosely defined character of the concept of fragility is a disturbing feature from both an academic and a policy-oriented perspective, as it produces an unwarranted perception of coincidence among rather different approaches which use the same jargon. Different underlying definitions of fragility can lead to identifying different countries as fragile, and they can induce the various proponents to argue in favour of diverging sets of priorities to be pursued by the donor community. (Bertoli & Ticci, 2012, p. 212)

Although most research on the political economy of international monetary relations is relatively recent, it has already given rise to interesting and important theoretical approaches, analytical arguments, and empirical conclusions. We summarize this work without attempting to cover exhaustively a complex and rapidly growing literature.… Two interrelated sets of international monetary phenomena require explanation. The first is national: the policy of particular governments towards their exchange rates. The second is global: the character of the international monetary system. (Broz & Frieden, 2001, p. 318)

While [previous quantitative] findings increase knowledge concerning factors associated with homeless-domicile transitions, they do not delineate the processes through which individuals achieved the positive outcome of stable housing. Therefore, building on this previous study, the authors employed qualitative methods to identify and query individuals who had successfully negotiated the exiting process in order to explicate the processes leading to success in achieving stable housing. The focus of this current analysis aimed to identify and describe the processes that empowered previously homeless individuals to exit homelessness and reach housing stability. (Thompson et al., 2004, p. 424)

Common Phrases Used to Describe a Research Gap

A research gap is often indicated with the word *however*, which is followed by a statement of some missing element, or what previous research has not done, or with the word *although,* which is followed by a description of what previous research has done and what it has not yet done. Below are some examples.

> However, **little is known about** the effect of globalization on income inequality.

> However, **little attention has been paid to** the role of foreign investment in income inequality.

However, **few researchers/studies have looked at** the role of exchange rate volatility in a dollarized economy.

However, **few attempts have been made to** investigate the causes of urban homelessness in developed countries.

However, **it remains unclear whether** fiscal decentralization reform can lead to better economic growth in China.

However, **previous research has not addressed** the relationship between trade liberalization and economic growth in Zambia.

However, **to date, researchers have been unable to clarify** the main cause of failure of administrative reforms.

Although previous research has examined the relationship between fiscal decentralization and growth in transition economies, evidence for a causal relationship is lacking.

Although several studies have explored the extent to which this approach might be effective in developed countries, similar research for developing countries is lacking.

Importance of Filling the Gap

A description of a gap is often preceded or followed by an explicit explanation of why filling the gap is important, either for research or for policy. One common way to explain the importance of filling a gap is to appeal to the unique characteristics of your setting or context. Here is an example.

The existing literature on the changing characteristics of international migrant households in the past and at present mostly focuses on Mexico-US migration. This is one of the largest migration corridors in the world (UN, 2015), and the research on this corridor has accumulated detailed longitudinal data on migratory patterns. Similar studies of other areas are needed to determine whether the changing pattern of migrant households found in the Mexico-US case can explain migration patterns in other parts of the world. Each migratory route is built on unique economic and social conditions within diverse institutional frameworks that affect labor mobility, so the characteristics of migrant households may differ substantially among regions. This study makes an inquiry into socio-economic characteristics of international migrant households using the case of Bangladesh. (Kikkawa & Otsuka, 2016, p. 5)

CONTRIBUTION OF THE STUDY

The word *contribution* in a research context refers to ways in which a piece of research extends our theoretical or practical knowledge about an issue. As I said earlier, to some authors, contribution and motivation are synonymous or at least very similar. To me, the difference is in how these two elements are described in a paper.

Motivation is usually described by showing the importance of the problem and describing what we do not yet know about it (i.e., a research gap). The focus is on what is lacking from existing research. In contrast, contribution is described by showing how the particular study extends, expands, or advances existing academic knowledge or how it adds to a policy debate. To put it differently, motivation answers the question, "Why did you do this study?" whereas contribution answers the question, "Why should we care about your study?"

The first question, Why did you do this study, is answered by showing that there has not been enough research on an important problem, that previous research findings have been mixed, and/or that previous research has had limitations. The second question, Why should we care about your study, is answered by describing the conceptual, methodological, or other advantages of the study and highlighting its results.

For example, a study may be motivated by the fact that there has been little research on a particular important issue; the contribution part will then describe in detail how the study adds to the existing literature and highlight its particular strengths such as the use of an improved methodology, a richer or more appropriate data set, or a more rigorous estimation strategy.

Below are some examples of how authors describe their studies' contribution. Go over them and underline the parts where the authors describe the contribution of their studies. Which words and phrases do they use?

In this paper, we will contribute to the existing empirical literature on the determinants of credit booms in a number of ways. First, previous studies focus their analyses on advanced and emerging market economies. Some of them even combine data from such countries together into pooled regression analyses, although these countries share broadly different characteristics and stages of development. Instead, our paper will focus on credit booms in developing countries and compare them with those in advanced and emerging market economies. Second, in addition to a binary response probit model, this paper provides the first attempt with a tobit regression model to provide a robustness check on the findings from the probit model and also to identify which factors may potentially trigger magnitude of the booms. Moreover, our econometric approach will focus on the role of domestic policies in curbing or developing credit booms, which are rarely highlighted in previous studies. Finally, we perform our analysis on a broader set of countries. (Meng & Gonzalez, 2016, p. 4)

The aim of this paper is to examine the long-run impact of health, education, exports, imports, R&D, and investment on economic growth for a panel of 5 South Asian countries, namely India, Indonesia, Nepal, Sri Lanka, and Thailand for the period 1974–2007. We consider these 5 Asian countries because they fall in a similar economic growth group. Our study takes the literature forward in a novel way. In studying the relationship between income, health, education, exports, imports, R&D, and investment, we take a production function approach and model the relationship within a panel unit root and panel cointegration with structural breaks framework in order to unravel the long-run relationships among the variables. The main motivation for studying the role of health in economic growth for Asian countries is that the growth of the bigger Asian countries, such as India, has been impressive in the last decade or so. Hence, the ensuing focus has been on determinants of economic growth and productivity in Asian countries in general. One limitation of the literature on the determinants of economic growth is that it has ignored the role of health in economic growth. The exception is Bloom et al. (2009), who examine the role of population health on economic growth in China and India and find improved health has been an important driver of economic growth. This paper aims to fill this research gap. (Narayan et al., 2010, p. 405)

The available literature on corruption and efficiency in customs suggests the extent of the impact of customs corruption and inefficiency on the economy and the importance of addressing this issue. However, despite serious implications of the issue, there have been few empirical studies conducted on the subject of corruption and efficiency in customs agencies. Most research that has been done in this area has been qualitative in nature (e.g., McLinden & Durrani, 2013; Michael & Moore, 2010; Michael et al., 2010; Ndonga, 2013; Stasavage & Daubrée, 1998; Tuan Minh, 2007; Widdowson, 2013). One reason for this is the difficulty in obtaining reliable data on corruption in customs (Michael & Moore, 2010). In this study I aim to contribute to the body of empirical literature on customs corruption and efficiency by analyzing the relationship between these two concepts more systematically. (Ibrahim, 2014, p. 1)

To assess the transferability of immigrants' education credentials, and better discern the drivers of potential native-immigrant differences in labour market outcomes, the returns to foreign and domestic education must be allowed to vary. However, the existing Australian studies do not distinguish between foreign and domestic education. This study addresses this gap. Drawing on the methodology of Friedberg (2000), this study builds on the conventional approach by allowing (i) the returns to foreign and domestic education to vary for immigrants, and (ii) the returns to domestic education to vary between natives and immigrants. Importantly, this analysis is undertaken separately for immigrants from English-speaking backgrounds (ESB) and non-English speaking backgrounds (NESB). As explained in detail later, there are several reasons to suggest that the transferability of human capital held by these cohorts is likely to be different. A further innovation of this study is the use of longitudinal data from the Household, Income and Labour Dynamics in Australia (HILDA) survey. This rich data source helps to address some of the shortcomings of Australian studies that use cross-sectional data. (Montgomery, 2017, pp. 1–2)

Common Phrases Used to Describe a Study's Contribution

Papers in economics and public policy often have a paragraph or a section that explicitly states the study's contribution to academic literature or policy debate. This section usually begins with a sentence announcing that the paper has made an important contribution or several contributions to the literature or policy debate and then describes the contribution in detail. Below are some templates for describing a contribution, which I created using a selection of published studies.

The present paper **contributes to the policy debate** on [name of the topic] **in three ways**. **First, we present** correlations between [some variables] using [describe your data set]. **The second contribution of this paper is** an attempt to identify causality in the correlations between [name your variables]. **The third contribution of our research is to** clarify the effectiveness of [specific] policies.

This paper **contributes to several strands of literature**. **First,** it adds to the growing literature on [name the topic] by [explain how]. **Second,** we add to the literature on [name another aspect of your topic]. **We also** offer a new hypothesis on [name another aspect of the topic].

A number of studies have investigated [my topic] and several theories have been put forward to explain [the relationship I am interested in]. In this paper, **I extend this literature in three directions**. First..., Second..., Third...

Our article adds to the current literature in at least three aspects. **First,** we investigate... So far, the literature on [our topic] has been restricted to.... **Second**, we document a new pattern/correlation/trend that has not yet been described in the economic literature. **Finally,** we demonstrate that [our results].

This paper makes three key contributions. **First,** we replicate/identify/summarize [our topic] by using [our methodology] in [our context]. **Second**, we show that [our findings and what they suggest/imply]. **Third**, we provide evidence on the role of X in Y/the importance of X to Y.

This paper makes a contribution to the literature on [my topic] by applying [my methodology]. **In addition, the findings of the analysis shed light on** the most appropriate economic policy for [the focus of my research] for governments/policymakers.

In an effort to shed light on [an important problem], this article examines [an important relationship]. We used [data and methodology] to identify factors that are most closely associated with [our dependent variables]. **Insights** into this [relationship/topic] **can assist** policymakers **in determining** the most effective interventions to [achieve an important goal].

Chapter 10

Theory and Theoretical Frameworks

Students who are new to graduate study often find the word *theory* confusing. Some equate theory with what great philosophers of the past have said; others believe that it is similar to a historical overview of the field or research area. The problem is compounded by the fact that the words *theory, theoretical framework, theoretical perspective,* and *model* may be used in the literature interchangeably, to mean the same or similar things, or differently by different authors to refer to different things. In this section, I will try to clarify what these terms mean and what you need to do in order to address theory in your paper.

WHAT IS THEORY?

In social sciences, theory has been variously defined as

- A **systematic explanation** for the observations that relate to a particular aspect of life (Babbie, 1998, p. 52).

- A **system of interconnected abstractions** or ideas that condenses and organizes knowledge about the social world (Neuman, 2004, p. 24).

- A set of analytical principles or **statements designed to structure our observations**, understanding and explanation of the world (Nilsen, 2015, p. 2).

What all these definitions have in common is the idea that theory is a means to organize our knowledge about the world in a systematic (=structured) and generalizable (=applicable to a broad class of things) way. Essentially, a theory is a simplified version of reality that shows how things are related and which factors are more important than others in a relationship. In economics, theories are used to represent economic processes; in political science, political process, and so on.

We use theories every day without realizing it. For example, a mother who says to her child, "If you study hard, you'll succeed," puts forward a theory that relates differences in life outcomes (e.g., job attainment, or income) to differences in schooling. However, our everyday theories are casual: They are neither explicit nor well-formed, and therefore, they are not testable. What does it mean, for example, "to study hard" or "to succeed"? How exactly is studying

How to Write about Economics and Public Policy. https://doi.org/10.1016/B978-0-12-813010-0.00010-7

hard related to success? Under what conditions might studying hard lead to positive outcomes? In contrast to casual theories, theories we use in social sciences are explicit—they state clearly how factors are related and under what conditions they may lead to certain outcomes.

In public policy and economics, we use theories to explain

- Why things happen the what they do;
- How economic, social, or political processes work;
- Why certain policies may lead to certain results;
- Why some policies may be more effective than others; and/or
- What we can expect when a particular policy is adopted.

COMPONENTS OF A THEORY

Social theories have these components:

- Concepts and variables,
- Relationships between concepts and variables,
- Predictions that can be derived from a theory, and
- The domain or scope to which a theory applies.

Concepts are abstract ideas—such as *globalization, economic development,* or *poverty*—that are generalized from particular occurrences. When they are defined in a measurable way, they become **variables**. For example, globalization is a concept that can be defined as the extent to which foreign capital dominates a host country's economy, and it can be measured as the ratio of foreign direct investment (FDI) stocks to GDP. The ratio of FDI stocks to GDP is a variable.

Concepts and variables are at the heart of a theory. In fact, one of the main purposes of having a theory in a research project is to identify concepts and variables that are relevant to the research, define them in a way that makes them measurable and researchable, and make a prediction about how they are related, in what contexts, and under what conditions.

For example, a theory of economic growth may have the following concepts: *labor productivity, capital intensity, labor efficiency, output per worker, saving rate, depreciation,* and *investment.* It may describe how the economy changes over time as a result of increased output per worker, which in turn results from labor force growth, investment, technological progress, and improved social organization. The theory may predict that investment would lead to capital intensity, and that technological progress would lead to increased labor efficiency. Finally, the theory may pertain to all countries, or it may pertain primarily to developed countries and may be less applicable to developing countries.

A theory of leadership may have the following concepts: *leader, follower, motivation, job satisfaction, public values, contingent rewards, extrinsic rewards,* and *employee performance.* It may postulate a positive relationship between a certain style of leadership and the outcomes of employee performance or a negative relationship between certain types of reward and employee job satisfaction. Furthermore, it may pertain to institutions rather than individuals or small groups, and it may be used to derive specific predictions such as that when leaders provide a clear vision, articulate clear performance expectations, and stimulate employees intellectually, the employees' performance and job satisfaction increase.

To theorize, therefore, means to make justifiable predictions (often called *propositions*) about how various concepts and variables are related, under what conditions, in what direction, how strongly, and, sometimes, why. **Justifiable predictions** are those that can be explained and supported. In economics and public policy research, this explanation can be narrative or mathematical. Narrative explanations draw on previous research (both theoretical and empirical) or on logical *if…then* statements, and sometimes, on both. Mathematical explanations use equations to show how, in theory, a particular process should work.

THEORY ACROSS DISCIPLINES

All research uses theory or is related to theory in one way or another; in fact, theory is one of the main attributes that distinguish research from other, less systematic, approaches to human inquiry. But disciplines differ greatly with regard to theory in at least three important ways:

- The kinds of theory that are used,
- How theories are used (e.g., to what phenomena a theory may apply), and
- How theories are described in a paper.

For example, economics operates from a tight body of well-established, formal theories such as

- **The Public Choice Theory**, a theory that explains government decision-making as a result of the actions of individual, self-interested public policy actors, who make decisions as civil servants or elected officials.

- **Game Theory**, a theory that explains how people make decisions in competing situations where the outcome depends on the actions of the other actors.

- **Utility Maximization Theory**, a theory that explains consumer behavior, or how consumers, who are assumed to be rational and trying to obtain the most value for their money, make decisions and allocate their limited resources.

Political science, sociology, and psychology also have many well-developed, formal theories, which provide a starting point for researchers working in these disciplines. For example:

- **Elite Theory**, a theory in political science that explains how power relations and the preferences of economic, cultural, and governing elites (e.g., Wall Street bankers, corporate executives, elected officials) affect public policy.

- **Conflict Theory**, a theory in sociology that views society as being in a state of conflict, where groups with competing interests struggle for power and where social order is maintained through domination and violence.

- **Cognitive Dissonance Theory**, a theory in psychology that explains how people who are forced to commit acts that violate their positive self-image modify their attitudes toward their own actions to avoid an uncomfortable state of mental suffering or discomfort.

However, researchers do not always make use of well-established, formal theories. Often, they use rather loose theories, which may not even be called theories, or may borrow theories from other areas. This is especially true of research in public policy, which is often interdisciplinary, combining research strands from different disciplines. Researching problems in public policy will often necessitate creating theoretical frameworks for the particular problem under study by borrowing theories, concepts, and perspectives from various disciplines or research areas.

Thus, instead of using a formal theory in a study, a researcher might use a *theoretical* or *conceptual framework.* These frameworks are simply statements made on the basis of some consistent findings of previous research, which has been organized in some way to show what concepts and variables are relevant to the particular research question and how those concepts and variables are related. In such a framework, researchers may discuss competing theories, definitions of relevant concepts and variables, specific approaches or strategies that have been used to study a problem, and their own expectations and predictions. All of these components will form a theoretical, or conceptual, framework for a study. In this sense, the terms *theoretical framework, conceptual framework,* and *theory* are often used synonymously and interchangeably and may differ only to the extent to which the theory that a researcher uses is a formally established one.

A related term that is often used with regard to theory is *theoretical perspective.* Some researchers use this term synonymously with the term *theoretical framework.* To others, however, it may have a broader meaning and denote the lens through which a researcher might look at a problem. The same problem can be looked at very differently from the perspective of different disciplines or different areas within the same discipline. The perspective that we adopt will determine our approach including how we frame the problem and design the study.

For example, a rise in obesity, traditionally an epidemiological problem, can be examined from different perspectives, including epidemiological, psychological, and economic. From an epidemiological perspective, we may frame the problem of obesity as a public health issue and focus on the patterns and time trends, associated diseases, obesity population dynamics, environmental causes, and the prevalence of obesity in certain populations. If we look at the problem from a psychological perspective, we may focus on the genetic influences of obesity, psychological outcomes of obesity such as mood disturbances, or social consequences of obesity such as stigmatization of people suffering from the disease. And if we look at the same problem from an economic perspective, we may focus on obesity-related mortality, frame the problem as a household health production function, and estimate the relationship between diet, health care, and obesity-related mortality using aggregate, rather than individual-level, data. In each of these cases, the specific questions that we will formulate, the factors that we will look at, and the tools that we will use will be different and will be motivated by the chosen theoretical perspective.

In economics, the terms *theoretical framework* and *theoretical perspective* may refer to yet another way to think about theory—as a series of if…then statements that are used to describe an economic or a decision-making process and justify particular expectations. These statements usually culminate in a series of hypotheses, which are then tested using empirical data.

ROLE OF THEORY IN RESEARCH

Why do we need a theory or a theoretical framework when conducting research? The main reason is the enormous complexity of the world around us and of the various phenomena that we may wish to study. Suppose that you want to investigate factors related to trade liberalization. There are literally dozens of such factors including the degree of a country's openness, exchange rate, population, GDP growth rate, gross capital formation, per capita GDP, and so on. How would you know which ones to include in your investigation? How would you know which ones may be more important than others and under what conditions? More important, which factors cause trade liberalization and which ones are caused by it? Which ones are merely associated with trade liberalization? And what exactly does trade liberalization mean? How can it be measured? Are some measures better than others? You need a theory to answer these questions.

Or how would you approach the relationship between women empowerment and economic growth? How would you know which causes which? Is it women empowerment that leads to economic growth or economic growth that leads to women empowerment? As it turns out, both are plausible scenarios. Again, to postulate a relationship between women empowerment and economic growth, you need to have a theory.

In a quantitative study, we use theory to postulate relationships, justify the choice of specific definitions and variables, and make predictions. For example, we may use a theory of electoral politics to justify the expectation of a particular outcome in recent Japanese elections by showing how various voter characteristics—such as age, gender, education, and social class—affect voting decisions. Or we may use a theory of decision-making to make predictions about individuals' responses to a particular policy initiative such as an initiative to raise the price of gasoline.

Here is an example of the use of a theoretical framework in a quantitative study. In a study of the relationship between competition policy and investment, Sasatra Sudsawasd (2010) examines the effect of market competition policy on investment in Southeast Asia. The main theoretical considerations in his study relate to the definition of competition policy and the choice of an investment model. Sudsawasd selects seven indicators of competition policy based on a broad definition of the concept in the IMD's *World Competitiveness Yearbook*: legal and regulatory framework, protectionism, public sector contracts, foreign investors, competition legislation, subsidies, and price controls; measures for these variables come from an executive opinion survey. Sudsawasd then extends an earlier investment model to include the seven selected measures of competition policy and evaluates the effect of this variable on investment. Together, the definition of competition policy, the seven measures selected as its indicators, and the modified investment model form a *theoretical framework* for the study.

In a qualitative study, theory may be used to shape the direction of the study. For example, a theory explaining why violent conflicts occur in particular countries at particular times and how political instability affects economic growth can be used to help choose a case study and formulate questions about pre- and postconflict politics and economy. Or a researcher may use a theory of power relations to examine the role of the defense industry in weapons procurement policy or the role of drug companies in healthcare policy.

Here is an example of the use of a theoretical framework in a qualitative study. In a study of successful economic reforms in Asia, Dennis Arroyo (2008) reviews approaches used by past Asian leaders to overcome political obstacles to economic reforms and identifies a range of political maneuvers that were effective. At the beginning of the paper, he provides a definition of economic reform, outlines its scope, and then lists, with reference to relevant literature, several obstacles to economic reform, or reasons that explain why economic reforms may be politically difficult. These reasons include ideological polarization of policy players, patronage, rent-seeking by vested interests, lack of support from the party center, bureaucratic inertia, and economic hardships associated with the reforms. Together, they provide a theoretical framework for the study: The author uses these reasons to examine past leaders' approach to economic reforms and show how the leaders minimized the impact of these obstacles. The author does not use the words *theory* or *theoretical framework* in the article, and yet, the literature-based framework he describes provides a clear direction for examining and answering the research question.

In another qualitative study, Lee (2016) examines Chinese foreign policy from the perspective of Social Identity Theory, an influential theory in social psychology that explains how social groups strive to maintain a positive identity. He uses the concepts of respect and disrespect to develop a theoretical framework for examining Chinese strategies and actions in international politics and applies this framework to the analysis of specific conflicts. He concludes that "China's rise would be more peaceful than threatening" (p. 29).

Do all empirical studies have a theoretical framework? Yes, in some form or other. Virtually all quantitative studies have a theoretical framework, which is stated more or less explicitly and contains, at the very least, definitions of key variables and statements about their expected relationships, which are supported with relevant literature.

With qualitative research, there may be more variability and less explicitness in the presentation of theory. However, as many researchers have pointed out (e.g., Merriam, 1998; Sandelowski, 1993), theory is always present in a qualitative study however implicitly—and it is evident in how a problem is framed and presented, how the literature is selected and reviewed, how the study is designed and executed, and what interpretations are made and conclusions, drawn.

Do nonempirical studies have a theoretical framework? That depends. Many nonempirical studies are essentially literature reviews and in such studies, there is usually no theoretical framework. However, some nonempirical studies are theoretical essays in which the author explores a phenomenon, describes changes and trends, or provides a theoretical analysis of a concept. Such studies usually have a theoretical framework, which delineates the scope and direction of the analysis. Here is an example.

In a qualitative, literature-based study of the role of management in organizational performance, Boyne (2004) looks at the impact of various public management variables on organizational performance in the public sector. He first develops a theoretical framework for assessing the impact of public management strategies on organizational performance, which consists of three broad groups of strategies that managers have at their disposal for improving organizational performance—change the environment, change the organization, or change the product. Boyne then reviews empirical studies on management and performance, assessing the importance of each of the variables he has identified as related to managerial performance. He concludes that management does matter for performance.

WHERE SHOULD MY THEORY COME FROM?

A theory for your study can come from the academic fields of economics, political science, psychology, sociology, or any other area of social science. Begin reading about your topic as early in your research as possible. Explore the existing body of knowledge to discover the theories that researchers use to explain phenomena in your research area. Keep in mind that disciplines and research areas differ on what specific theories they use and how they use them. Focus on studies that are as close to your research area as possible—they will provide the most useful models. Remember also that theory may not always be described as a theory in a study. It could be presented simply as a framework of consistent findings of previous research.

As you read the literature on your topic, note the following:

- Main concepts and variables that are related to your research question,

- Most common definitions for your concepts and variables,

- Consistent findings showing how your concepts and variables are related,

- Conditions or constraints that may modify these relationship, and

- Various predictions and expectations regarding the relationships between your concepts or variables and the specific contribution of each of your variables to these relationships.

Using this information, try to develop a theoretical framework for your own study. A graphical representation of all the relationships you have identified can be especially helpful.

THEORIES VS. MODELS IN ECONOMICS

How are models different from theories? As Nilsen (2015) points out, the difference between a model and a theory is not always clear. In fact, in economics, for example, theoretical models are often used synonymously with theory. Generally, however, models tend to be more specific and more precise than theories and they are derived from theories. For example, Neugeboren (2005) states that "a model is a theory rendered in precise, usually mathematical, terms" (p. 18). Other authors (e.g., Kraft & Furlong, 2015) point to the descriptive nature of models and argue that models are less concerned with explanation than theories are.

Models have two main uses: to predict and to simulate. In economics and public policy, models are often used to predict the effects of past or future policy actions. For example, how will climate change affect the environment? What will be the effect of a new housing subsidy on housing decisions? Will reduced class size improve students' achievement test scores? Prediction can also be backward-looking, as Neugeboren (2005) points out. In this case, the analyst would look at a past event and try to predict a particular outcome that has already occurred in the past. For example, the analyst may ask, "How did Hurricane Katrina affect housing prices in New Orleans?" The results of this estimation can then be used to forecast how major hurricanes may affect housing prices.

Models can also be used to simulate what might happen if there is a change in one or more variables, *other things being equal*. For example, using an economic model, economists can simulate, other things being equal, the effect of trade barriers on bilateral trade or the impact of productivity shocks in major crops on food security. As previous authors have pointed out, models generally work better for simulating changes than for predicting them. This is because in simulation, researchers usually manipulate a small number of variables and keep everything else constant. Prediction, on the other hand, requires making many assumptions about long-term trends and other uncertain developments. The further out the prediction, the less can be taken for granted and the harder it is to predict.

All models are based on **assumptions**, which reflect certain perspectives and views of reality. The validity of these assumptions—the extent to which they accurately reflect the real world—should not be taken for granted but should be assessed critically. In fact, economists sometimes create models that are based on assumptions that are violated in the real world. Pfleiderer (2014) has called such models *chameleons*. It is important to distinguish, however, between the validity of a model's assumptions and the precision of its predictions, which is a function of its internal consistency (Putt & Springer, 1989). A model may give a precise estimate of a 4% inflation for a given year, but if it is based on unrealistic or incomplete assumptions about how the economy will develop, its estimates will not accurately predict what will happen. As Putt and Springer have argued, to have value, models do not need to be 100% accurate representations of reality; however, the value of a model as a predictive device will often depend on the degree to which it accurately represents real-world behavior. If a model is based on unrealistic assumptions, its estimates will not be accurate, even though they may be precise.

PLACEMENT OF THEORY IN A PAPER

A research paper may not necessarily have a separate section called Theory or Theoretical Framework. This is because researchers often weave in their theory into the section where they review relevant literature, for example, in the Literature Review section, in the Introduction, or in a section with a thematic title. In fact, many, if not most, articles in economics and public policy do not have a separate section devoted to theory. Instead, they describe relevant theory (or several competing theories) and theoretical predictions in the same section where they describe previous research.

In a quantitative study, the theoretical framework is always described before the methodology because its purpose is to justify the selection of particular variables and their measurement and the hypotheses that will be tested. In a qualitative study, the place of theory in a paper is more variable and will often depend on the purpose and methodology used. For example, in many qualitative studies, theory is used to shape the direction of the study and the selection of the appropriate methodology. In this case, theory will be placed at the beginning of the study, much like in a quantitative paper. Alternatively, some qualitative research aims at developing a theory in order to explain particular observations. In this case, theory will be placed at the end of a study, usually in a special section, and it will be presented as emerging from the empirical observations. In such a study, the development of a theory is a main purpose of the study.

DESCRIBING THEORY IN A PAPER

There are three common ways of presenting a theory, theoretical model, or theoretical framework in a paper: by using a narrative, by using a visual, or by using mathematics (e.g., a series of simultaneous equations). By far, the most common way to present a theory or theoretical framework in a public policy or economics paper is by using a narrative. In fact, in my corpus of 400+ studies from 40 journals and several working paper series in public policy and economics, more than 90% used a narrative description or a narrative description with a visual model to present a theoretical framework. Less than 10% used equations, and those descriptions were usually limited to very technical, theoretical articles.

Narrative descriptions are sometime strengthened with visual models. This is a good strategy for three reasons. First, creating a visual representation of a complex relationship often helps you clarify the connections between the variables and understand the relationship more deeply. Second, visual models help readers grasp your points and understand your arguments better. Third, for some writers, it may actually be easier to describe a visual than to present clearly connected logical statements in a narrative description. This may be especially true of novice writers, especially those who are new to their discipline. Keep in mind, however, that all visuals that are included in a paper must be explained: Do not just assume that the reader will understand what your model represents; walk the reader through the model, explaining each part clearly.

Many descriptions of theoretical frameworks follow a similar pattern: An author begins by reviewing several alternative or competing theories, providing an evaluation of each theory's explanatory power for the problem under study. This evaluation can be more or less critical and can focus on how much empirical support a theory has received or how logical it is, or both. An example of such a description can be seen in a paper by Mariyam Rashfa (Box 24). Competing theories are often described beginning with the less plausible or applicable one(s), which will not be used in the study, and ending with the one that the author finds more plausible or applicable and that will be used in the study. This theory is often described in greater detail. Examples of this approach are Fafchamps (Box 25), Roberts (Box 26), and Li (Box 27).

Following an evaluation of a theory, authors often describe what the theory predicts. This description can be in the form of formal hypotheses or informal expectations. Sometimes authors will derive alternative hypotheses from each theory (Box 28); other times, they will use alternative theories to show that they all lead to the same prediction (Box 29).

Often, authors will describe an existing theory or theories and then suggest a modification—for example, by adding a new variable or variables. This approach is demonstrated by Zlotnick et al. (Box 30) and Maparara (Box 31). An alternative way to describe a theoretical framework is to focus on the variables rather than on the theories. Using this approach, an author may focus on variable selection and classification and/or on explaining how each predictor variable is related to the dependent variable(s), and, possibly, why. Examples of such frameworks are shown in Boxes 32 and 33.

Narrative Descriptions

This section shows examples of theoretical frameworks described in narrative form. They come from a wide selection of published and unpublished research in public policy and economics. Go over these frameworks and note the organization of these sections. What are the authors doing in each paragraph? What is their purpose? Formulate it clearly. Then look at the language that the authors use to achieve their purpose, paying special attention to the following aspects.

- The use of **modal verbs** (e.g., *may, might, can*). When do the authors use these verbs? What do you think is the purpose of using these verbs?

- The use of **linguistic markers** (e.g., *thus, consequently, similarly, as a consequence, assuming that, in principle*). As I explained in Chapter 1, these markers have many purposes including to help guide the reader through the flow of the text and show the author's attitude toward the information the author presents. As you go through the extracts, underline these markers and think about their specific purpose.

- The **verbs** used to present and discuss theories, describe expectations, and outline variables. Write them out. Which verbs are used most commonly? In what specific contexts are they used?

Box 24 shows a theoretical framework from a policy-oriented study of the determinants of inflation in the Maldives. This study was done by Mariyam Rashfa, a graduate student in Macroeconomic Policy. Notice the organization of her theoretical framework: She outlines three theories of inflation, briefly describes their predictions, and then evaluates each theory by summarizing empirical support for each.

Box 25 shows a theoretical framework from a study of the role of ethnicity in access to bank credit in African manufacturing conducted by Marcel Fafchamps (2000). The purpose of this theoretical framework is to explain how the main variables, allocation of credit and ethnicity, are related. Notice the organization of Fafchamps' framework: The author first names all relevant theories, providing citations, and then describes and evaluates each one. Notice that his description starts with those theories that he finds rather deficient and ends with the one that he finds more plausible and that will form the theoretical basis for his study. This is a common way to organize a review of theories in a study—proceeding from those that the author finds more deficient and that will not be used or tested to those that the author finds more plausible and applicable and that will be tested in the study. Notice also that Fafchamps devotes twice as much space to the theory that he will test than to the other theories.

Box 26 shows a theoretical framework from a qualitative study by Andrew Roberts (2009) examining healthcare reform in postcommunist countries in Europe. Notice that just as in theoretical frameworks in quantitative studies, here, too, the author does not merely describe various theories of health reform but also evaluates them against empirical evidence. Notice also that he starts with the less plausible ones and ends with the one that he believes is most applicable to his study.

Box 27 is a theoretical framework from a study by Xueyao Li (2017), a graduate student in Public Policy, on a topic in international relations—Japan's engagement in UN peacekeeping operations. Notice the organization of this framework. In the first paragraph, the author introduces the problem and names the more traditional theories that have been applied to the problem. In the second paragraph, she describes how each theory would view the problem under study. In the next paragraph, she gives an evaluation of these theories and argues that they cannot provide a satisfactory explanation for the problem. She then describes a more applicable framework and its advantages. Again, as we have seen previously, the framework that is the last to be described is the one that is used in the study.

Box 28 is a theoretical framework from a study of banking sector globalization by Amit Ghosh (2017). As you read, notice the tentative language the author uses to theorize about the relationship between banking sector globalization and economic growth, which is especially noticeable in the use of modal verbs.

Box 29 is a theoretical framework from a study of decentralization and terror by Alex Dreher and Justina Fischer (2011). Here, the authors review two alternative theories, both leading to the same prediction—that decentralization should reduce terror. Notice the tentative language the authors use when describing their predictions and the use of various linguistic markers. What do you think is the purpose of using such tentative language?

The framework shown in Box 30 comes from a study of homelessness by Cheryl Zlotnick and coworkers (1999). Here, the authors describe a model of homelessness that consists of four domains and connect it to a framework proposed by a previous researcher that predicts successful exists from homelessness. The previous framework consists of four broad concepts—dysfunction, human capital, disaffiliation, and cultural identification. The authors review each concept and explain, using previous research, how it is related to the outcome variable—achieving stable housing—and how it can be measured. Then, they extend this framework by adding a fifth dimension, economic resources, and test how well the new model predicts exits from homelessness in homeless adults. Notice how the authors describe the relevant concepts, their indicators, and possible measures. Notice also how they propose a new component to be included in the existing model and how they explain why the proposed component might be relevant.

Box 31 is a theoretical framework from a study that investigated the direction of causality between government expenditure and economic growth for Southern African Development Community (SADC) countries. It was written by Itai Maparara, a graduate student in Public Finance. The author begins by reviewing several theories that explain the relationship between government expenditure and economic growth. Notice how the review moves from a more formal discussion of theories to a less formal discussion of the role of trade and how the author theorizes why trade may be related to economic growth. Notice also that he does not simply summarize the theories—he also tries to evaluate their usefulness, applicability, and the strength of empirical support. Finally, notice how he uses the discussion of the role of trade to justify the inclusion of one of the key variables in his study.

The framework shown in Box 32 comes from a study of determinants of parental saving, which was conducted by Don Hossler and Nick Vesper (1993). It is very short, and its purpose is to name and group the variables that the authors have identified as being related to the dependent variables as well as to outline predictions. In this paper, the authors used numbers for citations, which I removed for convenience.

Box 33 shows a theoretical framework from a study by Seema Narayan and coworkers (2010), who used the production function framework to model a relationship between health and economic growth. Here, the authors identify several variables that they hypothesize as being related to economic growth and explain why these variables should be included in the model.

BOX 24 Theoretical Framework from a Study of Determinants of Inflation

There is extensive literature on determinants of inflation and various models have been used by researchers to identify the causes of inflation in both developed and developing countries. One of the most well-known theories of inflation states that inflation is always and everywhere a monetary phenomenon (Friedman, 1963). Several empirical studies have found excess money supply to be a major determinant of inflation. For example, using a VAR model, Montiel (1988) found increases in the monetary base and exchange rate to be the main sources of inflation in Argentina and Brazil during their high inflation episodes, whereas Liu and Adediuji (2000) observed that excess money supply was the main determinant of inflation in the Islamic Republic of Iran. According to Lim and Papi (1997), inflation in Turkey was also found to be driven by monetary variables.

Another widely established view is the fiscal view of inflation, which states that the government budget constraint can create inflation if it is financed by increasing the monetary base (Fischer & Easterly, 1990). Although in their study of the economics of government budget, Fischer and Easterly found a low correlation between

Continued

BOX 24 Theoretical Framework from a Study of Determinants of Inflation—cont'd.

fiscal deficits and inflation (which was partly explained by the deficit reduction programs that were inflationary and the slow adjustment of the economy to inflation), they concluded, referring to the massive rates of inflation experienced by countries with high budget deficits, that high fiscal deficits sooner or later lead to increases in inflation. Meanwhile, Cottarelli, Griffith, and Monaghan (1998) concluded that there is a strong relationship between high fiscal deficits and an increase in inflation in countries where the government securities market is less developed. Also, Lim and Papi (1997) found government deficits to be important contributors to inflation in Turkey.

The exchange rate is another important channel that can contribute to wide swings in inflation according to the *balance of payments* view of inflation (Ghosh, Gulde, Ostry, & Wolf, 1996; Montiel, 1989). Although pegged exchange rate regimes are widely associated with low and stable rates of inflation relative to the rates with more flexible regimes, countries with less stable macroeconomic policies — which often lead to frequent parity changes— are often subject to more volatile and higher inflation rates. This finding was supported by Ghosh et al. (1996) in a cross-sectional study of exchange rate and inflation, which found that inflation averaged 7 percent in countries with fixed exchange rate regimes, 13 percent in countries that had frequent revisions of exchange rate parity, and 17 percent in countries with more flexible regimes. According to Ghosh et al., (1996) low inflation from pegging the exchange rate comes from both the disciplinary effect (arising from the cost of abandoning the peg, which forces governments and central banks to pursue only policies that support the peg) and the credibility effect (which increases the demand for foreign currency). Furthermore, using a recursive VAR, Louganis and Swagel (2001) analyzed sources of inflation in developing countries and concluded that monetary variables had a smaller impact on inflation in countries with fixed exchange rate regimes compared with those with flexible exchange rate regimes. In analyzing inflation in the Gulf Cooperation Council countries using a Vector Error Correction Model, Kandil and Morsy (2009) found that, with the exception of Kuwait, the depreciation of the US dollar against the major trading partner currencies contributed to inflation in these countries. Further empirical support for the balance of payments view comes from Montiel (1989), who argued that nominal exchange rate devaluation can contribute to high and persistent inflation as experienced by Argentina and Brazil. (Rashfa, 2012, pp. 8–9)

BOX 25 Theoretical Framework from a Study of Ethnicity and Access to Credit

Conceptually, there are several ways by which ethnicity may influence the allocation of credit, (e.g., through taste for discrimination, Becker, 1971; Akerlof, 1985), erroneous expectations or 'prejudice' (e.g., Yinger, 1998), difficulties of communication across cultural boundaries (e.g., Cornell and Welch, 1996; Loury, 1998), statistical discrimination (e.g., Arrow, 1972; Coate and Loury, 1993), and network effects (e.g., Saloner, 1985; Montgomery, 1991; Taylor, 1997). There is widespread disagreement as to the relative empirical contributions these mechanisms make to ethnic and gender bias in labor and credit markets. Becker (1971), for instance, has argued that prejudice and taste for discrimination are costly and should result in lower profits. In a competitive environment, he argues, firms that discriminate on the basis of taste or maintain erroneous expectations should, in the long run, be competed out by more open-minded, better informed businesses. Becker's view has not gone unchallenged, however.

Unlike prejudice and tastes, statistical discrimination is perfectly compatible with the profit-seeking motive and cannot, therefore, be competed out. Whenever firms cannot assess clients and suppliers directly, it is rational for them to screen on the basis of whatever observable information they can collect. If groups of different race or gender differ in unobservable attributes, statistical discrimination will arise. The role that it plays in explaining actual ethnic bias has, however, been the object of much debate. In addition, the presence of statistical discrimination is extremely difficult to prove since it requires the econometrician to have as much if not more information about applicants than employers themselves (e.g., Darity, 1998).

Network effects have received somewhat less attention in the discrimination literature, but they have long been studied in labor markets (e.g., Granovetter, 1995). The basic idea is that information about opportunities for exchange and agents' types circulates along interpersonal networks. People talk with their friends and professional acquaintances about jobs, bad payers, and arbitrage opportunities, and they refer job and credit applicants to each other. In such environment, individuals with better networks collect more accurate information, which enables them to seek out market opportunities more aggressively and to better screen prospective employees and credit recipients. A rapidly growing literature has modeled these processes and has shown that, in a world of imperfect information, they provide an economic advantage to better connected agents (e.g., Kranton, 1996; Taylor, 1997; Fafchamps, 1998).

To the extent that members of a particular group cultivate close links with each other, be it for historical or cultural reasons, the group will be seen to perform better than others in market exchange. If this group recruits its members primarily along ethnic or gender lines, ethnic or gender bias will occur although, strictly speaking, agents need not have a taste for discrimination and they need not rely on statistical discrimination. Network effects thus put the emphasis on patterns of socialization as an alternative explanation for ethnic or gender bias. The primary objective of this paper is to assess how much of the observed ethnic and gender bias in African enterprise credit can be attributed to network effects. (Fafchamps, 2000, pp. 207–208)

BOX 26 Theoretical Framework from a Study of Healthcare Reform

What do existing theories have to say about choices among these alternatives? Early works focused on the causal impact of rising national income; richer states spend more on healthcare (Wilensky, 1975). But these theories were inadequate for explaining the distinctive institutional forms that healthcare takes. Concerning Eastern Europe, these theories would point out that they had 'premature welfare states'; they spent more on healthcare than other states at similar income levels (Kornai and McHale, 2000). One would thus expect them to cut spending when they were exposed to the free market. In fact, healthcare spending remained stable or grew in the three countries considered here; over the first five years of the transition, sspending rose from 5.0 per cent to 7.8 per cent of GDP in the Czech Republic, from 5.2 per cent to 6.9 per cent in Hungary, and from 3.5 per cent to 4.9 per cent in Poland (Chelleraj et al., 1996).

A second wave of theories has emphasized the power of interest groups, particularly physicians (Starr 1982). Physicians are an important force in policy making because their livelihoods are most directly affected by healthcare institutions. Patients for their part are more concerned with coverage than with complicated financing and payment schemes whose effects are not always clear. Immergut (1992) put a useful twist on these accounts by noting that what physicians want to avoid is a government monopsony. Confronting multiple purchasers increases their bargaining power.

While such accounts are correct in putting physicians at the center of the policy process, differences in doctors' socio economic position do not correlate well with cross-national differences (Immergut, 1992). Physicians are similarly organized and have similar resources in most advanced democracies. This applies as well to Eastern Europe where physicians had a similar place in the occupational hierarchy and were present in similar numbers. Even differences in the willingness of physicians to engage in contentious action do not alter this conclusion. Polish physicians were the most strike-prone in the region, but the least successful at getting their way (Ekiert and Kubik, 1999). While the power of physicians is important, it does not explain different policy choices.

In place of these theories, something of a consensus has emerged that political institutions determine whether a country can alter its healthcare system. If political institutions give doctors the ability to veto changes in the direction of greater state control, they will do so. Immergut thus found that countries with more veto points tend to have more market-oriented health sectors (also Maioni, 1998; Steinmo and Watts, 1995). Institutions like referenda, separation of powers, and fragmented party systems allow societal actors, particularly physicians, to block moves away from the market-oriented status quo and towards statist healthcare. Stable parliamentary majorities and executive dominance have the opposite effect. Tuohy (1999) introduces an important wrinkle in these accounts, arguing that reforms can only take place during relatively rare windows of opportunity; otherwise interest groups have a relatively strong veto over major reforms. Institutions in short provide the points where interest groups—particularly physicians but latterly health insurers—can block change.

BOX 26 Theoretical Framework from a Study of Healthcare Reform—cont'd.

What is less emphasized in these, and in fact many institutionalist accounts, is an explanation of the motive forces for change. Most studies persuasively show how changes are blocked, but they do not explain why or how they come about (though see Hacker, 1997). They typically assume constant pressures towards greater state control, which may or may not be blocked by physicians and insurers. What is needed is a better understanding of the motive forces for change, of how actors get access to the policymaking arm of the state. Institutions are important not only in providing blocking points, but in opening windows of opportunity for change. (Roberts, 2009, pp. 308–309)

BOX 27 Theoretical Framework from a Study in International Relations

Japan's engagement in United Nations (UN) peacekeeping operations as an element of Japan's foreign policy is often examined within the framework of International Relations (IR) theory. Realism, liberalism, and constructivism are the main theoretical tools used to analyze the rationale underlying Japan's peacekeeping policy.

Realists argue that the Japanese state, as a rational and interest-driven actor, makes calculated moves to use its engagement in UN peacekeeping operations to enhance its national influence and to strengthen its bilateral ties with the US (Hatakeyama, 2014). Liberalists maintain that the UN provides a legitimate platform for its member states to contribute to peace and security through military, economic, and humanitarian means, which will in turn benefit all states (Mochizuki, 2007). From the liberalist perspective, then, Japan's contribution to UN peacekeeping operations is an expression of its obligation to create favorable conditions, in cooperation with other member states, for common prosperity. The increasingly popular constructivist approach places strong emphasis on Japan's norm-driven policy changes, focusing on both Japan's internalization of international norms and its own security identity shifts, urged by domestic political leaders and gradually endorsed by the general public (Dobson, 2003).

Each of these three IR approaches contributes in some way to an understanding of the rationale behind Japan's policy shift from non-participation to participation in UN peacekeeping operations. Nevertheless, these approaches do not provide a satisfactory explanation of the unique factors that characterize Japanese peacekeeping contribution at a given time. Arguably, it would be more appropriate to examine the rationale behind a state's peacekeeping policies by examining both the motivating and constraining factors that inform the state's decision-making process. Such an examination could create a foundation for further exploration of policy options, which capitalize on the motivating factors and catalyze change regarding the constraining factors.

Bellamy and Williams (2013) have developed a new theoretical framework based on the findings of various case studies for understanding the rationale underlying a state's peacekeeping policies. This framework identifies both the motivating and constraining factors in five different domains, namely, political, security, financial,

Continued

BOX 27 Theoretical Framework from a Study in International Relations—cont'd.

institutional, and normative. Compared with the approaches inherent in the traditional IR theories, this theoretical framework takes into consideration the influence of different factors on a state's decision-making process, but does not attach any arbitrary weighting to the effect of those factors on the state's peacekeeping policies; this leaves room for a contextual analysis of the state's actual decision-making. Given these advantages of the Bellamy and Williams theoretical framework, this study will use this framework to explore the rationale behind Japan's peacekeeping policy by synthesizing a number of relevant studies within this framework. (Li, 2017, pp. 4–5)

BOX 28 Theoretical Framework from a Study of Banking Globalization and Economic Growth

Conceptually foreign banks may positively influence economic growth both directly and indirectly. By bringing additional capital, energetically seeking profitable use of these funds, exerting corporate control, and facilitating better risk management practices, foreign banks may directly boost capital accumulation and efficiency of resource allocation in ways that accelerate growth (Levine, 1996). Foreign banks may also spur growth indirectly by intensifying competition. By contesting markets and sharpening competition, foreign banks can raise the overall level of banking sector efficiency. Their entry forces domestic banks to provide better services; domestic banks also become better at mobilizing savings, vigorously seeking profitable use of these savings, exerting better corporate control, and easing risk management in ways that accelerate economic growth (Demirguc-Kunt et al., 1998; Tschoegl, 2005).

In stark contrast to these viewpoints, those against the entry of foreign banks into host countries argue that foreign banks tend to "cherry pick" the most profitable borrowers, leaving the small and medium sized firms unattended who are likely to be informationally opaque. If this argument is justified, a high level of foreign bank penetration may hurt the economic growth of host countries since small and medium sized firms represent usually the largest group of total enterprises and hire a large share of employees (Cull & Peria, 2007; Berger, Miller, Petersen, Rajan, & Stein, 2005). Foreign banks may also lack local information; a major problem in low income countries (LICs) and even to an extent in emerging and developing market economies (EMs) where asymmetric information problems are severe and legal enforcement is weak (Acharya, Sundaram, & John, 2004; Petersen & Rajan, 1995). In addition foreign banks are often large organizations and reluctant to decentralize decision power. However, decentralization is necessary if lending decisions need to be based on soft information, based on relationships of banks with prospective local clients and knowledge about local market conditions. This is often the case when dealing with small firms, dominant in LICs and EMs. As a result, the local branches of foreign banks may specialize in funding large firms and overlook small firms. Such neglect may create concerns that foreign bank presence may be detrimental to the financing and growth of small and young businesses (Giannetti & Ongena, 2012). This may actually lower overall economic growth, especially in LICs and EMs. (Ghosh, 2017, pp. 83–84)

BOX 29 Theoretical Framework from a Study of Decentralization and Terror

According to the theory of Frey and Luechinger (2004), decentralization reduces terror. Frey and Luechinger argue that decentralized countries are politically and administratively more stable than more centralized states, and have more efficient markets — "a polity with many different centers of decision-making and implementation is difficult, if not impossible, to destabilize" (ibidem, p. 512). Thus, decentralization may stabilize the polity by reducing the damage terror can exert on a country's ability to govern its affairs, letting countries with strong local governments and administrations recover more quickly. Consequently, terrorists' perceived benefits of attacks decrease with government decentralization.

Similarly, according to traditional public choice arguments (Brennan and Buchanan, 1980; Tiebout, 1961), decentralization can yield efficiency gains in government activities and increase the effectiveness of deterring terror through national security policies: Decentralization permits residents to express their disagreement with local security policies by moving to a different jurisdiction in a Tiebout fashion (Tiebout, 1961), indirectly exerting control over local decision-makers by inducing incentives for competing local governments to innovate, to work efficiently and to target their security policies effectively (Brennan and Buchanan, 1980). As a consequence, the marginal costs of terrorism are increased.

Assuming that terrorists are rational decision-makers who weigh the expected costs against the benefits of their terrorist activities (see Lichbach, 1987), less terror should occur in countries with stronger local governments and administrations. This hypothesis has been confirmed with data on transnational terror in Dreher and Fischer (2011). In principle, it should also hold for domestic terror, as the goals of destabilizing the polity and economy are common to both transnational and domestic terrorists (Frey and Luechinger, 2004). (Dreher & Fischer, 2011, p. 223)

BOX 30 Theoretical Framework from a Study of Homelessness

A number of models have been presented to illustrate the onset, perpetuation, and termination of homelessness. Grigsby and colleagues (1990) propose four domains that perpetuate homelessness: (a) affiliation with others who are homeless, (b) functioning outside traditional roles, (c) isolation and dysfunction, and (d) continuing diminished level of social support. Sosin, Colson, and Grossman (1988) described homelessness as a problem representing three levels of society: individual, community, and social system. At the individual level, homeless adults may be characterized by the extent and nature of their "human capital" including education, work experience, and skills; "pathologies" such as mental illness or alcoholism; and "alienation" suggesting withdrawal from society and identification with street culture. In a later work, Westerfelt (1990) blends several theories to develop a framework predicting exits from homelessness: (a) dysfunction, (b) human capital, (c) disaffiliation, and (d) cultural identification. Both theoretical models share common concepts.

Continued

BOX 30 Theoretical Framework from a Study of Homelessness—cont'd.

Researchers have conceptualized dysfunction to incorporate aspects of a person's life that may impair functional status in society including mental illness, substance abuse, and physical disability. Ostensibly, possession of human capital should help protect against homelessness, and in turn, enhance one's ability to exit homelessness. Human capital has been conceptualized to include education and employment (Piliavin, Sosin, & Westerfelt, 1989; Sosin et al., 1988; Westerfelt, 1990).

Disaffiliation encompasses experiences of life disruption, severed relationships, and intensified distrust of others. Disaffiliation usually is reflected in three primary areas: household formation (e.g., living alone or no history of marriage or having children), limited or no associations with others (e.g., family, friends), and limited or no involvement in or interaction with various traditional social institutions or systems (e.g., religious or social groups, employment, welfare, mental health treatment systems) (Bahr & Garret, 1978; Grigsby et al., 1990; Sosin et al., 1988). Disaffiliation also has been operationalized by different experiences including childhood out-of-home placement, criminal history, and working at temporary "off-the-books" jobs (i.e., jobs such as panhandling, or selling recyclables or blood); all of these may interfere with one's ability to exit from homelessness (Bahr & Caplow, 1973; Bahr & Garret, 1978; Herman, Susser, Struening, & Link, 1997; Koegel, Melamid, & Burman, 1995; Sosin et al., 1988).

Westerfelt (1990) and Piliavin et al. (1989) conceptualized cultural affiliation with homelessness to indicate self-identification as a homeless individual or identification with the norms that develop in the context of homelessness. However, Westerfelt (1990) failed to find any association between identification with a homeless culture (operationalized as self-identification as homeless or interaction with homeless persons) and ability to exit from homelessness. Alternatively, some investigators have suggested that self-identification as homeless is more likely among persons with longer histories of homelessness (Grigsby et al., 1990; Robertson, Zlotnick, & Westerfelt, 1997; Sosin et al., 1988).

Researchers have had limited success in identifying variables that contribute to exits from homelessness. However, just as researchers have considered the onset of homelessness to be multidimensional, such may also be true for the exits from homelessness. One domain often described, but not yet tested as a component of the model, is economic resources.

Many studies have documented the low monthly and annual incomes reported by homeless adults (Bassuk, Rubin, & Lauriat, 1986; Breakey et al., 1989; Burt & Cohen, 1989; Fischer, Shapiro, Breakey, Anthony, & Kramer, 1986; Koegel, Burnam, & Farr, 1990; Milburn & D'Ercole, 1991; Miller & Lin, 1988; Wood, Valdez, Hayashi, & Shen, 1990; Zlotnick & Robertson, 1996). Although few homeless adults report regular formal-sector employment, many who have regular formal-sector employment, report that the work pays poorly and is temporary or sporadic (Zlotnick & Robertson, 1996). Another source of income is entitlement benefits (Breakey et al., 1989; Calsyn, Kohfeld, & Roades, 1993; Koegel et al., 1990; Sosin, 1992; Zlotnick & Robertson, 1996). Estimates of the number of homeless adults currently receiving entitlement benefit income vary between 25%–60% (Koegel et al.,

BOX 30 Theoretical Framework from a Study of Homelessness—cont'd.

1990; Zlotnick & Robertson, 1996). However, few studies indicate how many individuals are able to sustain entitlement income over time (Jahiel, 1992; Segal, 1991; Zlotnick, Robertson, & Lahiff, 1998) and whether sustained entitlement income contributes to exits from homelessness. Therefore, this article adds a fifth domain to the model, economic resources, and tests the association of all five model domains to obtaining and sustaining housing among homeless adults. Specifically, we propose to test whether temporary or permanent housing is associated with human capital, dysfunction, disaffiliation, cultural identification or economic resources. Because duration of homelessness differs among men, women, and women with children, household composition has also been included. (Zlotnick et al., 1999, pp. 211–212)

BOX 31 Theoretical Framework from a Study of Government Expenditure and Economic Growth

There is a plethora of literature dating back several centuries on government expenditure and economic growth and the interest in the subject has not declined with time. The neoclassical growth model propounded by Ramsey (1928) and further developed by Solow (1956) posits that economic growth results from capital accumulation through household savings. Such accumulation continues until the stage of unconditional convergence as diminishing marginal returns to capital set in. In the long run, population growth and technology will exogenously determine growth (Barro, 1996). Although this representation is plausible, the model falls short in accounting for public policy and institutional factors that characterize government expenditure in influencing economic growth (Bassanini & Scarpetta, 2001). Such deficiency, together with a lack of basis for long-run economic growth determined within the model itself necessitated the development of "new growth theories" or endogenous growth theories (Mankiw, 2013).

The new growth theories postulate that technology is endogenous because it relies on the decision to invest in research and development and diffusion (Bassanini & Scarpetta, 2001). Endogenous growth theories predict increasing returns to scale in technology, which translate into long-term knowledge-based growth (Cortright, 2001). By relaxing the hypothesis of exogenous savings and capital formation of Solow (1956), these theories allow policy and institutional factors to shape economic growth (Bassanini & Scarpetta, 2001). In his working paper, Barro (1996) argued that differences in growth rates are a result of differences in propensity to save, access to technology, and government policy. Governments that allocate increased expenditure to alleviating market distortions, enforcing property rights, providing infrastructure services, and ensuring better financial markets generate efficiencies that translate into growth. However, the endogenous growth theories are still to be supported by empirical literature (Barro, 1996).

Continued

BOX 31 Theoretical Framework from a Study of Government Expenditure and Economic Growth—cont'd.

Keynes' hypothesis

Keynes (1936) argued that the total income of an economy, in the short run, depends on the spending patterns of households, businesses, and government. Challenging the neoclassical views that aggregate supply alone affects the total output, he claimed that increasing expenditure will increase output because prices are "sticky" in the short run (Mankiw, 2013, p. 312). He considered government expenditure to be exogenous in his model (Peacock & Wiseman, 1961). Keynes posited that the increase in government expenditure will increase output, which further increases money demand. As money demand increases, interest rates will adjust upward to clear the market, thus crowding out investment. If the economy is an interest rate taker on world financial markets, this will result in trade deficits in the domestic economy. The resulting effect of government expenditure on economic growth, known as the multiplier, is positive but below unity, meaning that an increase in government expenditure of 1% results in an increase in economic growth of less than 1%. Keynes' views are still recognized in present day economics, which is evidenced by "The Obama Stimulus" policy of 2009 when the United States of America rolled out an expenditure package close to USD800 billion, which was meant to kick start economic recovery from a recession (Mankiw, 2013). The question that arises is: What determines the size of the multiplier? Empirical findings are inconclusive and in some cases, do not support Keynes' hypothesis.

Wagner's inference

The law of increasing state activity (Wagner's law) developed by Wagner (1893) resulted from his empirical analysis of government expenditure and economic growth for five Western European countries. It states that government spending increases faster than economic growth in progressive economies. Wagner (1893) contended that such trends are evident because governments suffer pressure from social progress, which demands changes in relative spheres of private and public economy. As governments respond to such demand, their expenditure increases. He further asserted that since governments are financially handicapped, growth of public spending cannot precede economic growth. In other words, the basis for financing additional expenditure is the growth of the economy (Peacock & Wiseman, 1961). His views support the expectation that the direction of causality should flow from economic growth to government expenditure. However, Wagner (1893) analyzed data from a century ago and for countries with governments that were different from those of today. The role of government has gone through transitions that warrant a reexamination of the empirical evidence for this claim.

The role of trade

International trade is one of the driving forces behind regional groupings such as SADC and it has implications for both economic growth and government expenditure. Openness to international trade has the effect of increasing efficiencies in

BOX 31 Theoretical Framework from a Study of Government Expenditure and Economic Growth—cont'd.

markets, thus regenerating social welfare that is otherwise lost through imposition of trade tariffs and quotas (Begovic & Ciftcioglu, 2008). The benefits of trade include a wide market for domestic goods while increased competition from foreign firms forces greater innovation by firms as they fight for survival, ultimately leading to more and cheaper products. Moreover, openness allows transfer of technologies and creates opportunities to learn from abroad. Trade can increase government expenditure through demand for trade facilitation services. A greater economy allows governments to generate more revenue through taxation and this translates into increased public expenditure. In a study of determinants of economic growth using data for 100 countries for the period from 1960 to 1990, Barro (1996) found that trade was significantly and positively related to economic growth. However, he noted that it was not a key element for economic growth in poor countries such as the countries of Sub-Saharan Africa. Trade is included in this study to assess if countries within the SADC region have benefited economically from their grouping and to reexamine Barro's (1996) perception. (Maparara, 2016, pp. 2–3)

BOX 32 Theoretical Framework from a Study of Determinants of Parental Savings

There is little previous empirical work on the factors associated with parental saving for postsecondary education. However, economists have been concerned about parental household savings since the emergence of capitalist economies and especially since the industrial revolution [citations]. Drawing upon previous econometric studies and research on college choice, we posit that parental saving for postsecondary education is a function of the financial ability to save, parental motivation to save, parental postsecondary aspirations for their children, and the ability of their children to benefit from postsecondary education. Based upon research on household savings and student college choice we have identified factors that might be expected to influence parental saving. These factors include an array of variables which we have grouped under the categories of background characteristics, student and parental aspirations and activities, and information and incentives. Background characteristics include: family income, family size, gender, race, parental education, and student ability [citations]. The student and parental attitudes and values we have included are parental educational aspirations and encouragement and student aspirations and activities [citations]. The informational variables are related to parental knowledge of postsecondary costs and student financial aid [citations]. (Hossler & Vesper, 1993, pp. 141–142)

BOX 33 Theoretical Framework from a Study of Health and Economic Growth

Good health can contribute to economic growth in a number of ways. First, a healthy workforce is associated with higher productivity because workers are more energetic and mentally more robust. Moreover, absenteeism at work is low since both the workers and their family members enjoy good health. Low absenteeism raises production. This argument is embedded in the theoretical models of nutrition-based efficiency wages. Leibenstein (1957), for instance, argued that those who consumed more calories relative to the poorly nourished workers are more productive, and that better nutrition is associated with increasingly higher productivity. Healthier workers with higher productivity earn higher wages (Strauss & Thomas, 1998). Higher wages in turn contribute to higher consumption and savings, which by virtue of improving the well-being and happiness of people contribute to economic growth.

Second, improvements in health raise the incentive to acquire schooling, since investments in schooling can be amortised over a longer working life (Kalemli-Ozcan, Ryder, & Weil, 2000). Healthier students tend to be associated with lower absenteeism and higher cognitive functioning, and thus receive a better education for a given level of schooling (Weil, 2001). It follows that better health contributes to increased schooling and knowledge accumulation, which improves the quality of a country's human capital; thus, contributing positively to economic growth.

Human capital is important because it improves productivity through several ways. First, the human capital theory views schooling as an investment in skills, which contributes to improvements in productivity (see, for example, Becker, 1975; Schultz, 1960; Schultz, 1961; Schultz, 1971). The growth accounting literature posits that education, through increasing the human capital stock of individuals, improves their productivity and therefore contributes to economic growth. The endogenous growth literature, popularised by the work of Romer (1990), assumes that the creation of new designs/ideas is a direct function of human capital, which is reflected in the accumulation of scientific knowledge. Therefore investment in human capital, by improving research and development, generates growth in physical capital, which results in economic growth (Asterious & Agiomirgianakis, 2001; Romer, 1990). Moreover, persistent accumulation of knowledge by individuals, either with intentional efforts as explained by Lucas (1988) or with learning by doing as explained by Azariades and Drazen (1990) enhances labour and capital productivity, thus contributing to economic growth.

Second, human capital improves adaptability and allocative efficiency, in that skilled workers allocate resources more efficiently across tasks and are more able to respond to new opportunities (Heckman, 2005; Nelson & Phelps, 1966; Schultz, 1971). Third, human capital not only improves the productivity of labour but it also produces spill over benefits, meaning that apart from benefiting the individual who receives education, it also benefits the society (Self & Grabowski, 2004).

Theoretically, investment contributes to economic growth by generating technological diffusion (see, Borensztein, Gregorio, & Lee, 1998; Obwona, 2001). Balasubramanyam, Salisu, and Sapsford (1998), Li and Liu (2005), and De Mello (1999), among others, explain that foreign direct investment is a composite bundle of capital stock, know-how and technology, which has the capacity of improving existing stock

**BOX 33 Theoretical Framework from a Study of Health
and Economic Growth—cont'd.**

of knowledge through labour training, skill acquisition and diffusion, and the introduction of alternative management practices and organisation arrangement.

The causal relationship between exports and economic growth is known as Export-Led-Growth (ELG) hypothesis. This hypothesis suggests that export-led outward orienting trade policy stimulates economic growth; see Wilbur and Haque (1992), Richards (2001), Marin (1992), Yamada (1998), and Awokuse (2003). As explained earlier, exports stimulate economic growth by contributing to aggregate output, through an efficient use of resources and capital formation through foreign exchange that increases imports of capital goods and stimulates economic growth.

On the supply side, Import-Led-Growth (ILD) hypothesis emphasise[s] modernisation and transfer of advanced technology through acquisition of more advanced capital which in turn affect the growth of total factor productivity, see Iscan (1998), Marwah and Klein (1996), and Marwah and Tavakoli (2004).

Technology and technological advancements are key components of economic growth (Grossman & Helpman, 1994). R&D investments are regarded as the key to secure technological potential which leads to innovation and economic growth (Trajtenberg (1990). Investments in R&D increase the possibility of a higher standard of technology in firms, leading to the production of high quality products. This will ensure higher levels of income; see Romer (1990) and Lichtenberg (1992). (Narayan et al., 2010, pp. 406–407)

Visual Models

Visual models come in two forms, depending on whether they are theoretical or empirical. A theoretical visual model is typically presented in the form of "graphs with lines and curves that tell an economic story" (Evans, 1997, p. 1). Such models are common in textbooks and theoretical papers. An empirical visual model, in contrast, is commonly presented as a conceptual map—a map showing all the relevant concepts and their relationships. Such models can be very simple or they can be rather complex; regardless of their complexity, their purpose is to help the reader quickly grasp the relationships between relevant variables.

Box 34 shows a very simple visual model explaining two mechanisms that connect electronic filing of taxes (predictor variable) and government revenue (the dependent variable). It comes from a study conducted by Fadhila Douglas Mshindo (2017), a graduate student in Public Finance. Her topic was electronic filing (e-filing) of taxes and its effect on government. In her conceptual framework, she tries to show, using a simple diagram, two mechanisms through which e-filing might affect revenue.

BOX 34 Example of a Visual Model

E-filing is a system that allows taxpayers to submit their tax returns to the revenue authorities electronically (Azmi & Kamarulzaman, 2010). Revenue authorities in both developed and developing countries have been adopting such systems in an attempt to increase their revenue. Conceptually, this revenue enhancement may be mediated by two mechanisms, which are shown in Figure 1. The first mechanism is an increase in taxpayers' compliance, or the degree to which taxpayers voluntarily comply with tax laws (Simon & Clinton, 2004). The degree of noncompliance can be evaluated through the tax gap, which is the difference between the actual revenue collected and the amount that would have been collected if there were 100% compliance. The second mechanism is a reduction in taxpayers' compliance costs, or costs incurred by the taxpayers in meeting the requirements of the tax law and revenue authority, which are costs that are over and above the actual payment of tax (Sandford, 1986, 1995). With the adoption of e-filing, theoretically, less time should be spent by VAT traders on submission of tax returns; errors can also be reduced by the use of the system. These two mechanisms should in theory lead to an increase in revenue collection. (Mshindo, 2017, p. 2)

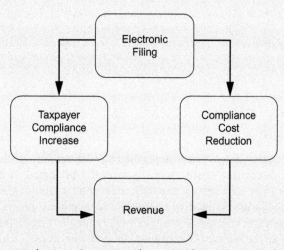

Figure 1. Two Mechanisms Connecting Electronic Filing and Increased Government Revenue.

Chapter 11

Situating a Study: The Literature Review

Academic knowledge is not an objective reality that is "out there," waiting to be discovered; rather, it is something that academics actively construct. And as any constructed entity, knowledge, too, can be accepted or rejected by members of the academic community. The task of any academic writer, therefore, is to persuade the reader to accept his or her claims to knowledge as credible and legitimate.

To be accepted as credible and legitimate, new knowledge must build on prior, existing knowledge. Researchers show that their study builds on prior knowledge by posing questions that are warranted by the current state of research, by employing theories and methodologies that are sanctioned by the discipline and its academic community, by using definitions that have been accepted by the researchers working in the target area, and by basing their expectations on previous research—in other words, by situating their study within the body of existing academic literature and demonstrating that it fits that literature.

Textbooks on academic writing often use the term *literature review* to refer to the idea of situating a study within the existing body of knowledge. Yet, the term *literature review* is somewhat confusing because it does not clearly convey what the writer needs to do. Students who are new to graduate study often take the term literally and interpret it as an instruction to write a detailed, often chronological, account of everything that has been said on their topic in order to demonstrate familiarity with existing research. Such literature reviews are often recognizable by their organization: Every paragraph is a review of a separate study, starting with "Author so and so investigated..., Author so and so found..., or According to Author so and so,.... ." There is no attempt to show how all of those studies are related, and, especially, how they are connected to the student's work.

In fact, rather than reviewing existing literature on the topic for the sake of demonstrating familiarity with it, what authors need to do is make an argument or a series of arguments that would persuade the reader to accept the author's own study as necessary, valid, and perhaps even interesting. Recall from Chapter 5 that an argument is a claim that is supported by evidence—in this case, evidence from previous research. Thus, what you need to do is use

How to Write about Economics and Public Policy. https://doi.org/10.1016/B978-0-12-813010-0.00011-9

previous literature to make and support your arguments. These arguments may be about, among other things,

- The importance or timeliness of your topic,
- The state of current knowledge on your topic (both theoretical and empirical),
- The use of specific approaches or methodologies in your area,
- The variables that you have selected to include in your model,
- The specific expectations, and/or
- The definitions you have chosen for your concepts.

A literature review, then, could best be thought of not as a review of existing works on a topic, but as an argument that provides a very selective account of what is known on a particular topic and helps the author build a case for his or her own study and justify his or her own choices and expectations.

The use of literature in an academic study is critical because previous research acts as a way of legitimizing a study and persuading the reader to accept it as needed. There are, however, large differences among studies in how academic literature is organized and presented and how much of it is used in a given study. These differences reflect the requirements of various journals or degree programs, the wishes of individual professors acting as students' advisors, and to some extent, the individual preferences of the authors. Crucially, however, these differences reflect the conventions of different disciplines and research areas.

In this section, I give some general suggestions on situating a study in the context of previous research in public policy and economics. However, because the specific ways in which the literature is used in a study, its organization, and the language that authors use to make arguments about the state of research will depend on the discipline and research area you are working in, make sure to check papers that are most relevant to your research. Study them to learn how authors working in your area use literature to situate their study—what claims they support, how they organize the literature, and where exactly in their paper they talk about the work of others.

SUGGESTIONS FOR USING THE LITERATURE

Use (Mostly) Disciplinary Literature

Perhaps the most important criterion for selecting literature for a study is the relevance of the literature you select to the discipline or research area to which your study will be contributing. If you are contributing to a research area in economics, then most of the literature in your study should be related to economics; if you are contributing to a research area in sociology, then most of your literature should come from sociology.

The difficulty, of course, is that many problems in public policy are interdisciplinary and their research often necessitates pooling together concepts, theories, or tools from several disciplines or research areas. For example, the problem of school attainment can be examined from an economic perspective as an educational production function; however, you may also want to employ a psychological theory of motivation to gain further insights into the problem or use research in sociology to identify important school-related variables to include in your model. In this case, you should use literature from all relevant disciplines. However, the extent to which you will use literature from a particular discipline should be proportionate to the importance of that discipline in your research. Ultimately, you should ask yourself who your readers will be: If your research will be read primarily by economists, then you should relate it to research in economics and use mostly economic literature.

Prefer Empirical Literature to Nonempirical

As I explained earlier, there are two kinds of academic literature: empirical studies, which can be quantitative or qualitative, and nonempirical literature, which comes in a wide variety of forms, from theoretical studies to systematic literature reviews to policy-oriented argumentative essays. When researching a problem, you can use both kinds of literature to get an idea about the state of research on your problem. However, when using literature to support claims about the state of current knowledge (e.g., what has and has not been investigated, what is more or less important, what affects what), prefer empirical literature to nonempirical unless you are summarizing theories or theoretical positions.

The use of empirical literature as support for a claim is especially important if you use nonintegral (or parenthetical) citations—citations that are not included in the running text and that usually appear in parentheses at the end of a claim. In fact, readers in many disciplines often *assume* that the parenthetical citations that they see at the end of authors' claims refer to empirical work. For example, the following statement would be interpreted by many readers as an argument that is being made on the basis of an empirical study:

> In post-communist countries, privatized organizations appear to be more efficient than government-controlled organizations (Smith, 1999).

That is, to many readers, this sentence would mean that Smith conducted an empirical study of privatization, in which he found that privatized organizations were more efficient than those controlled by the government, and that the author of this sentence is using Smith's findings to support this claim. If, however, Smith did not conduct an empirical study but merely made a claim somewhere about privatized organizations being more efficient than government-controlled ones, then the use of the parenthetical citation to support this claim may be confusing.

If you use nonempirical literature—for example, a researcher's theoretical arguments—to support your claims, make it clear in your narrative that the work you are referring to is nonempirical. Instead of using parenthetical citations at the end of the sentences, consider integrating citations into the text by using signal phrases such as: *Smith argued in his review..., Brown theorized...,* or *Miller proposed a view.... .* For more on integral and nonintegral citations and their use in different disciplines see Chapter 16.

Consider if You Need a Separate Section for the Literature

Students often ask if they should have a separate section dealing with the literature. The answer depends on the type of paper you are writing and the requirements of the journal or educational program to which you are submitting your paper. Many empirical articles in economics and public policy that appear in academic journals do not have a separate literature review section; instead, authors make arguments about the importance of their research, the inclusion of particular variables, or the appropriateness of their approach and methodology in the Introduction. The part that deals with existing literature in such studies can be quite short—as short as a few paragraphs.

Master's theses and especially doctoral dissertations dedicate much more space to situating the study in previous research and usually have separate sections devoted to reviewing relevant literature. In economics papers, it is also common to break a literature review into two parts—theoretical literature and empirical literature—and review theoretical and empirical literature separately. Nonempirical papers almost never have a separate section devoted to the literature because they are usually based entirely on the literature. Such papers are often organized thematically.

Support All Claims that Are Not Based on Your Own Findings

In an academic study, claims that are not based on your own findings should be supported with literature—primarily empirical literature. Recall from Chapter 1 that an academic paper is a dialog in which the author is trying to persuade the reader to accept his or her study. In this dialog, readers can easily reject an author's claims if they find them inappropriate or baseless. The writer's job, therefore, is to anticipate readers' questions or objections and respond to them in an acceptable way.

Novice students sometimes hold mistaken beliefs about the use of literature in a study, thinking that if they cited a lot of studies in their paper, their advisor would think that they were unoriginal. But it is important to realize that a study's originality and, in fact, its usefulness can only be judged by what the author actually did—by the study's design and execution, and not by its claims and citations.

In fact, supported claims look stronger than unsupported claims and they make writing appear more professional because they show that the author has researched the issue and has found evidence to support his or her claims. To see that, compare the following two passages. In the first passage, all citations have been removed and the claims are left unsupported; in the second one, all claims are supported with citations. Which one looks more credible to you?

Passage 1

Although women are achieving greater equity in certain labor sectors, they are not making much progress in the higher echelons of the business world. Women account for about 5% of senior management in corporate America. While the earnings differential between male and female managers has decreased in recent years, this gap continues to exceed that reflected in the labor force as a whole. In one 1991 study, the greatest salary gap between men and women occurs with managerial positions, where women in full-time management jobs receive only 61% of the salaries received by men in similar positions. (Tsui, 1998, p. 364)

Passage 2

Although women are achieving greater equity in certain labor sectors (Blau, 1994), they are not making much progress in the higher echelons of the business world. Women account for about 5% of senior management in corporate America (Bickley, 1996). While the earnings differential between male and female managers has decreased in recent years, this gap continues to exceed that reflected in the labor force as a whole (Jacobs, 1992). In her 1991 analysis, Crispell reported that the greatest salary gap between men and women occurs with managerial positions, where women in full-time management jobs receive only 61% of the salaries received by men in similar positions. (Tsui, 1998, p. 364)

In Passage 1, there are no citations, and as readers, we may wonder, quite naturally, where all this information comes from. Why should we accept the author's claims, for example, that "women are achieving greater equality" or that "the earnings differential between male and female managers has decreased"? In contrast, in Passage 2, we can see plenty of supporting evidence, which is shown in the form of citations. We can even check this evidence to see if the author's interpretation is accurate or if we agree with that interpretation. These citations increase the author's credibility in the eyes of the readers and the readers' confidence in the author's knowledge of the subject matter. Situating a study, therefore, means framing it as a response to the ultimate readers' questions: What is the basis for your claims? Where is your evidence?

Evaluate Rather than Merely Describe

Situating a study in previous research means not only describing relevant research but also, crucially, evaluating it—or, as Feak and Swales (2009) put it, "taking a stance toward the literature" (p. 71). In fact, a review of the literature without some sort of evaluation is hard to imagine as such a review would be difficult for readers to interpret. How, for example, can readers interpret the fact that Smith found one thing, Brown found another thing, and Miller found something else?

Evaluation helps the author organize the material and present disparate studies as coherent arguments showing what is more or less important, significant, or well-established; how common a particular finding or approach is; or if there is another view on the problem. Evaluation also helps the author show his or her own stance toward the literature as a whole or toward a particular study. For example, authors may describe a question as "big" or "important," an analysis as "accurate" or "myopic," or a consensus as "lacking" or "overwhelming," thereby indicating their own position toward what they are describing, which may encompass a wide range of feelings, from criticism to admiration.

To see the importance of evaluative statements, compare these two sentence openings:

1. *There is some literature that shows that...*

2. *A **large and growing literature** has shown that...*

In the first sentence, the author merely states the fact that there are studies showing something. Such a statement would be difficult to interpret beyond its literal meaning and it might leave at least some readers wondering, *So, what?* In the second sentence, however, the author makes an **evaluative statement** about the body of existing literature: the words "large and growing" show the author's own assessment of the state of the field and his or her belief that there may be a potential consensus. Such a statement also helps the reader quickly grasp the state of the field and see how the author's study fits into it.

Note that evaluative statements are typically followed by nonintegral (parenthetical) citations to studies that have found support for the author's claims or by explanations and examples from relevant studies, which in turn are followed by citations to those studies. This is important because many readers would find it difficult to accept unsupported evaluations.

Below are some examples of evaluative statements. Read them and notice how they help the author organize the literature. What stance toward the literature does the author show in each statement?

A **large and growing literature** has shown that maternal health determines offspring's health and productivity.

Aid effectiveness has been **a subject of much debate in the past decade.**

There is **a considerable lack of consensus** on the importance of nonfarm activities to the incomes of rural households.

The empirical work on the relationship of land reform and economic growth **is mired in controversy.**

The early literature on economic development **was strongly influenced by** the work of Brown (1965).

In **a pioneering contribution,** Brown (1998) **demonstrated** a strong association between economic development and life expectancy.

Tsang (2002) argues that in China, unified inflation targeting may not be the optimal solution because differences in inflation rates among the provinces may undermine the effectiveness of a unified inflation-targeting monetary policy. His arguments, however, **are based on an empirical analysis of a rather limited set of data.** Furthermore, in his analysis, Tsang did not compare social welfare loss under different inflation targeting policies, which **significantly weakens** the overall conclusion.

ORGANIZING THE LITERATURE TO MAKE A POINT

Situating a study in previous research typically requires making three kinds of statement. They are briefly described below.

Statements about the Overall State of the Field

Statements about the overall state of the field include statements about the direction in which the field is going, its major findings, its consensuses and disagreements, its main theoretical positions, and so on. The purpose of these statements is to summarize current research in a succinct manner in order to **establish a niche** (Feak & Swales, 2009) for the author's study. These statements are usually made on the basis of empirical work and they take the form of claims followed by nonintegral, parenthetical citations to studies that support those claims. For example:

Do elections increase public spending? Some say yes (citations) and others say no (citations).

Several studies suggest that the new policy has several benefits including a reduction in child mortality (citations), improved maternal health (citations), and a greater access to sanitation facilities (citations).

The root causes of corruption in politically centralized systems reflect not only economic realities but also perceived cultural norms (citations).

If you look closely at these statements, you will notice that they summarize relevant research by imposing some sort of order on the literature—by grouping and presenting studies according to some criterion. This is how the overall state of research in a field is usually described.

Common criteria for grouping studies include

- Approaches or methods that have been used to study a problem or phenomenon (e.g., experimental vs. observational methods or the use of one particular model vs. another);

- Major findings, especially if they have been mixed (e.g., some studies have found a positive effect and others, a negative effect);

- Main controversies (e.g., different opinions about the threshold value of inflation needed for inflation to exert positive effect on economic growth);

- Main theoretical positions (e.g., neoclassical view vs. Keynes's view of the relationship between government expenditure and economic growth);

- Different kinds of determinants of some outcome (e.g., policy-related vs. other determinants of economic development);

- Different views of a phenomenon (e.g., linear vs. nonlinear view of economic development); or

- Different settings (e.g., predictors of economic growth in developed vs. developing countries).

The way you organize and present relevant literature should help you frame your study in relation to that literature. For example, if you wish to frame your study as an attempt to resolve a controversy, focus on mixed results and present relevant literature according to whether it shows a positive or a negative effect of some variable on another variable or variables that you are interested in. If you wish to present your study as an attempt to extend existing knowledge about the determinants of some outcome from developed to developing countries, you may want to group studies by economic status. You may further want to show that there are important differences between studies conducted in developed and in developing countries and that these differences may account for the different results that have been obtained. Or if you are interested in the effects of a particular policy, you may want to organize your literature according to the type of effect that the policy has had.

Below are two examples from published studies showing how authors impose order on the material they present. In the first example, the authors review two types of argument on gender wage differences. In the second example, the authors present studies of privatization that have been grouped by study design. Notice the use of citations to support claims in both examples.

Example 1

The economic literature on gender wage differentials has identified multiple reasons why women and men have generally different levels of earnings. Basically, there are two types of arguments. The first is concerned with differences in human capital. Due to the higher incidence of expected career breaks, women make different human capital choices (both education and on-the-job training choices), and this in turn leads to job segregation. Many studies have shown that segregated labor markets are the main reason for gender wage differences (e.g., Meyersson-Milgrom et al., 2001; Korkeamäki and Kyyrä, 2006; Wolf and Heinz, 2007). The other main argument is based on labor market discrimination.

PRP [performance-related pay] increases wages due to its impact on selection and effort (Lazear, 2000; Pekkarinen and Riddell, 2008). Tying pay to performance attracts high-ability employees and provides incentives to increase their effort. Thus, PRP may affect the gender wage gap through several mechanisms: (1) discrimination, (2) segregation, (3) differences in selection effects between sexes and (4) differences in effort effects. We now consider each of these mechanisms in turn. (Kangasniemi & Kauhanen, 2013, p. 5133)

Example 2

The assumption behind privatization in many parts of the world is that private ownership improves corporate performance. The empirical evidence for this assumption comes from two kinds of studies. The first, exemplified by Megginson, Nash, and Van Randenborgh (1994) and La Porta and Lopez-de-Silanes (1997), compares pre- and postprivatization performance of selected privatized firms. The second focuses on comparing the performance of state firms with either private (Boardman and Vining 1989) or privatized (Pohl et al., 1997) firms operating under reasonably similar conditions. (Frydman et al., 1999, p. 1153)

Statements about Most Relevant Studies

Statements about the overall state of the field and major findings are usually followed by more detailed reviews of empirical studies that are particularly relevant to your research. Rudestam and Newton (2001) call such studies "very relevant literature" (p. 64) and explain that these are empirical studies that focus largely on the same relationship as the one you are interested in, incorporating all or most of the variables that you will focus on in your own study. These studies form the foundation on which your study will build and they are used to justify expectations, definitions, or the choice of particular variables, measures, methods, or models. Authors usually devote considerable space to reviewing very relevant studies, describing how a study was done (i.e., its methodology), what results were obtained, and what those results mean.

Often, you will need not only to review very relevant studies but also to evaluate them and explain why they are insufficient—and why, therefore, your study is needed. One way to do that is to point to the differences between those studies and your own study, which may be differences in purpose, focus, or methodology. Another common approach is to point out flaws in the design of the most relevant studies and show how your study will fix those flaws. Below are examples from research papers showing how authors review most relevant studies. The first two come from student papers and the last one, from a published paper.

The first example comes from a paper by Efita Fitri Irianti, a student in Economics, Planning, and Public Policy, who examined the relationship between fiscal decentralization and human development. She begins her review with a statement that implies the importance of her topic: *Several studies have examined....* She then describes in detail the purpose, design, and results of a most relevant study before offering her interpretation of the study's results in the last sentence. Read this example and notice the phrases she uses to review the study and draw her own conclusion.

Several studies have examined the relationship between fiscal decentralization and human development. For example, Habibi et al. (2003) studied the impact of fiscal decentralization on human development in Argentina using health (infant mortality rates) and education (secondary school enrollment) as dependent variables. The authors used panel data analysis at the provincial level over a period of 25 years from 1970 to 1994. The variables included as independent variables were per-capita income of public employees, per-capita total expenditure, ratio of provincial taxes to own revenue, ratio of own revenue to total revenue, ratio of royalties to own revenue, and ratio of conditional transfers to total transfers. They found that infant mortality rates had a significant negative association with the ratio of provincial taxes to own revenue and the ratio of own revenue to total revenue. For educational output, the ratio of provincial taxes to own revenue and the ratio of own revenue to total revenue were positively and significantly associated with secondary school enrollment. These results imply that fiscal decentralization may have a positive impact on human development. (Irianti, 2014, pp. 4–5)

The second example is from a paper by Itai Maparara, a student in Public Finance, who examined the direction of causality in the relationship between government expenditure and economic growth. In his theoretical framework, Itai outlined several theoretical views on the relationship he was interested in including those of Keynes and Wagner (see his extract in Chapter 10). Here, he reviews two empirical studies to show how they are related to those theories and to justify his own approach. Notice the use of the word "interesting" to describe the second study. Why do you think he uses this word? Also notice that after reviewing this study, he interprets its findings in a way that helps him justify his own research.

Examining the case of a developing country, Nasiru (2012) employed a bound test to cointegration and Granger causality tests to determine causality in Nigeria for the period from 1961 to 2010. The study categorized government expenditure into capital and recurrent expenditure. The results show that no causality exists for these expenditure categories in the long run. However, in the short run, causality flows from government capital expenditure to economic growth, thus supporting Keynes' views. The study concluded that government can influence economic growth by shifting expenditure from recurrent to capital formation.

One interesting study was carried out by Loizides and Vamvoukas (2004). The study examined causality in a bivariate and trivariate framework using an error correction model and a Granger causality test, enabling the comparison of results from different frameworks. In the bivariate framework, data analysis supported Keynes' views for the United Kingdom and Ireland in both the short and long run whereas the data for Greece validated Wagner's inferences. However, when causality was examined in the trivariate framework by adding inflation as a third variable, the UK data supported Wagner's views. These results imply that omitting certain explanatory variables may influence results on the direction of causality.

Therefore, the present study directly proceeds into the trivariate framework of analysis in order to confirm the findings of Loizides and Vamvoukas (2004). This study will also employ error correction model and Granger causality tests as a strategy. The uniqueness of this study is the choice of a third explanatory variable, trade, included in the model. By including trade, the study can examine whether the regional group has influenced government expenditure and economic growth in its member countries through agreed-upon trade policies. (Maparara, 2016, pp. 3–4)

Statements about Other Authors' Arguments or Theoretical Positions

Although empirical studies often constitute the bulk of the literature that authors review in order to situate their study, nonempirical literature is also often used. For example, authors may need to describe theories or theoretical positions, theoretical or policy-related arguments advanced by others, or conclusions from a comprehensive literature review on their topic.

Nonempirical literature is often used to support theoretical definitions of concepts, various classifications, or theoretical views and expectations. For example, in a study of political instability and economic growth, you may use theoretical literature to support a definition of conflict or political instability; in a study of farmers' motivations to convert to organic farming, you may use a comprehensive literature review to derive a classification for those motivations, dividing them, for example, into economic and noneconomic ones. However, nonempirical literature should generally not be used to support claims about empirical relationships unless you are deriving predictions from a theoretical study.

As I explained earlier, you should make it clear for the reader when you use nonempirical literature. Avoid the use of nonintegral, parenthetical citations at the end of sentences when reviewing nonempirical literature; instead, introduce nonempirical works with signal phrases (e.g., *Brown argued..., Smith contends...*) and briefly indicate the type of study you are referring to: *Brown's (1999) theoretical analysis has shown that...; Using a systematic review of relevant literature, Smith (1999) derived....*

When reviewing nonempirical literature, it is important to explain how it is related to your purpose. This often requires that you evaluate and critique authors' arguments in relation to your own study. For example, if you are summarizing a theoretical view, explain how it relates to your expectations or why it may or may not be applicable to your particular context; or if you are describing several possible definitions, evaluate them in relation to your methodology and explain which one is preferable in your context and why.

Below are some examples from research papers showing how authors use nonempirical literature to situate and justify their study. The first example comes from Itai Maparara's paper on the relationship between government expenditure and economic growth. Here, Itai describes a theory relating government expenditure and economic growth. Notice that after describing Wagner's views, he also explains what they mean for his own study. Notice also how he justifies the need for his study in the last sentence. What argument does he make?

The law of increasing state activity (Wagner's law) developed by Wagner (1893) resulted from his empirical analysis of government expenditure and economic growth for five Western European countries. It states that government spending increases faster than economic growth in progressive economies. Wagner (1893) contended that such trends are evident because governments suffer pressure from social progress, which demands changes in relative spheres of private and public economy. As governments respond to such demand, their expenditure increases. He further asserted that since governments are financially handicapped, growth of public spending cannot precede economic growth. In other words, the basis for financing additional expenditure is growth of the economy (Peacock & Wiseman, 1961). His views support the perception that the direction of causality should flow from economic growth to government expenditure. However, Wagner (1893) analyzed data from a century ago and for countries with governments that were different from those of today. The role of government has gone through transitions so that a reexamination of the empirical evidence for his claim has become imperative. (Maparara, 2016, p. 2)

In the second example, Nana Mensah Otoo, a student in Public Finance, summarizes theoretical arguments that connect intellectual property rights (IPR) protection and foreign direct investment (FDI). Notice that after reviewing these arguments, he tries to explain what they mean and gives an overall evaluation. Notice also that he uses another author's argument to support his assertion that theory may not provide a clear insight into the relationship between IPR and FDI. Why do you think he does that?

It is useful to briefly review why IPR protection might matter for FDI theoretically. IPR protection is often discussed in the context of innovation and creative activity. According to Maskus (2004), intellectual outputs have the characteristics of a public good: once produced, they are available on a nonexclusive basis. The author further indicates that intellectual outputs are also nonrivalrous in use, that is, additional par- ties can benefit from them at zero additional cost. Hence, these factors make it difficult for producers of intellectual outputs to appropriate the returns to their investments and recoup costs. Maskus stresses that in the absence of property rights, the market for intellectual outputs would fail or yield an inefficient supply of output. Regarding the connection to FDI and trade, Braga and Fink (1998) have argued that because many producers of intellectual output are engaged in both domestic and foreign markets, risks of unauthorized copying and imitation exist both at home and abroad. The authors argue that in regions where IPR protection is weak, incentives to market (via trade or FDI) might also be weak. Moreover, weak IPR protection (and smaller markets as a consequence) may adversely affect incentives to innovate and produce, thereby affecting the potential to export and invest abroad. Similarly, the theoretical study by Taylor (1994) indicates that stronger patent protection increases technology transfer when competition exists between foreign and domestic investors. However, theory does not necessarily provide clear insights into the IPR/FDI relationship, as Maskus (2000) noted in the case of patents and trade:

> Theoretical models do not clearly predict the impacts of variable patent rights on trade volumes. Much depends on local market demand, the efficiency of imitative production, and the structure of trade barriers. Also important are the reactions of imperfectly competitive firms. Thus, a clear picture can emerge only from empirical studies. (p. 113).

(Otoo, 2013, p. 2)

The above suggestions for organizing the literature apply in equal measure to short reviews presented in Introductions and to longer reviews presented in separate sections. In the Introduction, one or more statements about the overall state of research in the field are often followed by a more detailed focus on just a few studies, which are reviewed in detail and critiqued. In papers where there is a separate section for reviewing the literature, detailed reviews and critiques of relevant studies are usually presented in the Literature Review section whereas statements about the overall state of research are presented in the Introduction.

The specific organization of the literature will also depend on whether the paper is quantitative or qualitative. If you are writing a qualitative paper, your literature review can be organized thematically. A common strategy is to break down the main research question into subquestions and use those subquestions as section headings in the literature review.

If you are writing a quantitative paper examining a relationship between variables, you may want to have two separate sections, a theoretical framework section and an empirical evidence section. In the theoretical framework section, review the theory on which your study is based. If there is currently a theoretical debate on your topic, review both sides of the debate and explain the expectations from both sides. In the empirical evidence section, group studies describing the background of your research according to the criteria that are relevant to your purpose, for example, the context in which the studies were done (e.g., developed vs. developing countries) or the time period in which they were done (e.g., before or after the introduction of a policy).

COMMON PROBLEMS

Below are some common problems that students who are new to graduate study may have when working with academic literature and reviewing studies in order to situate their own research. Some of these problems have been described earlier in this chapter; here, I summarize them in one place.

Not imposing order on the material. The student reviews disjointed studies without imposing any order on the material—without showing how the studies are related to one another and/or to the student's own study.

Flipping dependent and independent variables. The student writes a paper about the role of X in Y (e.g., urban poverty in childhood obesity). Here, the hypothesized direction of causality is from X to Y (from poverty to obesity). However, the literature review focuses on studies that have examined the *causes* of urban poverty—in other words, on studies that treated urban poverty as the dependent variable and that would be largely irrelevant to the relationship between urban poverty and obesity. Thus, when reviewing literature, always keep in mind the direction of the hypothesized relationship—what are you hypothesizing to affect what?—and make sure to review studies that bear directly on that relationship.

Using the wrong literature. Sometimes students use literature that is almost exclusively policy-related or that is not disciplinary. Other times, a student may include studies that, while being on the same topic as the student's paper, do not actually support the student's arguments. If you are writing an academic paper, make sure that most of your literature is scholarly rather than policy-related, that most of it comes from the discipline you are contributing to, and that it actually supports your claims.

Not developing an argument. A common mistake is simply to review a study, describing what was done and/or what was found and leave it at that. Such a review is rather difficult to interpret, making readers wonder what the author is trying to say. Use literature to develop an argument, not just show that you have read it. This means drawing conclusions from studies; interpreting them; explaining what they mean, individually or collectively; and evaluating and critiquing them.

Presenting a claim without any evidence. It is often difficult for novice researchers to know which claims do, and which ones do not, require literature support. As a general rule, assume that all claims that are not a result of your own investigation require support from the literature. For example, consider the following statements:

Women are less financially literate than men.

Globalization leads to inequality.

Firms with employee-friendly work environments achieve greater innovative success.

All of these claims require some sort of support. If you are using them to justify the importance of your topic or your expectations, support them with previous research. If these arguments are based on your own findings, indicate this in the narrative by using such phrases as

We/I find that...
Our/my study indicates... Our/my results suggest...

Supporting claims with other claims. Students sometimes believe that as long as there were a parenthetical citation at the end of their claim, their claim would be valid. This is not necessarily true. As I explained earlier, evidence in academic research usually means empirical evidence, so claims should be supported with empirical evidence rather than with other people's claims or opinions.

Presenting evidence and making illogical claims. Sometimes students misunderstand what a study really shows; other times they may misinterpret a study's findings or make an illogical claim from a perfectly legitimate study. To avoid such mistakes, check carefully what the study you are reviewing really shows, what its author(s) claim, and whether the study does support your own arguments.

Criticizing rather than critiquing. Students often know that when reviewing the literature, they need to critique it. However, some confuse critiquing with criticizing. The difference is that the former focuses on analyzing and evaluating, whereas the latter focuses on finding faults. In your review of the literature, focus on critiquing and avoid criticizing.

Chapter 12

Literature Review: Models and Examples

The purpose of this chapter is to show some models and patterns for using academic literature in papers in economics and public policy. Some of the extracts shown in this chapter come from published studies, whereas others were taken from student work. Most of the extracts have been annotated to show what the author is doing in each paragraph. Go over these extracts first, paying attention to the following.

- **Structure and organization**. Notice how the authors organize their literature review and what order they impose on the material. How do they group the studies they review? What type of statement do they make about the literature (e.g., statements about the overall state of the field, statements about individual studies, or statements about other authors' views or theoretical positions)? Where in the review do they place each type of statement, and how do they develop their arguments?

- **Use of language markers,** especially
  - Hedges and boosters,
  - Transition and frame markers,
  - Self-mention, and
  - Attitude and engagement markers.

  Notice how these markers help the authors engage the reader, direct the reader to what is more or less important, show proper respect for the reader, and present themselves as an authority. See Chapter 1 for a review of these markers and their purpose.

- **Use of citations**. Notice how the authors use citations. Do they prefer integral citations (citations that have been integrated into the text and introduced with a signal phrase) or nonintegral citations (parenthetical citations placed at the end of sentences)? What signal phrases are most common in these extracts?

- **Verbs**. What verbs do the authors use most frequently when presenting other authors' arguments and/or findings? Which verb tense is more common, Present Tense or Past Tense?

How to Write about Economics and Public Policy. https://doi.org/10.1016/B978-0-12-813010-0.00012-0

- **Summaries.** How do the authors summarize the work of others? What information do they include in the summary? How much space do they devote to a description of previous studies' methodology vs. findings?

- **Length.** Notice how much space the authors devote to reviewing individual studies and what kind of details they include (e.g., purpose, methodology, main arguments).

After reviewing the annotated extracts, review those that have not been annotated and analyze them using the same approach.

ANNOTATED EXTRACTS FROM PUBLISHED STUDIES

The first extract comes from Jeffrey Kentor's (2001) article on the long-term effects of globalization on income inequality, population growth, and economic development, in which Kentor examines multiple relationships in a single model. The literature review in Kentor's study is divided into several subsections, and each subsection is devoted to examining a particular bivariate relationship such as the relationship between foreign investment and economic development, the relationship between foreign investment and income inequality, and the relationship between foreign investment and population growth. This is a common way to organize a literature review in a study examining multiple relationships or looking at multiple predictors of an outcome. When going over Kentor's review, pay special attention to the use of language markers. Notice how these markers help Kentor present himself as an authority on the subject and at the same time show respect for the readers.

Perhaps the most widely explored, and contested, of the relationships under study is the impact of foreign investment dependence on economic development (Bornschier, 1980; Bornschier and Chase Dunn 1985; Chase Dunn, 1975; Dixon and Boswell, 1996; Firebaugh, 1992, 1996; Kentor, 1998; Soysa and Oneal, 1999). Researchers on both sides of this debate cite apparently "definitive" results supporting opposite conclusions. [**Author introduces the relationship of interest and explains why it is important. Notice the citations in parentheses—their purpose is to support the claim that the relationship under study has been widely explored and that it is contested. Notice also the use of quotation marks with the word "definitive." These are so-called** *scare quotes* **and they are used to show the author's own attitude—in this case, that of disagreement.**] In this literature a key distinction is made between simple foreign investment (inflows of foreign capital) and what is referred to as foreign capital dependence. It is not foreign investment, per se, that has a negative impact on the host economy. Negative consequences arise when the host economy becomes dependent upon foreign capital for its development. [**Author explains an important distinction between two related concepts to show which one is relevant to his own argument.**]

The question of whether foreign investment is a panacea or an albatross on a host economy was first addressed empirically by Christopher Chase Dunn (1975), who found that his measure of foreign capital penetration (debits on investment income) had a negative effect on economic development. Bornschier, Chase Dunn, and Rubinson (1978) furthered Chase Dunn's work by constructing a new measure of foreign capital penetration (PEN), a ratio of foreign capital stocks to investment flows, which also exhibited a negative effect on economic development. These findings were replicated by Bornschier (1980) and Bornschier and Chase Dunn (1985). It was variously argued in these works that foreign capital had a wide range of negative consequences.

Foreign investment tended to be concentrated in a single product that dominated the host economy, resulting in commodity, trade, and partner concentration. This concentration allowed the investing country to obtain and maintain a significant advantage over its dependent partner (Galtung, 1971). Further, profits from foreign investments tended to be repatriated, rather than reinvested in the host country (Bornschier, 1980), resulting in decapitalization and a lack of forward and backward economic linkages (Dixon and Boswell, 1996). Finally, it was argued that there were a host of long-term ancillary negative effects, the "negative externalities" that arose in the host country's social structure (Dixon and Boswell, 1996). [**Author traces the beginnings of an academic debate on the relationship of interest. Notice the use of citations after virtually every sentence. Notice also the use of hedges ("tended to") and attitude markers ("a panacea or an albatross" and "vigorously argued."**]

Firebaugh (1992, 1996) rejected Bornschier and Chase Dunn's (1985) findings, and the subsequent findings of those who used their "PEN" measure of foreign capital penetration, as a statistical artifact, the well-known "denominator effect." Firebaugh argued that a correct analysis of these data indicated that foreign investment actually had a positive effect on economic development, albeit weaker than the effects of domestic investment. Dixon and Boswell (1996) reanalyzed Chase Dunn's model with a new measure of foreign capital penetration (foreign investment stocks/GDP) that addressed Firebaugh's concerns and were able to replicate the earlier negative findings. [**Author reviews another important argument. Notice the use of the strong word "rejected" here, followed by a summary of an explanation proposed by the original author.**]

Kentor (1998) examined the long-term lagged effects of foreign capital penetration on economic development. In a cross-national study of less developed countries between 1940 and 1990, Kentor found that two separate indicators of foreign capital penetration (debits on investment income and foreign investment stocks/GDP) had initial short-term positive effects on per capita GDP growth followed by a long-term (20 + year) negative effect. He argued that the short-term positive effects reflected the initial beneficial effects of capital flows into the host country, while the long-term negative effects were the consequences of trade distortions, decapitalization, lack of forward and backward linkages, and the "negative externalities" discussed by Dixon and Boswell (1996). [**Author reviews his own earlier study. Notice how he interprets its findings in relation to another relevant work.**]

Most recently, Soysa and Oneal (1999) reported that, in their reassessment of earlier models, foreign investment had a positive effect on economic growth between 1980 and 1990. In fact, according to Soysa and Oneal, foreign investment is actually two and one-half times as productive as domestic investment. However, Soysa and Oneal fail to address the question of the impact of long-term lagged effects described by Kentor (1998). In fact, their results would be consistent with Kentor's findings that foreign investment had a short-term positive effect followed by a long-term negative one. [**Author reviews a recent study that contradicts some of the previous findings and places it in the context of his own earlier study. Notice how he tries to reconcile the results of that study with those of his own in the last sentence.**]

While a detailed discussion of Soysa and Oneal's work is beyond the scope of this paper, there is one aspect of this research that warrants mention. Their failure to examine these long-term effects reflects more than an empirical omission. It suggests a lack of understanding of the concept and mechanisms of structural dependence (Cardoso and Faletto, 1979). This term refers to the development and/or restructuring of the host economy to make it attractive to foreign investment, which affects a wide range of social, political, and economic structures. These include laws permitting foreign ownership, convertibility and repatriation of currencies, favorable labor laws, lax environmental standards, and favorable tax treatments, among others. There is also an ideology that is legitimated concerning the value of foreign investment and incorporation into the global economy. These effects reproduce and exacerbate the negative effects of foreign investment far beyond, the commercial life of a given foreign investment. [**Author argues that a previous study should be disregarded. Notice the use of rather strong words in this criticism (e.g., "failure to examine," "more than an empirical omission," and "a lack of understanding." Notice also that he provides a careful, detailed explanation for his position.**]

How are we to interpret these conflicting analyses? [**This question signals that a conclusion is coming.**] In spite of those who dismiss the validity of negative findings of foreign capital penetration by simply referring to Firebaugh's (1992) critique of this body of work, an impartial review of the literature suggests otherwise. First, Firebaugh's critique refers only to Bornschier, Chase Dunn, and Rubinson's PEN measure of foreign capital penetration. Firebaugh does not address Chase Dunn's (1975) earlier results using debits on investment income (subsequently supported by Kentor 1998). Nor is Soysa and Oneal's myopic analysis of the short-term impact of foreign investment a valid rejection of the overall long-term negative effects found by Kentor (1998). In short, none of the critiques of these negative findings provide a basis for rejecting the basic tenet that dependence on foreign capital has negative consequences for the host economy. [**Author concludes with a clear description of an expected result. Notice the persuasive, authoritative tone of his conclusion, especially when he argues that a particular earlier result should not be taken into account.**] (Kentor, 2001, pp. 436–438)

Kentor devotes a large space—more than 4 out of 17 pages of the main text—to reviewing the literature in his study. This is rather uncommon for studies in economics, where authors would typically devote just a few paragraphs in the Introduction to a review of the state of current knowledge about the problem. Such reviews would often begin with 1–2 opening sentences announcing that studies have been conducted on the topic and giving a general evaluation of the state of research in the area. After these opening sentences about the state of research, the author may review individual studies or groups of studies, highlighting their limitations or differences from the proposed study. Here is an example from a study by Eric Bonsang (2007), who examined the determinants of financial and time transfers from adult children to their older parents.

Several studies have examined substitution between financial and time transfers from adult children to older parents. While some agreement exists concerning financial transfers, time transfers are more subject to debate. Zissimopoulos (2001) using US data (Health and Retirement Study (HRS)) finds that an increase in an adult child's income and wealth increases transfers to parents, while an increase in wage rate leads to an increase in financial transfer and a decrease in time transfer. Ioannides and Kan's (1999) estimates from the Panel Study of Income Dynamics (PSID) indicate a positive effect of head of household hourly earnings on financial transfer to parents and a negative one for time transfer. Sloan et al.'s (2002) results from the HRS suggest that financial assistance responds positively to an increase in the wage rate, while it exhibits no significant effect on time assistance to elderly parents. McGarry and Schoeni (1995) also used the HRS and showed that the household income of the respondent is positively associated [with] financial transfers to parents, while there is no significant impact on time assistance given. Arrondel and Masson (2001) analyze upward financial and time transfers from French data (the "Caisse Nationale d'Assurance Vieillesse" survey) using a bivariate probit and find no sign of substitution between financial and time transfers made by adult children to their parents. [**Notice that for each study mentioned here, the author indicates what data were used and where the data came from. This is very common in economics articles, because knowing what kind of data a study is based on helps the reader evaluate the validity and strength of the author's claims.**] (Bonsang, 2007, p. 172)

A common way to review a large amount of literature is to make general statements about certain aspects of the topic and support them with citations to relevant studies. This is a very economical way to cover a large amount of literature in just a few sentences, and it is particularly common in journal articles, where space is limited. Below is an extract from a study of homelessness by Zlotnick et al. (1999), in which the authors summarize research on incomes of homeless individuals. Notice that rather than reviewing individual studies one by one, the authors make general statements about what the current research shows and support them with citations. Virtually all of these citations are to empirical studies.

Many studies have documented the low monthly and annual incomes reported by homeless adults (Bassuk, Rubin, & Lauriat, 1986; Breakey et al., 1989; Burt & Cohen, 1989; Fischer, Shapiro, Breakey, Anthony, & Kramer, 1986; Koegel, Burnam, & Farr, 1990; Milburn & D'Ercole, 1991; Miller & Lin, 1988; Wood, Valdez, Hayashi, & Shen, 1990; Zlotnick & Robertson, 1996). Although few homeless adults report regular formal-sector employment, many who have regular formal-sector employment report that the work pays poorly and is temporary or sporadic (Zlotnick & Robertson, 1996). Another source of income is entitlement benefits (Breakey et al., 1989; Calsyn, Kohfeld, & Roades, 1993; Koegel et al., 1990; Sosin, 1992; Zlotnick & Robertson, 1996). Estimates of the number of homeless adults currently receiving entitlement benefit income vary between 25%–60% (Koegel et al., 1990; Zlotnick & Robertson, 1996). However, few studies indicate how many individuals are able to sustain entitlement income over time (Jahiel, 1992; Segal, 1991; Zlotnick, Robertson, & Lahiff, 1998) and whether sustained entitlement income contributes to exits from homelessness. [**Notice here how the authors support every sentence with multiple citations. The first sentence is a rather general statement indicating the importance of the topic. The next three sentences describe specific results. The last sentence establishes a niche for the authors' study.**] (Zlotnick et al., 1999, p. 212)

Here is another example from a study by Arum and LaFree (2008) of educational attainment and the risk of adult incarceration in the United States. Notice how the authors impose order on the literature by grouping studies according to the specific result they show. This helps the reader quickly see the connections between previous research and the proposed study.

As jail and prison populations in the United States have reached levels that are both historically and comparatively unprecedented, there has been increasing interest in better understanding the determinants of incarceration. Accordingly, recent research has explored the effects of a wide range of macrolevel variables on incarceration rates, including unemployment (Chiricos & Delone, 1992; Grant & Martinez, 1997; Western & Beckett, 1999), economic inequality (Garland, 1990; Greenberg, 1999), electoral cycles (Beckett, 1997; Jacobs & Carmichael, 2002), welfare spending (Greenberg & West, 2001), and race relations (Greenberg & West, 2001; Jacobs & Carmichael, 2002; Pettit & Western, 2004). However, with few exceptions (Arum & Beattie, 1999; LaFree & Arum, 2006), researchers have not examined the possibility that school characteristics are associated with the risk of incarceration in adulthood. [**Authors state the topic and show its significance ("there has been increasing interest"). Then, in just one sentence, they summarize what is known about the topic by focusing on predictor variables. This is a common strategy for summarizing a large amount of literature in a very succinct manner.**]

This situation is surprising because educational attainment has become an increasingly important determinant of life-course outcomes, including employment, marriage, and incarceration (Fischer & Hout, 2006; Goldin & Katz, 2000; Mare, 1991; Pettit & Western, 2004), and in modern societies, sociologists have long recognized that schooling functions as the primary nonfamilial social institution that is responsible for socializing children and young adults to behave in a conventional law-abiding fashion (Durkheim, 1925/1973). [**Notice the use of the word "surprising" here. This is an attitude marker and it helps the authors highlight the importance of their own study.**] Indeed, prior research has consistently shown that delinquent and criminal behavior are [*sic*] strongly associated with a variety of education-related variables, including grades (Hirschi, 1969; Kercher, 1988), dislike for school (Gottfredson, 1981; Sampson & Laub, 1993), misbehavior in school (Wilson & Herrnstein, 1985), and educational attainment (LaFree & Drass, 1996; Lochner & Moretti, 2001). But despite the institutional importance of schools and their centrality to explanations of crime, little is known about their association with the risk of incarceration. [**Authors explain why educational attainment, the main predictor variable in their study, may be related to the dependent variable, risk of incarceration, by arguing that schooling is related to many important life outcomes including delinquency.**] (Arum & LaFree, 2008, pp. 397–398)

In economics articles, authors often place the emphasis in reviewing the literature on showing how their own study is different from the previous ones and what their own contribution to the field is. Here is an example from Charles and Hurst (2003), who examined the correlation of wealth across generations. The literature in this study is described in the last part of the Introduction section, which has the following structure:

- Purpose of the study,
- Outline of the authors' study (e.g., what the authors did),
- Description of main results and arguments, and
- Description and evaluation of previous research.

This structure—when the literature is reviewed at the end of the Introduction after a description of the purpose, methodology, and results—is rather unique to economics articles, where it is fairly common.

Aside from Mulligan (1997), the few previous authors who have studied the intergenerational wealth association have used samples from very specialized sub-populations drawn from the late nineteenth and early twentieth centuries. Although wealth was not the primary focus of his analysis, Mulligan reports estimates of the elasticity in log wealth between parents and their children of between 0.32 and 0.43. However, he does not attempt to separate between different explanations for the parent-child wealth relationship. [**Authors describe previous attempts to examine the topic. Notice that the emphasis here is on the fact that there have been few such attempts and that there are limitations in previous research. Presenting previous research in this way helps the authors frame their own study as an attempt to fill an existing gap and make an important contribution to the field.**]

Of the intergenerational relationships that can affect the similarity in parent-child wealth, the one that has received the most independent attention is the intergenerational relationship in income. The consensus is that the elasticity of log child earnings with respect to log parents' earnings is between 0.4 and 0.6, after one accounts for measurement error (Mulligan 1997; Solon 1999). Few papers have looked at how the growth rate and variances of parents' and child's incomes are related, and no one has studied how much of the intergenerational wealth relationship is attributable to the aspects of lifetime income emphasized in the theoretical literature. [**Authors indicate a consensus in the field and describe a gap. Notice how they connect the gap with theoretical literature.**]

... Only a handful of papers have looked at direct evidence on the extent of heterogeneity in household savings preference parameters, although none examines whether these preferences are related between parents and children (Lawrance, 1991; Barsky et al., 1997; Samwick, 1998; Warner and Pleeter, 2001). Work on intergenerational correlations in portfolio composition is equally sparse (for exceptions, see Chiteji and Stafford [2000] and Hurst and Lusardi [2002]). [**Authors show that there is a clear need for their study by carefully evaluating the state of current knowledge and describing a gap.**] (Charles & Hurst, 2003, pp. 1157–1158)

In a similar pattern, authors may describe relevant literature in the part of the Introduction where they talk about the contribution of their own study to the existing body of research. In this case, they would often describe previous research in relation to their own contribution to the field, emphasizing what they did rather than what other researchers have done. This is a fairly common way of presenting existing literature in economics papers. Here is an example from a study by Atkin (2016), which examined the differences in caloric intake between local residents and migrants in India. This study appeared in one of the most prestigious economics journals, the *American Economic Review*. As in the previous example, the literature review in this study appears in the last paragraphs of the Introduction, following a description of the purpose and a summary of the study's methodology and results.

This paper contributes to several literatures. First, it adds to the growing literature on the importance of culture, a topic surveyed in Guiso, Sapienza, and Zingales (2006), Fernández (2011), and Alesina and Giuliano (2015). In using the behavior of migrants to examine the influence of culture on household decisions, it is particularly closely related to Carroll, Rhee, and Rhee's (1994) study of savings behavior; Fernández, Fogli, and Olivetti's (2004) and Fernández and Fogli's (2009) studies of female labor force participation; and Giuliano's (2007) study of family living arrangements. In contrast to this strand of the literature, which typically demonstrates that culture can influence behavior, my approach allows me to quantify the costs that culture can impose. [**Author establishes connections between his study and previous studies and highlights his own contribution. Notice how in just a few sentences, he manages to cover a very large literature on the topic. He achieves this by imposing order on the literature—by grouping studies according to their focus.**]

Second, I add to the literature on the persistence of food preferences initiated by Staehle (1934), with recent contributions by Logan and Rhode (2010) and Bronnenberg, Dube, and Gentzkow (2012). Although these papers document that migrants bring their food preferences with them (and in the latter case, the consequences for brands' market shares) none of these papers explore the nutritional consequences and hence the costs of such preferences. Finally, this study is related to Nunn and Qian (2011). Their finding, that over hundreds of years the Old World adopted New World crops with consequent nutritional improvements, suggests that the persistent food culture I find may weaken over many generations. [**Author reviews more relevant studies and highlights a gap. Notice how in the last sentence he tries to place his own results in the context of the existing literature.**]

Atkin (2013) provides theoretical and empirical evidence for the existence of regional food preferences in India. The two papers differ in that Atkin (2013) lays out a model in which the combination of agroclimatic endowments and habits generate regional food tastes that favor the locally abundant foods and explores the implications of this correlation between preferences and endowments for the size of the gains generated by trade. In contrast, this paper takes India's regional food preferences as given, interprets these as cultural phenomena, and furthers our understanding of the importance of culture by quantifying the calories households are willing to forgo to accommodate their cultural preferences. [**Author explains the differences between his current paper and his earlier paper. Notice how this helps him build on his previous study and at the same time highlight the contribution of the current study.**] (Atkin, 2016, pp. 1147–1148)

ANNOTATED LITERATURE REVIEW FROM A STUDENT PAPER

The extract below comes from a paper written by Ruopeng An, a student in Transition Economy, on the topic of income inequality and the role of technology and migration in income convergence. Notice how the review goes from more general to more specific—from studies that have been conducted in different parts of the world to those that have focused on China, the main focus of the current study. Notice also how the author moves from general statements about the research area to a more specific description of the relevant studies and, finally, to an evaluation of those studies.

During the past decade, accelerated income inequality has been as outstanding as the Chinese growth miracle. From 1991 to 2004, China's real gross domestic product (GDP) tripled while its regional Gini coefficient increased by 22.4% to 0.465. According to the World Development Indicators released by the World Bank (2005), the top quintile of the Chinese population earned half of the total income in 2003, a ratio higher than that of the United States of America (U.S., 45.8%) or India (43.3%), and close to that of Philippines (52.3%). Furthermore, a substantial part of this disparity lies in the income gap between the coastal and the interior provinces, which exhibits a U-shaped pattern with the year 1990 as its turning point (Long, 1999). What does the long-run trend of the regional disparities suggest? Will this inequality increase over time as poor provinces lag further behind? What are the driving forces of economic divergence across Chinese provinces? Are there any policy reforms that can deal effectively with the current problem and thus contribute to economic convergence? This paper explores these core questions. [**Author describes the problem and the main questions his study will address.**]

Regarding the research approach, this paper belongs to the growing literature on economic convergence. As suggested by the neoclassical model of economic growth (Solow, 1956), poor economies would grow faster than rich ones, and thus the poor and rich economies would eventually converge. The 1980s and 1990s experienced an explosion of research on convergence across countries, regions within a country, and economic sectors (Barro & Sala-i-Martin, 1991a, 1991b, 1992a, 1992b, 1995, 1998; Baumol, 1986; Bernard & Durlauf, 1995; Dowrick & Nguyen, 1989; Lucas, 1988; Mankiw, Romer, & Weil, 1992; Quah, 1993; Romer, 1986). Although the empirical results seem to be rather mixed, in general, evidence is increasing of conditional convergence across similar economies after controlling certain variables that affect the steady-state output level.[1] **[Author situates his study within the existing scholarship and theories of growth and describes the current state of research and its main findings.]**

The study of convergence in the Chinese economy began relatively late due to a lack of provincial data. However, it has grown rapidly since the mid-1990s as official statistics have become largely available and the increasing inequality has become a hot issue in both academic circles and in politics.[2] **[Author traces the development of the field.]** Three main studies have been conducted in this field. Following the cross-sectional approach, Jian, Sachs, and Warner (1996) examined the convergence of per capita income across Chinese provinces during the period of 1952–1993. Their results suggested convergence since 1978, when China's Reform and Open-up Policy (*Gaige Kaifang Zhengce*) began, but divergence during the Cultural Revolution of 1965-1978.[3] Chen and Fleisher (1995) examined convergence of per capita income across provinces from 1978 to 1993 and estimated the speed of absolute convergence to be 0.9% per year and the speed of conditional convergence to be 5.7% per year after controlling for physical/human capital investment, employment growth rate, foreign direct investment, and coastal location. Raiser (1998) used both cross-sectional and panel data to test the speed of absolute and conditional convergence during the period of 1978–1992 and found that it ranged from 0.8% to 4.2% in various subperiods. **[Author provides a detailed description of the most relevant studies. Notice that he also describes their methodology to help the reader evaluate those studies.]**

The above studies have established a sound basis for further research in provincial convergence in China and have offered alternative methods and results that this paper uses to make comparisons. Nevertheless, three main limitations in the current research need to be identified. First, these studies did not pay sufficient attention to the dynamics of convergence over time, focusing instead on finding significant convergence rates within the whole period under investigation. Jian, Sachs, and Warner's (1996) study is an exception to this trend; however, limited by the sample size obtained before 1978, these researchers could not accurately measure the convergence trends.[4] Second, the driving forces behind convergence and the evolution of their effectiveness have received little attention. Third, the role that technology has played in provincial disparity since 1990 and the influence of migration on convergence have so far been neglected.[5] **[Author evaluates the most relevant studies. Notice how he acknowledges the important contribution of those studies before critiquing them. This is a common way to introduce a critique.]**

By addressing the above gaps, the present study provides a new look at the convergence dynamics across Chinese provinces from 1952 to 2004. This paper contributes to the convergence literature in the following six ways. First, by analyzing the trend of σ convergence and decomposing the Theil Inequality Index, it establishes a theoretical basis for identifying the breakpoints that are used to examine the evolution of β convergence. Second, it focuses on the influence of macroeconomic policies on provincial disparities. The roles of physical and human capital investment, population growth, international trade, and fiscal transfer during different periods are highlighted. Third, both the β convergence of personal income and that of labor productivity are modeled and their respective results are compared.[6] Furthermore, the use of the endogenous economic growth model makes it possible to incorporate technology into the Barro and Sala-i-Martin model, which solves the omitted variable problem of the traditional cross-sectional approach. In addition, the role of interprovincial migration in China is, for the first time, analyzed within the convergence framework. Finally, the statistical data used in this paper come mainly from the *China Compendium of Statistics*, 1949-2004, the latest official data in which many key economic indicators have been readjusted and standardized. **[Author describes the contribution of his study to the literature on convergence. Notice how he tries to highlight the strengths of his dataset and his approach.]**

Notes

1. For example, Barro and Sala-i-Martin (1992a) found the speed of conditional convergence to be 1.84% per year in 98 countries during the period of 1960–1985.
2. See Yao and Weeks (2000) for a detailed discussion of the evolution of the Chinese statistical reporting system.
3. The official period of the Cultural Revolution was from 1966 to 1976. For research purposes, they set this period to be between 1965 and 1978.
4. In their paper, only 15 provinces were included in the analysis of delta convergence and beta convergence during the period of 1952-1978.
5. Yao and Weeks (2000) examined the impact of technology and its progress rate on convergence by applying a panel data approach. However, their methodology had certain flaws, which are discussed in Section 6.
6. In this paper, real GDP per capita is used as a proxy for personal income, and real GDP per worker is used as a proxy for labor productivity.

(An, 2006, pp. 1–2)

MODEL LITERATURE REVIEWS FROM STUDENT PAPERS

This section shows three model literature reviews written by graduate students on different topics in public policy and economics. Go over these reviews and analyze their structure, organization, language, and the use of citations.

The first extract is a revised version of a literature review written by Zhang Jiaxin, a student in Macroeconomic Policy. In her paper, she investigated the relationship between fiscal decentralization and economic growth in China. As you go over this extract, pay attention to the highlighted words and expressions and try to determine their purpose. How do they help the author make her arguments?

The debate regarding the relationship between fiscal decentralization and economic growth continues across empirical studies. The picture is mixed in both cross-country and single-country studies. Some scholars have argued that fiscal decentralization has a positive effect on economic growth because it promotes efficiency in the allocation of resources, especially the allocation of public goods, and because it stimulates local government performance. For example, in a study of fiscal decentralization in the U.S. using state-level data, Akai and Sakata (2002) found that fiscal decentralization contributed to economic growth. The particular strength of that study is the use of multiple indicators of fiscal decentralization. For China, too, a number of empirical studies have shown significant positive effects. For example, Lin and Liu (2000) used provincial data from 1970 to 1993 to demonstrate that fiscal decentralization had a positive effect on Chinese economic growth. Ma (1997) also showed that fiscal decentralization benefited economic growth in China. In a later study, Zhang and Gong (2005) analyzed data from 1986 to 2002, which reflected many socio-economic changes in China including the introduction of a tax-sharing system in 1994. They found a positive relationship between fiscal decentralization and economic growth after the implementation of the tax-sharing system. Using provincial-level panel data from 1980 to 2004, Wen (2006) found that fiscal decentralization promoted China's economic growth overall, although there were significant geographical differences.

In contrast, Davoodi and Zou (1998) found a significant negative relationship between fiscal decentralization and economic growth in developing countries. Their study used data for 46 countries across the world from 1970 to 1989. Zhang and Zou (1998) used panel data for China covering the period following the reforms in the late 1970s and found that fiscal decentralization led to segmentation, which increased local government corruption and had a negative impact on the sustainable development of the economy. Yin (2004) further argued that fiscal decentralization aggravated the imbalances of economic growth among different regions in China.

A number of studies have failed to find a strong link between fiscal decentralization and economic growth or could only demonstrate uncertain results. For example, Davoodi and Zou's (1998) study showed no significant relationship in developed countries and Xie, Zou, and Davoodi (1999) found no significant effect of fiscal decentralization on economic growth in the U.S. Jin, Qian, and Weingast (2005) found a weak positive relationship between the level of fiscal decentralization and provincial economic growth in China, but the relationship was not statistically significant. Furthermore, Wang and Qin (2007) found differential effects of fiscal decentralization on the economic growth of different regions in China. (Zhang, 2010, p. 2)

The second extract comes from a study by Tatsuya Takeda, a student in Macroeconomic Policy, in which he investigated opportunity costs of holding foreign currency reserves for Japan. Notice how he carefully groups previous studies and how he uses previous research to support his own arguments rather than simply describe what previous studies have found. As you go over the extract, highlight the words and expressions that help Tatsuya organize previous studies and make his own arguments.

There has been a considerable amount of research devoted to foreign exchange reserves. The literature has focused on two aspects of foreign exchange reserves in particular. The first one is the reason, or the motives, for holding foreign exchange reserves, and the second one is the costs and benefits of such holding in pursuit of finding the optimal level of foreign exchange reserves.

The motives for holding foreign exchange reserves are generally categorized into two kinds. The first kind is a natural extension to and interpretation of the financial reserves held by governments against undesirable events and it is called *precautionary motives* in the literature on foreign exchange reserves. The study of precautionary motives has a relatively long history, going back to Heller (1966), and many theoretical and empirical studies have been conducted to elucidate these motives. Frenkel and Jovanovich (1981) and Ben-Bassat and Gottlieb (1992a), for example, argue that foreign exchange reserves are held to smooth consumption and fill the gap created by sudden moves in the capital markets.

Precautionary motives have been more extensively studied since the turn of the century, reflecting the intensified globalization and experiences of the Asian currency crisis. Aizenman and Marion (2002), for example, develop a buffer stock model and argue that loss aversion of society makes large reserves welfare-improving even in the presence of significant opportunity costs associated with holding such reserves. Lee (2004) extends this insurance aspect developed by Aizenman and Marion (2002) and uses an options pricing technique to estimate the insurance value of precautionary foreign exchange reserves.

While the precautionary motives may well explain the behavior of small developing countries, which need to guard against external shocks, the recent drastic increase in foreign currency reserves held by some developing countries is puzzling. Based on the precautionary motives, the demand for reserves is "self-insurance against costly output contraction incurred by sudden stops and capital flight" (Aizenman & Lee, 2007, p. 192) and an increase in the trading flow of goods and capital calls for larger reserves (Baker & Walentin, 2001). Aizenman and Marion (2003) also show that increasing the level of risk aversion and volatilities increases the demand for foreign currency reserves.

Yet, because precautionary motives alone cannot explain the recent build-up in reserves held by some developing countries (Hauner, 2006), a different perspective in understanding the motivations behind such an increase is called for. According to a mercantilist view, reserves are "a by-product of mercantilist motives to keep the real exchange rate undervalued" (Hauner, 2006, p. 186) and countries accumulate foreign exchange reserves "in order to prevent or mitigate appreciation, with the ultimate goal of increasing export growth" (Aizenman & Marion, 2003, p. 196).

Government intervention in the global capital markets has introduced some rigidity in the market place and the world has started to resemble the Bretton Woods era (Dooley, Folkerts-Landau, & Garber, 2003, 2004). This mercantilist view is supported by central bankers. Former chairman of the Federal Reserve Bank Mr. Greenspan says that "a mercantilist view of trade…perceives trade surplus as somehow good, deficits bad. Since in the short run, if not in the long run, trade balances are affected by exchange rates, rates that are allowed to float freely are few and far between" (Greenspan, 1999, p. 1).

Empirical studies of the motives of foreign exchange reserve holdings have produced mixed and inconclusive results. Aizenman and Lee (2007) claim that there is more evidence to support the precautionary view compared to the mercantilist view while others (e.g., Hauner, 2006; Neely, 2000) disagree. The difficulty for such an empirical study comes from the fact that "[b]road country coverage...comes at a cost: detail on individual country cases may get lost" (Hauner, 2006, p. 185) and that some countries use foreign exchange market intervention for domestic monetary policy operations (Neely, 2000). More recently, Nor, Azali, and Law (2011) conducted extensive panel data analyses and concluded that, while current account balances are positively correlated with foreign exchange reserves for all Asian countries, for non-ASEAN countries (i.e., Japan, China, Taiwan, and Korea), short-term external debts and international reserves have positive correlations whereas for ASEAN countries, the opposite is true (Nor, Azali, & Law, 2011, p. 89). This seems to suggest that economically stronger countries tend to hold foreign exchange reserves with precautionary motives.

Another major topic in the literature on foreign exchange reserves is cost-benefit analysis, which also dates back to Heller (1966). Benefits of reserve holdings are closely related to the motives while the costs of such holdings have been analyzed using various approaches. These costs might be substantial if calculated properly and "[a] model that accurately measure[s] the cost of the necessary increase in reserve holdings may find that the predicted gains from greater trade are significantly reduced, and possibly eliminated altogether" (Baker & Walentin, 2001, p. 6).

In order to derive the cost in value terms, one needs to estimate both the unit cost and the amount of reserves because the product of the unit cost and the amount of reserves give the total cost in value terms. On the unit cost side, early works focused on the funding cost of reserves (Baker & Walentin, 2001). However, since the pioneering work of Ben-Bassat and Gottlieb (1992), the opportunity cost has become the core component for the unit cost estimation of foreign exchange reserves in cost analysis. These authors define the opportunity cost as the real rate of return on capital, using the maximum of the real productivity of capital in the private and public sectors as the overall real productivity of capital and consider it to be the opportunity cost for holding foreign exchange reserves. Hauner (2006) further elaborates this cost analysis and decomposes the costs into four groups. The first one is opportunity costs resulting from the foregone returns from alternative use (Hauner, 2006, p. 172). This is exactly the same as what Ben-Bassat and Gottlieb defined as the opportunity cost. The second group is financial gain or loss created by the reserve assets (Hauner, 2006, p.173). Since foreign exchange reserves are held in some kind of financial assets, typically a short maturity government bonds denominated in hard currencies, they yield current returns and their values fluctuate with the moves in exchange rates and interest rates. The third group is the "savings from a lower interest bill to the extent that higher reserves lower the spreads and thus the interest rate on external debt" (Hauner, 2006, p. 173). A country can choose to pay down external debts using the assets held as foreign exchange reserves or continue borrowing, just like corporates can have cash and debts at the same time. The borrowing cost should be lower if the lenders feel safer with the existence of large reserves. The fourth group is the "cost through the present cost of past sterilizations undertaken to offset the monetary impact of reserve accumulation" (Hauner, 2006, p. 173). Purchase of foreign currency for reserve accumulation requires sale of domestic currency, and the added liquidity in the market must be absorbed by the issuance of government debts, directly or indirectly, by the central bank, if the authorities intend to keep the monetary policy unchanged.

On the amount side, it may not be a straightforward procedure to convert what is reported as reserves into the base amount for cost calculation. Reserves are held in multiple currency denominations and because of the exchange rate fluctuation, "[i]n practice, adjusting reserves for valuation changes is very difficult" (Neely, 2000, p. 26). Furthermore, foreign exchange reserves may be held not just in government bonds such as US Treasury Notes but also in gold and SDR. However, the data available for developed countries seem adequate for detailed study.

The literature on foreign exchange reserves has focused mostly on developing countries. Developing economies do need foreign exchange reserves since their own currencies are typically not accepted as a means for payment in international trade. In contrast, there appears to be no strong reason for developed countries to have large foreign exchange reserves because their currencies are accepted in international trade (Williams, 2005). There should be little reason for developed countries to hold foreign exchange reserves for precautionary motives and, as Williams (2005) points out, developed countries should intervene in foreign exchange markets only for the purpose of "ensuring orderly conditions" (Williams, 2005, p. 2). In fact, the International Monetary Fund's Article IV, Section 1 prohibits "attempts to remedy balance of payments problems by manipulating exchange rates" (Neely, 2000, p. 20). Therefore, there should not be many cases of developed countries holding sufficiently large reserves to necessitate detailed study.

However, it is widely understood that Japan has been an exception. Various studies either assume or conclude that Japan has been aggressively purchasing the dollar for mercantilist reasons of keeping the yen undervalued (Dooley et al. 2004; Greenspan, 1999; Williams, 2005).

Mercantilist motives make the discussion of optimal reserve holdings difficult because the reserves are a by-product of interventions and not the goal in itself. As Williams (2005, p. 1) points out, "[s]ince the holding of reserves ... generally means that the home country is financing investment and development of other people's countries, ... countries should hold no more foreign exchange reserves than they think is necessary." Furthermore, calculating opportunity costs for holding foreign exchange reserves is challenging as Ben-Bassat and Gottlieb (1992) and Williams (2005) have pointed out, especially for large and complex economies like the U.S. and Japan.

In the case of Japan, there has been no discussion about the optimal level of foreign exchange reserves, given their mercantilist origins. Yet, given the size of the reserves and the current fiscal conditions of Japan, the costs and benefits for the foreign exchange reserves in Japan should attract more attention. This paper aims to estimate the opportunity costs of Japanese foreign exchange reserves following the approach initially developed by Ben-Bassat and Gottlieb (1992a) as a first step in the study of Japanese reserve holdings. (Takeda, 2012, pp. 4–9)

The last extract comes from a study by Itai Maparara, a student in Public Finance. This is his review of empirical literature on the direction of causality between government expenditure and economic growth. A part of this review was used as an example in the previous chapter. Here, you can see the entire literature review section from his paper. As you read, notice the amount of detail Itai includes in the description of previous studies and his attempt to relate the findings of these studies to specific theoretical positions. Highlight the words and expressions that help Itai organize previous studies and make his own arguments.

Empirical evidence on the direction of causality between government expenditure, whether in whole or in sub-categories, and economic growth has generated mixed results. Magazzino (2011) examined the relationship between disaggregated public spending and GDP for Italy using 1990 to 2010 data. He employed cointegration plus error correction model and Granger causality test to determine the direction of causality. His results supported Wagner's law in four subcategories of public expenditure, namely, defense, public order and safety, economic affairs, and housing community amenities. A bidirectional flow was detected for public service and education. Magazzino (2011) concluded that policy makers can reduce public expenditure in the four subcategories without the move affecting the growth rate of the economy. Kolluri, Panik, and Wahab (2000) examined the direction of causality between government expenditure (consumption + transfer payments) and economic growth for G7 countries using data for the period from 1960 to 1993. They used a cointegration procedure, error correction model, and Granger causality tests. Their results supported Wagner's law for all countries, showing that government expenditure was increasing at a faster rate than was economic growth and that it was resulting from economic growth. They concluded that such a trend is an outcome of a forward-looking budgetary process, which reflects deterministic strategic goals supported by sound taxation and expenditure policies. Ono (2014) used a different approach to examine the case of Japan for the period from 1960 to 2010. Employing the autoregressive distributed lag (ADL) test for a threshold cointegration procedure developed by Li and Lee (2010) and a threshold Granger causality test, he showed that Wagner's law holds for Japan, thus striking consistency with Kolluri et al (2000) findings in the G7 case. Ono (2014) examined causality in a trivariate framework, adding population as an explanatory variable in the regressions.

Cetin et al. (2014) used panel data for 60 countries covering the period from 1976 to 2010. The study was based on a pooled mean group strategy, that is, a panel-based error correction model, and the countries were sub-categorized on the basis of their economic growth rates. The categories comprised low (below 3%), medium (3% to 5%), and high (above 5%) growth rates. Their findings were that high growth rate economies had a significant relationship between government expenditure and economic growth, both in the short and long run. The coefficient for government expenditure was positive and significant. For middle growth economies, only a long-run relationship was supported, whereas no relationship was detected for low growth economies. Arpia and Turrini (2008) used the same strategy on data for EU countries for the period from 1970 to 2003. Their categories were catching-up countries (e.g., Portugal, Spain, and Ireland), fast-ageing countries (e.g., Belgium, Finland, and Portugal), low-debt countries (e.g., Luxembourg, Finland, and Spain), and countries with weak numerical rules for expenditure control (e.g., Austria, Greece, and Italy). They concluded that government expenditure and economic growth were linked by a stable long-run relationship and that the direction of causality followed Keynes' views.

Examining the case of a developing country, Nasiru (2012) employed a bound test to cointegration plus Granger causality tests to determine causality in Nigeria for the period from 1961 to 2010. The study categorized government expenditure into capital and recurrent expenditure. The results show that no causality exists for these expenditure categories in the long run. However, in the short run, causality flows from government capital expenditure to economic growth, thus supporting Keynes' views. The study concluded that government can influence economic growth by shifting expenditure from recurrent to capital formation. One interesting study was carried out by Loizides and Vamvoukas (2004). The study examined causality in a bivariate and trivariate framework using an error correction model and Granger causality test, enabling the comparison of results from the different frameworks. In the bivariate framework, data analysis supported Keynes' views for the UK and Ireland in both the short and long run, whereas the data for Greece validated Wagner's inferences. However, when causality was examined in the trivariate framework by adding inflation as a third variable, the UK data supported Wagner's views. These results imply that omitting certain explanatory variables may influence results on the direction of causality. Therefore, the present study directly proceeds into the trivariate framework of analysis in order to extend the findings of Loizides and Vamvoukas (2004). This study will also employ an error correction model and a Granger causality test as a strategy. The uniqueness of this study is the choice of a third explanatory variable included in the model, which is trade. By including trade, the study can examine whether the regional group has influenced government expenditure and economic growth in its member countries through agreed-upon trade policies. (Maparara, 2016, pp. 3–4)

Chapter 13

Data and Methodology

RESEARCH QUESTION AND METHODOLOGY

Methodology is the "how" of research—a means for answering a research question. In this book, I use the word *methodology* in a broad sense, to refer to the overall approach that the researcher takes in order to answer the research question. In a qualitative study, methodology usually refers to case selection and data collection methods (e.g., semistructured interview); in a quantitative study, methodology often encompasses the following aspects of a study:

- Variables and their definitions,
- Data and sampling,
- Empirical (i.e., econometric) model, and
- Empirical (i.e., estimation) strategy.

A cardinal rule of research is that a particular research question implies a particular methodology—for example, a particular type of data, model, and empirical strategy. This means that once you have formulated a research question, you are no longer entirely free to choose any methodology you wish. Rather, what you should do is ask yourself, "What sort of evidence do I need in order to answer my research question in the most persuasive way?" The answer to this question will guide you in the selection of the most appropriate methodology. A good methodology is, therefore, one that allows you to test your hypothesis and answer your research question in the most persuasive way.

It is beyond the scope of this book to describe the various methodological options that exist for quantitative and qualitative studies. However, it is important to point out that you should think about your methodology as soon as you have a research question. Much of your ability to pursue your research question will be determined by data availability—whether you will be able to collect or obtain data. All too often students invest a lot of time in developing a research question only to discover that the data they wanted to use are not available or that they do not possess the proper technique for analyzing the type of data they have obtained. Think about your methodology while still reviewing the literature on the topic you have chosen. As you read, note what kind of data and empirical strategy previous studies have used. If you are not sure whether you can obtain the same kind of data, seek help from your advisor.

How to Write about Economics and Public Policy. https://doi.org/10.1016/B978-0-12-813010-0.00013-2

THE IDEAL VS. THE REAL METHODOLOGY

When students are taught about methodology, they are usually told about what research should be like, ideally. Yet, reality is almost always different from that ideal. Despite being presented in many textbooks as a step-by-step process, research never is; in fact, it is a process that is characterized by advances and retreats, trials and errors, false starts, and innumerable problems. For example, you may not be able to secure as big a sample as you need or obtain the data that you need; participants may drop out from a longitudinal study; you may discover half way into the analyses that the model or strategy you have chosen is not sufficiently robust, or that there is an alternative explanation for which you forgot to control, and so on. Research in public policy may be particularly messy because policy researchers deal with real-world problems, which are complex and multifaceted and which involve multiple actors and often call for an interdisciplinary approach. Researching such problems almost always necessitates making compromises.

Unfortunately, most textbooks would not tell you how to deal with unforeseen problems, especially problems that occur after the data collection. Journals further perpetuate an idealized view of research—that it is sequential and linear, with no place for confusion or mistakes. Take any published article and look at the methodology section—what you will see is a neat, logical description of a sequence of steps that the researchers went through in conducting their study, from collecting or obtaining data to testing their model.

It is important to distinguish, therefore, between what researchers actually do when conducting a study and what they write about what they did. Not everything you will do as part of your study will be, or even needs to be, described in a paper. In a way, what you will need to do is create a narrative that imposes order on your research process and that makes it appear logical and linear, even though in reality it almost never is. At the same time, you must be honest in reporting your research and discuss important challenges and problems you have encountered and how you overcame them.

In this chapter, I will show how researchers in public policy and economics present their methodology in a convincing way: which elements they include, how they describe them, and how they talk about the problems that they have encountered. However, you should take the guidelines and examples presented in this chapter as a starting point and do your own analysis of methodology sections from articles that are most relevant to your research area.

METHODOLOGY SECTION IN A PAPER

All empirical articles have a methodology section and usually, the methodology is described in great detail, like a recipe for a study. A detailed description of the methodology is important for two reasons—to enable replication and to convince the reader that you have followed accepted procedures and used established techniques in order to ensure the validity and reliability of your findings.

There are, however, some important differences between quantitative and qualitative studies regarding what the authors focus on when describing their methodology. In a quantitative study, the focus is on the data, model, and empirical strategy, and the goal is to persuade the reader that you have done everything that could be done to eliminate or minimize bias. In contrast, in a qualitative study, the focus is on case selection and description, and the goal is to persuade the reader that the case or cases you have selected are adequate for the purpose of the study and that you have examined these cases in-depth.

Do literature-based studies have a Methodology section? That depends. Studies that are based on a nonsystematic review of the literature are usually nonempirical and do not have a separate methodology section; instead, there may be a brief paragraph or two in the Introduction explaining what the study is based on. Studies that are based on a more systematic review of the literature devote more space to the methodology, explaining how the reviewed studies were selected and analyzed. Studies that are based on a review of policy documents may or may not have a Methodology section, and this will often depend on the specific research area the paper belongs to, the type of paper, and the publication requirements.

Keep in mind that the methodology in a study can be described under many different headings. In quantitative studies using available data, there is almost always a section called Data, a section called Model Specification (or Econometric Model), and a section called Empirical Strategy (or Strategy Specification). Often these sections appear under the overall heading Methodology. In quantitative studies using data collected by the researchers, there is also often a section called Sample and Procedure. In studies where new measures are constructed or the measures used are nonstandard in some way, there may be a section called Measures or Variables. In shorter studies, there may be just one section devoted both to the methodology and results, which may be called Empirical Analysis or Data, Methodology, and Results.

CONCEPTS AND MEASURES

In Chapter 10, I talked about the importance of concepts to the theoretical framework of a study and I said that one of the main purposes of having a theoretical framework in a paper is to identify relevant concepts and define them in a way that makes them measurable and researchable. In the Methodology section, you need to describe how, precisely, your concepts are measured. As I explained earlier, concepts are abstract ideas; they do not exist in the real world, so they cannot be observed or measured directly. We can only observe and measure indicators of concepts, e.g., *amount of foreign investment* as an indicator of globalization, or *GDP* as an indicator of economic growth. Most concepts have multiple indicators, and this is why it is critical to specify exactly what you mean by your concepts. This is done in a study by providing operational definitions.

Operational definitions specify the exact empirical indicators that represent a concept. These definitions should be distinguished from conceptual or theoretical definitions, which clarify the meaning of a concept by means of other concepts, and which are part of the theoretical framework of a study. Operational definitions, in contrast, are measurement procedures that are used to measure concepts. Operational definitions may be based, among other things, on

- Responses to a questionnaire in a survey or interview,
- A score on a test,
- A way of observing people in the field, or
- Social indicators and other existing statistics such as crime rates, infant mortality rates, or volume of exports.

For example, *poverty* is a concept, which can be operationalized as responses to the question, *"How much money do you make per month?"* Respondents can then be classified based on a chosen threshold into poor and nonpoor. *Knowledge of economics* can be operationalized as a score on a final examination; the higher the score, the more knowledgeable one can be considered. *Citizen initiative* can be operationalized as speaking up in a meeting; participants can then be classified into high-initiative and low-initiative groups based on how many times they spoke up during a series of meetings. *Crime* can be operationalized as the most recent crime rate statistics or as the perceptions—measured through a survey—of people living in a certain neighborhood of how dangerous the neighborhood is. Box 35 shows the difference between conceptual and operational definitions for another common concept in public policy, *corruption*.

Here is an example of moving from a conceptual to an operational definition taken from a study of homelessness by Rossi et al. (1987). Rossi and his coworkers conducted a study to estimate the size and characteristics of the homeless population in Chicago. One of the main difficulties that the researchers faced was how to define the homeless—at the time of the study, there was no agreed-upon definition. The researchers first drew a distinction between the literally homeless and the marginally housed and limited their study to the literal homeless. Then they provided a conceptual definition of the homeless: Literal homeless are persons who do not have access to a conventional dwelling (which was also carefully defined). Then, to estimate the size of the homeless population and the characteristics of the homeless, they conducted two surveys, a shelter survey and a street survey. An important step in each of these surveys was to define homeless in operational terms—who, exactly, should be counted as homeless in each case? In the shelter survey, the researchers simply assumed that all persons who were in the shelter at the time of the survey were literally homeless. In the street survey, homeless were defined as all persons who were encountered between 12 a.m. and 6 a.m. on the sampled blocks and who said that they did not have access to a conventional

BOX 35 Operational and Conceptual Definitions

The concept of *corruption* has been variously defined in public policy literature as

- Destruction of integrity in the discharge of public duties by bribery
- Inducement to wrong by unlawful means
- Abuse of public office for private gain
- Behavior on the part of a public official involving the misuse of public power
- Behavior on the part of a public official with the goal to improperly and unlawfully enrich themselves

But what do all of these definitions mean? What is "destruction of integrity," "inducement to wrong," or "abuse of public office?" What instances of behavior should be countered as "corruption" in each of these cases? This is what you need to clarify in the operational definition. For example, if corruption is defined conceptually as the abuse of public office for private gain, the operational definition should specify what is meant by "abuse," what is meant by "private gain," and what will be counted as instances of "abuse for private gain" when you look at specific behaviors.

One way to operationalize corruption is to look at the law: Which abusive actions would be considered violations of the law? You may find that this definition includes such actions as bribery or exchanging favors for money but excludes other actions such as nepotism. Another way to define corruption is to treat it as a perceptual phenome-non and to focus on the *perceived* level of corruption, as determined by opinion surveys. Corruption can then be measured by using Transparency International's *Corruption Perception Index*; in this case, however, you will not be measuring the actual levels of corruption but rather, people's perceptions of corruption. Or you could focus on *the institutional framework* (e.g., anti-corruption institutions) and its ability to fight corruption and use the presence or absence of anti-corruption institutions as a proxy for levels of corruption in a given society.

housing unit, which in turn was defined as apartments, houses, rooms in hotels, and mobile homes.

In quantitative studies, researchers often talk about variables, rather than concepts. A **variable** is a concept that varies, or takes on different characteristics (called *attributes*) or values. For example, *gender* is a variable and it has two attributes, *men* and *women*, which allow us to classify observations into categories; *consumer spending* is a variable and it can take a whole range of values. In some cases, concepts and variables may be identical, such as in the case of *age*. In other cases, researchers may view concepts as more general than variables. In economics research, the term *variable* is often preferred to the term *concept* and an empirical study would usually include a table of variables showing their operational definitions and sources.

The important thing to keep in mind is that there are multiple ways to measure a concept and some are better than others or are more acceptable. But how do you make a decision about which measures to use? These decisions should be guided by two things—previous research (or theory) and data availability.

The operational definitions you choose for your concepts must be justified, which is done primarily by appealing to previous research. It is, therefore, a good idea to select definitions that are well accepted and agreed upon in the literature.

Whenever possible, rather than creating your own measures, choose existing, or standardized measures such as economic, social, political, or demographic measures developed by the government (e.g., poverty indicators, unemployment rates, crime rates). Box 36 shows examples of common

BOX 36 Common Measures of Concepts in Economic and Public Policy Research

Concept	Conceptual Definition	Operational Definition
Income inequality	The extent to which household income is distributed unevenly among a population	GINI Index
Unemployment	Proportion of unemployed people in the labor force	Proportion of adults in the labor force who do not have a job, have actively looked for a job in the past four weeks, and are available for work
Economic development	Literacy (often used as a proxy of economic development because both correlate almost perfectly)	Literacy rate
Globalization	The extent to which foreign capital dominates a host country's economy	Ratio of stocks of FDI to GDP
Globalization	Export commodity concentration	Value of a country's single largest export commodity divided by its total exports
Globalization	Foreign investment partner concentration	Foreign investment stocks of a country's largest investment partner divided by total foreign investment stocks
Poverty	Not having enough money to meet basic needs such as food, clothing, and shelter	Income of less than $1.25 per day
Economic growth	Increase in aggregate output	GDP per capita
Inflation	Change in the price of a market basket of commodities consumed by a typical consumer	Consumer price index (CPI)

measures of concepts from economic and public policy research. Notice how specific each operational definition is. Notice also the three ways of defining *globalization*. What would be the implications of using each of these definitions for data collection?

Sometimes, however, you may not be able to find data for your desired variables. In this case, your decision about operational definitions will be guided by data availability. It is not uncommon for researchers to find themselves in a situation when they cannot obtain data on the measures that make the most sense for their study and, therefore, have to compromise. In the worst case, you may need to revise your hypotheses so that you can test them with the available data. If you end up using less than ideal measures for your concepts, you may need to explain your decisions. Try to justify them on theoretical or logical grounds (e.g., Why are the proposed measures a good substitute for the more standard measures used in research on your topic?), rather than simply by appealing to data availability.

Where should you put operational definitions in your paper? In a quantitative study, operational definitions are placed in the Methodology section, usually in the section where you describe your model or estimation strategy. In economics articles, it is common to place a table of variables and their measures in an Appendix. In qualitative studies, there are usually no operational definitions; in fact, one of the goals of conducting a qualitative study is often to develop a more precise definition of a particular concept or phenomenon, which would emerge from the data. Instead of operational definitions, conceptual definitions may be used in a qualitative study to delimit it in some way and to shape its direction.

Box 37 shows how Ganesh Pandeya, the author of a qualitative study of decentralization and decision-making in local government, defines a key concept in his study, *citizen participation*. Notice how he goes from a rather broad, theoretical definition of the concept to a more narrow one and, finally, to a rather specific one, which he uses in his paper. Although not an operational definition, it does help him to delineate the scope of his research. Notice the language expressions that Ganesh uses to move from the more general to the more specific (I have highlighted them in bold). Notice also that the definitions he uses are supported with citations from relevant literature.

BOX 37 Conceptual Definition in a Qualitative Study

Broadly speaking, citizen participation **has been defined** as a process of citizen involvement in civic affairs to influence and control public policy decisions that affect them (citations). **More specifically, it can be defined as** a collaborative and deliberative process of capturing public sentiment with respect to policy decisions (citations). **In this study,** citizen participation **refers to** a process through which citizens can have access to, or influence over, the process of making decisions in local government that affect them. (Pandeya, 2014, p. 2)

DATA

What Are Data?

The word *data* is often defined in dictionaries as statistics or facts. This definition gives the impression that what researchers do in data collection is collect objective facts. This view of data is quite misleading. As Greenlaw (2009) and others have pointed out, data in economics and public policy are constructed, rather than collected, and are therefore affected by how the concepts have been defined and measured. Concepts such as *poverty, efficiency,* or *corruption* are often defined and measured differently by different governments or organizations or at different times. Even such "standard" economic concepts as inflation or unemployment can be measured differently and these differences will have implications for the outcome of an analysis. Furthermore, data collection is almost always plagued by problems such as attrition (participants dropping out), missing values, or lack of group comparability and as such, necessitates making various choices. These choices affect the resulting data. Even qualitative data are constructed rather than collected because qualitative data, too, are influenced by the questions that the researchers ask, by how they ask them, and, especially, by how they interpret respondents' answers.

Data should be distinguished from literature. Students who intend to do qualitative literature-based research often think of literature as their data. Yet, literature (and even policy documents) can only be data if it is analyzed in some way, rather than merely summarized. For example, in a systematic literature review, previous studies become data when they are subjected to quantitative analyses. In a qualitative paper, policy-related documents can be data if they are analyzed to support an argument.

Data are crucial to any study because, together with the research design, data allow the reader to judge the validity and reliability of the study's findings and the author's claims. It is therefore important to give the reader as much detail about the data as he or she would need in order to be able to evaluate the study's claims. In fact, an increasing number of journals in economics require that authors submit, along with their manuscript, the complete data set that they have analyzed in their study.

Data in a Quantitative vs. Qualitative Study

Data in a quantitative study are always **numeric,** but they can be either **continuous** or **discrete.** Continuous data are quantitative, or interval; these data are measured on a scale with numbers reflecting the amount of the variable. Examples include *GDP, price, annual income,* and *years of education.* These variables can be used in statistical analyses directly. Discrete data, in contrast, are qualitative, or nominal, and these data exist in categories. Examples include *type of company* (public vs. private), *privatization status* (privatized vs. non-privatized), or *political affiliation* (liberal-democratic vs. democratic). Discrete variables need to be recoded into **dummy variables** for analysis. There are also some limitations on the types of analyses in which such variables can be used.

Data in a qualitative study usually come in the form of **quotations** obtained from participants or **notes** made by the researcher during observations.

Primary vs. Secondary Data

Primary data are data collected by the researchers specifically for the purposes of a study—for example, in an experiment or in a small-scale survey. Secondary data, in contrast, are data that have been collected by others—by other researchers or organizations, usually in large-scale surveys. Research in public policy and economics typically relies on secondary data collected in large-scale—and assumed to be representative—surveys. Master's students in particular almost always have to rely on secondary data in their research as there is simply no time to collect primary data.

Both types of data have advantages and disadvantages. The main advantage of primary data is that data collection instruments can be tailored to the particular research context, enabling you to collect precisely the data you need. The main disadvantage is that collecting your own data is a very time-consuming process. The main advantage of secondary data is that these data have already been collected, are available, and often have a known reliability. The disadvantage is that the available data may not be in the form or at the level of aggregation needed for your analyses and they may require complex transformations. Perhaps even more important, as Babbie (1998) points out, when you use available data, you do not know what problems may have occurred during data collection or how the data may have been manipulated. It is, therefore, important to make sure that the data come from a reputable organization and that there is detailed documentation about data collection procedures.

Data Collection Methods

There are seven major data collection methods in public policy and economics. They are

- Tests,
- Surveys,
- Interviews,
- Focus groups,
- Observation,
- Use of existing statistics, and
- Documentary research.

All of these methods can be used in public policy and economics research; however, the two most common tools in quantitative research are existing statistics (collected through large-scale surveys) and, to a lesser extent, surveys designed by the researchers; in qualitative research, the most common tools are interviews (i.e., semistructured, open-ended interviews with probing questions) and documentary research.

Sampling

Sampling refers to the drawing of a sample from a population in order to collect information quickly and economically. Sampling is widely used in public policy research, for example, in political polls, public opinion surveys, and surveys of production and consumption of goods.

In quantitative sampling, the goal is to draw a representative sample, a sample that has similar characteristics to those of the target population from which it is drawn. Samples are drawn from a **working population**, or a specific pool of cases the researcher is interested in. The characteristics of a sample are called *statistics*, whereas the characteristics of the population from which the sample is drawn are called *parameters.* Population parameters are always unknown and one of the purposes of analyzing samples is to estimate these parameters.

There are several important elements of a sample that must be reported in a quantitative study. If your study is based on a sample, make sure to report these elements. If you are using existing statistics obtained from an organization, make sure to check this information before using the data to determine the quality and applicability of the data.

- **Sampling frame** refers to a list of all members of a working population from which sample members are drawn. For example, it can be a list of property owners, or a list of welfare recipients.

- **Sampling technique** is the method used to select cases. In quantitative research, we often use probability samples (or samples selected by using a method based on the probability theory) because the goal is to generalize from the sample to a wider population.

- **Sampling error** is the amount of difference, or deviation, of the sample from the true parameters of the population.

- **Response rate** is the percentage of people, out of all the people in the sample, who responded to the survey.

Qualitative sampling (or case selection) is different from quantitative sampling. Qualitative sampling is purposive and samples are selected not to be representative of a wider population but rather because they are unique, be-cause they can provide necessary information, or because they are important in some way to your particular purpose. Qualitative samples are nonprobability (also called *haphazard* or *convenience*) and they should not be used to generalize findings to a wider population.

How Many Observations?

Quantitative research requires large data sets—often comprising dozens or even hundreds of observations or data points. Statistical textbooks often cite 30 as the minimum number; however, the specific number of observations often depends on the type of analysis: Analyses of Variance (ANOVA) with experimental data, for example, could be performed with just a handful of observations; regression analysis, on the other hand, would require close to a hundred data points and often more, if there are multiple predictors. As a general rule, if you are conducting a survey-based, observational study, keep in mind that the more predictor variables you include in the model, the larger the data set you will need.

Qualitative researchers usually use small samples, but this again varies depending on the purpose. The minimum sample size in a qualitative study is one.

Types of Data

There are generally four types of data that can be used in a study; three are quantitative and one, qualitative. Each type of data has advantages and disadvantages. Your choice should be guided by the research question and theory; it is also often guided by data availability.

- **Cross-sectional data**. Researchers collect observations on a variable or variables at one point in time. An example of a cross-sectional study is a one-shot study of predictors of maternal health in a rural area, where data are collected on multiple variables at one point in time. The unit of analysis in cross-sectional studies is often the individual person, household, organization (e.g., hospital), or country.

- **Time-series data**. Researchers collect observations on the same variable across multiple time points. Time-series data can be measured at different frequencies—daily (exchange rates), monthly (consumer price indices), quarterly (unemployment rate), or annually (GDP). An example of a time-series study is a study of energy consumption and economic growth, where energy consumption and economic growth are measured annually and then energy consumption is used to predict economic growth. The unit of analysis in time-series studies is the time point (e.g., day, month, or year).

- **Longitudinal panel data**. Researchers collect the same type of information from the same people or other units across several time periods. An example of a panel study is a study of determinants of school enrollment in which data are collected yearly for each school in a region or country over a 10-year period.

- **Case study data**. Researchers collect information about the features of one case over a period of time, several cases at one time, or several cases over a period of time. Case study data are qualitative data. An example of a case study is a detailed study of how a new policy on decentralization has affected decision-making in a community.

Data Limitations and Transformations

Data obtained or collected for a study often have limitations, which may be big or small. Some of the more serious limitations in quantitative data include

- Missing values or missing variables,
- Lack of normality,
- Lack of linearity,
- Heteroscedasticity (i.e., unequal variability across a set of predictor variables, which is often caused by nonnormality of one or more of the variables or by measurement error at a particular level of a predictor variable), or
- Multicollinearity (i.e., high correlation among the variables).

Because all statistical tests have assumptions about the data, it is important to screen the data for any problems prior to analyses and to make sure that the data are appropriate for the empirical test that is being planned. There are numerous techniques for dealing with various data limitations, which often require transforming data into a different form. For example, in economics, data are often transformed into logarithmic form before performing regression analyses because such transformation helps with data linearity and makes interpretation easier. A very good resource showing how to screen data and make transformations is *Using Multivariate Statistics* by Tabachnick and Fidell (2013).

Data transformation may be necessary for another reason—to make the data comparable. This is especially important in international comparisons. Different governments and organizations may use different criteria to measure the same concepts and the resulting numbers may not be comparable. Unemployment rate is an oft-cited example. In 2003, the official unemployment rate in the United States was 6% and in Japan, it was 5.5%. However, these numbers were based on very different criteria for counting the unemployed. Had they been based on the same definitions and measurement criteria, they would have been much more different.

Sources of Secondary Data

Appendix C lists a large number of sources where survey and other data could be found, often for free. Check these sources to see if they may have the type of data you need for your study.

Describing Data in a Study

When using quantitative data that have been obtained from a database, authors often describe the following elements in the Data section:

- Type of data (e.g., cross-sectional, time-series, or panel)—if that is not otherwise clear;

- Database from which the data were obtained;

- Time period covered by the data;

- Place of data collection (e.g., countries, regions, organizations);

- Who collected the data, when, and how; if a survey was used, details about the survey; and

- Characteristics of the sample and whether it is representative of the target population.

In addition to these elements, for quantitative data that authors collect by themselves, it is common to describe the following:

- Sampling techniques and procedures that were followed to draw a sample;

- If a self-constructed questionnaire was used, how the questionnaire was constructed and what exactly it measures; the entire questionnaire may be included in an appendix or sample questions may be shown in the main text or in a table; and

- How the questionnaire was administered and if there were any problems during the administration.

Below are three examples of data description taken from published studies. The first one comes from a study by Engström and Hagen (2017) on income under-reporting among the self-employed; the second one, from a study by Lago-Peñas and Lago-Peñas (2010) on tax morale; and the third one, from a study by Cohen et al. (2012) of black-market medicine in Israel. The first two studies are based on data obtained from a database whereas the third one, on data collected by the authors using a self-designed questionnaire. Go over these examples and note how the authors describe their data, sample, and measures (in Example 3). What specific details do they include and why? Notice the language expressions the authors use in these descriptions and the verb tenses they use when describing the data.

Example 1 (Engström and Hagen, 2017)

Data

Consumption survey (HUT)

The consumption data come from the Swedish Household Budget Survey (Hushållensutgifter, HUT). The household data is [sic] presented annually by Statistics Sweden. Around 4000 randomly selected households are approached each year, of which slightly more than half participate in the survey. We use data from 2003 to 2009 with a total number of households of 15,044. The HUT data contain no panel elements.

The participating households are asked to report their consumption expenditures during randomly selected two-week periods using a detailed expense manager. The expenditures are then multiplied by 26 to represent annual consumption. The households should also note whether the expenditures are associated with a certain household member. Various other questions are asked [so] as to get information on household characteristics, including employment status, age, occupation, type of housing, and number of children.

Income data (LINDA)

To calculate household income, we use the register-based longitudinal database LINDA, constructed to be cross-sectionally representative of the Swedish population each year. The data set is large; it contains 3.35 percent of the Swedish population each year corresponding to over 300,000 individuals. Information about individuals' incomes comes from official tax reports, so that the income variables are free from measurement errors that are common in survey data. Swedish register data on income are of very high quality because they are automatically third party reported (for wage earners) and are reported separately for different types of income.

We use LINDA from 2000 to 2012, which means that we can observe both past and future income streams of the households in the consumption survey. An additional advantage of using register data for incomes is that we may directly interpret the results in terms of tax evasion/avoidance. Most studies using the PW method rely on survey data instead of register data. It is not obvious, however plausible, that a tax evading self-employed individual also underreports incomes in surveys. See Hurst et al. (2014) for an in-depth discussion on this matter. The consumption survey used in this paper does not contain any self-reported measure of household income because of the access to register-based incomes.

Because LINDA is at the individual level, we aggregate income for the members of a given household to get household income. By construction of the HUT survey, one household member, referred to as the "sampled individual," is always part of LINDA. However, since LINDA and HUT use different household definitions, the remaining household members are not always part of LINDA. HUT households are self-reported and consist of individuals who share residence and have a common household budget. In LINDA, individuals must share residence and be registered as partners, or have children, in order to form a household. We will restrict the sample to households whose members are all part of LINDA. (pp. 95–96)

Example 2 (Lago-Peñas and Lago-Peñas, 2010)

Individual-level responses on tax morale, gender, age, education, religion, income, employment status, satisfaction with democracy, trust in politicians, and ideology were taken from the second wave of the European Social Survey. The ESS provides data on socio-political attitudes, trust in institutions, financial and household circumstances and, crucial for the purposes of this study, a module on economic morality for residents of 17 European nations. The survey is designed to provide methodological consistency and is therefore ideal for comparative and cross-national analysis. Fieldwork was conducted between autumn 2004 and winter 2005. The surveys are representative of all persons aged 15 and over (no upper age limit) who reside within private households in each country, regardless of their nationality, citizenship, or language. The sample is selected by strict random probability methods. Finally, the minimum "effective" sample size is 1500. Response rates vary by country, with a median of 62% overall and with most countries exceeding 60%. (p. 452)

Example 3 (Cohen et al., 2012)

Sample and procedure

In order to obtain quantitative and qualitative evidence for the existence of BMM [black-market medicine] in Israel, we conducted a public opinion survey and interviews with decision-makers. The quantitative data were collected during the spring of 2010 using questionnaires distributed to a sample of 507 adults from the Israeli–Jewish population. Interviewers met the participants in various locations such as public venues, governmental institutions, and private homes. We used a random quota sampling, and sampled various cities and other communities based on geographic location and the size and structure of the population. Response rate was approximately 60 percent due to our sampling method. The response rate was calculated as the ratio between those participants who ultimately took part in the study and those who agreed to listen to our explanation of the study and reviewed the questions.

Of the respondents, 54.3 percent were men, 45.3 percent were women (compared to 50.58 percent of women in the overall population according to the Central Bureau of Statistics), and 0.4 percent did not report their gender. The average age in this sample was 32.27 years (STD: 15.68). With regard to education, 41.9 percent of the interviewees in the sample reported a high school education, another 39.4 percent were undergraduates or graduate students, and 10.2 percent had second or third degrees. With regard to income, 45.8 percent earned a gross monthly wage of 4,000 NIS or less, 26.8 percent earned between 4001 and 8000 NIS per month, while 15.4 percent had a monthly income of between 8,001 and 14,000 NIS, and 10.6 percent of respondents earned 14,001 NIS or more. The average monthly wage for employees in Israel in July 2010 was 8,602 NIS (Central Bureau of Statistics, 2010a). As for religious observance, 22 percent of respondents were secular, 37.4 percent were religiously traditional, 25.8 percent were religiously observant, and 24 percent were ultra-Orthodox.

Even though the demographic characteristics of the sample do not completely match the population distribution (i.e., women are over-represented in the sample and participants are better educated than the general population), the demographics of the sample are relatively representative of the general Israeli population (Central Bureau of Statistics, 2010b).

The qualitative data for this research is based on 24 interviews with politicians, bureaucrats, and leading scholars from the field of health care policy. The interviewees' sample was based on the snowball sampling method, which has proven effective in reaching and involving hidden populations (Cohen & Arieli, 2011).

Measures

Measuring BMM care is a very difficult task. Usually there is no documentation of this activity, which is normally done secretly. Given that this practice is illegal, people tend to avoid questions on this subject or lie when asked about these activities. Even gray market payments are usually offered in private, making the collection of data about monetary amounts difficult (Gaal *et al.*, 2006: 259; Lewis, 2000: 11). Hence, in this study we did not ask people about their actions or past events. Rather, we chose to focus on the declarative aspect, asking the interviewees about their perceptions and beliefs on this subject and about their willingness to make black-market payments.

The survey questionnaire asked respondents to indicate the degree to which they agreed or disagreed with 89 statements. Participants ranked their responses on a Likert scale ranging from 1 to 5, where 1 indicated 'strongly disagree' and 5 indicated "strongly agree." The participants had the option to choose 'Do not know' in every statement. The questionnaire included 56 statements that represented four main measures as part of a large-scale project. Reliability tests (Cronbach's α) were conducted to verify the measures' suitability. The two measures under discussion here are *attitudes toward the welfare policy* and *attitudes toward BMM*.

Attitudes toward the welfare policy was measured by a 28-item scale composed of two sub-indexes as follows:

1. *state intervention*: a 17-item scale indicated the desired level of state intervention in the economy and in the individual's life ($\alpha = 0.781$) (see questions 1–17 in Table 3); and

2. *extra taxes*: an 11-item scale indicated the willingness to pay for the welfare state ($\alpha = 0.919$) (see questions 18–28 in Table 4).

Attitudes toward BMM was measured using four items designed to test the willingness to *make extra payments* or *use personal connections* in order to obtain better access to health care services or improve the quality of these services for themselves ($a = 0.670$). As can be seen in the wording of questions 29–32 in Table 1, these items indicate (potential) behaviour as compared to general attitudes towards BMM strategies (detailed in questions 33–36 in Table 2). (pp. 733–735)

For both types of data—data obtained from a database and data collected by the researchers specifically for the purposes of their study—it is common for authors to describe any data-related problems and limitations, such as missing values, inadequate sample size, or an unrepresentative sample, as well as how these problems were fixed or why they can be ignored. Below is an example from a study by Borge et al. (2015) of the relationship between public revenues and efficiency in the production of local public goods. Notice how the authors describe the problem of missing observations and how they explain why it can be ignored. Notice how they support their arguments with citations. Why do you think they do that?

Our measure of local government efficiency is a modified version of a measure developed by Borge et al. (2008), which is also applied by Bruns and Himmler (2011) and Revelli and Tovmo (2007). The point of departure for the measure is an indicator of output from the six main service sectors: care for the elderly, primary and lower secondary education, day-care, welfare benefits, child custody and primary health care. These service sectors account for about 75% of total expenditures. The output measure captures both quantity and quality of the services delivered and is available for the period 2001–2007. We refer to Borge et al. (2008) for a more detailed description of the output measure.

The yearly number of observations varies between 357 and 387, representing 86% of all local governments on average. The major cause for missing observations is failure to report data on indicators required to calculate output. Small local governments are overrepresented among the missing observations. However, other observable characteristics for the observations with missing efficiency measure are on average comparable to the non-missing observations. Using the terminology of Rubin (1976), we assume that the missing data are "missing (conditionally) at random" (MAR). Data are then missing for reasons related to completely observed variables in the data set, e.g., population size, and we can ignore the reasons for missing data in the analysis (Pigott, 2001). (Borge et al., 2015, p. 103)

In quantitative papers, it is common to include a table showing all the variables, their definitions, and sources. Box 38 shows an example of such a table from a paper by Mariyam Rashfa, a student in Macroeconomic Policy, who examined inflation in the Maldives. It is also common to include a table of **summary statistics** for the variables, showing the means, standard deviations, and

BOX 38 Variables, Their Definitions, and Sources

Variable	Definition	Source
CPI	Consumer Price Index for Maldives	Maldivian Monetary Authority (MMA)
FCPI	Foreign Consumer Price Index, at trade-weighted CPI in major importing countries of Maldives	Author's own estimations using data obtained from the MMA and online databases of the IMF and OECD
RDGP	Real Gross Domestic Product	Online database of International Financial Statistics of the IMF
YGAP	Output Gap calculated as the difference between the actual level of output and the trend output (derived using the Hodrick-Prescott filter)	Online database of International Financial Statistics of the IMF
GB	Fiscal balance as a ratio to GDP	MMA
M2	Money supply	MMA
NEER	Nominal Effective Exchange Rate, a trade-weighted index of exchange rate of major trading partners expressed in terms of foreign currency per Rf where an increase indicates an appreciation and a decrease indicates a depreciation.	Author's own estimations using data obtained from the MMA and the online database of the IMF

Note. IMF = International Monetary Fund; OECD = Organization for Economic Cooperation and Development, Rf = Maldivian rufiyaa.

maximum and minimum values for both the dependent and independent variables. Such a table should be briefly descried in the text and the most important numbers should be interpreted. All abbreviations or acronyms should be explained in the accompanying notes under the table—the reader should not have to guess what the names of your variables refer to. Both the table with variables and their sources and the table with summary statistics can be placed in an appendix.

In a qualitative paper, the focus in describing the data is often on sample characteristics, procedures of data collection (i.e., interview procedures), and the overall themes that were the focus of the interviews. Here is an example from a qualitative study of homelessness by Thompson et al. (2004).

Twelve subjects were recruited from participants at a multi-service agency serving the mentally ill homeless population in St Louis, Missouri. The subjects represent a convenience sample of individuals whose location was known to agency staff and had at least 24 consecutive months of continuously stable housing after being homeless. All subjects provided written consent after the procedure had been fully explained and were paid $10 for their interviews.

The participants were part of a larger sample of 58 formerly homeless individuals from the service agency. Additional detail on the larger sample is available in previous publications (Pollio et al., 1997, 2000). The original sample was approximately 40 (SD ± 9.7) years of age, predominately male (78%), and African–American (76%). More than half (59%) had completed high school or received a general equivalency diploma. Two-thirds of the original sample (67%) had a substance use disorder, 17% had schizophrenia, and 12% had a personality disorder. Participants in this current study included nine men (75%) and three women (25%); nine were African–American (75%) and observationally averaged 40 years of age.

Interview protocols were developed and critiqued by a panel of researchers to minimize potential biases introduced by the wording of questions. Interviews focused on three major areas through three open-ended questions: (1) what was it like to be homeless, (2) what helped (or did not help) you exit homelessness, (3) tell me about important people in your life in the past and current. Interviewers were trained in non-directive interview techniques, emphasizing non-verbal prompting and key phrase repetition as primary procedures to elicit information. They were not associated with the agency and had little previous contact with staff or service providers within the agency; the interviewers also had never met any of the participants before the interview session. (Thompson et al., 2004, pp. 424–425)

QUANTITATIVE VS. QUALITATIVE DATA ANALYSIS

There are many different strategies and techniques for data analysis in public policy and economics; some are more common in a particular research area than others. The choice of the particular strategy for data analysis is dictated largely by the purpose of your study—by its research question—and by the type of data that are used.

Quantitative research questions usually ask about relationships among multiple variables, and data are usually observational rather than experimental. By far, the most common tool used to analyze such data is **multiple regression analysis**. Multiple regression analysis allows researchers to assess the strength of the relationship between an outcome (the dependent variable) and several predictor variables as well as the importance of each of the predictors to the relationship, often with the effect of other predictors statistically eliminated.

It is important to point out, however, that multiple regression analysis is a statistical technique, not a research design, and as such, it does not establish causation. This is because multiple regression builds on correlation, which shows mere associations between variables. To infer a causal relationship, re- searchers need to eliminate bias resulting, for example, from variables that cannot be observed. This can be done by design—through experimental manipulation of variables, or by using statistical controls. The second option is much more common in studies of public policy and economics. Various approaches can be used to minimize bias due to reverse causality and omitted variables. Panel regression with fixed effects is one example of a commonly used approach in economics research. However, panel regression requires the use of panel data, which may not always be available, and they, too, have limitations. It is, therefore, wise to keep in mind when interpreting results, that even under the best of circumstances, statistical controls are never fool-proof.

Qualitative data analysis in public policy depends on whether the study is data-based or literature-based. In data-based studies (e.g., studies based on data collection through interviews, focus group discussions, or participant observation), data analysis involves transcribing and coding participants' responses and/or the researcher's notes by identifying certain themes or patterns in the data that help answer the research question(s). In many ways, qualitative data analysis is an attempt to reduce a very large amount of qualitative data—participants' responses and comments—to a few themes. For example, if your study has looked at how poor women in rural areas cope with violence, you may want to analyze the women's responses to identify the strategies that they have used. You would have to make many subjective decisions about what the women's responses really mean and you would need to be very clear about how you made those decisions. Using multiple sources of data (e.g., interviews +documents+observation) in a qualitative study is one strategy to reduce subjectivity.

In literature-based studies, there are usually no data and a paper may be based solely on summarizing an often arbitrary selection of studies or other documents. In such studies, it is common for authors to explain how the literature was located, how the specific studies and documents were selected, and how they help answer the research question(s).

DESCRIBING A QUANTITATIVE METHODOLOGY

Conceptual vs. Empirical Models

It is important to distinguish between conceptual and empirical (or econometric) models. Conceptual models are theoretical models—they are used to simulate economic behavior and they allow researchers to derive predictions about the behavior of individuals, households, or institutions. Such models are often mathematical—they describe precisely the quantitative changes in a particular variable in response to changes in the environment (Stokey & Zeckhauser, 1978).

Empirical models, in contrast, are statistical models, and they are used to specify and test a statistical relationship predicted by a theoretical model. For example, a theoretical model may predict a positive relationship between economic growth and the rate of poverty reduction in developing countries. This model can then be tested empirically to estimate by how much a particular increase in economic growth would increase the rate of poverty reduction.

A wide range of empirical models can be used in economics and public policy; however, all models share the following features:

- They have assumptions, which may be more or less general or more or less realistic. Assumptions are crucial to any model because they influence the resulting estimates: Models based on different assumptions often result in different predictions.

- They have exogenous variables, or inputs, which may or may not be related to policy. An example of a policy-related variable is government spending and an example of a policy-unrelated variable is political stability. Exogenous variables are independent variables; they affect the model but are not affected by it—they are "determined 'outside' the model... [and] are assumed not to change over the period of analysis" (Neugeboren, 2005, p. 18). In other words, their values are independent of the values of other variables in the model.

- They have one or more endogenous variables, or outputs, which the model tries to estimate. Endogenous variables are the dependent variables; their values are determined by the other variables in the model.

- They have coefficients showing how a dependent variable will change in response to a certain change in one or more of the independent variables. These coefficients are often based on historical data.

Some variables—such as *gender* or *age*—are always exogenous; however, in many cases, the same variable can be used as exogenous in one model and as endogenous in another. For example, in a study looking at the effect of poverty on child development, poverty is exogenous; but in a study looking at the effect of remittances on poverty reduction, poverty is endogenous. Decisions about which variables should be included in the model as exogenous and which ones, as endogenous should be guided by theory.

Model Specification

Model specification refers to describing a series of equations that constitute a model. Graduate students and novice researchers seldom construct their own models from scratch. Usually, they use existing models, sometimes with modifications (e.g., by adding a variable). In such papers, it is important to state the source of the model—what it is based on or what it is derived from. If you make modifications to an existing model, it is important to describe them and explain why they were made. If the use of a particular model is not straightforward, you may need to explain and justify the choice of the model. This is done by appealing to relevant research literature and building an argument to show why using that particular model in that particular case makes sense.

In economics papers, models are presented in mathematical (or algebraic) form. If you use several models, describe them separately. State your model's assumptions, starting with the most general ones and moving to the more specific. Below are two examples taken from the papers written by graduate students in Public Finance. The first one comes from a paper by Blessings Majoni, who tested the applicability of Okun's law—a law predicting an inverse relationship between real gross domestic product and unemployment rate—to 10 Southern African countries. The second one comes from a paper by Perfect Ahamadzie, who investigated the impact of Single Window (SW), a cross-border mechanism that allows parties involved in trade to use a single entry point for all import, export, and other regulatory requirements, on customs revenue and the time it takes to clear shipments by customs in 43 African countries. As you read these examples, notice the amount of detail in the model descriptions, the use of the first-person pronoun, and the use of the verbs and verb tenses to present the model. Notice also the use of citations. Why do you think they are needed?

Example 1 (Majoni, 2015)

There are three main versions of the model that can be used in the quantitative analysis of Okun's law: the dynamic version, the gap version, and the difference version. As did Okun, for the short run, I use the gap version to estimate the gap between the actual and potential output against the gap between the actual and potential unemployment rate. I also use the difference version for the first differences in output and unemployment rate. I use the Hodrick Prescott (HP) Filter to separate temporary and permanent changes in real GDP and unemployment rate. For the long run, I estimate the cointegrating relationship between output and unemployment and use the Engle Granger two-step method to test for cointegration. I also estimate an error correction model, which indicates another short-run relationship between the variables. The cointegration test shows whether there is a relationship between the two variables in the long run. The data used in the models covers a period from 1991 to 2014 for each of the ten Southern African countries. The models are described below.

The first model is estimated using a simple gap equation proposed by Harris and Silverstone (2000) for the short run effect. A necessary assumption for this version is that inflation will not lead to any differences in the results. As such, it can be taken as a constant so that production is at full capacity when all labor is employed. By taking the natural log of real GDP, I obtain the following gap equation:

$$(Y_t - Y_t^*) = b(U_t - U_t^*) + \varepsilon_t \tag{1}$$

where
Y_t is the actual real GDP level,
Y_t^* is potential real GDP level,
U_t is the actual unemployment rate,
U_t^* is the natural rate of unemployment around which the economy fluctuates,
ε_t is a random error term, and
b is expected to be < 0. The inverse of b will show how much of the change in unemployment rate is attributable to a change in real GDP. This is my main parameter of interest as it will show the magnitude of the percentage change in unemployment rate that will impact real GDP.

$$\text{Okun's coefficient} = 1/b \tag{2}$$

The potential GDP and the natural rate of unemployment are estimates of the general trends of the two variables.

The second model is estimated using the difference equation proposed by Knotek (2007). By taking the first differences in unemployment rate and real GDP, I obtain the following equation:

$$Y_t - Y_{t-1} = \alpha + \beta(U_t - U_{t-1}) + \varepsilon_t \tag{3}$$

where
Y_t is real GDP level at time t,
$Y_t - 1$ is real GDP level at time $t - 1$,
U_t is unemployment rate,
$U_t - 1$ is unemployment rate at time $t - 1$,
α is a constant,
β is Okun's coefficient, and ε_t is a random error term. (pp. 4–5)

Example 2 (Ahamadzie, 2015)

The main regression model is given by the following equation:

$$Y_{it} = \beta_0 + \beta_1 SW_{it} + CONTROLS_{it} + YEAR_t + COUNTRY_i + \mu_{it} \tag{1}$$

Here, Y_{it} is a log-linear specification of (customs revenue)$_{it}$, and time$_{it}$. Customs revenue is one of the two dependent variables I use in this study, and it is measured here by the number of imported goods and services as a percentage of GDP. Previous research has also measured customs revenue using import duties such as value-added tax, but due to the unavailability of data, import duties were not included. Clearance time was the other dependent variable; it was defined as time to import (days) and measured as the time necessary for obtaining all documents as well as for inland transport and handling, customs clearance and inspection, and port and terminal handling. This variable did not include ocean transport time spent by importers prior to the release of their cargoes after importation. Here, β_0 is the constant term and β_1 is the estimated difference-in-differences (DID) average coefficient. (p. 4)

Variable Specification

All variables used in the analysis, along with their measures, should be described in the Methodology section even if you have already described them somewhere else in the paper. Start with the dependent variable(s), go on to the explanatory variables, and finish with the control variables. If your dependent variables can be measured in different ways, explain the choice of the measures.

It is common in economics and public policy papers to justify the inclusion of particular control variables you have selected. This is done by referring to one or more of the following:

- **Theory**: What does your theory suggest about variables that might correlate with the variables you are measuring?

- **Previous research**: What have other researchers included?

- **Your own logic**: Can you think of any alternative explanations? If you can, you need to control for them.

Here is an example of variable specification taken from the study by Perfect Ahamadzie, whose model specification was shown earlier. Her methodology is based on the use of difference-in-differences regression. As you read, notice how detailed Perfect's description is for all the variables she includes in her model. Notice also that she uses the results of previous research to support and justify the inclusion of the control variables in her study.

Explanatory Variables

In this study, the independent variables are Single Window (SW), year and country, and control variables. Out of the 43 African countries used in this study, only 16 have implemented SW. In my regression, I used one (1) for the 16 countries that have implemented SW and zero (0) for the remaining 27 countries that have not implemented SW. Control variables include tariff rate, trade liberalization (openness), exchange rate, inflation, population growth, GDP per capita, and political stability. Year represents year fixed effects and country represents country fixed effects. The fixed effects control for omitted variable bias arising from unobservable variables that are constant over time and across countries.

Further, μ_{it} is the error term, which contains all other factors that are likely to influence customs revenue and which are not controlled for in this study. Two regressions were estimated in this study: The first regression estimated the impact of SW on customs revenue; the second regression estimated the impact of SW on the time required to clear goods by customs at the port. Finally, control variables were used to control for omitted variable bias that may result in a biased estimation. The control variables are explained below.

Justification for the Use of Control Variables

The variables that are controlled for in this study because of their potential influence on the dependent variables are tariff rate, trade liberalization (openness), exchange rate, inflation, population growth, GDP per capita, and political stability of the African countries. The sources and description of the controlled variables are shown in Table 2. Tariff rate refers to the rate applied to a commodity to determine its import value. The role of tariff rate in the generation of import revenue appears to be beneficial. According to Pritchett and Sethi (1994), changes in a tariff structure significantly affect revenue collection. An increase in tariff rate significantly raises customs revenue collection. It is, therefore, an important factor that affects import revenue collection. In contrast, Irwin (1998) argues that a higher rate lowers customs revenue—as Adam Smith pointed out in *The Wealth of Nations*: "The high duties which have been imposed upon the importation of many different sorts of foreign goods, in order to discourage their consumption in Great Britain, have in many cases served only to encourage smuggling: and in all cases have reduced the revenue of the customs below what more moderate duties would have afforded" (p. 63). This means that tariff rate, if not controlled for, may give a biased estimation.

Population growth refers to the annual growth of the population of the African countries used in this study. Codrington (1989) showed that population growth results in a significant difference in revenue when he compared countries with small populations and those with large populations, supporting the findings of Tait et al. (1979). Okafor and Eiya (2010) and Craigwell, Thomas, Thomas, and Craigwell (2008) also argue that population has a positive impact on government revenue, and that larger population size is associated with higher revenue. This makes it important to control for population growth when assessing customs revenue because African countries have different population sizes.

GDP per capita measures how many goods and services an economy produces for the people in a country and it is a proxy for sustained economic development. Agbeyegbe and Stotsky (2004, p. 20) argue that GDP per capita is expected to have a positive relationship with tax-to-GDP ratio because higher income countries tend to have a more monetized economy and better tax administration.

Trade liberalization refers to trade openness within a country. Trade openness according to David (2007) is measured as the total volume of imported goods and services plus exported goods and services as a share of GDP. Zakaria (2014) and Santos-Paulino (2002) concluded that trade liberalization on both import and export of goods and services increases in the era of liberalization to a greater extent than in the era without liberalization. Because trade openness enhances competition and promotes larger markets, it should be included in this study.

Political stability is another important variable. A stable political environment improves revenue collection (Alesina et al., 1992). For African countries that have a stable government, the chances of an economic collapse are significantly lower than for African countries without a stable government. This implies that political instability may cause a shortage in revenue collection and also that any changes in the political environment of a country may have great consequences for its socioeconomic systems (Alesina et al., 1992; Ghura & Mercereau, 2004; Mutascu et al., 2011). Therefore, evaluating customs revenue collection without controlling for political stability in African countries will likely give rise to bias.

Another important variable to control for is inflation. Measured by the consumer price index, it "reflects the annual percentage change in the cost to the average consumer of acquiring a basket of goods and services that may be fixed or changed at specified intervals" (World Bank, 2016). Researchers (e.g., Immervoll, 2000; Samimi & Jamshidbaygi, 2011; Samimi et al., 2012; Tafti, 2012) have measured the effect of inflation on revenue using CPI values. According to Qadirpatoli (2012), changes in inflation caused revenue to increase. Therefore, increases in revenue are greatly responsive to changes in inflation. This implies that inflation has a significant role to play in revenue collection and as a result, it should be taken into account in this study.

Exchange rate is another important variable. Imported goods are affected by changes in the exchange rate (Jabara, 2009). For example, Peree and Steinherr (1989) found that an increase in exchange rate had an adverse influence on the volume of trade. Mckenzie and Brooks (1997) and Hwang and Lee (2005) found a positive effect of exchange rate on trade. However, Akhtar and Hilton (1991) and Baileys et al. (1986) found nonsignificant and mixed effects. Ozturk and Kalyoncu (2009) found a significant relationship between exchange rate and trade for the Republic of Korea, South Africa, Poland, and Pakistan. Taking into account these mixed findings, it is important to control for exchange rate when evaluating customs revenue. (Ahamadzie, 2015, pp. 4–5)

Estimation Strategy

Empirical models are estimated. To estimate a model means to estimate the relationship you are interested in by testing your hypothesis. Many testing strategies can be used for empirical estimation, which differ by the empirical test that is used to estimate a relationship. In economics, some of the most common estimation strategies include

- Ordinary least squares estimation,
- Difference-in-differences estimation, and
- Maximum-likelihood estimation.

How do you choose among the available options? First of all, the choice will depend on the purpose of your study and the relationship you are trying to estimate. Second, all tests come with assumptions about the data such as assumptions of linearity, normality, and random sampling; violating these assumptions would render the tests uninterpretable. It is, therefore, important to make sure that the particular empirical test you want to use can, in fact, be used with your data. The final advice, given by both Greenlaw (2009) and Jacobsen (2014), is this: Choose the simplest testing strategy that does the job. Here is how Jacobsen explains the advantage of choosing a simple technique:

> The advantage of simple techniques, like measuring correlations, differences in means tests, or regressions, is that everybody understands them. That means that everyone can follow your story and signal possible flaws in your thinking. Moreover they tend to be very general. OLS regressions (with White standard errors or Newey-West standard errors) are hard to beat... (Jacobsen, 2014, p. 21).

It is often a good idea to explain why you chose a particular strategy. The more complex the analysis, the more space you will need to devote to describing it and explaining your rationale. It is also a good idea to support your decisions with references to the literature.

MATHEMATICAL WRITING: BASIC PRINCIPLES

Studies in economics and public policy often use mathematics to present methodology. In this section, I explain some very basic principles of using mathematical expressions in a paper. It is important to keep in mind, however, that every field has its own conventions for the style and usage of mathematical expressions. Thus, you should treat these principles only as suggestions and consult relevant papers in your research area to learn how to use mathematical expressions correctly. You may also wish to consult the following books that cover mathematical writing in some detail:

- William Thomson's A *Guide for the Young Economist*, which is a very useful resource for economists.

- *The Chicago Manual of Style*, which is an excellent resource for writers in various social sciences as well as in mathematics.

Use of Statistics

Statistics can be presented in text or in a table. If you have a small number of statistics to present (3–4 or fewer), present them in sentence form in the main text; if you have more statistics to present, present them in a table.

Commonly used statistics do not require a reference; however, less common statistics may need one. Ask yourself would your readers be familiar with your statistic. If you think that some readers may not be familiar with it, provide a reference. In a similar vein, do not provide formulas for common statistics in your field. However, if a statistic is not common and your readers may not be familiar with it, provide a formula.

Statistical symbols denoted by Latin letters—for example, N, SS, SE, t, or F—are usually italicized; statistical symbols denoted by Greek letters—for example, α or β—are not.

Mathematical Expressions

Integrating equations into the text. Empirical articles in economics and public policy use a lot of prose around the mathematics; in such articles, equations and other mathematical expressions interact grammatically with the text—they read as grammatical parts of a sentence and often have direct verbal translations, for example:

$a + b = c$ reads "a plus b equals c."
Let $x = 5y$ reads "let x equal $5y$."
When we set $XF = XI$ reads "when we set XF to be equal to XI."

Further, research papers almost never present mathematical sequences without some sort of textual guidance. Rather, authors use equations by integrating them into the surrounding text. For example, Shaw (2006) describes several common ways in which equations are integrated into sentences.

Apposition to a noun phrase: The equation $x = y$
Object of a verb: We set $x = y$
Complement: Given by $x = y$; expressed by $x = y$
Finite clause: Where $x = y$
Nonfinite clause: Let $x = y$
Main clause: Thus, $x = y$

Spacing. Mathematical expressions are usually spaced in the same way as words are—by using one space between each symbol.

Presenting equations. Equations can be presented in the line of text or displayed. Present very short equations that do not go above or below the line in the text:

The total revenue, R, made from selling the units is given by the equation $R = pq$, where p is the price at which each unit is sold and q is the quantity....

Let us denote $PTt = Bt \times PRTt$ and $PNt = Bt \times PRNt$ for the total capital case and the net equity case, respectively.

Displaying equations. Display all complex equations and those that would project above or below the line even if they are short. Display equations on a new line with additional spacing above and below the equation. Number equations consecutively by placing the number in parentheses near the right margin of the page (more common) or the left margin of the page (less common):

$$(yrs_{it}) = \alpha + \beta_1 DRA_{it} + \beta_2 XPEDU_{it} + \beta_3 Pov_{it} + \beta_4 Dlocation_{it}$$

Numbering equations. In the text, refer to equations by number. In some fields, the number is put in parentheses and in others, it is not. For example: Eq. (1) *shows*...or *as shown in* Eq. (1)..... Do not write the *first equation, the second equation*, and so on.

Use of pronouns. It is common to use "we" rather than "I" when explaining equations even in papers with a sole author. For example: By using Eq. (1), we obtain [...]. However, "I" may also be used.

Notation

Conventions. Follow closely the conventions of your field. Check relevant literature to see what notation is commonly used in your area and follow the standard notation. If you need to use your own notation, make it as clear and self-evident as possible.

Consistency. Notation should be used consistently—the same symbol should be used to denote the same term or operation throughout the paper. This also concerns the use of capitalization or italics—be consistent with using lowercase, uppercase, and italicized symbols.

Usage in text. William Thomson (2011) gives wonderful advice for using notation in economics papers. Here, I summarize some of his points. If you are working in an area of economics, you may find his book very useful in your work.

- Choose easily recognizable notation.

- Choose mnemonic abbreviations for assumptions and properties.

- Do not introduce notation that you will use only once or twice.

- Respect the hierarchy of the different parts of a paper: Do not refer in the main text to terms or ideas introduced in a footnote.

- Choose notation resulting in uncluttered mathematical expressions.

Generally, mathematical notation should not be used at the beginning of a sentence. Spell out what it stands for. For example, instead of

X is countable if [...]

write,

The set X is countable if [...]

Adjacent mathematical expressions should generally be separated by words:

...if for any $y \in Y$ there exists an $x \in X$ with $f(x) = y$...

Here is an example of the use of notation from a paper by Tatsuya Takeda (2013), a student in Macroeconomic Policy, who investigated the costs of holding foreign currency reserves for Japan. Notice the use of the plural pronoun *us* in the introductory sentence.

Let us use the following notations. Returns are all annualized and the subscript t denotes the observation year.

T_t: US Treasury Notes' annual rate of return

E_t: Foreign exchange rate, expressed in the units of yen for dollar

g_t: Rate of change in Et, defined as $E_t/E_t - 1 - 1$

B_t: Japanese foreign exchange reserves in yen

PRT_t: Japanese private sector's return on total capital (equity and debt)

PRN_t: Japanese private sector's return on net capital (equity only). (Takeda, 2013, p. 11)

DESCRIBING A QUALITATIVE METHODOLOGY

In qualitative studies, it is common to focus on explaining the following elements.

- **Case selection** (e.g., setting, participants): Why was that particular case selected? How does it help answer the research question? Case description in a qualitative paper is crucial to persuading the reader of the validity of the study, so authors spend considerable time describing the rationale behind their case selection.

- **Characteristics of the case(s)**: What are the specific characteristics of the case? These should be described in detail, with a focus on the most relevant ones. For example, if you are looking at a particular person or group of people, provide a summary profile of your respondents. If you are looking at the role of a particular policy in some outcome in a particular country, focus on that policy rather than on the country in general.

- **Strategy of inquiry**: What strategy was used to collect data? If semistructured interviews were used, for example, explain the procedures and the protocol that was followed. How were the data recorded, by whom, and in what context? Keep in mind that qualitative research is often based on collecting data from multiple sources, using multiple strategies. You would need to explain all sources and strategies used in data collection.

- **Data coding and analysis**: How were the data coded and analyzed? If several researchers participated in the coding to ensure reliability, to what extent did they agree?

- **Data accuracy**: Was the accuracy of the data verified in some way? How? For example, what did you do to confirm that the themes and patterns you have identified were, in fact, correct?

Here is an example of qualitative data description from a study by Irvine (2011) on the influence of sick pay and job flexibility on absence due to sickness. Go over the extract and underline the parts where the author describes data collection, sample characteristics, and data coding and analysis. Notice the use of Passive Voice throughout the description. Why do you think the author prefers Passive Voice over Active Voice?

The data drawn upon in this article are taken from a study of people's experiences of managing mental health and employment (Irvine, 2008). The study involved qualitative interviews with 38 individuals who considered themselves to have experience of a mental health condition and had sustained employment for at least the past 12 months. A range of recruitment strategies was used, including approaches via employers and employment support organizations. This resulted in a large geographical spread, including participants living and working in Scotland and various regions of England. Most people lived in urban or suburban areas. Slightly more than half were female and a majority were in their mid-30s to late 40s. There was a range of household types, with couples slightly outnumbering single people. Half the study group had dependent children living with them, a third of whom were lone parents. Table 1, above, provides an overview of the study group characteristics.

Data were gathered through individual in-depth qualitative interviews. A semi-structured topic guide was used, covering key areas of: personal, employment and health background; managing in work and experiences of absence from work; talking to others about mental health problems; support from others (in and outside work); long- and short-term impacts on employment and income; suggestions for improvements and future plans. Most interviews were conducted face to face, either in participants' homes or at their workplace (according to participant preference) with a small number being conducted by telephone.

Interviews were audio recorded (with participants' permission) and transcribed verbatim. Data were then summarized under a set of thematic headings and managed using the qualitative data analysis programme MaxQDA. Analysis involved detailed examination of the data for emerging themes and categories within each of the study's research questions. Analysis and reporting [were] grounded in the narratives and language of the study participants.

There were no preset health/medical criteria for the sample selection; volunteers participated according to their own assessment of whether their personal experience of mental health difficulties fitted with the broad study objectives. The majority of participants recounted experiences of anxiety and/or depression, which they often associated (at least in part) with work related stress. A small number of people had diagnoses of bipolar disorder or had experienced episodes of psychosis. At the time of the research interviews, some people were reflecting on past experiences of anxiety or depression from some distance in time, while others felt that they continued to experience episodes of poorer mental health as part of an ongoing, fluctuating condition. For most people, however, there was a key episode in their narratives—the time when they had been most acutely affected by mental ill health—which some people described as a 'breakdown'. At this point, many people in the study group had taken a relatively long period of time off sick from their job. Just under half had spent a period of one month or more off sick, several having been absent for four to six months and some for up to 12 months. However, some people had not taken any time off sick due to mental ill health.

Although the study had endeavored to include participants in a range of employment circumstances, variable response rates from the various recruitment routes meant that the achieved study group predominantly comprised people who worked for large employers (in the private and public sectors), many of whom had been with their employer for several years (see Table 1) and had reached relatively senior positions. Virtually everyone in the study group had a permanent contract of employment and an entitlement to six months' occupational sick pay at full salary, with a further period at half pay before moving to statutory sick pay or social security benefits. Thus, these individuals could be seen as having "secure employment" (Davidson and Kemp, 2008) to the extent that they benefited from a contractual and financial safety net at times when they felt too unwell to be at work. Additionally, most of the participants in this study were in desk-based managerial or administrative roles and had a relatively large amount of autonomy and control in organizing and managing their workload. (Irvine, 2011, pp. 756–757)

Chapter 14

Results, Discussion, and Conclusion

RESULTS IN AN EMPIRICAL STUDY

Recall that conceptually, an empirical paper consists of three main parts—background, methodology, and findings and arguments. The first part—background—sets the scene for the research and serves to justify the study, situate it in the appropriate literature, and explain theoretical expectations. The purpose of that part is to persuade the reader that the study is needed and that it is making an important contribution to the field. The second part—methodology—explains how the study was conducted, and its purpose is to convince the reader that all appropriate procedures have been followed and that the findings of the study should, therefore, be accepted as reliable and valid. The last part—findings and arguments—is the main part of an empirical study because this is where authors make claims to knowledge. It is often the longest part of a study.

In an empirical paper in public policy and economics, authors usually do the following in this part of the paper:

- Report main results,
- Interpret results, especially in relation to policy,
- Discuss results in relation to previous research or theory,
- Describe implications and/or provide policy recommendations,
- Describe limitations of the study (and offer suggestions for future research), and/or
- Summarize main arguments in a conclusion.

These elements would be present in various forms in most empirical studies, both quantitative and qualitative. However, even though the elements may be the same, there are considerable differences between quantitative and qualitative studies in *how* results are reported, discussed, and interpreted. These differences stem not only from the differences in the kinds of data used in quantitative and qualitative research but also, and perhaps more important, from the logic, purpose, and design of quantitative and qualitative studies because the specific features of quantitative and qualitative research determine what readers find convincing. There are also important differences that stem from the

How to Write about Economics and Public Policy. https://doi.org/10.1016/B978-0-12-813010-0.00014-4

specific conventions of the particular disciplines and research areas. In this chapter, I show how authors report results of both quantitative and qualitative studies in a variety of research areas in public policy and economics. However, because quantitative research is much more common in public policy and economics, the focus of this chapter will be on reporting and discussing results in a quantitative study, especially in a multiple regression study.

WHERE TO DESCRIBE RESULTS?

In an empirical paper, results are almost always described in a Results section, which may be called Results and Discussion, Analysis and Results, or Findings. In economics papers, there may also be a section or subsection called Robustness Checks following Results—this is where researchers test alternative explanations to confirm their findings. In such papers, it is also common to include a summary of results—and sometimes a brief discussion of results in relation to the existing literature—in the Introduction.

Many published papers in economics and public policy do not have a separate Discussion section and report and discuss results in the Results section. In contrast, most theses and dissertations do have a separate Discussion section as a requirement of the thesis/dissertation format adopted by the particular school or department. If you do need to have both a separate Results and a separate Discussion section, use the Results section only to report results and the Discussion section, to interpret and explain them, compare them with the results of previous research, discuss their implications, and describe limitations of your study.

In nonempirical papers, there is no Results or Discussion section, just like there is no Methodology section. Arguments in nonempirical papers are based on a selective review of the literature and are typically presented under thematic headings and subheadings. It is sometimes possible to follow the author's argument just by looking at the structure of the paper and its headings and subheadings. The conclusion in such a paper is always tentative, usually calling for more research.

RESULTS IN A QUANTITATIVE STUDY

There is a lot of variability in how results of quantitative analyses are reported. The specific statistics that are reported and the way they are reported depend on many factors including the purpose of the study, the statistical procedures that were used, the specific research area, and so on. And even the same statistical procedure in the same research area may be reported somewhat differently in different journals or by different researchers.

As a general rule, the more complex the procedure, the more detail you would need to provide about your analyses and results. Results of a simple regression can be reported in a few paragraphs. However, many questions in economics require performing multiple statistical procedures such as tests for unit roots and cointegration as a prerequisite for running regressions, Granger causality tests, or variance decomposition analysis, especially if the goal is to make causal inferences. These tests can be quite complex, requiring careful explanation in the text. Even though most readers reading economic journals—and almost certainly your advisor—would be familiar with standard econometric procedures such as the Augmented Dickey Fuller test for stationarity, you still need to walk the reader through your analyses and results. This is because in order to persuade the reader to accept your results, you need to show that you have performed all the necessary procedures, that you have performed them in an appropriate way, that you have interpreted the results of these procedures correctly, and that you have made the necessary adjustments.

Which Results to Report and in How Much Detail?

What would be an adequate set of statistics to report in a quantitative paper? That depends on the statistical technique you are using, the type of paper you are writing (a paper for publication or a thesis), and the conventions of your discipline or research area.

As a general rule, assume that your readers have a professional knowledge of statistics and that they are familiar with tests that are commonly used in your area. At the same time, give your readers sufficient information about the decisions you have made and the tests you have performed so that they can understand the analyses you have conducted and be able to evaluate the validity of your claims. This may be especially important if you are writing a thesis or a dissertation as you would need to demonstrate to your advisor both your statistical competence and knowledge of disciplinary conventions.

In a quantitative study, there are generally three types of result that need to be reported.

- **Results of prerequisite tests**. Recall that all statistical tests have assumptions. If these assumptions are violated, results will be uninterpretable. It is therefore important to make sure that the data meet the assumptions of the tests you are using. The specific prerequisite tests that you need to perform depend on the statistical technique(s) you are using to test your model. In public policy and economics, many statistical techniques require prerequisite testing for autocorrelation (serial correlation among the errors), heteroscedasticity (constant variance among the errors), multicollinearity (high correlation among explanatory variables), or nonstationarity of variables (nonconstant mean, variance, or autocorrelation structure). Results of prerequisite testing are often reported in the Methodology section but can be reported in the Results section, especially in economics papers. The amount of detail that should be reported depends on whether the data had significant problems and required transformation. Data sets used in public policy and economics often contain problems and require adjustment before use. These problems and adjustments should be described, especially in theses and dissertations.

Box 39 shows two examples of reports of prerequisite testing. The first one is an extract from a paper by Itai Maparara, who examined the relationship between government expenditure and economic growth for countries of the Southern African Development Community (SADC). In this extract, Itai describes the use of a test of cointegration as a prerequisite for regression analysis. Notice that he does not simply report the results of the test—he carefully explains them and what they mean. As you go over this example, notice the highlighted words and phrases, which help Itai explain and interpret his results. The second

---

BOX 39 Reporting Prerequisite Test Results

Example 1 (Maparara, 2016)

Johansen test of cointegration with a constant and time trend was carried out using the results of lag order selection. Table 3 reports eigenvalues and maximum rank values against the critical values (column 7) at the 5% significance level. Maximum rank shows the number of existing cointegration vectors in the model. **As shown below**, eight countries reported a maximum rank of 0, **implying that** the null hypothesis of no cointegration relationships among logRGDP, logGE, and logtrade could not be rejected at the 5% significance level. The eight countries are Angola, Botswana, Democratic Republic of Congo, Malawi, Mauritius, Swaziland, Seychelles, and Zimbabwe. **This means that** no common long-run equilibrium exists among these variables. OLS regression of filtered variables I(0) will generate consistent estimates. The last column in the table **indicates that** a VAR model is recommended for such cases. Lesotho, Madagascar, Mozambique, Namibia, and Zambia reported a maximum rank of 1, **implying that** the null hypothesis of at least one cointegration relationship could not be rejected at the 5% significance level. **In this case**, there exists one cointegrating vector among the variables under examination **suggesting** a common long-run equilibrium. VECM in first difference I(1) was employed to produce consistent results. Tanzania and South Africa reported a maximum rank of 2, **implying that** the null of at least two cointegration relationships among the variables could not be rejected at the 5% significance level. **This outcome means that** there exist two cointegrating vectors through which variables adjust to maintain a long-run equilibrium. VECM was used in first difference I(1) to estimate the coefficients. (p. 6)

Example 2 (Majoni, 2015)

In order to use ordinary least squares (OLS) methods, four assumptions must be met: stationarity, orthogonality, full rank condition, and martingale difference sequence (MDS) (Hayashi, 2000). The first three assumptions ensure consistency and the last one ensures asymptotic normality of the results. This paper used the Dickey Fuller test to verify stationarity and the Engle Granger test to check for a cointegrating relationship between the variables for each of the 10 countries. (pp. 5–6)

example is an extract from a paper by Blessings Majoni, who tested the validity of Okun's law for a set of African countries. Notice that Blessings supports her argument with a reference to a previous study.

- **Summary statistics.** These are descriptive statistics such as means, standard deviations, and minimum and maximum values. Descriptive statistics should be reported for all the variables. They are usually presented in table form and can be put in the Methodology or Results section. In economics papers, they are usually presented in the Methodology section under Data. In published papers, they may be put in an appendix. There are several things to keep in mind when presenting summary statistics in a table.

  - You should use the names of the variables, not their acronyms or abbreviations that you used in your analyses or in the model specification. For example, INF should be spelled out as "inflation," IND-COMP should be spelled out as "individual tax compliance," and DUTYTAX should be spelled out as "tax revenue." Acronyms that are very common in your area—such as FDI, for example—may be used as such but in this case, make sure to spell them out in the note under the table (e.g., FDI = foreign direct investment).
  - Remind the reader what measures you used for the variables. You can do this in a note under the table (e.g., tax revenue = ratio of total tax revenue to GDP).
  - Indicate the form of the variables that have been transformed. Log-transformed values are often shown by putting *ln* in front of the variable: *ln*(land in acres).
  - Summary statistics should be interpreted, and not just presented. Explain what the values mean. This is especially important if there are some unusual statistics (e.g., high standard deviations) or if the groups included in the sample are very heterogeneous.

For an example of how to report and interpret summary statistics, see Chapter 15, which shows models and examples of reporting results.

- **Main results.** Statistical analyses in social sciences are performed using computer software such as SPSS or STATA. These software programs generate output in the form of tables containing various statistics. For example, for multiple regression analysis, SPSS generates the following tables:

  - Descriptive statistics
  - Correlations
  - Variables entered/removed
  - Model summary
  - ANOVA summary table
  - Coefficients

Novice researchers often feel overwhelmed when they see all this computer output. Should all these statistics be reported? If not, which ones should be reported? How to choose? In the next section, I show which main results are usually reported with one of the most commonly used statistical techniques in public policy and economics—multiple regression analysis (MRA).

Results of Multiple Regression Analysis (MRA)

Recall that MRA is a statistical procedure that assesses the relationship between a dependent variable and several predictor variables. The estimates generated by MRA are called *coefficients*. Using MRA, we can calculate the amount of variance in the dependent variable that is accounted for (= explained) by the variation in each of the independent variables. This calculation shows the relative importance of each independent variable to the relationship.

It is beyond the scope of this book to provide a detailed treatment of MRA as a statistical technique. For a basic interpretation of MRA results in economics, consult Greenlaw (2009). For advanced information on MRA and other statistical techniques, you may wish to consult Tabachnick and Fidell's *Using Multivariate Statistics*.

In an MRA study, the following information generated by regression software is usually reported.

- The **size** and **sign of regression coefficients**. The size of regression coefficients shows how much each predictor variable contributes on its own to the variance in the dependent variable after the effects of all the other predictor variables in the model have been statistically removed. In their standardized form (as β), regression coefficients are a measure of the importance of each variable, allowing researchers to compare the relative importance of the predictors. In economics and public policy, the sign of regression coefficients is also important and it is discussed in comparison with the expected (or hypothesized) sign predicted from theory: Do the explanatory variables have the expected sign?

- **Statistical significance** for each estimated coefficient, which is determined by comparing the p-value (or significance probability) associated with a coefficient with the chosen level of significance. If the p-value is smaller, the coefficient is interpreted as being statistically significant; if it is greater, the coefficient is interpreted as being nonsignificant, or as not being significant. There are many variations in the reporting and interpretation of null hypothesis significance testing in public policy and economics. For example, in economics, three significance levels are commonly used: 1%, 5%, and 10% and results are often described as being "statistically significant at the 1% (or 5%, or 10%) significance level." The 10% significance level is uncommon in other disciplines, for example, in sociology or education, where results with p-values that are greater than .05 (5%) are interpreted as being nonsignificant.

Alternatively, when reporting statistical significance, researchers may simply indicate whether the generated p-values are smaller than the level of significance. In this case, authors indicate statistically significant values with asterisks—a single asterisk (*) for $p < .01$, a double asterisk (**) for $p < .05$, and a triple asterisk (***) for $p < .1$—and use a note under the table to show what the asterisks refer to.

In some research areas, authors may provide the exact p-values (e.g., $p = .58$). Providing the exact p-values is especially common in psychological and educational research, but it is fairly uncommon in economics. In some areas, confidence intervals are commonly used to indicate significance levels.

Because of the great variability among disciplines in reporting statistical significance, it is important to find out what is common in the particular area you are working in and report statistical results using the conventions of your field.

- **"Goodness-of-fit" statistics.** These statistics show how well the model you are testing explains the data: How much variance in the dependent variable is explained by the combination of the predictors? The F-statistic is used to determine if all the coefficients in the model are statistically significant, whereas R^2 (or adjusted R^2) is used to determine the overall amount of variance in the dependent variable that is explained by all the predictor variables in combination.

  Greenlaw (2009, p. 217) gives good advice for interpreting R^2: "R^2 for cross-section data is generally less than R^2 for time-series data. Econometricians typically consider a time-series regression to be "good' if it results in an R^2 of 0.8 or higher. By contrast, a cross-section regression is considered "good" if it has an R^2 of only half that: 0.4 or above."

Regression results are always presented in table form. A typical regression table includes the following information: regression coefficients, standard errors (in parentheses), statistics indicating significance, and goodness-of-fit statistics. It is important to stress here that regression tables that are included in a paper are always constructed and never copied directly from regression output provided by the regression software. Later in this section, I give suggestions for formatting tables in a quantitative study.

HOW TO REPORT RESULTS IN A QUANTITATIVE STUDY

In your Results section, you should guide the reader throughout the presentation of your most important results. Do not assume that the reader would remember the details of your research question or that he or she would understand your results without careful and detailed guidance.

A Results section usually opens with a brief summary of the purpose of the study and its methodology. If space is limited, at the very least, provide a one-sentence description of what you examined in your analyses or remind the reader what was regressed on what. Below are two examples taken from two published studies. Notice the highlighted words and phrases—they help the authors guide their readers throughout their explanation.

One goal of our analysis is to identify borrower characteristics that are correlated with the elasticity of demand for microcredit. If elasticity can be linked to client or loan characteristics, then credit rationed populations can be identified and targeted. **As a first step, we focus on** easily observable borrower demographic characteristics (age, education, vocational training, dependents in elementary school, community involvement, Haitian relatives, religiosity, access to water, survey treatment dummy variables, Esperanza branch dummy variables, and interviewer dummy variables). (Bogan et al., 2015, p. 745)

We study the impact of public debt on subsequent credit growth using different econometric methods. **We start with four regressions that include** time dummies (see the left-hand part of Table 4). (De Bonis & Stacchini, 2013, p. 297)

Organize your results around your research questions. Report results for each research question separately, in a separate subsection. Title the subsections thematically to reflect what they are about. For example:

The Relationship between Government Expenditure and Economic Growth

Infrastructure Development and Poverty Reduction

Results of quantitative analyses are often reported in the following three steps.

1. **Refer the reader to the relevant table or figure** and tell the reader what to look for by directing the reader's attention to the appropriate column or value. For example:

   Figure 2 **shows/illustrates/demonstrates** the distribution of income across the provinces.

   Table 6 **shows/presents/provides/summarizes** the findings/results of our analyses.

   The most common types of behavior **are shown in** Table 3.

   The details of the questionnaire **are presented in** Table 4.

   The results of the policy experiment **are shown in** Figure 2.

Notice the use of Present Tense in these sentences. In public policy and economics, visuals are always presented using Present Tense.

2. **Describe the result**. Answer your research question(s) or state whether your hypothesis (or your null hypothesis) should be accepted or rejected. If you are reporting regression coefficients, indicate whether they have the expected sign, whether they are statistically significant, and how big they are. When talking about statistical significance, use the word "significant" only to mean "statistically significant." Avoid ambiguous phrases such as *highly*

significant, very significant, almost significant, slightly significant, or *marginally significant.* For results that have failed to reach statistical significance, economists often use the word *insignificant*; in many other disciplines, it is more common to use the word *nonsignificant.* Here is an example. Notice how the authors guide the reader throughout the description of their results.

In this subsection we will address the problem that self-employment status is not permanent. **As seen from Table 3** there is rather high persistence in the employment status. **The results from the table can be summarized as follows**: if a household is self-employed in period *t*, the chance that it is self-employed in *t* + 1 or *t* − 1 is roughly 85 percent. The persistence in self-employment status is thus high but still far from permanent. (Engström & Hagen, 2017, p. 100)

---

3. **Interpret the result for the reader**—explain what the result means. For example:

> Table 3 **shows that** home owners are the most likely voters in general elections.

> Figure 2 **indicates that** the experimental results may be biased.

> The results presented in Figure 1 **indicate that** 94% of all businesses in the area were affected by the disaster.

> The trends described in Table 5 **suggest that** there has been a shift in demand.

> **As shown in** Fig. 1, the companies used in the survey varied significantly in geographical location and size.

> Table 2 **summarizes** the approaches to capacity building revealed by the participants from the two organizations studied. The table **shows that** all participants favored similar approaches to capacity building and that they used similar strategies to strengthen links with policy makers.

Again, notice the use of Present Tense in the interpretation of results.

To provide additional information or explanation, authors often use **code glosses**—phrases that restate or further explain the original idea. Below are two examples.

At the same time **this means that** medical insurance is least available to those who need it most, for the insurance companies do their own "adverse selection". (Akerlof, 1970, p. 494)

In one direction, development alone can play a major role in driving down inequality between men and women; in the other direction, continuing discrimination against women can, as Sen has forcefully argued, hinder development. Empowerment can, **in other words**, accelerate development. (Duflo, 2012, p. 1053)

It is also common to use **hedges** when interpreting results. These are phrases that allow authors to present their views in tentative ways. Below are some examples. For more about hedges, see the corresponding section at the end of this chapter.

Opinion surveys further confirm this analysis. **Table 2 suggests** that economists have in general less regard for interdisciplinarity than their social scientific and even business school brethren. (Fourcade et al., 2015, pp. 94–95)

More important, the constant aside, every common coefficient and its t-value in these equations is increased in absolute value, and the coefficient of the synchronous real stock price is positive, as the substitution effect would imply, and statistically significant. Hence, **these regressions suggest** that there is both a wealth effect and a substitution effect, with the wealth effect the stronger. (Friedman, 1988, pp. 232–234)

These two examples suggest that just reducing the grip of poverty on these households or helping them to deal with crises could improve the welfare of women of all ages. (Duflo, 2012, p. 1055)

REPORTS OF QUANTITATIVE RESULTS: EXAMPLES

Box 40 shows examples of how authors describe and interpret results. Go over these examples and identify the places where the authors

- Refer the reader to a visual,
- Describe results, and
- Interpret results.

Pay attention to the highlighted words and phrases, which the authors use to guide their readers throughout the presentation and interpretation of their results and to show their own attitude toward these results. Notice the use of hedges in some of the extracts. Why do you think the authors want their claims to sound more tentative than definitive? Notice also the use of verb tense. Which verb tense is commonly used in results interpretation?

BOX 40 Examples of Results

Table 1 shows the results for our two indicators of expenditure decentralization. **Columns 1 and 2 show that** fiscal decentralization reduces the number of domestic terror events. **This is in line with our *a priori* hypothesis that** decentralized structures **may increase** the opportunity costs and direct costs of domestic terrorists, on the one hand, but equally that it **may decrease** the marginal benefit from such a terror act, as decentralization stabilizes the polity and the economy. Calculating the marginal effect (at the sample mean, with the country and year dummies equal to zero), **the results in column 1 show that** the number of terror events in a country declines

BOX 40 Examples of Results—cont'd.

by 0.001 as decentralization increases by ten percentage points. The calculated elasticity of almost 2.5% **is socially relevant.** (Dreher & Fischer, 2011, p. 224)

In all four regressions public debt **has a negative and significant coefficient.** This is true using either the between estimator or the pooled estimator. Fixed effects (the within estimator) and the sGMM estimator **confirm** the negative influence of public debt on private credit growth. The sGMM estimate (-0.36) **indicates that** a 10% increase in the debt-to-GDP ratio is followed by a deceleration of 0.7% points in the annual change of the credit-to-GDP ratio. (De Bonis & Stacchini, 2013, p. 297)

The coefficients [sic] estimates obtained using on one hand the Ferrer-i-Carbonel and Frijters (2004) and on the other hand the Das and van Soest (1999) estimation strategy are relatively similar. For males there are two differences; the Das and van Soest estimation **yields insignificant and significant estimates** for poor health and public sector employment, respectively. The key economic variables – the hourly wage and hours (part-time work) – **remain significant,** albeit the precision of the Das and van Soest estimates is lower. For females, **none of the estimated coefficients** with the Das and van Soest procedure **differ significantly from zero. Thus,** the determinants of reported job satisfaction **clearly differ** between the genders. (D'Addio et al., 2007, p. 2421)

Table 5 reports our proxy of survey over-reporting: the simple survey-validation differences, with p values from a t test of the difference from zero. Negative values **indicate** survey under reporting, **assuming the validator measure is more accurate of course. As noted above,** we have the statistical power to detect differences greater than about 17% of the survey mean. (Blattman et al., 2016, p. 109)

We begin by discussing the results from the unrestricted specification, **that is,** we define self-employed households as households in which at least one member was self-employed in year t. **The results are reported in Table 2. The estimates of γ are** positive and significant in all four specifications. **The interpretation is that** self-employed spend around 7 percent more on food relative to wage earners with the same reported income. The γ estimates are roughly stable when moving toward permanent income. (Engström & Hagen, 2017, p. 99)

Overall, variables that relate to entrepreneurial drive and skill-level **emerge with** a positive correlation to elasticity. Education and vocational training **indicate** elastic demand. Additionally, clients who report that they were more likely to take risks in order to increase profits **carry significantly more** elastic demand ($p < .10$). **Alternatively, the model suggests** that clients who depend primarily on wage-labour income and/or have low monthly sales have more inelastic demand. Further, **a variable that could correlate** with financial literacy **emerges as** negatively related with elasticity. Clients who display an understanding of interest rates by reporting a rate on their actual Esperanza loan, even if that rate was incorrect, have significantly more inelastic demand ($p < .01$). (Bogan et al., 2015, p. 747)

HOW TO REPORT RESULTS IN A QUALITATIVE STUDY

Earlier I said that there is a lot of variability in how results of a quantitative study are reported. There is even more variability in the presentation of results in a qualitative study. This is because qualitative research usually generates more data and more varied data than does a quantitative study; these data may include transcripts of interviews, meetings, and focus group discussions; policy and other documents; field notes; and various artifacts. This is also because qualitative analysis procedures are more subjective than quantitative ones and because there is less emphasis on objective description in presenting results.

Recall that data analysis in a qualitative study involves data coding in order to reduce a very large amount of data to just a few manageable categories or themes. There are many approaches to qualitative data analysis and many procedures have been described for data coding. If you plan to do a qualitative study, it might be a good idea to obtain a guide to qualitative analysis and follow it. A good starting point is Rudestam and Newton (2001), where you can find a summary of several approaches to qualitative analysis as well as useful references. Briefly, qualitative analysis proceeds as follows.

1. The researcher reads and rereads the obtained data to extract **meaning units**—words, phrases, or sentences that represent a particular experience or phenomenon.

2. These meaning units are then combined into **themes** and, later, larger **categories**.

3. The researcher then extracts **quotations** from the data that illustrate a particular experience or phenomenon most vividly. These quotations are used in the presentation of results to support specific claims.

4. Depending on the purpose of analysis, qualitative researchers may create a **conceptual framework** to show the connections among the identified themes and categories. This framework is then compared against the data as well as existing theoretical frameworks, revised and modified as needed, and finally presented as an explanatory framework for the observed phenomena.

The presentation of qualitative results in a paper differs considerably from the presentation of quantitative results. Below are some of the main differences.

- **Organization.** In a quantitative study, results are typically presented as an answer to a research question; in contrast, in a qualitative study, results are presented organized into themes or categories that have emerged from the data. One important consequence of this organization is that it is impossible to plan in advance how qualitative results will be presented—simply because you cannot predict what themes and patterns will emerge. In fact, when qualitative researchers complete data analysis and begin writing, they often change or modify not only the outline of the paper, but also the main questions, frameworks, and the entire approach to presentation as they review the data and critically engage what others have written on the topic in light of the emerging themes. Thus, if you are writing a qualitative paper, be prepared to make major changes to your original outline and ideas.

- **Argument support**. In a quantitative study, arguments are supported with statistics obtained in the analysis. In a qualitative study, arguments are supported with quotations obtained from participants or relevant policy or other documents. These quotations can be quite long and the same argument may be supported with multiple quotations from different participants or other sources.

It is important to keep in mind that different research areas may have different conventions for the use of quotations. In Chapter 16, I give some general guidelines for using quotations in research papers in public policy. However, you should check papers in your particular area to see how authors have used quotations.

- **Use of visuals**. In a quantitative study, results are almost always described by referring the reader to a corresponding table or figure. In a qualitative study, visuals are not as commonly used and when they are included, their purpose is to present the coding scheme, the categories that the researcher has identified, or the researcher's conclusions.

- **Discussion**. In a quantitative study, results are usually presented and discussed separately, often in separate sections or subsections. In a qualitative study, the researcher would often present and discuss results at the same time, supporting his or her claims with quotations from participants and references to published research. Thus, the presentation of results in a qualitative study often follows this pattern:

Claim + support with quotations from participants or documents + the author's interpretation/discussion

Below are two examples of qualitative results presentation. As you go over them, notice the organization and structure of the extracts and try to divide them into the three parts described above—claim, support, and interpretation/discussion. Notice the language the authors use to make claims and to introduce and interpret the quotations.

The first example (Box 41) is from a paper written by Ganesh Pandeya, a visiting researcher from Nepal. Ganesh wanted to know if citizen participation in local government decision-making improved local planning in Nepal. His research strategy was semistructured interviews with 52 stakeholders, a survey of 88 purposefully selected local citizens, focus group discussions with 25 district representatives, and participant observation of community meetings, where he took detailed field notes. In addition, he examined official documents, policies, memos, records, and progress and study reports related to the local governments in the target districts. The key questions he asked were: How do

BOX 41 Describing Results in a Qualitative Paper: Example 1

The second most-oft cited constraining factor for effective participation was absence of elected representatives in local governments for more than a decade. This appeared to be a major stumbling block for promoting effective participation in three ways: (a) by constraining citizens' voice, (b) by reducing local government's responsiveness, and (c) by impeding two-way communication. In fact, many informants believed that a long-term political void limited considerably the voices and incentives of citizens to fight for spaces and resources in the participatory sphere. An ex-minister explained, for example, that "[a]s there was no trusted ally to listen to [the citizens'] grievances, it was natural that their degree of participation in, and influence over, local planning was low and so were their voices." He suggested that elected representatives may have a greater incentive to hear citizens' voices and address their needs. These views were supported by many participants. Informants also believed that this void created many deficiencies in responsiveness, leading to unaccountable and irresponsible local governments. An ex-secretary, for example, stated that a long-term political void "resulted in a most fragile situation for accountability and responsive culture in LGs," apparently because, as one political representative explained, "those who need not be elected by people, need not be responsive to people." These findings are in line with the arguments made by Yang and Callahan (2007) and Yang and Pandey (2011) that the presence of elected representatives is an important factor for effective citizen participation. In summary, these findings suggest that the formal rules of the game should be understood as part of a social context within which they are embedded. In fact, structural conditions for citizen participation appear to determine whether positive outcomes are achieved or whether participation creates only punishingly high costs. This argument is well supported by Gaventa and Barrett (2010), Huntington (1968), Kabeer (2005), and Julnes and Johnson (2011). For instance, Huntington (1968) argued that citizen participation could lead to various economic, social, and political costs when there is an absence of broad-based participation, representative democracy, and strong institutional safeguards to set and enforce rules. (Pandeya, 2014, pp. 34–35)

citizens participate in local planning? What difference does this participation make to planning outcomes? Does participation lead to better planning and more equitable access to resources? What are the key enabling and constraining factors that affect citizen participation?

For his study, Ganesh collected data over the course of several months and then transcribed all the interviews, discussions, and field notes. He then coded participants' statements using an open coding method (Creswell, 2014). Initially, he clustered the statements into 25 categories based on the various themes and patterns he identified in the data. After rereading the transcripts, comparing them with his own field notes, and consulting with the participants, he was able to collapse these categories into just a few main categories related to positive and negative outcomes and factors that enabled or constrained citizen participation.

Under each category, he further created several subcategories into which he clustered the participants' statements. To verify the reliability of his interpretations, Ganesh conducted confirmatory discussions with some of the participants and additional consultations with practitioners and academic experts. The final step was to verify those findings against established theories of citizen participation as well as research findings for Nepal. The extract in Box 41 describes one of the factors that constrain citizen participation in local decision-making in Nepal. Notice the structure of the extract: First, Ganesh makes a claim, then he presents quotations from the participants to support it, and then he interprets the finding by relating it to previous research and theory.

The second example (Box 42) shows an extract from a published study by Izuhara and Forrest (2013). In this qualitative study, the authors examine intergenerational dynamics and provision of support in contemporary families in two East Asian societies—China and Japan. The study was based on semistructured, in-depth interviews with purposively selected participants in Tokyo and Shanghai. As you read the extract, notice its structure: In what way is it different from the structure of the extract shown in Example 1 in Box 41?

BOX 42 Describing Results in a Qualitative Paper: Example 2

While de-familization is evident among the older generation, there is also increasing dependence among the current younger generation (adult children) in both societies (Zhu, 2012; Hirayama, 2012). Due partly to the wealth created by the middle generation, especially in Shanghai, and more competitive and precarious labour markets, parents continue to support their adult child(ren) in co-residency sometimes well into their 30s. Prolonged dependence regarding co-residency and increased financial support in various aspects of adult children's life are new phenomena which add a different dimension to intergenerational dynamics, and the role of families, in the transitional welfare systems. While a 'new middle class' with greater financial independence has emerged in the Chinese market economy, many are still supported substantially by their parents' newly created wealth, rather than through the state or the market:

"The situation is the other way round. We are taken care of by our parents. My parents come here nearly every day or every other day to prepare all our dinner . . . We also give them some money but we do not feel good. They as our parents might think it is their responsibility to help children and we are their only child. But, as a child, we feel guilty and try to find a way to compensate them even little – to give them some money is simply what we can do now. What they have done for us is far more than this." (Young Zhao, 27, female, married, Shanghai)

"I want to leave my parental home by age 30. I do not give my parents any money. Although I do not receive pocket money from them, my mother cooks for me and does everything. I would like to repay the debts." (Young Yamashita, 27, female co-resident, Tokyo) (Izuhara & Forrest, 2013, p. 534)

Tables can be a very effective way to present the overall results of a large qualitative study, especially a comparative one. One such example is shown in Box 43. In that qualitative study, Schmitz et al. (2015) looked at drivers of economic reform in Vietnam. The study was based on qualitative interviews with

BOX 43 Presenting Results in a Table

Drivers	Bac Ninh	Hung Yen	Dong Thap	Ca Mau
Central government	Connections with central government & proximity to Ha Noi probably useful but not dominant driver	Central government has been only mainstay of reform, but without a local champion, reform has flagged	Central government has been supportive but not a major driver	Central government is a key driver, particularly of administrative reform
Provincial government – Leaders – Bureaucracy	Provincial leadership played a critical role in the later stages of reform	Provincial leadership has constantly changed, leaving policy uncertainty & lack of direction	Provincial leadership has been critical driver	Provincial leadership has been mediocre and is not key driver of change
Large business	Big firms play important role throughout, working closely with provincial government	Big firms have not played key role in driving reform. Indeed, lack of leadership from business may be one reason for lack of governance reform	Big firms have focused on their own needs rather than generalized reform	Big firms have been influential in driving reforms, but only for issues of concern to them
Small business	SME association was main driver in early stage but had less influence later on	SMEs have had very little influence over reform	Good SME/ government relationships (& political links) have helped reform to be more broad- based	SMEs have had virtually no influence on reform

Source: Schmitz, H., Tuan, D.A., Hang, P.T.T., McCulloch, N., 2012. Who Drives Economic Reform in Vietnam's Provinces? (Research Report No. 76). Institute of Development Studies, Brighton, United Kingdom. Retrieved from: http://www.ids.ac.uk/files/dmfile/Rr76.pdf (Accessed 3 March 2017).

carefully selected participants from both the public and private sectors in four Vietnamese provinces. The authors cross-checked the obtained information within each province and compared the findings across the four provinces. They present their overall findings in a table taken from their earlier study: The left-hand column lists the drivers of reform that they have identified—central government, provincial government, large business, and small business; the other four columns show what role each of these drivers played in each of the provinces. This is an efficient and readily understandable way of presenting the findings of a large qualitative study because it allows readers to quickly grasp the overall results. Notice that there are no cryptic or abbreviated entries in the table—the authors use complete sentences and phrases that are easy to understand in every cell. Notice also that most sentences in each row begin with the same subject. This is important to ensure clarity, avoid confusion, and make comparisons among cells more easily understandable.

HOW TO DISCUSS RESULTS

It is common for theses and dissertations to have a separate Discussion section. However, most published studies in public policy and economics do not have such a section and instead, present and discuss results in the same section (e.g., Results).

Students who are new to graduate study are often unsure about what "discussing results" means. In policy papers, in particular, students often focus on recommendations and provide a long list of actions their government should take—sometimes regardless of whether those actions are related to what they have found. Keep in mind, however, that you are writing for an academic audience and that your purpose is to persuade your audience to accept your claims. To do that, your discussion needs to follow disciplinary conventions for both content and style. So what does discussing results mean in an economics or public policy paper? In this section, I will show some of the most common things authors do when they discuss results: i.e., explain and evaluate, comment, draw implications, and address limitations.

Explain and Evaluate

Authors explain and evaluate their results by relating them to previous research or theory and comparing them to the findings of other researchers and/or to their own theoretical predications or expectations. Are the obtained results consistent or inconsistent with the results of previous research, theory, or expectations? If the results are consistent, no further explanation may be necessary although authors will often provide details of previous studies when comparing them to their own results. Below are two simple templates that can be used to present results that are consistent with those of previous research or theory.

These results are **consistent with previous research** on [topic]. For example, [give details on one or two most relevant studies and include references].

These results **support earlier findings** showing that [describe the earlier findings].

If results differ from those of previous research or theory, a careful explanation of possible reasons for the discrepancy is usually necessary. It is common in this case to offer several possible explanations. If you offer several explanations, start with the least plausible and end with the most plausible one. Make sure to explain your logic and why you believe a particular explanation is more plausible than others. Below are two templates that can be used to present results that are inconsistent with those of previous research or theory.

We can offer **two possible explanations** for the observed discrepancy. **The first possibility** is that [explain]. However, we believe that this is unlikely because [explain]. **The second possibility** is that [explain]. This **appears to be more plausible** because [explain]. In fact, this interpretation **would be consistent with** [previous research].

The evidence **seems inconsistent with** the theoretical expectations. [Give details]. **One possibility** is that [explain]. However, [explain why this may not be a good possibility]. **Another possibility** is that [explain]. We believe that this is **the more likely explanation** because [explain].

Note that authors often need to provide some basis for their explanations. Sometimes, the explanation may be based on theory; more often, however, authors support their arguments with previous empirical research and include references to relevant studies. Below are three examples; the first two come from published studies and the last one, from a student paper, in which the student, Dwi Rahmahapianti, investigated the effect of infrastructure development on poverty reduction in Indonesia.

The results from Table 4 show that the house price indices **appear to have** different integration orders across cities. **Possible explanations could be** the presence of structure breaks (Chen et al., 2007; Chien, 2010), nonlinearity implied by the nature of the data (Cook, 2003; Cook and Speight, 2007), new real estate policies, or the financial crisis that generated structural change to housing prices. (Chen et al., 2011, p. 320)

In another paper (Cardenas, 2001), I discuss how for these same 10 groups one can correlate the social efficiency achieved at the end of the experiment with the percentage of players with their main income being from extractive activities, or negatively with the percentage of players having land as their main income source. **A second possible explanation for a positive sign** between wealth and level of free-riding is that wealthier participants **may** show smaller marginal utilities from the cash earned in the experiment, and **therefore** their marginal net utility from the effort to promote and enforce a cooperative agreement would be much lower, or the marginal value of potential losses is again smaller than for the poorer participants. (Cardenas, 2003, p. 278)

Surprisingly, results show that regional income **has no statistically significant impact** on the poverty rate at the national level and in provinces outside of Jawa and Bali, although it is statistically significant at the 1% significance level in Jawa and Bali. The 1.14% decrease in poverty rate in Jawa and Bali indicates that the welfare of the poor responds quite strongly to the overall income growth (Balisacan et al., 2002). On the other hand, the economic growth in regional provinces outside of Jawa and Bali **appears** not to have made that much of an impact on poverty rate compared to its impact in Jawa and Bali. Suryahadi, Raya, Marbun, and Yumna (2011) **suggested several reasons for this result** including lack of productive opportunities, weak human capabilities, and inadequate social protection. (Rahmahapianti, 2014, p. 15)

There is a fine line, however, between offering a reasonable explanation to reconcile discrepancies with previous research or explain unexpected findings on the one hand and purely speculating on the other. Be sure to support your explanations with at least some evidence from previous research and avoid entirely unsupported speculation. Present all explanations that are not directly warranted by the evidence using tentative language and state explicitly that you are speculating.

Here is an extract from a published study in which the author looked at factors that predict a person's willingness to contribute ideas to a group. Notice that the author bases her explanation on earlier findings. Notice also how tentatively she presents her explanations. She ends with a call for more research to test her proposed explanation.

We can only speculate as to what additional factors **may contribute** to the gender differences we observe, **as the experiment was not designed to test other** stories. **That said, it seems valuable to think about what other theories might speak to our results.** In her work on social role theory, Eagly (1987) explains that gender roles are not only positive (descriptive of our perceptions of men and women) but also normative (proscriptive of how men and women should behave). **With this in mind, it seems plausible that** the utility an individual derives from contributing to a group **may depend** on whether the domain is gender congruent. An individual **may prefer** to contribute in a gender-congruent area because it is more consistent with her own and others' expectations about how she should behave. **This could potentially explain why** even controlling for beliefs about own ability, women **are less likely** to contribute in stereotypically male domains. **To better understand this channel, it would be useful to conduct additional research** in which we exogenously manipulate the salience of an individual's gender identity or the gender stereotype of the category. (Coffman, 2014, pp. 1657–1658)

Because there are clear similarities between the part where authors review relevant literature and outline their expectations and the part where they discuss whether those expectations have been met, it may be easier for some writers to write their Introduction/Literature Review and Discussion sections together, at the same time—or at least have an outline of the main points covered in the review of the literature that need to be addressed in the Discussion. The important thing to remember is that when discussing results, you should always try to embed them within the theoretical and/or conceptual context presented in the earlier part of the study. The example below shows how authors can explicitly connect their results with the expectations they described in the introductory part of the paper.

To summarize, whatever specification we adopt, government debt has a negative and statistically significant influence on loan growth. **As anticipated in the introduction, our results might reflect three linked phenomena. The first interpretation** is a typical crowding-out effect: in countries where the government has a large involvement in the economy, greater shares of bank assets may flow toward government securities and state-owned firms, reducing loans to the private sector. **Secondly**, according to the public finance approach to financial repression (Giovannini and de Melo, 1991; Roubini and Sala-i-Martin, 1995), issuing government securities is a way for the state to collect revenues, especially when the proceeds from legal taxation are difficult or costly to obtain and banks are forced to invest in government securities. **Thirdly,** the recent tensions in the euro area have confirmed that the direction of causality may run from the condition of the public finances to banks' financial position. In many European countries the increase in the yields on public debt securities implied a higher cost and a deceleration of bank funding: a slowdown of credit followed. **Our results are consistent with those obtained by** Hauner (2009), who found a negative link between public debt held by banks and financial development in middle-income countries. (De Bonis & Stacchini, 2013, p. 299)

Comment

When discussing results, authors often comment on the importance, significance, unexpectedness, and other features of those results. These comments show the authors' attitude toward the proposition he or she offers.

In order to interpret results in an appropriate way, however, it is important to distinguish between statistical significance of a result and its significance for policy. As has been noted previously by many authors, statistical significance and policy significance are different things and it is incorrect to describe results as important solely on the basis of their statistical significance. Statistical significance means only that the observed difference is rare; it does not say anything about how big or how important the difference is, or what implications it may have for policy. In economics and public policy, in particular, where large samples are commonly used, even small results may be statistically significant but this does not mean that they would be automatically important for policy.

With this caveat in mind, let us look at how authors comment on their results. Three strategies are commonly used, often in combination.

1. **Showing one's attitude toward a result**. This is achieved by using attitude markers such as *unfortunately, surprisingly, more important, remarkable* [result], [this point is] *worthy of note*, or *striking* [finding]. You should, however, avoid melodramatic language such as "amazing," "unbelievable," or "fantastic." Below are some examples.

Figure 5 tracks the development of corporate profits to GDP over the past 15 years. In the United States, profits to GDP increased by a **remarkable** five percentage points since 2000. (Ferguson & Schularick, 2007, p. 222)

The figure thus confirms that the employment entry rate is quantitatively **more important** a factor than the employment exit rate in adjustments of the size of French firms. (Abowd et al., 1999, p. 177)

Perhaps this result is unsurprising. The Michigan index captures a mix of first-moment and second-moment concerns, as expressed by households in survey data. The relationship between "confidence" and uncertainty is **murky**, and the two concepts are tightly linked at a deep level in some theoretical models, for example, Ilut and Schneider (2014). (Baker et al., 2016, p. 1631)

In this light **it is interesting and perhaps ironic** that the same multilateral institutions which pursued the "structural adjustment" agenda in the 1980s and 1990s, with its attendant "good governance agenda," also promoted forms of regional economic integration which require relatively strong states to implement them. (Draper, 2010, p. 13)

Therefore, many believe that a special effort is needed to educate girls, and that educating girls would have **tremendous** spillover effects. **Unfortunately, the evidence for this is not as strong as is commonly believed**. (Duflo, 2012, p. 1065)

---

2. **Showing one's certainty toward a result**. This is achieved by using boosters such as *clearly, obviously,* or [the data] *demonstrate*. Below are some examples.

Meanwhile, the favoured country will gain as regional industry relocates to its soil and real wages rise as a result. **Clearly** these effects would generate substantial political tensions over time which in turn would undermine integration processes. (Draper, 2010, p. 18)

The statistics in tables 5 and 6 **demonstrate** that matching may be an important issue on the French labor market, in particular for those skill levels with less education and, therefore, little signal given by schooling. (Abowd et al., 1999, p. 179)

These results, the first to use a consistent methodology across countries, **confirm** previous studies and **demonstrate clearly** that the wage premium is much larger in the two less developed economies.... (Hijzen et al., 2013, p. 179)

3. **Expressing tentativeness**. This is achieved by using hedges, or words and expressions that help the author qualify his or her claims. Below are some examples. For more on hedges, see the last section of this chapter.

Because of the very short nature of our time series, **we are reluctant to draw strong conclusions from these analyses**; however, **it is worth noting that these results are not obviously contrary** to Davis and Haltiwanger's (1990) or Anderson and Meyer's (1994) results on cyclicality. (Abowd et al., 1999, p. 182)

There, firms that deal anonymously with suppliers receive longer credit terms. **One possible interpretation is that** the presence of a credit reference bureau makes it possible for firms to deal at arms length. (Fafchamps, 2000, p. 223)

Despite all the attention to lowering tax rates and increasing a pro-business climate, **the evidence suggests** that these factors have little effect on economic growth, while actually decreasing the potential for economic development (Goetz et al., 2011; Hungerford, 2012). (Feldman et al., 2016, p. 12)

Overall, much of the gains from the coup occurred before the coup itself due to speculation from top-secret information. **This suggests that** estimates of the value of the coup to a company that only considered the stock price reaction to the coup itself **would be** dramatically understated. (Dube et al., 2011, p. 1407)

More important, the constant aside, every common coefficient and its *t*-value in these equations is increased in absolute value, and the coefficient of the synchronous real stock price is positive, as the substitution effect would imply, and statistically significant. Hence, **these regressions suggest** that there is both a wealth effect and a substitution effect, with the wealth effect the stronger. (Friedman, 1988, pp. 232–234)

Draw Implications

After comparing their results with those described in the literature, authors often draw implications or provide recommendations for research and/or policy. You should keep in mind two things when drawing implications or providing recommendations.

- Implications and recommendations must be warranted by the results. This means that if you found a negative result, you should not recommend actions that ignore that result. This also means that you should not raise issues that have not been addressed in the research and that you should not speculate—your implications and recommendations should be directly supported by your findings.

- It is a good idea to present implications and recommendations tentatively, using hedges. Avoid strong statements, especially with the verb "should"—they often invite criticism. Compare, for example, the two paragraphs shown below. In the first one, the author uses "should" to make recommendations, whereas in the second one, the author makes recommendations in a much more tentative way. The second example would be more appropriate in an academic paper.

Example 1

The results of this study show a negative relationship between welfare assistance and efforts to seek employment. The government should develop more effective policies to reverse this negative trend. The government should also increase welfare benefits to people who have lost their jobs or are unable to work because such people cannot survive without assistance. This study shows how important it is to support the poor and the unemployed.

Example 2

The results of this study are consistent with Adam and Baker's (2004) findings of a negative relationship between welfare assistance and efforts to seek employment. This study extends their findings to a younger population and **suggests** that this relationship **may be even stronger** than has been thought previously. However, this result **should be interpreted with caution** because of a relatively small sample used in this study.

Below are two examples from published studies in which the authors draw implications for policy. Again, notice how tentatively they word their recommendations.

Example 1

It is worth considering which of these results is most useful for policy purposes. One policy objective could be to use the CLASS to identify effective teachers (for example, for promotion). In this case, the OLS results are most relevant. Moreover, there is no obvious disadvantage to using contemporaneous (rather than lagged) CLASS scores, and observing a teacher multiple times is likely to produce more accurate measures of her effectiveness than observing her once only.

> **Another policy objective might be to** estimate how much learning outcomes **could** increase if teacher behaviors, as measured by the CLASS, **were to** improve (say, through an in-service training program targeting those behaviors) or to understand the sources of differences in teacher effectiveness. **In that case, the IV results might be more informative (subject to the caveat that** the coefficients in both the OLS and IV regressions **may not** have a causal interpretation). (Araujo et al., 2016, p. 1441)

Example 2

> By focusing on the microeconomic foundation of the economy, economic development offers **perhaps the best, and maybe the only,** policy prescription for sustainable economic growth. (Feldman et al., 2016, p. 7)

Address Limitations

Virtually every study in public policy and economics—in fact, in most research fields and disciplines—would have limitations, which may be quite significant. These limitations may be a result of using imperfect data, research designs that preclude causal inferences, or various problems that occurred during data collection or analysis. It is important, therefore, to acknowledge these limitations in your work. Acknowledging limitations performs two important functions.

- It positions the author as a competent researcher, one who understands the complexities of research and the equivocal nature of research findings.

- It protects the author from overstating his or her case and inviting criticism from the readers.

The focus in describing a study's limitations is often not just—or even not so much—on describing the problems but also on explaining why, despite those problems, readers should accept the author's interpretations and conclusions as valid. It is also common here to suggest directions for future research. Below is an example.

> **Without multiple treatment arms, I am unable to pin down the exact mechanisms** through which job fairs affect labor market outcomes. **However,** the information results, combined with the absence of increased interest or steps to migrate as a result of attending the fair, **suggest that it is unlikely** job fair attendance increases the perceived returns to overseas job search. . . . **For researchers, this paper highlights** the presence of incomplete information among job seekers in domestic and overseas labor markets, and **it indicates** that additional exposure to labor market opportunities can be important to reduce these information gaps. **It demonstrates the effectiveness of a randomized encouragement design** in generating exogenous variation in job-fair attendance, and **it outlines a clear agenda for future research** into the impact of job fairs: **pursuing a similar research design across multiple** job fairs, focusing on domestic employment, **will permit a more detailed analysis** of the mechanisms through which job fairs affect individual labor market decisions. (Beam, 2016, p. 40)

WRITING A CONCLUSION

Most papers in public policy and economics have a separate Conclusion section. In an empirical paper, especially in a quantitative paper, this section is usually rather brief and it does the following:

- Reminds the reader about what the authors did and what they found.
- Summarizes main arguments and their implications.

Here is an extract from Cohen and Levinthal's (1989) quantitative study of the role of R&D (research and development) in learning and innovation. Notice the organization of this paragraph, where the authors first present their hypotheses and then describe their results. Notice also the language the authors use to summarize their main arguments and results.

We have argued that firms invest in R&D not only to pursue directly new process and product innovation but also to develop and maintain their broader capabilities to assimilate and exploit externally available information. Recognition of the dual role of R&D **suggests that** factors that affect the character and ease of learning will affect firms' incentives to conduct R&D. **We hypothesised that such factors** include the degree to which knowledge is targeted to a firm's needs, and, more generally, the character of knowledge within each of the scientific and technological fields upon which innovation depends. **Our analytic model suggests** these factors should both exercise a direct effect on inventive activity, and condition the influence of more conventionally considered determinants. (Cohen & Levinthal, 1989, p. 593)

In a qualitative paper, especially in a nonempirical, literature-based one, the Conclusion section usually

- States that the paper has summarized research on a particular topic,
- Highlights main directions of this research, and
- Calls for more research.

For example, in a paper summarizing literature on the political economy of international monetary relations, Broz and Frieden (2001) conclude that the "theoretical and empirical status of [many existing] arguments remains undecided" (p. 340) and that further research is needed; in a study of antidumping policy in developing countries, Niels and Kate's (2006) main conclusion is that more research is needed.

Below is an example from a literature-based paper examining the relationship between women empowerment and economic development. As you go over this example, notice how tentative much of the conclusion is, both in content and in form.

Women's empowerment and economic development are closely interrelated. While development itself will bring about women's empowerment, empowering women will bring about changes in decision making, which will have a direct impact on development. **Contrary to what is claimed by some of the more optimistic policymakers, it is, however, not clear** that a one-time impulsion of women's rights will spark a virtuous circle, with women's empowerment and development mutually reinforcing each other and women eventually being equal partners in richer societies.

On the one hand, economic development alone is insufficient to ensure significant progress in important dimensions of women's empowerment, in particular, significant progress in decision-making ability in the face of pervasive stereotypes against women's ability. **On the other hand,** women's empowerment leads to improvement in some aspects of children's welfare (health and nutrition, in particular), but at the expense of some others (education).

This suggests that neither economic development nor women's empowerment is the magic bullet it is sometimes made out to be. In order to bring about equity between men and women, **in my view a very desirable goal in and of itself, it will be necessary to continue to take policy actions that** favor women at the expense of men, and **it may be necessary to continue doing so for a very long time.** While this **may result** in some collateral benefits, **those benefits may or may not be sufficient** to compensate for the cost of the distortions associated with such redistribution. **This measure of realism needs to temper the positions of policymakers on both sides of the development/empowerment debate.** (Duflo, 2012, p. 1076)

USING VISUALS: TABLES AND FIGURES

Different disciplines and publications have different rules for formatting and presenting figures and tables in a paper, and it is important that you find out what these rules are and follow them. There are, however, some basic principles for presenting visuals that apply to many papers in public policy and economics. They are described below.

1. Figures and tables included in a paper should generally be made by you. If you have to use a figure or a table from a published source, clearly state this in a note, indicating where the table or figure comes from. Do not include statistical output generated by statistical software as is; create a table or a graph using only the most important information from that output—information that helps you make a point. If you are reporting results of several regressions, consider consolidating them and presenting them in one table.

2. Visuals included in a paper must be described and interpreted in the text. Students sometimes include tables that are not mentioned anywhere in the text, justifying this practice by the desire to "just give the reader some additional information." But this additional information would not be useful or helpful unless it is interpreted. Remember, if you include a visual, you need to tell the reader what the visual shows and what it means.

3. Visuals must be understandable on their own, without the main text. This means that you should spell out all abbreviations and acronyms, give your variables clear, readily understandable names, and provide detailed notes under the table explaining everything that may be unclear or confusing to the reader.

4. Do not assume that the visuals are self-explanatory and that the reader would know what to look at. Use special expressions in the text—such as previews and action markers—to direct the reader to a visual. For example:

Previews: **We show** in Table 5... **As shown in** Figure 3...

Action markers: **To illustrate the size of this effect, consider** the values shown in Table 5.

5. It is common in public policy and economics papers to refer to all tables as tables and to all graphs, photos, boxes, histograms, distributions, scatter plots, time plots, and so on as figures.

6. All tables and figures require a number, a caption, and notes.

- **Captions**. Table and figure captions may go above or below a visual and may or may not be italicized. That depends on the specific editorial style used in your research area or by the journal you are submitting to. Make sure to check the conventions of your field and/or journal. It is also very important to ensure that you use a consistent style for all the visuals. A good table/figure caption presents the names of all the major variables and type of analysis. If you have many variables, use the word "predictors" or "determinants" in the caption. For example:

    Table 1. Predictors of Academic Achievements Among High-School Students

- **Numbers**. Tables and figures are usually numbered consecutively throughout the paper using Arabic numerals (e.g., Table 1, Table 2). However, do check what is customary in your field.

- **Notes**. Notes are placed under the visual and indicated with the word *Note*. Two types of notes are used for tables and figures: general notes and statistical notes. General notes provide information referring to the table/figure as a whole, such as the meaning of the abbreviations used or the source of information; statistical notes indicate statistical significance of the results. These notes are usually placed below the general notes. Use asterisks to indicate the probability levels (when not stating the exact probabilities):

    $*p < .05$, $**p < .01$. (Notice that the symbol p is italicized.)

HEDGING IN PUBLIC POLICY AND ECONOMIC WRITING

Research that has examined argumentation styles in various academic disciplines shows that writers in virtually every academic discipline tend to qualify their claims and present their arguments merely as possibilities rather than facts. Such qualified statements are called *hedges*. The use of hedges in English academic writing is ubiquitous, and it is perhaps one of the main features that distinguish academic writing from other types of writing including general-purpose and popular-science writing. For example, Hyland (2008, p. 74) argues that experienced academic writers use hedges every 50 words, or every 2–3 sentences.

Why are hedges so common in academic writing? Hyland (2008) gives three reasons (pp. 76–78).

- **Precision.** Hedges help writers to express their ideas with greater accuracy because they allow writers to convey different levels of certainty. Arguments can be made in proportion to the strength of the evidence on which they are based. Compare the following statements. Which one would be most accurate as a general statement about the focus of federal expenditures?

Federal expenditures **always focus on** activities that have national implications.

Federal expenditures **focus on** activities that have national implications.

Federal expenditures **tend to focus on** activities that have national implications.

- **Protection**. Hedges protect writers from overstating their claims. Strong claims are more likely to be challenged by readers, especially if the evidence for them is not very compelling. Hedges allow writers to express claims more cautiously. Compare the following statements. Which one would be less likely to invite criticism as an overstatement?

Keynesian analysis **recognizes the possibility** that high tax rates may stifle an economy because they reduce disposable income and spending.

Keynesian analysis **clearly demonstrates** that high tax rates may stifle an economy because they reduce disposable income and spending.

- **Politeness.** Hedges help writers be polite and show respect toward their readers. Politeness conventions in English call for elaborate syntactic and lexical modification of messages to make them less strong, more tentative, and therefore more acceptable to readers. This is especially important when authors offer criticism.

Cross-cultural research on politeness indicates that nonnative English writers tend to be more direct when expressing ideas and may not sufficiently mitigate criticism of other authors—a quality that readers may find threatening and as a result, evaluate the writer more negatively. Compare these pairs of statement. In your opinion, which ones are more polite and would be easier to accept? Highlight the part that softens the claims.

We then proceed to delineate why these two positions should mutually reinforce each other	We then proceed to delineate why, **in our view**, these two positions should mutually reinforce each other.... (D'Ippoliti & Roncaglia, p. 1)
In order to implement genuinely sustainable community development, practitioners should integrate in their practice the principles of ecological economics and sustainability	**We suggest that** in order to implement genuinely sustainable community development, SCD practitioners should integrate the principles of ecological economics and strong sustainability into their theory and practice. (Hamstead & Quinn, p. 142)
The simulation described by Smith and Miller *overstated* the shift in the distribution of emissions towards non-OECD countries	The simulation **may have overstated** the shift in the distribution of emissions towards non-OECD countries to the extent that existing energy subsidies in many of these countries...were assumed to remain unchanged over time. (Nicoletti & Oliveira-Martins, 1992, p. 13)
Cultural values are a fundamental source of identity for governments and for individuals	Cultural values **may be** a fundamental source of identity for governments as much as for individuals, with consequences for highly material arenas of policy choice. (Simmons & Elkins, 2004, p. 187)

Hedges may be used in all sections of an academic paper but they are especially common in sections where authors interpret and discuss results, draw implications, and make arguments based on their own results or the literature. Below are examples of hedged statements in the description of results that come from both published studies and student work.

The main finding **suggests** that trade openness has a negative effect on economic growth in Fiji. (Lai See Sue, 2011, p. 12)

Results further **suggest** that FDI inflows to SSA **tend to be** distribution-oriented as well as natural-resource-based and that IPR protection may not necessarily be of any benefit. (Otoo, 2013, p. 1)

Summarizing our results, **we find the strongest evidence** for the theory that biased managers interact less with minority workers and assign them to new tasks—even unpleasant ones—less often. **This may be because** they feel less comfortable around minorities, they are concerned with appearing biased, or they believe there is a low return to expending effort managing minorities. (Glover et al., 2017, p. 1251)

Biased managers **do not appear** to treat minorities poorly. Instead, they seem to simply interact less with minorities, leading these workers to exert less effort. By making minorities less productive, manager bias **appears to** generate statistical discrimination in hiring. (Glover et al., 2017, p. 1257)

The results suggest that elevated policy uncertainty in the United States and Europe in recent years **may have harmed** macroeconomic performance. (Baker et al., 2016, p. 1633)

HOW TO QUALIFY CLAIMS

Swales and Feak (2012) describe several ways to qualify, soften, or moderate a claim in an academic paper (pp. 160–163). I summarize some of them below.

Express Probability

- It is **possible** that...
- It is **(highly) likely/unlikely** that...
- There is **a strong possibility** that...

Distance Yourself From the Data

- Based on the limited data available, ...
- According to this preliminary study, ...
- Based on an informal survey of...

Qualify the Subject or the Verb

- **Many** immigrants have suffered some form of trauma.
- **In many parts of the world**, immigrants suffer from discrimination.
- Immigrants **tend to** suffer from social discrimination.

Use a Weaker Verb

- The regression coefficients **suggest** that the policy has had an effect.
- The results of this study **indicate** that protecting intellectual property rights **may be** more important in developing countries.
- **As suggested by our data**, nonprofit organizations **may not have** sufficient resources to accomplish their goals.

Chapter 15

Data, Methodology, Results, and Discussion: Models and Examples

This chapter shows models and examples for describing data, methodology, and results and for presenting discussion in quantitative papers in economics and public policy. Some of the extracts shown in this chapter come from published studies; others, from student work. Go over these extracts, paying attention to the following.

- **Structure and organization**. Notice how the authors organize their text and how they describe their data, methodology, and results. How much detail do they include? What elements do they emphasize in their description? How much space do they devote to the description of data, model, and empirical strategy? How do the authors describe their visuals (i.e., tables)? How do they draw the reader's attention to important elements in the text as well as the visuals?

- **Use of language markers,** especially

  - Hedges and boosters
  - Transition and frame markers
  - Use of self-mention
  - Attitude and engagement markers

  Notice how these markers help the authors engage the reader, direct the reader to what is more or less important, show proper respect for the reader, and present themselves as an authority. See Chapter 1 for a review of these markers.

- **Use of citations**. Notice how the authors use citations. Do they prefer integral citations (citations that have been integrated into the text and introduced with a signal phrase) or nonintegral citations (parenthetical citations at the end of sentences)? What signal phrases are most common?

- **Verbs**. What verbs do the authors use most frequently when describing data, presenting results, comparing their results with those of previous research, and referring to visuals? Which verb tense do they use (e.g., Present, Present Perfect, or Past)?

How to Write about Economics and Public Policy. https://doi.org/10.1016/B978-0-12-813010-0.00015-6

I have included some questions in the description of the extracts, which you might want to consider as you read the extracts. The purpose of these questions is to help you reflect on the writers' purposes and how they were accomplished. In some of the extracts shown below, I have also highlighted what would generally be considered standard academic phrases and expressions. These are skeletal elements that are commonly used in research studies in public policy and economics to describe data, methodology, and results. Use these phrases to improve your own academic vocabulary.

DESCRIBING DATA AND MEASURES

The extract below is from a study of performance-related pay and gender wage differences conducted by Kangasniemi and Kauhanen (2013). Here, the authors describe a data set they obtained for their analyses. Notice how detailed their description is, showing where the data come from, what industries and time period the data cover, and what information the data include. Notice that the authors include many numbers here, showing not only the total number of observations but also the average number of observations per person. As you go over the language of this extract, notice that the word *data* is plural and that it requires a plural verb.

We use wage **data from** the Confederation of Finnish Industries (EK), which is the central organization of employer associations. **The main** industries **covered by the data** are manufacturing, construction, energy and transportation. Member firms of EK employ the majority of employees in manufacturing and roughly every third Finnish employee. Wage **data are based on an annual survey of** employers and, except for the smallest firms, a response is mandatory for member firms. Wage **data are used in** collective bargaining and form the basis of the private sector wage structure data maintained by Statistics Finland, the country's statistical authority. **The information we use here thus comes from** the wage records of firms and **is highly reliable. The data cover the years** 1998 to 2007 **and contain** 3 019 278 **observations and there are** 590 809 **unique persons** (414 601 men and 176 208 women) and 3768 **unique firms**. An average man has 7.3 observations and the corresponding figure for women is 7.0.

   The data include detailed information on wages, working time and individual characteristics as well as unique person and firm identifiers. Thus, it [sic] forms a linked employer–employee panel that allows for following persons over time, possibly in different firms. (Kangasniemi & Kauhanen, 2013, p. 5135)

The extract below is from a study of trade openness, capital openness, and government size conducted by Liberati (2007). Notice how the author calls for caution in interpreting results. Why does he do that? What specific language expressions does he use? Notice also how the author describes a problem in the data—the presence of outliers—and how it was dealt with.

Data on exports, imports and capital flows (foreign direct investments and port-folio investments) **are taken from** the International Financial Statistics (IFS) of the International Monetary Fund (IMF). **The same source provides for data on** con-solidated *central* government expenditures, **which are mainly used for the analysis. To get reasonably long series on** *general* government expenditures (i.e., including intermediate and local government levels), **recourse has been made to** OECD data. **When interpreting results, therefore, caution must be used as, in some cases, data from different sources are combined.** The definition and source of all variables used in this paper are reported in Table A.2 in Appendix.

As discussed in Section IV.I, **the core of the analysis will be based on** the use of central government expenditures. **Data used cover** a reasonable number of years and countries—with the exception of Germany, observed only after the re-unification process—while the use of general government expenditures generates a nonnegligible loss of observations. **Outliers have been identified and dropped according to the method proposed by** Hadi (1992) for multivariate analysis. **This has led to identifying** 1 outlier in the measure of trade openness, 15 for FDI open-ness, 2 for portfolio openness, 1 for government deficit and 3 for current account balance. (Liberati, 2007, pp. 223–224)

The extract below is from a study of the relationship between government debt and bank credit conducted by De Bonis and Stacchini (2013). Notice how the authors justify the choice of countries in their sample and how they describe the problem of an unbalanced dataset. Notice also how they describe and justify the data transformation they conducted. As you go over the extract, notice that *dataset* is one word here. Some authors, however, prefer to use *data set*.

Our sample includes 43 countries: 23 are members of the OECD while 20 are classified as upper income non-OECD countries (see Table 1). **The choice of countries was dictated by the availability of statistics. The dataset is unbalanced** as some countries do not provide statistics for the entire time span under scrutiny. **The analysis covers the period** 1970–2010, and **the data were originally recorded annually. As we are interested in the long-term consequences of** public debt levels, short-term fluctuations were smoothed by generating five-year nonoverlap-ping windows. **The final dataset has** a short-time dimension and a larger country size as it is made up of eight observations for 43 countries. (De Bonis & Stacchini, 2013, p. 292)

The extract below is from a study of firm-level corruption in Vietnam con-ducted by Rand and Tarp (2012). Notice the details the authors include in their description of the two surveys (e.g., time, place, number of enterprises and their types, stratification strategy, sampling strategy, and data cleaning). Notice also how they explain the reduction of observations in their study from 2600 to 1659. What specific reason(s) do they give for this reduction?

The two SME **surveys on which we rely in this article were conducted in** 2005 and 2007. Both **surveys covered around** 2,600 enterprises in 10 provinces (Ho Chi Minh City [HCMC], Hanoi, Hai Phong, Long An, Ha Tay, Quang Nam, Phu Tho, Nghe An, Khanh Hoa, and Lam Dong). In both years and all areas covered by the surveys, **samples were stratified by** ownership form **to ensure that all types** of nonstate enterprises, including both officially registered (with a business registration license) formal household, private, cooperative, limited-liability, joint-stock enterprises, and nonofficial (informal) household firms, **were represented. For reasons of implementation, the surveys were confined to specific areas** in each province/city. Subsequently, **stratified random samples were drawn from** a consolidated list of formal enterprises and an onsite random selection of informal firms. While **the sampling was adjusted over time to** accommodate the rapidly changing business environment in Vietnam, **other aspects**, including the questionnaires, **were maintained virtually identical. After cleaning the data and checking consistency of time-invariant variables between the two survey rounds, we were left with a balanced panel of** 1,659 firm observations in each year. **It is especially a lack of** financial accounts **that reduced the number of observations**. (Rand & Tarp, 2012, p. 573–574)

The extract below is from a study that looked at the relationship between the choice of a firm's name and the firm's quality, which was conducted by McDevitt (2014). In this extract, the author describes the construction of one of the main measures he used in the study, firm's quality. Notice how much space the author devotes to explaining the process of filing complaints with the Better Business Bureau and how much detail he includes. Why do you think he does that?

The primary measure of firm quality **used throughout this paper** is the number of complaints filed against the firm with the Better Business Bureau. **The data for each** plumbing firm operating in Illinois **come from** a June 2008 download of the Better Business Bureau's website, **which lists a historical record of** complaints filed against a business during the preceding 3 years. As its main function, the Better Business Bureau acts as an intermediary between consumers and firms to resolve disputes through a formal process. First, a staff member reviews each complaint filed with the Better Business Bureau and forwards it to the accused company within 2 business days if deemed legitimate. Next, if the company has not responded within 14 days, the Better Business Bureau makes a second attempt to resolve the issue. Finally, after two unsuccessful attempts at resolution, the complaint becomes a part of the business's record with the Better Business Bureau. (McDevitt, 2014, p. 913)

DESCRIBING METHODOLOGY

The extract below is from a paper by Wilson Gakuya, a student in Public Finance, who investigated the impact of intellectual property rights on economic growth in Sub-Saharan Africa in the post-TRIPS (Agreement on Trade-Related Aspects of Intellectual Property Rights) era. Notice how he explains the regression methodology and the variables included in the model and how he justifies the use of the particular approach he chose.

This paper uses a fixed-effects **regression approach to investigate the effect of** intellectual property rights (IPR) protection on economic growth. **This method is used to prevent econometric problems that may emerge, such as problems of** endogeneity and measurement error in the data matrix (Maskus & Penubarti, 1995). **For instance,** a simultaneous causality problem may arise whereby strong IPR protection enhances economic growth and economic growth promotes IPR protection. **It is also possible that** some of the explanatory variables are related to the error term (Falvey et al., 2006). **To eliminate these problems,** fixed-effects regression is used. In this analysis, time fixed effects and entity fixed effects **are used to control for** the unobservable time- and entity-(country) variant factors.

To analyze the effect of IPR protection on economic growth, **as a starting point, the following** simple multivariate OLS growth equation (Model 1) **is used:**

$$Gdp/capita\,growth_{it} = \beta_0 + \beta_1 Log(Gdp/capita)2001_{it} + \beta_2 Trade_{it}$$
$$+ \beta_3 Investment_{it} + \beta_4 Inflation_{it} + \beta_5 Secondary schooling_{it} \quad (1)$$
$$+ \beta_6 Log(Population)_{it} + \beta_7 IPRi_{it} + \mu_{it}$$

where $Gdp/capita\,growth_{it}$ is GDP growth per capita and it is the dependent variable and a measure of economic growth for country i in year t, where $i =$ country and $t =$ year; β_0 is the constant term; β_1's to β_7's are the coefficients to be estimated; $Log(Gdp/capita)2001_{it}$ is the log transformation of initial GDP per capita for the year 2001; $Trade_{it}$ is a measure of openness of an economy and it is indicated by the total volume of exports and imports for a country as a percentage of GDP at a given time; $Investment_{it}$ is a measure of gross capital formation; $Inflation_{it}$ is the real rate of inflation and it is included as a control variable for economic stability; $Secondary schooling_{it}$ is the level of secondary schooling, which is used as a proxy for human capita development; $Log(Population)_{it}$ is the log transformation of total population; $IPRi_{it}$ is a measure of intellectual property rights; and μ_{it} is a regression error term.

In order to eliminate internal and external validity threats arising from endogeneity and measurement error in the sample, **the first model is extended to include** fixed-effects variables:

$$Gdp/capita\,growth_{it} = \beta_0 + \beta_1 Log(Gdp/capita)2001_{it} + \beta_2 Trade_{it}$$
$$+ \beta_3 Investment_{it} + \beta_4 Inflation_{it} + \beta_5 Secondary schooling_{it} \quad (2)$$
$$+ \beta_6 Log(Population)_{it} + \beta_7 IPRi_{it} + \beta_8 Z_i + \beta_9 T_i + \mu_{it}$$

Thus, entity fixed effects (Z_i) and year fixed effects (T_i) are included in the model. Here, Z_i **is used to capture unobservable country-specific variables that are assumed to be** time-invariant. **Such** country-**specific variables include** attitude of consumers in each country towards IPR protection as well as cultural characteristics of each country. **Omission of** the country fixed-effect **variable may cause**

omitted variable bias. The year fixed-effect variable (T_i) **is included to capture** time trends and **it is used to control for unobservable factors that are** constant across the countries but vary over time. **These factors may include** global economic crises affecting all the countries. **If such factors are not included in the model, omitted variable bias would result.** β_8 and β_9 are the coefficients of country-specific and year-specific effects, respectively. **The other variables are as described in** the regression equation in Model 1.

One of the concerns when analyzing panel data is the possibility of serial correlation of error terms (μ_{it}) within an entity (country). If serial correlation exists in panel data, **the estimated results are usually unbiased and consistent.** However, the OLS standard errors underestimate the true uncertainty. **To eliminate this problem,** heteroskedasticity and autocorrelation-consistent standard errors (HAC) are used. **This process is also known as** clustering. (Gakuya, 2015, p. 7)

The extract below is from a study of the relationship between tax rate and tax evasion in Ecuador. The study was conducted by Rodolfo Rommel Villamar Arreaga, a student in Public Finance. He uses an approach described in the literature to estimate the effect of tax rate on tax evasion. In this extract, Rodolfo describes his empirical model as well as the difficulty involved in investigating tax evasion. Notice how he supports all of his decisions with previous research and how he draws on previous research when providing variable definitions.

When it comes to studying tax evasion, **an inevitable question is how to measure** it. The difficulty is that by definition, evasion is not recorded or clearly observable. **My research follows the same approach adopted** by Fisman and Wei (2004). **The measure of** tax evasion **is** the ratio of the value of exports of the United States of America to Ecuador, defined as *export_value*, to the value of imports of Ecuador from the United States of America, defined as *import_value*. **This indicator corresponds to** the value of the gap in international trade between the analyzed countries. **In the absence of any** market failure such as evasion or errors in recording transactions, the indicator X/M should be equal to one.

As Van Dunem and Arndt (2009) **point out, this methodology completely ignores** smuggled products since they are not recorded either by the United States or by Ecuador. **Nonetheless, this methodology covers** products exported from the United States that somehow entirely bypass customs procedures in Ecuador, perhaps because they are declared as other products. **This is usually known as** "misclassification behavior" (Van Dunem & Arndt, 2009, p. 1013).

Below, **I adopt the same model specification used in the work of** Van Dunem and Arndt (2009, pp. 1013–1015): **The first simple model is defined as a** linear relationship between the gap in the value of international trade between the United States of America and Ecuador and the "*Taxes*" variable, i.e., all the taxes that

Ecuadorian importers have to pay in order to be able to bring a particular product into the territory of Ecuador. **The model is defined as follows:**

$$gap\_value_{it} = \log \left(\frac{export\_value_{it}}{import\_value_{it}} \right) \tag{1}$$
$$= \alpha_{it} + \beta Taxes_{it} + \varepsilon_{it}$$

where
  i **stands for** each product in the sample, and
  t **stands for** each year analyzed.
In Eq. (1), a positive β **indicates a positive relation between** tax evasion and tax rate. **The magnitude of β reflects the** elasticity or sensibility of tax evasion for a minuscule change in tax rate. **This can be expressed in terms of** derivatives:

$$\frac{dexport\_value_{it}}{export\_value_{it}} - \frac{dimport\_value_{it}}{import\_value_{it}} = \beta(dTaxes_{it})$$

However, in reality, things are not so easy. Fisman and Wei (2004) and Van Dunem and Arndt (2009) also discussed the problem that direct imports from the trade partner, the United States of America, **cannot always be seen or deduced accurately. Actually, what is really observed is** import_value*, **which consists of** both direct imports from the United States of America and transshipments from other sources, misreported as imports from America. **In accordance with the work done by** Fisman and Wei (2004), **I consider** misclassified imports **to be a subset of** genuine imports from the United States. Thus, misclassified indirect imports in the Ecuadorian case **can be expressed as**:

$$import\_value_{it}^* = (1 + \theta_{it})import\_value_{it} \tag{2}$$

For Eq. (2), **it is assumed, in accordance with** Fisman and Wei (2004) and Van Dunem and Arndt (2009), that θ_{it} is an independent and identically distributed random variable with intervals between 0 and 1. i represents one element of the set. Using Eq. (2) in Eq. (1), **I can redefine the baseline model as**

$$\log \left(\frac{export\_value_{it}}{import\_value_{it}^*} \right) = \alpha_{it}^* + \beta Taxes_{it} + \upsilon_{it} \tag{3}$$

where

$$\alpha_{it}^* \equiv \alpha_{it} + E(\varepsilon_{it} - \log(1 + \theta_{it}))$$

and

$$\upsilon_{it} = \varepsilon_{it} - \log(1 + \theta_{it}) - E(\varepsilon_{it} - \log(1 + \theta_{it}))$$
$$\sim N(0, \sigma^2)$$

The redefined model shown in Eq. (3) reveals a new constant term, α_{it}^*, and a new error term, υ_{it}, which are assumed to be identically and independently distributed (Fisman & Wei, 2004; Van Dunem & Arndt, 2009).

Adding Misclassification Phenomenon into the Baseline Model

Fisman and Wei (2004) and Van Dunem and Arndt (2009) **also addressed** the misclassification phenomenon. **In a similar manner, I look for statistical evidence of** misreporting the real codes of the products in Ecuadorian data. **To do that, it is necessary to add** one new regressor: *average taxes within similar products.* Fisman and Wei (2004) **defined the concept of** "similar products" **as** products whose codes bear the same first four digits. **Let** Avg(tax_sim) **be the variable that captures the** average tax rate for similar products. **This new variable is created by** grouping products whose codes bear the same first four digits. **I obtained the average of the variable** "*Taxes*" within each one of these groups **and derived the following regression equation:**

$$\log\left(\frac{export\_value_{it}}{import\_value^*_{it}}\right) = \alpha^*_{it} + \beta_1 Taxes_{it} + \beta_2 Avg(tax\_sim)_{it} + v_{it} \tag{4}$$

A negative and statistically significant β_2 **could explain** the misclassification phenomenon. According to Van Dunem and Arndt (2009), a highly taxed product among similar products with low taxes **can lead to an increase in the probability that** products might be mislabeled:

A high tax on the given product combined with a low tax on similar products enhances the incentives to misclassify our given product. The converse is also true. A low tax on the given product relative to the tax on similar products would tend to create overreporting of imports of the given product due to misclassification (Van Dunem & Arndt, 2009, pp. 1014–1015).

With regard to the regression equation used for measuring the gap in quantity, **I will use** the same functional form. **For this purpose, I have defined** *export_qty* **as the variable that captures** the quantity exported by the USA to Ecuador, and *import_qty* as the quantity imported by Ecuador from the United States. Then the model of the gap in quantities is:

$$gap\_quantity_{it} = \log\left(\frac{export\_qty_{it}}{import\_qty_{it}}\right) \tag{5}$$

$$= \alpha_{it} + \beta Taxes_{it} + \varepsilon_{it}$$

And **the model that incorporates** the misclassification variable **is defined as**

$$gap\_quantity_{it} = \log\left(\frac{export\_qty_{it}}{import\_qty_{it}}\right) \tag{6}$$

$$= \alpha_{it} + \beta_1 Taxes_{it} + \beta_2 Avg(tax\_sim)_{it} + \varepsilon_{it}$$

(Arreaga, 2015, pp. 6–8)

The extract below is from a study of the effects of tariff rates on skill intensity within firms and industries. That study was conducted by Tricia Ingrid Soberanis, a student in Public Finance. In this extract, Tricia describes her data and estimation strategy. Go over the extract and highlight standard academic phrases and expressions that Tricia used to describe her data and methodology. Notice how she describes her data sources, variables, and regression models, and how she supports her analysis decisions with citations to previous research.

The purpose of this study is to empirically investigate the effect of tariff rates on the skill intensity of firms. The study uses an unbalanced panel data set from 23 developing and less-developed countries. It was selected because of the availability of data on capital, machinery and equipment, sales, wages, and the number of nonproduction and production workers. The data were extracted from the *Productivity and Investment Climate Private Enterprise Survey (2002-2006)* conducted by the World Bank Group (2002). This survey provides data on firm productivity and any potential threats to investment climate from policies and programs that have been set in place. The data are categorized into different sections and include data on sales revenue, finance, labor relations, productivity, trade, number of employees, wages, compensation, assets and liabilities, capital, international transactions, and other indicators. Information on the experience of doing business is collected from private enterprises in door-to-door and face-to-face interviews and through surveys conducted by trained professionals and experts, and it is processed into data by certified analysts working at the World Bank. The surveys are conducted every three to four years and cover over 100 indicators that benchmark the quality of the business environment in some 126 countries; these indicators are computed as weighted averages of the business responses to the questions in the survey, using sampling weights at country-level aggregation. In my data set, I excluded countries with fewer than 100 observations and those with more than half of sales or labor values missing.

The data for the tariff variable was obtained from the World Bank Database for World Development Indicators for the period 2002–2006. Tariff data used in this study are the weighted average of tariff rates, which is computed as *(sum of (duty*import value))/sum of import values*. There are several limitations to using the weighted average tariff rates as explained by the World Bank because those weights tend to overestimate the importance of tariff lines that have low duties. In the case of imports entering under tariff lines with high applicable duties, the weighted average will tend to underestimate the real importance of a tariff line, which is somewhat similar to understating the level of protection.

The first dependent variable and one of the two main variables of interest in this study is skill intensity, represented as *skill_ints1* in Table 1 and measured as the share of nonproduction workers in total workers. Previous studies have also used share of nonproduction workers in total workers to estimate the shift toward more skilled labor and its wages (Autor, Katz, & Krueger, 1998; Berman, Bound, & Griliches, 1994; Berman, Bound, & Machin, 1998; Machin & Van Reenen, 1998). Here, I used the total number of nonproduction workers as a fraction of the average number of permanent workers in a one-year period; in cases where the countries did not have these data, I replaced the missing values with the average number of management and professional workers. The World Bank provides a detailed description of the indicators for the definition of nonproduction and production workers. Nonproduction workers are personnel engaged in supervision, installation and servicing of own products, sales, or delivery; professionals; technological, administrative, clerical, and executive staff; and those engaged in purchasing, finance, and legal work. In this paper, I refer to these workers as either nonproduction or skilled workers or laborers. In contrast, production workers consist of workers engaged in fabricating, processing, assembling, inspecting, and other manufacturing or production operations (such as packing, handling, warehousing, and shipping but excluding delivery, maintenance, and repair) and those who are labeled "unskilled workers or laborers."

The second dependent variable and the other main variable of interest in this study is wages, represented as *skill_ints2* in Table 2. It is measured using the wages of nonproduction workers in the total wage bill. In generating this variable, I used the total compensation of nonproduction workers, which consists of wages and all benefits, including food, transport, and social security (i.e., pensions, medical insurance, unemployment insurance). The tariff and firm-level data sets were merged in this study and the matching data were retained for analyses.

This analysis follows the share equation used by Berman et al. (1994), who used a cost function in the quasifixed form and linear-log transformation of variables as well as first-differencing. The regression equation was modified as

$$dS_{ij} = \beta_0 + \beta_1 d \ln \left(W_n / W_p \right)_j + \beta_2 d \ln (K/Y)_{ij} + I_j + \varepsilon_{ij}$$

where n and p indicate nonproduction and production labor, respectively; j indexes country-industry level; i indexes firm level; t is time (i.e. year); W_n and W_p represent the wages of nonproduction and production workers, respectively, and their ratio measures relative wages, which is the variable *lrwage*; K represents capital net value and Y represents total sales (as a proxy for value added). $(K/Y)_{ij}$ measures the capital-skill complementarity factor and helps to show firms' use of high-tech capital equipment complimented with skilled workers, which is represented by the variable *lkapital*. I is country-industry fixed effects. β_1 will be positive or negative according to whether the elasticity of substitution between production and nonproduction labor is greater than or less than 1. Capital-skill complementarity implies that $\beta_2 > 0$. β_0 is a measure of cross-industry average bias in technological change, while $\beta_0 + \epsilon_{ij}$ represent industry-specific bias. The equation for dS_{ij} is redundant.

Tables 1 and 2 show results of the regression analysis for the effect of tariff rates on skill intensity and wages. Regressions 1 to 6 explain the methodology for the results in Table 1.

Regression 1: The first regression in Table 1 is a multivariate Ordinary Least Squares (OLS) regression model. I regressed the log of capital, log of sales, and log of relative wage on skill intensity and controlled for country-industry specific factors and clustering.

$$Skill\_ints1_{ij} = \beta_0 + \beta_1 lkapital_{it} + \beta_2 lsales_j + \beta_3 lrwage_j + I_j + \varepsilon_{ij} \tag{1}$$

Regression 2: In the second regression, I also used a multivariate OLS model but removed the relative wages variable, *lrwage*, from the equation and continued to control for country-industry specific factors and clustering.

$$Skill\_ints1_{ij} = \beta_0 + \beta_1 lkapital_{it} + \beta_2 lsales_j + I_j + \varepsilon_{ij} \tag{2}$$

Regression 3: In this regression, I added the main independent variable of interest, *tariff*, to the equation and included relative wages, *lrwage*, as well as controlled for country-industry specific factors and clustering in the error term. Here, I still used a multivariate OLS regression model.

$$Skill\_ints1_{ij} = \beta_0 + \beta_1 tariff_j + \beta_2 lkapital_{it} + \beta_3 lsales_j + \beta_4 lrwage_j + I_j + \varepsilon_{ij} \quad (3)$$

Regression 4: In this regression, I again removed relative wages, *lrwage,* from the equation, controlling for country-specific factors and clustering. This is to observe what the effect of tariffs will be on skill intensity with relative wages in the error term.

$$Skill\_ints1_{ij} = \beta_0 + \beta_1 tariff_j + \beta_2 lkapital_{it} + \beta_3 lsales_j + I_j + \varepsilon_{ij} \quad (4)$$

Regression 5: In regression 5, because the intention is to find the effect of tariff rates on skill intensity when firms export, I performed regression analysis using the dummy variable *export*, which is 1 if firms export, and 0 otherwise. Not all countries are exporters and the tariff data used in this study are for import tariffs only. This regression uses a multivariate OLS regression model and controls for country-specific factors and clustering to correct for correlation within clusters.

$$Skill\_ints1_{ij} = \beta_0 + \beta_1 tariff_j + \beta_2 lkapital_{it} + \beta_3 lsales_j + I_j + \varepsilon_{ij} \quad (5)$$

Regression 6: This regression is a multivariate OLS regression model but the *export* variable is included in the equation because if it remains in the error term, it could be correlated with an explanatory variable, and the analysis will suffer from omitted variable bias.

$$Skill\_ints1_{ij} = \beta_0 + \beta_1 tariff_j + \beta_2 lkapital_{it} + \beta_3 lsales_j + \beta_4 export_j + I_j + \varepsilon_{ij} \quad (6)$$

The regressions presented in Table 2 are for the second dependent variable, wages, represented as *skill_ints2*. This analysis was conducted to find out not only if the use of skilled workers is increasing but also whether their wages are increasing as well. According to Berman et al. (1994), using wages as a share in the total wage bill is a good measure to capture the changes in wages due to skill intensity. In Regressions 1 to 4, I used the *tariff* variable and capital-skill complementarity variable, *lkapital.* The *tariff* variable is the main independent variable of interest and *lkapital* can show the presence of skill-based technological changes and if such changes have explanatory power for the wage gap between skilled and unskilled workers. In each of the four regressions shown below, I used a multivariate OLS regression model, controlled for country-specific factors, and used robust standard errors and clustering by country to correct for correlation errors.

Regression 1: In this regression, I regress capital-skill complementarity factor, total sales (proxy for value added), and relative wages on the share of nonproduction workers' wages in the total wage bill.

$$Skill\_ints2_{ij} = \beta_0 + \beta_1 lkapital_{it} + \beta_2 lsales_j + \beta_3 lrwage_j + I_j + \varepsilon_{ij} \quad (1)$$

Regression 2: In this regression, I excluded relative wage variable, *lrwage,* from the equation.

$$Skill\_ints2_{ij} = \beta_0 + \beta_1 lkapital_{it} + \beta_2 lsales_j + \varepsilon_{ij} \quad (2)$$

Regression 3: In this regression, I added the *tariff* variable, which is the main independent variable of interest, and the relative wage variable, *lrwage.*

$$Skill\_ints2_{ij} = \beta_0 + \beta_1 tariff_j + \beta_3 lkapital_{it} + \beta_3 lsales_j + \beta_4 lrwage_j + l_j + \varepsilon_{ij} \qquad (3)$$

Regression 4: In this regression, I dropped the relative wage, *lrwage*, to see what the effect of tariffs will be on the wages of nonproduction workers.

$$Skill\_ints2_{ij} = \beta_0 + \beta_1 tariff_j + \beta_3 lkapital_{it} + \beta_3 lsales_j + l_j + \varepsilon_{ij} \qquad (4)$$

(Soberanis, 2015, pp. 5–7)

The extract below is from a study investigating the relationship between government expenditure and economic growth. The study was conducted by Itai Maparara, a student in Public Finance, and I have used extracts from it in other chapters. In this extract, Itai describes his model, data, and estimation strategy. Notice how he opens his methodology section with a brief summary of what he did and an explanation for the chosen methodology. As you go over the extract, highlight standard academic phrases and expressions that Itai uses to describe his data, approach, and methodology.

Methodology

This paper employs a vector autoregression (VAR) model for countries with variables that are not cointegrated and a vector error correction model (VECM) where the series are cointegrated. Regression was done in a trivariate framework where trade assisted either government expenditure or economic growth in explaining the dependent variable, thus partially solving the problem of omitted variable bias. This method was chosen because it allows the key variables under study to affect each other where exogeneity is suspected. The Granger causality test was then performed to determine the direction of causality in both the short and long run. Time-series data for the period 1970 to 2014 were used in the study. All variables are observed annually; thus, there are 45 observations. Regressions were done on a country-by-country basis using Stata.

Data

Real gross domestic product (RGDP) is denoted as Yt. The growth transformation for RGDP (first difference) represents economic growth. Government expenditure (Gt) is final general government consumption expenditure (inclusive of transfer payments). The measure captures both recurrent and capital expenditure by central governments. Trade (Tt) is the value added on export goods, i.e., it is restricted to exports. There are various trade measures but this study uses this measure because it captures government policy on trade and, therefore, helps to explain the effect of trade policy on economic growth. All variables are in constant 1970 prices and are transformed into logarithmic form. Data for the fifteen SADC countries for the period from 1970 to 2014 were obtained from *World: Macroeconomic Research* (Kushnir, 2015).

Regression Methodology

This study employs the error correction model (ECM) as its principle method. In ECM, stationarity of variables is important for obtaining consistent results, thus testing for stationarity constitutes the first step. According to Granger and Newbold (1974), variables that are nonstationary may cause a spurious regression. The generated t-statistics appear significant and the $R2$ is high, but the regression has no economic meaning. This paper uses the Augmented Dickey Fuller (ADF) test to check for stationarity of the series and to determine their order of integration. The model is specified as:

$$\Delta Z_t = a_0 + \varphi_t + \beta Z_{t-1} + \sum_{i=2}^{p} a_i \Delta Z_{t-i} + \varepsilon_t$$

where a_0 is a constant and ϕ is time trend, Δ is a difference operator, Z_t is the variable tested for stationarity, α_i is a parameter, p is a preselected lag order, and ε_t is an error term. The hypotheses for the test are:

H_0: $\beta = 0$ (the variable contains a unit root, which implies that it is nonstationary).

H_1: $\beta < 0$ (the variable has no unit root, which implies that it is stationary).

When the ADF test shows that the series are integrated of order one I (1), the Johansen Test for cointegration (1991) is employed to check if the series are cointegrated. If the series are cointegrated, it means that they follow a common long-run trend. The Johansen procedure is represented as

$$\Delta A_t = \beta + \Gamma 1 \Delta A_{t-1} + \ldots + \Gamma_{k-1} \Delta A_{t-k-1} + \prod A_{t-1} + \delta_t$$

where A_t is a (n.1) vector of nonstationary variables in levels, β is a (n.1) vector of constants, δ_t is a vector of white noise, and Γ_k is a (n.n) matrix of parameters. In a trivariate framework, three hypotheses are tested with a maximum possible rank order of two. These are:

Rank 0, H0: there are no cointegrating relationships.

Rank 1, H0: there is at least one cointegrating relationship.

Rank 2, H0: there are at least two cointegrating relationships.

Rank 0 means that there is no cointegration in the series and the VAR model can be used to estimate the coefficients. However, a rank above 0 implies cointegration and the appropriate model for estimating coefficients is ECM.

When the exogeneity of a variable in a regression analysis is in doubt (as it is in this study), a system of equations which treat each variable symmetrically can be developed for analysis (Enders, 2004). This permits series Y_t time path to be affected by the current and past realizations of the Gt sequence and vice versa. When the variables are stationary, their error terms are white noise and uncorrelated, and each equation in the system can be estimated using ordinary least squares (OLS), a vector autoregression (VAR) model. However, where the variables Y_t, G_t, and other explanatory variables such as Tt in the model have unit roots and the stochastic terms are correlated, OLS will be a misspecification of the model and the estimates will be inconsistent. In that case, the error correction model (ECM), built upon the theory of cointegration, is useful. According to Engle and Grander (1987), two or more variables are cointegrated when they themselves are nonstationary I(1), but their linear combination is stationary I(0). The variables will follow a common long-run equilibrium relationship. ECM allows estimation of the short and long-run relationships among the variables. Therefore, if Y_t, G_t, and T_t are cointegrated, their ECM representation will be

$$\Delta Y_t = \alpha_0 + \alpha_1 E_{t-1} + \sum_{i=1}^{n} \alpha_{2i}(i) \Delta Y_{t-i} + \sum_{i=1}^{n} \alpha_{3i}(i) \Delta G_{t-i} + \sum_{i=1}^{n} \alpha_{4i}(i) \Delta T_{t-i} + \mu_t \quad (1)$$

$$\Delta G_t = \beta_0 + \beta_1 V_{t-1} + \sum_{i=1}^{n} \beta_{2i}(i)\Delta Y_{t-i} + \sum_{i=1}^{n} \beta_{3i}(i)\Delta G_{t-i} + \sum_{i=1}^{n} \beta_{4i}(i)\Delta T_{t-i} + \omega_t \qquad (2)$$

where i is the lag operator, E_{t-1} and V_{t-1} are error correction terms, μ_t and ω_t are white noise, α and β are parameters to be estimated, n is preselected lag order, and t is year. Equations (1) and (2) are VAR in the first difference augmented by the error correction terms. This means that if $\alpha_1 = \beta_1 = 0$, then the system reverts to VAR in the first difference. In this system, Y_t granger causes G_t if β_1 and/or β_{2i} are significantly different from zero and Gt granger causes Yt if $\alpha 1$ and/or $\alpha 3 i$ are significantly different from zero. (Maparara, 2016, pp. 4–5)

The extract below comes from a systematic literature review of the causes of civil war. This study was conducted by Dixon (2009). The methodology in this study is described in the Introduction; it is rather short and focuses on how the author obtained the studies for the review and what approach he used to compare the findings of previous research. Go over the extract and highlight standard academic phrases and expressions that the author uses to describe his methodology.

The approach used in this paper is simple comparison of the direction and significance of the findings of quantitative research on civil war initiation. Through the structured comparison of findings, it is possible to identify varying degrees of consensus within this research community on key questions of interest. Even when studies' findings are in disagreement, it is often possible to identify common conclusions; for example, even if half of quantitative studies find that population density makes civil war more likely and half fail to detect a significant effect, this nonetheless demonstrates a consensus that the relationship is nonnegative (that is, that population density does not reduce the likelihood of civil war). Therefore, this paper presents the findings themselves, along with their levels of statistical significance, so that scholars can identify both "settled" questions in the literature and questions that have yet to be addressed by quantitative research.

The studies reviewed in this paper were found using JSTOR, Academic Search Complete, Digital Dissertations, and recent conference papers. From 47 separate studies, 64 separate tables of findings were reviewed. Only studies with the dependent variables of armed intrastate conflict onset or civil war onset were selected for inclusion. Since it is common practice for a single table to present multiple statistical models, each of which differs only in the specific set of independent variables included, it was necessary to select which models were to represent the conclusions of the author. If the author favored a particular model, its results were given precedence over those of other models rejected by the author. Where the author did not specify a preference for one model over another, the one with the highest explanatory power as a whole (generally provided by Pseudo-$R2$, or significance of the model if this statistic was not provided) [was given precedence]. Results for excluded variables were drawn from each of the remaining models. In total, 99 statistical models are included in this review, including statistical results for a total of 203 independent variables. (Dixon, 2009, p. 708)

DESCRIBING RESULTS

The extract below comes from a study of the determinants of job satisfaction by D'Addio et al. (2007). The authors used longitudinal data for Denmark collected as part of the European Community Household Panel and estimated fixed-effects models using estimation methods described in the literature. Notice how the authors refer the reader to the visuals when describing results and how they highlight noteworthy results. Notice also the use of various attitude markers in the description and interpretation of results (e.g., decisively rejects, interesting patterns, it is worth remarking, clearly differ).

Turning now to the estimates, **which are set out in Tables** 3 and 4 for males and females, respectively, **we may first note that** the test of random effects *versus* fixed effects described in Section IV, **decisively rejects** the former. **As can be seen from the statistics** α and the likelihood ratio test reported at the bottom of Tables 3 and 4, **the null hypothesis is rejected** at the lower bound. The random effects ordered probit estimates **are in Table A1 in the appendix. A comparison of these** with the preferred fixed effects model estimates **reveals some interesting patterns.**

The first thing worth noting is that the key economic explanatory variables like income from work, training, poor health and temporary jobs **attach similar coefficient estimates.** Thus, **previous** job satisfaction **models have not been far from the mark in this respect. It is worth remarking**, however, that the coefficient to wage income for women is positive albeit insignificant in all specifications. **As the data** on working hours **are crude,** making a distinction between full- and part-time work only, **the insignificant signs** to this dummy variable **should not worry us much. Other similarities are found for** those explanatory variables the estimated coefficients of which are insignificant; i.e., when a variable does not differ from zero in the random effects model, it does not in the fixed effects models, either. **There is one exception,** however. According to the fixed effects estimations, for females employment in the public sector increases their job satisfaction. **This is not completely unexpected as there is** a negative wage premium for Danish public sector employees (Pedersen *et al.*, 1990) but at the same time more working time flexibility and less pressure on doing overtime work in the public sector. ...

A **second noteworthy observation is that** there are substantially fewer explanatory variables that differ from zero for female employees and that **this is in particular the case in the** fixed effects **estimations. In fact** in the latter, there is only one, public sector employment, and **as we will see below** this is not robust.

The coefficients estimates obtained using on one hand the Ferrer-i-Carbonel and Frijters (2004) and on the other hand the Das and van Soest (1999) estimation strategy **are relatively similar**. For males there are two differences; the Das and van Soest **estimation yields** insignificant and significant estimates for poor health and public sector employment, respectively. The key economic variables – the hourly wage and hours (part-time work)—remain significant, albeit the precision of the Das and van Soest estimates is lower. For females, none of the estimated coefficients with the Das and van Soest procedure **differ significantly from zero. Thus, the determinants of** reported job satisfaction **clearly differ between** the genders.

For male employees the number of nights spent in hospital and employer provided training **obtained** negative and positive **coefficients,** respectively. The first variable is a proxy for health status which is **plausibly** negatively **related to** job satisfaction as individuals in a good physical and psychic condition are likely to be able to earn more, to feel relatively more certain of their continued employment, to be more able to choose and carry out the type of work they like, and to have less difficulties with the number of working hours, placement of working hours, or with working conditions. **The second observation is also plausible** as training provided by the employer **implies** both improved future career prospects and increased job security. **The estimates do not lend support to notions that** temporary, fixed-term contract jobs are considered as bad. (D'Addio et al., 2007, pp. 2420–2421)

The extract below comes from a study of the impact of government decentralization on domestic terror, which was conducted by Dreher and Fischer (2011). Here, too, notice how the authors describe their results by referring the reader to the appropriate place in the tables and how they interpret these results to show whether they are in line with the proposed hypotheses.

Table 1 shows the results for our two indicators of expenditure decentralization. **Columns 1 and 2 show that** fiscal decentralization reduces the number of domestic terror events. **This is in line with our *a priori hypothesis that*** decentralized structures **may increase** the opportunity costs and direct costs of domestic terrorists, on the one hand, **but equally that it may decrease** the marginal benefit from such a terror act, as decentralization stabilizes the polity and the economy. Calculating the marginal effect (at the sample mean, with the country and year dummies equal to zero), **the results in column 1 show that** the number of terror events in a country declines by 0.001 as decentralization increases by ten percentage points. **The calculated elasticity of** almost 2.5% **is socially relevant.**

Regarding the vector of control variables, the number of domestic terror events decreases with political and civil freedom, at the 5 percent level at least, **consistent with** Li's (2005) **hypothesis.** In column 1, voting with the United States **is positively associated with** the number of domestic terror events (significant at the ten percent level). The remaining control **variables are not significant at conventional levels.**

In column 3 we exclude cases indicated as zero decentralization by our indicator (including grants, as in column 1), as these mostly refer to very small countries where there is no distinction between the central and the state/communal level (e.g., San Marino). In column 3, the coefficient on fiscal decentralization **remains significant at the five percent level.** In this sample, political freedom equally reduces domestic terror, also significant at the five percent level.

In column 4 we include the time-invariant political autonomy variable (and estimate a pooled model which excludes the country dummies). While **its** negative **coefficient would be in support of our hypothesis, it is far from being significant at conventional levels.**
In columns 5 and 6 we distinguish between severe and less severe terror events. However, **the regression focusing on** less severe events (column 6) **does not converge when** the year dummies are included, so we omit them. **As can be seen, our previous results have been driven by** severe events only. Severe terror events decrease with decentralization at the one percent level of significance, while less severe events are not affected by decentralization. (Dreher & Fischer, 2011, pp. 223–224)

And here is how Itai Maparara, whose methodology I included earlier, describes his results. Notice how he relates his empirical results to theory, indicating whether the theoretical predictions were confirmed, for which countries, and at which level of statistical significance. As you go over the extract, highlight standard academic phrases and expressions that the author uses to describe his results.

In the analyses, I ran unrestricted VAR for eight countries; results are reported in Table 4. A Granger causality test was subsequently performed to determine the direction of causality in the short run. First, no causality was detected between economic growth and government expenditure for Angola and the Democratic Republic of the Congo. Second, Wagner's (1893) inference that economic growth causes government expenditure was supported for Zimbabwe at the 10% significance level and for Malawi and Seychelles at the 1% significance level. Third, Keynes' views were supported for Mauritius at the 5% significance level and for Botswana and Swaziland at the 10% significance level.
The third column in Table 4 reports results for VECM regression analysis. In this model, the direction of causality was determined for both the short and long run. In the short run, no causality was detected for Lesotho, Mozambique, Namibia, and South Africa. There was bi-directional causality for Tanzania at the 5% significance level. Wagner's theory was supported for Madagascar at the 1% significance level, whereas Keynes' views were supported for Zambia at the 5% significance level. In the long run, economic growth and trade were observed to granger-cause government expenditure in Madagascar, Namibia, and South Africa at the 1%, 10%, and 1% significance level, respectively. A unidirectional flow from government expenditure and trade to economic growth was observed for Lesotho and Zambia at the 1% significance level. Finally, a bi-directional flow was observed for Mozambique and Tanzania at the 1% and 10% significance level, respectively. (Maparara, 2016, p. 7)

The last extract comes from a study conducted by Jessica Montgomery, a student in Public Policy, who investigated the extent to which the place of education explains wage outcomes of immigrants in Australia compared to native-born individuals. Below you can see Jessica's Abstract, Results, Discussion, and Conclusion. Go over Jessica's extract and highlight standard academic phrases and expressions that she uses to describe her methodology and results, present her discussion, and outline her conclusions.

Abstract
This study investigates the extent to which the place of education explains the wage outcomes of Australian immigrants compared to native-born individuals. A human capital earnings function is adjusted to account for differential returns between (i) the foreign and Australian education of immigrants; and (ii) the Australian education of natives relative to immigrants. The findings indicate that immigrants from English-speaking backgrounds receive the same returns to education as native-born individuals, regardless of whether they studied abroad or in Australia. Conversely, immigrants from non-English speaking backgrounds experience a wage disadvantage relative to native counterparts, which can be explained by their lower returns to Australian and foreign education. Policy recommendations should be informed by further research to identify the specific drivers of differential returns to education among immigrant populations, and between immigrants and natives.

Results
Empirical estimates presented in Table 2 provide a high-level comparison of wage outcomes between natives and immigrants. Column 1 presents estimates of Eq. (1), the standard specification, where returns to education are invariant to immigrant status and where it was acquired. The coefficient estimate for immigrant status shows that weekly earnings of male immigrant workers are approximately 13 percent lower than those for comparable native-born male employees. Assuming equal returns to education between natives and immigrants, we can see that an additional year of schooling is estimated to increase earnings by 6.8 percent, or by more than twice as does the estimate for work experience.

Regression coefficients in column 2, based on Eq. (2), underline the importance of allowing the returns to human capital to differ according to immigrant status. At first glance, immigrant earnings are estimated as being approximately 23 percent higher than the earnings of natives. However this wage advantage is eliminated, and indeed reversed in favor of natives, with increases in years of education. Coefficients on the education variables indicate that an additional year of education increases the earnings of natives and immigrants by approximately 7.6 and 5.3 percent, respectively. As a consequence of the returns to education for immigrants being approximately 2.3 percent lower than for natives, the wage advantage for immigrants gradually narrows over the first few years of education and it is eliminated at approximately 10 years of education. Beyond this point, natives assume a wage advantage.

Interesting, there is no statistically significant difference in returns to work experience between natives and immigrants. Assuming that there are no systemic differences in unobserved qualities such as ability and motivation, we can interpret this result as suggesting that education attainment is the most significant element of human capital in determining the different wage outcomes of immigrants and natives. More specifically, the results suggest that the native-immigrant wage differential depends on the level of education: Although immigrants have a wage advantage among lower educated workers, this becomes a wage disadvantage at higher levels of education.

Tables 3 and 4 compare English-speaking-background (ESB) and non-English-speaking-background (NESB) immigrants separately to native counterparts. In column 1 of Table 3, there is no evidence of a significant wage difference

TABLE 2 Wage Outcomes of Immigrants Compared to Those of Natives

	(1)	(2)
Immigrant	−0.131***	0.233**
	(0.039)	(0.089)
Years of education	0.068***	0.076***
	(0.004)	(0.005)
Years of education * immigrant	−	−0.023***
		(0.007)
Experience	0.030***	0.030***
	(0.003)	(0.003)
Experience squared/100	−0.046***	−0.045***
	(0.006)	(0.006)
Experience * immigrant	−	−0.001
		(0.001)
Experience sq./100 * immigrant	−	0
		(.)
Years since migration	0.001	0.00
	(0.001)	(0.002)
Partner	0.139***	0.136***
	(0.017)	(0.017)
City	0.000	−0.006
	(0.030)	(0.030)
Inner regional	−0.050	−0.052*
	(0.031)	(0.031)
Constant	6.604***	6.500***
	(0.076)	(0.084)

Note. Sample includes full-time male employees aged 15–65. Independent variable is log weekly wage, and year of survey and state were also controlled for in these analyses. Standard errors are in parentheses, and ***, **, and * indicate statistical significance at the 1%, 5%, and 10% levels.

TABLE 3 Regression Coefficients for ESB Immigrants Compared to Natives

	(1)	(2)	(3)
ESB immigrant	0.038	0.026	0.124
	(0.050)	(0.058)	(0.127)
Years of education	0.074***		
	(0.004)		
AUS years of education		0.074***	0.075***
		(0.004)	(0.005)
O/S years of education		0.074***	0.069***
		(0.006)	(0.007)
AUS years of edu * ESB			− 0.009
			(0.011)
Experience	0.030***	0.030***	0.030***
	(0.002)	(0.002)	(0.002)
Experience sq/100	−0.045***	−0.045***	−0.045***
	(0.005)	(0.005)	(0.005)
Experience * ESB		0.001	0.000
		(0.002)	(0.003)
Experience squared * ESB		0	0
Years since migration	−0.001	−0.002	0.000
	(0.002)	(0.002)	(0.003)
Partner	0.148***	0.148***	0.148***
	(0.018)	(0.018)	(0.017)
City	0.003	0.003	0.002
	(0.030)	(0.030)	(0.030)
Inner regional	−0.054*	−0.054*	−0.054*
	(0.030)	(0.030)	(0.030)
Constant	6.473***	6.474***	6.460***
	(0.087)	(0.086)	(0.090)

Note. Sample includes full-time male employees aged 15–65. Independent variable is log weekly wage, and year of survey and state were also controlled for in these analyses. Standard errors are in parentheses, and ***, **, and * indicate statistical significance at the 1%, 5%, and 10% levels.

TABLE 4 Regression Coefficients for NESB Immigrants Compared to Natives

	(1)	(2)	(3)
NESB immigrant	−0.245***	−0.072	0.155
	(0.047)	(0.080)	(0.118)
Years of education	0.070***		
	(0.005)		
AUS years of education		0.072***	0.075***
		(0.005)	(0.005)
O/S years of education		0.062***	0.052***
		(0.005)	(0.008)
AUS years of edu * NESB			−0.020*
			(0.011)
Experience	0.030***	0.030***	0.030***
	(0.003)	(0.003)	(0.003)
Experience sq/100	−0.046***	−0.046***	−0.046***
	(0.007)	(0.007)	(0.007)
Experience * NESB		0.000	− 0.003
		(0.003)	(0.003)
Experience squared * NESB		0	0
		(.)	(.)
Years since migration	0.002*	− 0.001	0.002
	(0.001)	(0.003)	(0.003)
Partner	0.144***	0.144***	0.142***
	(0.019)	(0.019)	(0.019)
City	0.016	0.015	0.013
	(0.027)	(0.028)	(0.027)
Inner regional	−0.039	−0.039	−0.040
	(0.029)	(0.029)	(0.029)
Constant	6.556***	6.525***	6.483***
	(0.076)	(0.080)	(0.081)

Note. Sample includes full-time male employees aged 15–65. Independent variable is log weekly wage and year of survey and state were also controlled for in these analyses. Standard errors are in parentheses, and ***, **, and * indicate statistical significance at the 1%, 5%, and 10% levels.

between natives and ESB male employees, assuming equal returns to education. An additional year of education is estimated to increase earnings by approximately 7.4 percent, whereas the return to experience is approximately 3 percent.

In column 2, the return to domestic and foreign education is allowed to vary. Australian education and immigrants' foreign education are estimated to have equivalent wage returns of approximately 7.4 percent. Similar to the results in Table 2, there is no statistically significant difference in the returns to immigrants' work experience compared to natives'.

Column 3 allows the return to domestic education to differ between natives and ESB immigrants. There is no evidence of Australian education being valued in the labor market differently for ESB immigrants compared to natives. Further, a Wald test confirms that the difference between the return to natives' domestic education and immigrants' foreign education is not statistically significant at the 5% level. Taken together, these results suggest that the education of ESB immigrants is valued similar to that of natives, regardless of whether their education was completed in Australia or abroad. Consistent with this, there is no significant difference between native and ESB immigrant workers.

Table 4 presents the results for NESB immigrants compared to native-born workers. Contrary to the experience of ESB immigrants, column 1 shows that NESB immigrants experience 24.5 percent lower wage earnings than natives. The estimated return to an additional year of education is 7.0 percent, assuming that the return is invariant to immigrant status and source country of education.

In column 2, Australian education is distinguished from the foreign education of immigrants. Despite the coefficient estimate for NESB immigrant status no longer being statistically significant, a wage disadvantage for NESB immigrants remains; however, it is now transmitted through the statistically significant lower returns to foreign education. The return to an additional year of domestic education is 7.2 percent, whereas the return to an additional year of education abroad is 6.2 percent.

Allowing the return to Australian education to differ between natives and NESB immigrants, as seen in column 3, delivers substantially different results to those for ESB immigrants, which are shown in Table 3. The return to an additional year of Australian education is considerably higher for natives (7.5 percent) than for immigrants (5.5 percent). This 2 percent differential is statistically significant at the 10% significance level. Further, NESB immigrants receive an even lower return of 5.2 percent per additional year of foreign education. These results point to a wage disadvantage for NESB immigrants compared to natives, which is greatest for those with foreign education. Notably, there is no statistically significant difference in the return to experience between NESB immigrants and natives, a result consistent with that obtained for the ESB immigrants. This suggests that the wage disadvantage is driven by the different returns to education.

Robustness Check

The results assume a linear relationship between years of education and earnings. However, if there are diminishing returns to education, lower returns to immigrants' domestic education may be expected because, by definition, it is completed after foreign education. Table 1 in Appendix B allows the return to education to vary according to level of qualification. These results are broadly consistent with those described in the preceding section, whereby NESB immigrants receive statistically significant lower returns to several higher-education qualifications, which can be assumed to have been completed in Australia following their domestic education. The difference in the returns to ESB immigrants' and natives' qualifications is not statistically significant.

Discussion

The results of this paper suggest that the place of education has different implications for the wage outcomes of ESB and NESB immigrants, relative to their native counterparts. Empirical evidence is provided in support of the two hypotheses of this paper:

(1) The returns to foreign education for ESB immigrants are higher compared to those for NESB immigrants and resemble natives' returns to Australian education.

(2) The returns to Australian education are higher for natives and ESB immigrants compared to those for NESB immigrants.

There are several possible explanations for these findings. First, the foreign education of NESB immigrants may be less compatible with the Australian labor market compared to that of ESB immigrants. This perspective implies that the "country-specific" element of education, related to language, culture, institutional structures, and so forth, is a "better fit" in the local labor market when it is attained in ESB countries (Friedberg, 2000). As a result, ESB immigrants may receive a higher return to their foreign education because they are better able to utilize the skills associated with their foreign education compared to their NESB immigrants. A simple example of this could relate to differing levels of English fluency among immigrants. A greater ability to communicate with colleagues and clients in the workplace may support higher levels of productivity, translating into higher returns to education. A more contentious example may relate to certain professions, whereby the specific skills provided in the origin country of NESB immigrants are incongruent to the skill needs within the Australian labor market (Chapman & Iredale, 1993).

Second, the lower returns to Australian education for NESB immigrants, compared to their ESB counterparts, may be similarly explained by the degree of resemblance between Australia and the immigrants' origin countries. Notwithstanding their diversity, the origin countries of NESB immigrants, compared to those of ESB immigrants, are likely to be less similar to Australia across various dimensions such as language, cultural norms, economic development, and occupational and industrial structures. In contrast, ESB immigrants originate from countries with the same native language, and more similar cultural, economic, and social backgrounds. The greater familiarity with Australian institutions and customs may provide ESB immigrants with a learning advantage, enabling them to derive greater productivity gains from a year of Australian education (Friedberg, 2000). Conversely, NESB immigrants may face more challenges in achieving the same level of productivity gains, due to their likely lower levels of country-specific knowledge. However, it is important to note that the Australian education of NESB immigrants shows higher returns compared to their foreign education. This suggests that acquiring Australian education may help to increase individuals' marginal productivity through enhancing their language abilities and familiarizing them with institutions, expectations in the workplace, and so forth (Basilio, Bauer, & Kramer, 2014).

Third, there may be differences in the quality of foreign education that translate into actual differences in the marginal productivity of ESB and NESB immigrants. This would suggest that ESB immigrants' foreign education is valued similar to natives' Australian education, because the respective skill endowments derived from a year of education are equal (Beggs & Chapman, 1991). Conversely, from this perspective, the lower returns to NESB immigrants' foreign education, compared to their domestic education as well as the education of ESB immigrants and natives, are fair and indicative of efficient labor market pricing mechanisms, whereby a lower return to education reflects lower skill level (Chapman & Iredale, 1993).

Fourth, the differential returns to foreign education may reflect a greater incidence of asymmetrical information regarding the education credentials of NESB immigrants. This implies that the foreign education of NESB immigrants may be discounted because employers are less familiar with the relevant educational institutions or qualifications (Kanas & Tubergen, 2009). As a result, the signaling value of foreign education, conveying to prospective employers the likely productivity of individuals (Patrinos, 2016), may be weaker for NESB immigrants compared to ESB immigrants. That being said, the higher returns to NESB immigrants' domestic education compared to foreign education suggest that Australian education may have a distinct signaling value for NESB immigrants. Undertaking Australian education may help these immigrants validate their foreign educational qualifications, or provide employers with greater confidence that the immigrants have sufficient understanding of the local labor market (Banerjee & Lee, 2015).

Finally, the premium associated with the foreign and domestic education of ESB immigrants, compared to that of NESB immigrants, could be driven by factors that are less relevant to the education itself. The higher returns to ESB immigrants' education, regardless of place of attainment, compared to NESB immigrants' education may reflect employer discrimination, or a preference among employers for the labor of ESB immigrants rather than of NESB immigrants. The general finding of equal treatment of natives and ESB immigrants in the labor market may also be considered evidence for this explanation. However, for this rationale to hold, it would presumably imply that the return to other elements of NESB immigrants' human capital, such as work experience, would also be discounted by employers. This explanation seems unlikely as the empirical results point to equal returns to experience between NESB immigrants and natives, in addition to those between ESB immigrants and natives.

Limitations

An implication of focusing on the relationship between earnings and education is that this paper only considers individuals employed in the labor market. However, immigrants and natives have different employment probabilities. With respect to Australian native-born individuals, foreign-born individuals are more likely to be unemployed (6.0 percent versus 5.8 percent in 2016) and less likely to participate in the labor force (74.7 percent versus 78.3 percent in 2016) (OECD, 2017). To the extent that these outcomes are driven by different labor market returns to immigrants relative to natives, the estimates in this paper may be biased (Islam & Parasnis, 2016).

Conclusion

This paper investigated the role of education in determining the wage outcomes of ESB and NESB immigrants in Australia, compared to those of native-born individuals. Most important, this analysis contributes to the Australian literature by determining the extent to which the source country of education impacts the respective earnings of ESB and NESB immigrants vis-à-vis their native counterparts. While Australian studies generally allow the returns to education to differ between natives and immigrants, very few studies, especially recently, have distinguished foreign from domestic education.

A key finding of this study is that the return to education for ESB immigrants is aligned with that of natives' Australian education, regardless of whether the education was obtained in their origin country or within Australia. Conversely, the place of education matters for NESB immigrants. The foreign education of NESB immigrants receives significantly lower returns compared to their Australia education, which in turn are lower than the returns to education for ESB immigrants and natives. Among the range of possible explanations for these results, the differing degrees of proximity between Australia and the source country of ESB and NESB immigrants in terms of language, institutions, economic development, and so on provide a useful basis for understanding how the productivity and signaling value of education may differ among the immigrant populations, as well as between immigrants and natives.

Consistent with findings in the Australian literature, these results point to a wage disadvantage for NESB immigrants, whereas ESB immigrants and natives are treated homogenously in the labor market. To outline the potential policy implications of this study, further research is required to determine the relative importance of the explanations offered for the differential returns to education between ESB and NESB immigrants. This will assist in determining the scope and type of policy intervention warranted by the results presented in this paper.

In particular, it is recommended that research be undertaken to determine the extent to which differential returns to education reflect *actual* differences in productivity, as opposed to perceived differences. For example, if lower returns to the foreign and domestic education of NESB immigrants reflect lower actual levels of productivity, then this would suggest that the labor of NESB immigrants has been appropriately discounted in the labor market, relative to that of natives and ESB immigrants. In such a case, policy intervention is likely to distort efficient pricing mechanisms within the labor market.

Conversely, research of this nature could point to the undervaluing (or potentially overvaluing) of immigrants' educational qualifications in the labor market. Further quantitative analysis and potential surveying of employers could help to identify specific market frictions obstructing immigrants' education from being appropriately valued in the labor market by employers. This would be especially valuable in assisting policy makers to develop policy initiatives that address the source of the problem and ensure maximum skill utilization in the economy.

For instance, it could be found that employers find it relatively more difficult to assess the value of foreign education credentials from specific regions. This would suggest that there is possible merit in enhancing investment or promoting immigrants' participation in programs to improve the transferability of foreign-acquired education. For example, further consideration could be given to the functioning of the government's "Qualification Assessment," a voluntary program that aims to "help organizations, such as a prospective employer, understand the educational level of an overseas qualification in the Australian context" (Australian Government, Department of Education and Training, 2017). A review of program take-up and potential obstacles to use could assist in determining avenues to enhance immigrants' participation and employers' awareness of the service. Potential actions may include an information campaign targeting employers and recently arrived immigrants, or reducing the fee-for-service to enhance accessibility for immigrants.

Given the diversity of immigrants, further analysis should also be undertaken based on country of origin or regional cohorts of immigrants to identify the specific barriers preventing educational qualifications from being directly transferable to the local labor market. For one country of origin grouping, language may be the most relevant barrier; however, for another, the most significant problem could be the quality of educational attainment as perceived by employers. Policies can be developed to address these barriers. (Montgomery, 2017, pp. 13–24)

Chapter 16

Writing Skills

The premise of this book is that each discipline or research area has its own unique characteristics and approaches not only to conducting research but also to presenting argumentation, and that these characteristics reflect disciplinary conventions and the way members of the particular discipline go about creating and constructing knowledge. The language of an academic text, then, is to a large extent determined by the members of the particular discipline for whom the author is writing. To produce writing that readers in that discipline would find acceptable, authors need to know the ways and approaches of their discipline and make sure that their writing conforms to the discipline's conventions. In the preceding chapters, I have tried to show how authors in economics and public policy go about organizing, structuring, and presenting various sections of a research paper in ways that their readers would find acceptable and persuasive. In this chapter, I focus on the more general skills of academic writing—such as using and citing sources, quoting, and summarizing. Keep in mind, however, that even such "general" skills as citing sources or writing in formal style are often discipline-specific: What may be considered good style in one discipline or research area may not be considered appropriate in another. The best way to learn the conventions for language use that exist in your research area is to read papers written by researchers working in that area.

USING AND CITING SOURCES

Earlier in this book, I talked about the various sources that are used in public policy and economics research and drew a distinction between scholarly literature, policy literature, and popular literature (i.e., mass media sources). Here, I draw another distinction—one between print and Internet sources. Understanding this distinction is important because students who are new to graduate study often treat the Internet as a source. Yet, the Internet is not a source; it is a place, just like a library, but without the gatekeepers to evaluate what should be included and excluded.

Print sources are those that are found in a library or bookstore. These include books, edited books, scholarly journals, government reports, dissertations, newspapers, and magazines. Although some academic print sources, such as journals, can be located and accessed online through a database, they are still considered print sources, which also happen to be available online.

How to Write about Economics and Public Policy. https://doi.org/10.1016/B978-0-12-813010-0.00016-8

Internet sources are those that are available only on the Internet. These include online journals and magazines, organizational websites, press releases, and similar sources. Internet sources should be used with great caution because (1) they are not generally peer-reviewed, and (2) there is often no quality control over what is published on the Internet. Anyone can put anything on a website. It may be of poor quality, highly biased, or fraudulent.

To assess the credibility of a source found on the Internet,

- Always look for the author and publisher of the source. If you cannot determine who wrote the material and/or who owns the website, do not use it!

- Check the author's professional affiliation and that the publisher is a recognized authority in the field. The domain tags *.edu*, *.org*, and *.gov* tend to publish reliable work by expert authors, but you should exercise caution.

Citing Sources

A citation is a reference to a source of information or ideas. A common style of citation in the social sciences is the in-text (author-date) citation. For example:

---

1. Brown (1999) described two main causes of management failure.

2. A true experiment is a process of carefully controlled observation and inference (Smith, 1987).

Citations can be integral or nonintegral. **Integral citations** are integrated into the running text (as in the first example) whereas **nonintegral citations** are placed in parentheses inside a sentence or at the end of a sentence (as in the second example), or included in footnotes. Nonintegral citations are not grammatically integrated into the text and are not part of a sentence. Both types of citation are used in public policy and economics, but often for different purposes. Integral citations are common when authors present other authors' arguments, theories, interpretations, and so on, or when they describe other authors' work and findings. Below is an example I created to show how integral citations can be used in a text.

Additional evidence supporting the general claim that privatization is effective comes from studies of the postcommunist transition economies. Earlie and Brown (1999) and Adams (2003) examined the effectiveness of privatization of shops and other small establishments in Central Europe and Russia and found that, on average, privatized firms had higher growth rates than state-run enterprises of a comparable size. Studies that examined privatization of large enterprises have also reported various advantages of privatized firms over nonprivatized. For example, Kollo (1995) compared privatized and state-run firms on 11 different factors in three countries in Central Europe and found that, on average, privatized firms enjoyed greater international exposure, were more cost-efficient, and achieved greater productivity.

Nonintegral citations are common when authors summarize a body of research to show the current state of knowledge. Such citations can also be used to support theoretical arguments. Below is an example showing how nonintegral citations can be used in a text.

As jail and prison populations in the United States have reached levels that are both historically and comparatively unprecedented, there has been increasing interest in better understanding the determinants of incarceration. Accordingly, recent research has explored the effects of a wide range of macrolevel variables on incarceration rates, including unemployment (Chiricos and Delone, 1992; Grant and Martinez, 1997; Western and Beckett, 1999), economic inequality (Garland 1990; Greenberg 1999), electoral cycles (Beckett 1997; Jacobs and Carmichael, 2002), welfare spending (Greenberg and West, 2001), and race relations (Greenberg and West, 2001; Jacobs and Carmichael, 2002; Pettit and Western, 2004). (Arum & LaFree, 2008, p. 397)

Citations should be placed as close as possible to the material being cited to prevent ambiguity. The reader should not have to guess what exactly a particular citation refers to and should be able to see clearly which ideas are yours and which ideas belong to the author(s) you cite. To see the difference between ambiguous and unambiguous citations, compare these two examples that I created.

Example 1

Evidence of the impact of the Autonomous Revenue Authority (ARA) model on revenue collection has been mixed. Some earlier studies have shown negative and inconclusive results, whereas more recent studies have shown positive results. It appears, therefore, that the ARA model may be a viable alternative for Sub-Saharan African countries (World Bank, 2011).

Example 2

Evidence of the impact of the Autonomous Revenue Authority (ARA) model on revenue collection has been mixed. Some earlier studies (e.g., Fjeldstad & Moore, 2009; Gupta & Tareq, 2008; Hadler, 2000) have shown negative or inconclusive results. However, more recent studies (e.g., Kloedan, 2011; Taliercio, 2004; World Bank, 2010), which have assessed the impact of the model after it had been used for a considerable length of time, have found positive results. It appears, therefore, that the ARA model may be a viable alternative for Sub-Saharan African countries.

In the first example, it is unclear what exactly the author's citation refers to. Did the World Bank paper summarize all of those studies? Did it make the claim about the earlier vs. the more recent studies? Or the claim that the ARA model may be a good alternative? In the second example, however, the author puts citations directly after the information is cited and there is no ambiguity.

Why do we need to cite? Although some authors identify multiple reasons for citation, there are three main ones: to support claims, to show the origin of ideas, and to give credit to the original author.

1. **Supporting claims**. New knowledge builds on existing knowledge. When we want to make a claim about the world, we need to support it with evidence and this is what citations are for.

2. **Showing the origin of ideas**. It is important for academics to be able to trace the origin of ideas in order to evaluate the strength of the evidence presented in support of a claim. Citations direct readers to relevant studies that they can check.

3. **Giving credit**. Citations allow us to give credit to the original authors when borrowing words or ideas. Failure to cite violates the rights of the original authors and constitutes plagiarism, which is a serious offence in an academic environment. Serious consequences may result from both intentional and inadvertent plagiarism.

WHAT REQUIRES A CITATION

Specific Words and Phrases that You Borrow

- Enclose exact words and phrases in "quotation marks" and provide the page number.
- If paraphrasing, make sure that the paraphrase is sufficiently different from the original.
- In either case, provide a citation with the author's name and date of publication.

Information and Ideas that You Take from Sources

- Numbers and other numeric data taken from a source (e.g., GDP growth rate; population statistics; survey results; census data)
- Explanations or examples taken from a source
- Definitions
- Graphs, tables, or figures that have not been created by you
- Laws, regulations, resolutions, decrees, treaties, or agreements
- Information taken from encyclopedias and other reference books
- Theories and models
- Classifications, typologies, and other ordering systems that have not been created by you
- Ideas about the causes of a phenomenon, steps in a process, specific methods or techniques, characteristics of a condition (e.g., poverty), interpretations

of a fact, origins of a phenomenon, condition, or problem, and other ideas taken from any source.

- Your own ideas that have been published previously

Even when using your own words to paraphrase a source, you need to cite the source.

WHAT DOES NOT REQUIRE A CITATION

Your Own Ideas, Experiences, and Results

- Your recommendations for how to achieve something
- Your opinion about an author's argument or interpretation
- Your agreement or disagreement with an author
- Results of your own analyses
- Your experiences working somewhere
- Your impressions of something
- Anything else you have observed with your own eyes

Factual Information

- Geographical facts (Moscow is the capital of Russia)
- Historical facts (birth date of a leader)
- Dates of important events

Commonsense Observations

- Statements that members of a particular discipline generally accept as uncontentious (**BUT:** Such statements are discipline-specific! What may be commonsense in one discipline may not be so in another.)

Common Phrases of Academic English

- These results seem to suggest....
- However, more research is needed to evaluate....
- These results are statistically significant.
- The survey was conducted in....
- Recent research demonstrates that....
- There was a weak correlation between X and Y.
- I investigated the relationship between X and Y to determine Z.

CITING INFORMATION FROM SOURCES YOU HAVE NOT SEEN

Sometimes you may need to use information (data, arguments, findings, or descriptions) that is cited in a source that you are reading. It is best to locate the original source, read it, and cite the information directly from that source. However, this may not always be possible. If you cannot locate the original source, your only option to use the information you need is to describe it in your own words from the source that you have read and then cite *your* source. Do not simply copy your source's summary and citation; rather, do the following.

1. Paraphrase the sentences you want to use.

2. Make it clear that you have not seen the original source by using the words "as cited in." (See the models shown below.)

3. List the source *you* have read in the reference list. Do not include the original source in your reference list.

Here is an example. Below is an excerpt from Fey and Denison's (2003) "Organizational culture and effectiveness: Can American theory be applied in Russia?"

> Many organizational researchers have examined corporate culture as a source of competitive advantage (Barney 1986, Ott 1989, Pfeffer 1994, Wilkins and Ouchi 1983), but explicit theories are few and empirical evidence is limited (Denison and Mishra 1995). The theories that do exist (Denison 1990, Kotter and Heskett 1992, O'Reilly 1989) have been developed and applied only in the United States. (Fey & Denison, 2003, p. 686)

Here are three ways to use Denison and Mishra's claim about limited empirical evidence.

Model 1. Highlight the information from the original source with a paraphrase and put both studies in the in-text citation using "as cited in":

> Some researchers working in the area of organizational effectiveness have highlighted the dearth of empirical evidence on the role of corporate culture in company performance (Denison & Mishra, 1995, as cited in Fey & Denison, 2003).

Model 2. Highlight the original source by mentioning it in your sentence and paraphrasing its findings. Show where you obtained the information in the in-text citation by using "as cited in":

> According to a review conducted by Denison and Mishra in 1995 (as cited in Fey & Denison, 2003), there is a dearth of empirical evidence on the role of corporate culture in company performance.

Model 3. Highlight your source by summarizing its argument and show how it uses the original source to support its statement:

> Fey and Denison (2003) have indicated a clear need for more research on the relationship between corporate culture and competitive advantage. They cite a review conducted by Denison and Mishra in 1995 in which the authors show a dearth of empirical evidence on the subject.

The reference list entry is *your* source only:

Fey, C. F., & Denison, D. R. (2003). Organizational culture and effectiveness: Can American theory be applied in Russia? *Organization Science, 14*(6), 686–706.

REPORTING VERBS AND VERB TENSES

Every discipline has its own preferred set of reporting verbs—verbs used to report results and present authors' arguments. Disciplines also differ as to which verb tense is commonly used to talk about the state of current knowledge, one's own purpose, methodology, and results, or a study's implications. The following reporting verbs are very common in public policy and economics:

Find: Miller (2012) finds that…
Show: Smith and Adams (2010) show that…
Argue: Brown (2002) argues that…
Suggest: Brown (2002) suggests that…
Estimate: Another study estimates….

Box 45 shows the verb tenses commonly used for various purposes in research papers in public policy and economics.

BOX 45 Verb Tenses Used in Public Policy and Economics Papers

To talk about...	Use...	Examples
State of current knowledge	Present Perfect	A substantial amount of research **has shown** that readily observable teacher characteristics—experience, education, and contractual status, among others—explain very little of the differences in teacher quality (Rivkin, Hanushek, and Kain 2005; Hanushek and Rivkin 2012). (Araujo et al., 2016, p. 1416)
	Simple Present	The qualitative evidence on links between business and coup planners **is** substantial. (Dube et al., 2011, p. 1379)
Summary of previous research	Present Perfect	Moreover, most of the evidence on the short-term effects of teachers **has focused** on test scores in math and language. (Araujo et al., 2016, p. 1416)

Continued

BOX 45 Verb Tenses Used in Public Policy and Economics Papers—cont'd.

There **has been** extensive theoretical investigation of the determinants of the capability of elected representatives and government agents (McKelvey and Reizman, 1992; Banks and Sundaram, 1998; Aragones and Palfrey, 2004; Caselli and Morelli, 2004; Acemoglu *et al.*, 2010; Egorov and Sonin, 2011; Iaryczower and Mattozzi, 2013; Krasa and Polborn, 2015; Mattozzi and Merlo, 2015). Empirical investigations **have tried** to disentangle accountability and competence in elections (Alt *et al.*, 2011), and **have further established** links between more capable elected officials and higher intra-party competition (Besley *et al.*, 2013; Folke *et al.*, 2014), higher inter-party competition (Banerjee and Pande, 2007), higher wages (Ferraz and Finan, 2011a; Kotakorpi and Poutvaara, 2011; Dal *et al.*, 2013; Gagliarducci and Nannicini, 2013), smaller budgets (Brollo *et al.*, 2013), and more democratic institutions (Besley and Reynal-Querol, 2011). (Beath et al., 2016, p. 935)

Purpose of own study	Simple Present	In this article we **study** the impact of teachers using unusually rich data from Ecuador, a middle-income country. (Araujo et al., 2016, p. 1417)
		To investigate the role of policy uncertainty we first **develop** an index of economic policy uncertainty (EPU) for the United States and examine its evolution since 1985. (Baker et al., 2016, p. 1594)
		In this article, we **explore** what determines whether an individual contributes her ideas to a group. (Coffman, 2014, p. 1626)
Previous studies (what researchers did and what they found)	Simple Past	A compelling illustration of such support issues is provided by Carrell *et al.* (2013). Results based on naturally occurring variation in peer composition at the U.S. Air Force Academy **indicated** that freshmen from the lowest one-third of the prior ability distribution would gain from being grouped together with freshmen from the highest one-third of the ability distribution (see also Carrell *et al.*, 2009). The authors then **conduct** a randomized experiment to test this and **find** that low-ability students are actually harmed by the policy which was predicted to benefit them. (Booij et al., 2017, p. 548)
	Simple Present	
	Simple Present	Michael et al. (2010) **estimates** a loss of about $2 billion in trade taxes caused by corruption in customs

BOX 45 Verb Tenses Used in Public Policy and Economics Papers—cont'd.

		globally. This figure does not include the loss of value added taxes and excise taxes collected by customs. Another study **estimates a** loss of at least $700 billion worldwide due to customs corruption (Michael & Moore, 2010). (Ibrahim, 2014, p. 3)
Methodology	Simple Past	Finally, participants **were asked** the following demographic questions: gender, year of birth, race, whether they attended high school in the United States, student/employment status, which categories they liked/disliked, and which categories they know the most/least about. (Coffman, 2014, p. 1635)
	Simple Present	Customs revenue **is** one of the two dependent variables **I use** in this study and **it is measured** here by the number of imported goods and services as a percentage of GDP. (Ahamadzie, 2016, p. 4)
Design/ Analysis	Simple Present	We **use** a 2 x 2 across-subject design. First, we **vary** whether the participants received feedback about Part B performance. (Coffman, 2014, p. 1635)
		In what follows, we **restrict** our analysis to respondents who are not retired at the time of the survey. This **reduces** the size of the sample to 4336 observations. (de Coulon & Wolff, 2010, p. 3323)
Results	Simple Present	We **find** that SYEP participation increases earnings and employment in the year of the program.... At the same time, we **do not find** that youth employment has a positive effect on subsequent earnings or on college enrollment. (Gelber et al., 2015, p. 4)
		Unsurprisingly, women **are** more likely than men to devote time to their parents. This kind of help **tends** to decrease with the age of the donors, presumably due to declining physical capacity. Moreover, adult children with poor health **have** a lower probability of giving time transfers to parents. The level of education of the adult children **increases** the probability of giving time assistance to their parents. (Bonsang, 2007, p. 181)
		It is evident that the instrument **has** a positive and statistically significant effect on total revenues. (Borge et al., 2015, p. 107)
		In all four regressions public debt **has** a negative and significant coefficient. (De Bonis & Stacchini, 2013, p. 297)

Continued

BOX 45 Verb Tenses Used in Public Policy and Economics Papers—cont'd.

Tables and Figures	Simple Present	Figure I **plots** the resulting index, which **shows** clear spikes around the Gulf Wars, close presidential elections, the 9/11 terrorist attack, the stimulus debate in early 2008, the Lehman Brothers bankruptcy and TARP legislation in late 2008, the summer 2011 debt ceiling dispute, and the battle over the "fiscal cliff" in late 2012, among other events and developments. (Baker at al., 2016, p. 1599)
		Table 4 **presents** the characteristics for the three intended location choices. (de Coulon & Wolff., 2010, p. 3324)
Discussion and Interpretation	Simple Present	Our results **are consistent** with those obtained by Hauner (2009), who found a negative link between public debt held by banks and financial development in middle-income countries. (De Bonis & Stacchini, 2013, p. 299)
		This **implies** that our result **is** not a consequence of public revenue being endogenous, a main concern in the existing resource curse literature. (Borge et al., 2015, p. 108)
		Our estimates **suggest** that the country of residence of children and other family members is necessary to understand the intended location of immigrants when retiring. (de Coulon & Wolff., 2010, p. 3330)
Future Research	Simple Present	More research **is needed** to determine the optimal conditions for decentralization. (Author's example)

ACADEMIC STYLE FOR REFERENCES AND CITATIONS

Citations and lists of sources in an academic paper must follow a recognized academic style. Two styles that are commonly used in public policy and economics are the style of the *Publication Manual of the American Psychological Association* (the so-called APA style) and that of *The Chicago Manual of Style* (the so-called Chicago style). However, your particular research area, journal or advisor, may have other preferences, so always check what style you should use. It is also important to be consistent and use the same style throughout the entire paper.

A reference list is associated with in-text (author-date) citations formatted according to *APA* or a similar author-date system. If you use in-text citations, you may want to format them according to *APA* and list your sources in a reference list at the end of the text. A bibliography is associated with source notes (footnotes or endnotes) formatted according to *Chicago* or a similar footnote/endnote system. If you use notes to cite sources, format them according to *Chicago* and list sources in a bibliography at the end of the text.

Both *reference list* and *bibliography* refer to an alphabetized list where the reader finds full information on every source mentioned in the text including:

- name of author(s) or editor(s)
- date of publication
- title of work
- journal name (if a journal article)
- place of publication and name of publisher (if a print source)
- web address (if an online source)

QUOTING AND SUMMARIZING

A quotation is a phrase, sentence, or passage that is quoted, i.e., repeated exactly as it was used in the original source. Such borrowed wording is enclosed in "quotation marks." Quoted material requires both quotation marks and a citation, including the exact page number of the quotation.

Different disciplines and research areas have different preferences and conventions for the use of direct quotations. In economics, direct quotations are extremely rare and are usually used to refer to short descriptions or characterizations of hypotheses, tools, models, and so on. Below is an example.

> According to Imai (1997), KAIZEN is a commonsense, low-cost approach to management. Its goal is to help enterprises attain the higher quality of products and services, lower costs, and timely delivery. It is a process-oriented approach based on a belief that "processes must be improved for results to improve" (Imai,1997, p. 4). (Sonobe & Otsuka, 2014, p. 9)

In other areas of public policy, quotations are more common, especially in qualitative studies, and they are often used to present other authors' arguments. Below is an example.

> In this context Pachauri (2006: 3) suggested that dangerous climate change "is no doubt a question that must be decided on the basis of value judgment: what is dangerous is essentially a matter of what society decides", and that a fundamental principle of such a decision "is, of course, universal human rights". (Adger, 2010, p. 287)

HOW TO QUOTE

Below are some general suggestions for the use of quotations in academic papers. These suggestions are based on the principles described in the APA and Chicago manuals. Depending on the research area you are working in, you may need to adjust them for your own purposes. Again, the best way to learn how—and how often—quotations are used in your research area is to check published papers.

General Principles

- Direct quotations must be accurate. The wording, spelling, and interior punctuation should be as in the original, even if the original is incorrect.

- If you add or change words for purposes of clarification, enclose them in brackets: [ ].

- Use three spaced ellipsis points . . . to indicate any omission within a quoted sentence and four points . . . . to indicate omission between two sentences. Do not use ellipsis points at the beginning or end of any quotation even if the quoted material begins in the middle of a sentence in the original.

- Provide the author, year, and page number in the in-text citation or footnote.

Within-Sentence Quotations

Within-sentence quotations are those that are incorporated into the running text.

1. Enclose quotations in double quotation marks.

2. Enclose quotations within the quotation in single quotation marks.

3. You may change the case of the first letter of the first word to uppercase or lowercase to fit the quotation into your sentence without the use of brackets.

   Original: Reliability is one of the most important criteria in survey research.
   Quotation: According to Author (date), "reliability is one of the most important criteria in survey research" (p. xx).

4. The quotation must fit into your sentence grammatically.

   Original: Such an error is not unique to historical explanations.
   Quotation: Neuman (2004) argued that "such...error[s] [were] not unique to historical explanations" (p. 97).

Block Quotations

Block quotations are those that are set off from the main text as a block of text by using indentation. Because they are indented and set off from the main text, they are easily recognizable visually.

1. Start the quotation on a new line. Indent the entire quotation, but do not indent the first line further even if it is the beginning of a paragraph.

2. Do not use quotation marks.

3. Include citations embedded within the original material but do not include these citations in your reference list. Or you may omit them and use ellipsis points to indicate the omission.

4. Use a signal phrase to incorporate the quotation into your text.

5. Include the page number in parentheses at the end of the quotation.

Below is an example of a block quotation taken from Young's (1999) book chapter "Complimentary, supplementary, or adversarial? A theoretical and historical examination of nonprofit-government relations in the United States" (p. 53).

As nonprofit organizations became more dependent on government funding in the 1960s and 1970s, the nature of the relationship between government and nonprofits changed in other ways as well:

> Historically, government purchased services from charitable organizations and attached few strings beyond those common to many other service purchasers. Today governments contract for whole programs, and even create providers where they otherwise do not exist. There is more contracting today than ever before, and the terms of contracting are more demanding. If in the past government went to the private sector for limited services, today its purchasing power is such that it is often in a position to shape the sorts of services offered by private providers. (Smith and Lipsky, 9–10)

Three Ways to Incorporate a Quotation in the Text

Here, I show three models for incorporating a block quotation in the text. The quotations and introductory sentences come from Young's book chapter "Complimentary, supplementary, or adversarial? A theoretical and historical examination of nonprofit-government relations in the United States" (Young, 1999, pp. 42–45).

Model 1. Introduce the quotation with a summary of what it demonstrates. For example:

On one level, the relative roles of government and nonprofit organizations in the United States may be appreciated by examining how nonprofits have attended to collective needs left unaddressed by government:

> Americans had a long experience in founding voluntary agencies to perform tasks which individuals could not accomplish alone and which public bodies, for one reason or another, were not able to undertake. (Bremner 1988, 176)

Model 2. Introduce the quotation with a statement of what its author claims. For example:

Nielsen (1979) claims that the late nineteenth and early twentieth century was the period in which private initiative peaked in its prominence:

> ...in the last decades of the nineteenth century and the first decades of the twentieth century, many Third Sector institutions—in addition to the churches—developed private sources of support and simultaneously an ideology of separateness which affected the policies of both private agencies and government (14).

Model 3. Make your own claim and use the quotation as supporting evidence. For example:

The role of women was especially important in creating voluntary associations that addressed social needs in this era of weak government:

> While wealthy businessmen such as John D. Rockefeller and Andrew Carnegie lavished massive donations on growing crops of foundations, universities, museums, and think tanks created in the corporate image of their business ventures, women—even very wealthy women—continued to build their own organizations through an economy of time, rather than cash.... [These] voluntary associations were unusually influential in weak governmental systems, such as that of the United States in this era.... (McCarthy 1997, 145–146)

HOW TO SUMMARIZE

Summarizing is an essential skill for academic writing. It is important to keep in mind, however, that we do not summarize just for the sake of summarizing. We summarize to make a point—to support a claim, explain a view, or offer an interpretation. For example, we may summarize definitions to argue for the most appropriate one or to point out important limitations and then suggest our own; we may summarize previous findings to support particular expectations; or we may summarize and compare different authors' views or ideas to point out similarities and differences or to show how these views and ideas are relevant to our study.

In papers in public policy and economics, four kinds of summary are common.

1. **Summaries of the state of current knowledge**. These are typically sentence-long claims about the state of our knowledge about a particular topic or relationship. These summaries are followed by multiple citations. For example:

Recent studies of the impact of Mexico's drug war have also documented the significant negative effects of violent crime on economic outcomes, such as the lack of growth among businesses, regional growth convergence, employment, and labor earnings (Dell, 2015; Enamorado et al., 2014; Robles et al., 2013; Velásquez, 2014). (Enamorado et al., 2016, p. 129)

Poverty is a consequence of the low endowment of assets and the low returns to such assets (Baulch and Hoddinott, 2000; Barrett, 2005; Carter and Barrett, 2006). (Yamano & Kijima, 2010, p. 2)

2. **Summaries of individual (usually empirical) studies**. These are descriptions of what a particular author did in a study and what he or she found. In economics, such summaries often contain details about the methodology. For example:

Trpcevska (2014) examined the effect of the implementation of the single window and simplified customs procedures in Macedonia and found that these procedures had helped save time and human resources. She also found that the introduction of various trade facilitation measures was necessary to assist companies to compete more effectively in the international market; however, this research also used a qualitative approach. (Ahamadzie, 2016, p. 3)

Yang et al. (2008) investigate the impact of the petroleum price hike and an increase in biofuel production using a computable general equilibrium (CGE) model, based on the Global Trade Analysis Project (GTAP) database Version 6 (Table 2). Mitchell (2008) examines its impacts on the…cost of wheat and maize production in the US and [on] their domestic transportation costs. Charlesbois (2008) estimates the influence of export restrictions on crops using a multicountry dynamic partial equilibrium model. Rosegrant (2008) measures the impacts of biofuel production on these crops using a partial equilibrium model by assuming different biofuel production growth rates. Yang et al. (2008) also quantify its impact on prices of wheat and maize and find similar results to those [obtained] by Rosegrant (2008). These studies consistently show [that] real-side factors have only limited explanatory power for the crop price hikes. (Tanaka & Hosoe, 2011, p. 3)

3. **Summaries of arguments**. These are descriptions of other authors' claims and views, existing theories and definitions, and other nonempirical statements. For example:

There are several possible explanations for these surprising results. Rose and Spiegel (2011) suggest that it is not the event itself or the resulting tourism or advertising that increases exports, but rather that the very act of bidding serves as a credible signal that a country is committing itself to trade liberalization that will permanently increase trade flows. Brückner and Pappa (2015) theorize that the announcement of a bid for the Olympics represents a news shock predicting increases in future government investment. (Baade & Matheson, 2016, p. 213)

Xing (2012) argued that the processing imports of China represent external demand and should fall, not increase, as the yuan appreciates, and he demonstrated how processing imports would decrease 5.0% for a 10% real appreciation of the yuan against the US dollar. (Xing, 2016, p. 3)

4. **Comparative summaries**. These are summaries of various arguments, views, positions, or findings that authors pull together to support their own argument. The point here is not to summarize what different authors have said separately on a topic but to show how different authors or studies compare on various aspects of the topic and/or where the field stands as a whole. Below is an example from Conner and Rabovsky (2011).

Prior to the last decade, only a few studies attempted to explain higher education funding policy, and they generally tended to either ignore or downplay the importance of political variables and explanations. However, there have recently been a number of works that have begun to focus on the importance of politics in shaping appropriations decisions (Archibald & Feldman, 2006; Doyle, 2007; Lowry, 2001b; Nicholson-Crotty & Meier, 2003; Rizzo, 2004; Tandberg, 2006). Furthermore, during the last two years, a series of articles have built on this literature to integrate theories from public policy and political science into an understanding on higher education funding (Dar, 2010; Dar & Spence, 2010; McLendon, Mokher, & Doyle, 2009; Trostel & Ronca, 2009). For instance, McLendon, Hearn, and Mokher (2009) and Tandberg (2010, 2009) each focus heavily on the role that interest groups, institutional arrangements (such as term limits and gubernatorial power), and partisanship play in influencing the amount of money that states appropriate to higher education. All three articles find strong evidence that funding for higher education increases in the presence of a weaker governor, a larger percentage of Democratic control in the legislature, and as the number of higher education interest groups increase relative to other lobby groups in the state. Surprisingly, they also find a positive relationship between term limits and higher education support, which suggests the need for further research to explore the role that legislative experience plays in shaping principal-agent relationships between the state legislators and public universities (McLendon et al., 2009).

As state appropriations continue to decline relative to other sources of revenue, questions surrounding the potential implications of privatization in higher education have emerged as a central theme. Organizational scholars have long wrestled to understand how (and if) public and private organizations differ from one another along important dimensions such as efficiency and equity (Boyne, 2002; Bozeman, 1987; Bozeman & Bretschneider, 1994; Niskanen, 1971), and as public support for higher education decreases relative to private streams, these concerns have been raised with regards [to] higher education in the United States. In particular, many have argued that public support for higher education is vital to increase access, improve equity, and promote social progress (Heller, 2001b; Mumper, 2003; Ryan, 2004; Titus, 2006a). In an edited volume by Morphew and Eckel (2009), a collection of scholars approach the issue of privatization in higher education from a variety of disciplinary perspectives, including education, political science, economics, and organizations. Together, their works address a number of important questions regarding the extent to which privatization has occurred over the last decade and the impacts that continuing trends of privatization are likely to have on students, faculty, university administrators, and state policy makers in America during the decades to come. (Conner & Rabovsky, 2011, p. 97)

PARAGRAPH WRITING

The unit of academic writing is the paragraph and in this respect, academic writing is different from many other types of writing, such as business writing, where lists of bullet points are common, or journalistic writing, where articles often consist of a collection of loosely connected sentences.

Writing in paragraph form may be especially difficult for non-English students, particularly from cultures where there are no strict rules or conventions for paragraph writing. In the space below, I briefly explain what a paragraph is and give suggestions for composing paragraphs.

In English academic writing, a paragraph is a piece of writing that has the following characteristics:

- It contains more than one sentence.
- It contains one main idea, which needs development.
- It develops the main idea by explaining it, illustrating it with examples, supporting it with evidence, or comparing or contrasting some of its aspects.
- It begins on an indented line.

Often—but not always—a paragraph contains a topic sentence, a sentence that

- Introduces the main idea of the paragraph,
- Acts as an umbrella for all the other sentences in the paragraph, and
- States or implies the purpose of the paragraph.

Here is an example of a paragraph with a topic sentence (highlighted in bold):

The financial crisis in Thailand had severe effects on the economy. The confidence of depositors in the banking system was completely destroyed. Many firms, including banks and financial companies, were forced into bankruptcy. The financial system was stunned by problems involving liquidity and nonperforming loans.

In a section consisting of several paragraphs, the first paragraph often acts as a topic sentence for the entire section, introducing main ideas which are then elaborated in the paragraphs that follow.

Tips for Writing a Good Paragraph

- Avoid statements of fact in the topic sentence because these are difficult or impossible to develop. A good topic sentence should express a claim, which the sentences that follow should then develop.

- Do not start a topic sentence with "I think," "In my opinion," or similar phrases.

- Avoid using quotations in the topic sentence because quotations may be difficult to interpret.

- To develop a main idea in a paragraph, think of possible questions that your readers may have and try to answer them in the paragraph.

- Provide cohesion between the sentences in a paragraph with the help of linking words and phrases.

STYLE, GRAMMAR, AND EXPRESSION

Academic writing is formal writing and as such, it follows many rules and conventions for formal writing. Below I summarize some of the most common rules and conventions that apply to writing in many areas of public policy and economics. You may also wish to check a style guide such as *APA* or *Chicago* for more detailed rules that are used in your research area.

Rules and Conventions	Examples
It is common to spell out contractions or use a verb that does not require the use of a contraction in academic papers. However, in some research areas, contractions may be used even in formal writing.	**Less formal:** These methods **can't** identify all the variations in parental attitudes. **More formal:** These methods **cannot** identify all the variations in parental attitudes. **More formal:** These methods **fail** to identify all the variations in parental attitudes.
We tend to avoid the use of *etc.* and other run-on phrases in formal writing. A better alternative is to use *and* + a *summary word*.	**Less formal:** These methods make it possible to predict fatalities, injuries, property damage, **etc.** **More formal:** These methods make it possible to predict fatalities, injuries, property damage, **and other adverse consequences.**
In formal writing, we tend to avoid expressions of personal opinion (e.g., *in my opinion, I think, as I recall, I would guess, I imagine*).	**Less formal: In my opinion,** global warming is a serious problem. **More formal:** Research evidence suggests that global warming is a serious problem (citations).

Rules and Conventions	Examples
Be careful with the use of synonyms—they may introduce a difference in meaning that can be confusing to the reader.	**Confusing:** This paper describes a new research **method**. This **technique** enables.... **Better:** This paper describes a new research **method**. This **method** enables....
We tend to avoid informal prepositional verbs and prefer their more formal, single-word counterparts.	**Less formal:** Economists have **come up with** a number of methods to measure the effect of the new policy **More formal:** Economists have **developed/established** a number of methods to measure the effect of the new policy. **Less formal:** An unexpected problem **showed up/came up** during the experiment. **More formal:** An unexpected problem **was discovered/found** during the experiment. **Less formal:** Our purpose is to **find out** the optimal threshold for inflation targeting. **More formal:** Our purpose is to **determine** the optimal threshold for inflation targeting. **Less formal:** A funding policy was **set up** to prevent misuse of funds. **More formal:** A funding policy was **established** to prevent misuse of funds.
Avoid long noun strings (several nouns used to modify a final noun) because such strings may be confusing.	**Unclear:** US energy consumption investigation approach **Better:** An approach to investigating US energy consumption.
When using comparisons, make sure that it is clear what is being compared to what.	**Incorrect:** A well-functioning financial market is more important to agricultural development **than** urban development. **Correct:** A well-functioning financial market is more important to agricultural development **than to** urban development.
Use objective-case pronouns with these prepositions: *among, between, to, with, of, from*, and *for*.	**Incorrect:** Submit your responses to Dr. Goodwin and **I**. **Correct:** Submit your responses to Dr. Goodwin and **me**.
Make sure that the verb agrees in number with its subject, especially when there are intervening phrases such as *together with, including*, and *as well as*.	**Incorrect:** The **size** of the coefficient **as well as the sign confirm** our expectation. **Correct:** The **size** of the coefficient **as well as the sign confirms** our expectation.

Continued

Rules and Conventions	Examples
In sentences beginning with *there*, the verb agrees with the real subject, which comes after the verb.	**Incorrect**: There **has** been **many studies**... **Correct**: There **have** been **many studies**...
The word *data* requires a plural verb.	**Incorrect**: The data **was** obtained.... **Correct**: The data **were** obtained...
The word *phenomena* requires a plural verb.	**Incorrect**: These phenomena **was** studied. **Correct**: These phenomena **were** studied.
Avoid misplaced and dangling modifiers. Place the adjective or adverb as close as possible to the word it modifies.	**Incorrect: When introducing new policies, efficiency** should be a priority. **Correct: When introducing new policies, the government** should make efficiency a priority.
Present parallel ideas in parallel form.	**Incorrect:** We found that formally recruited workers were more productive **and received** higher wages. **Correct:** We found that formally recruited workers were more productive **and that they received** higher wages.
Make sure that all elements in a series are parallel in form.	**Incorrect:** The process is **safe, economical**, and **has high reliability**. **Correct:** The process is **safe, economical**, and **highly reliable.**
Avoid run-on sentences, or sentences in which two or more main clauses are written one after another without connecting words or correct punctuation.	**Incorrect:** There is no alternative to the current policy**, however,** there are several adjustments that could be made. **Correct:** There is no alternative to the current policy**; however,** there are several adjustments that could be made.
Avoid sentence fragments. A group of words is a complete sentence when it has a subject and a verb and when it expresses a complete thought.	**Fragment: As Smith shows in his article in which** he analyzes the effectiveness of financial assistance to Ghana. **Sentence: In his article, Smith analyzes** the effectiveness of financial assistance to Ghana and shows that financial assistance can significantly improve access to medical services and education. **Fragment: As we can see that** developed countries have a long history of problems with taxation. **Sentence: We can see that** developed countries have a long history of problems with taxation. **Fragment: As shown in Table 1 that** more than 62% of respondents were satisfied with their economic situation. **Sentence: As shown in Table 1**, more than 62% of respondents were satisfied with their economic situation.

PUNCTUATION

Colon	Use between a grammatically complete introductory clause (one that could stand as a sentence) and a clause that illustrates the preceding idea:
	The new policy had two goals: to introduce cost recovery measures and to improve efficiency.
Semicolon	Use to separate two independent clauses that are not joined by a conjunction:
	In 1999, the government launched a radical educational reform in order to create more equitable access at all forms and levels of education in the country; it also changed the structure of the school system, reducing the length of secondary education from 8 to 9 years.
Comma	Use to
	Separate a series of three or more elements:
	We need to consider efficiency, reliability, and cost.
	Set off a nonrestrictive relative clause (a clause that, if removed, would not change the grammatical structure and meaning of the sentence):
	The response rate was 27%, which is considered low for this type of surveys.
	Separate two independent clauses joined by a conjunction:
	These findings are unexpected, but they support our original theory.
	Separate a subordinate clause from an independent clause (beginning with *although, if,* or *whereas*):
	Although the results were unexpected, they supported our original theory.
	Separate a nonfinite clause from an independent clause (one that cannot stand on its own grammatically):
	After receiving the instructions, participants began reading immediately.

COMMON COLLOCATIONS
Multiple-Word Prepositions

according to	for the purpose of	owing to
along with	in addition to	prior to
as a consequence of	in case of	regardless of
as a result of	in comparison with	subsequent to
aside from	in connection with	with reference to
by means of	in contrast to/with	with regard to
contrary to	in favor of	with respect to
for the benefit of	on account of	with the exception of

Verb + Preposition

add to	consist of	divide into
agree with	invest in	engage in
associate with	focus on	learn from
attribute to	define as	model after
believe in	depend on	regard as
blame for	derive from	result in
concentrate on	distinguish from	specialize in

Adjective + Preposition

associated with	equal to	qualified for
aware of	impressed by	related to
capable of	inferior to	satisfied with
committed to	known for	similar to
composed of	pleased with	superior to
confined to	puzzled by/at	surprised by/at
confused about	conscious of	

Appendix A

Citation Guides

APA Style Guide: In-text Citations and Reference List

Part 1. In-text Citations (author, publication date)

Citations usually appear at the end of the sentence.

In the late 1970s, Japan began to fix ODA commitment levels in its medium-term plans (Martinussen, 2003). By the early 1990s, Japan was disbursing aid at a faster pace than other donors (Kobayashi, 1999; Petersen, 1997). Sunaga (2004) argues that throughout this period, ODA functioned as a key instrument of Japan's foreign policy. However, others have pointed out that Japan has been very selective in using aid to directly influence or punish another country's behavior (Soderberg, 1996, 2003). One example was in 1995 when, "under pressure from public opinion at home," Japan cut aid to China to protest its testing of nuclear weapons (Adams, 1996, p. 22). Although Japan is no longer the leading ODA donor, foreign aid is still a key foreign policy instrument.

You may refer directly to the author in your sentence.

If you include a quotation, give the exact page number.

Works by different authors in the same citation are alphabetized and separated by a semicolon.

Two or more works by the same author can be included in the same citation.

This is how to cite different types of authors

1 author	(Green, 2001)
2 authors	(Cohen & Spencer, 1994)
3 to 5 authors	First citation: (Pratkins, Breker, & Green, 1989) Subsequent citations: (Pratkins et al., 1989)
More than 5 authors	(Kneip et al., 1993)
Editor(s)	(Migdal, Kohli, & Shue, 1994)
Organization as author	First citation: (World Health Organization [WHO], 2005) Subsequent citations: (WHO, 2005)
Institution as author *The parent body precedes the subdivision.*	First citation: (People's Republic of China, Ministry of Finance [MOF], 2006) Subsequent citations: (MOF, 2006)
No author *Use the first few words of the title*	Book: (*Oxford*, 1996) [Full title: *Oxford essential world atlas*] Article: ("Book fuels mistrust," 2004) [Full title: Book fuels mistrust of meritocracy]

No date *Use n.d.*	(Smith, n.d.)
A source you have not read *Cite the source **you** read.*	Prasad's study (as cited in Yang, 2005)
2 or more works by the same author in the same year *In the reference list, alphabetize by title.*	(Shaw, 1999a, 1999b)
2 or more authors in one citation	(Green, 2001; Yang, 2005)

Part 2. The Reference List

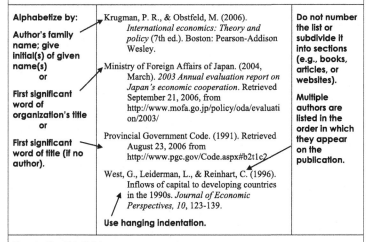

| Alphabetize by:

Author's family name; give initial(s) of given name(s)
or
First significant word of organization's title
or
First significant word of title (if no author). | Krugman, P. R., & Obstfeld, M. (2006). *International economics: Theory and policy* (7th ed.). Boston: Pearson-Addison Wesley.

Ministry of Foreign Affairs of Japan. (2004, March). *2003 Annual evaluation report on Japan's economic cooperation.* Retrieved September 21, 2006, from http://www.mofa.go.jp/policy/oda/evaluation/2003/

Provincial Government Code. (1991). Retrieved August 23, 2006 from http://www.pgc.gov/Code.aspx#b2t1c2

West, G., Leiderman, L., & Reinhart, C. (1996). Inflows of capital to developing countries in the 1990s. *Journal of Economic Perspectives, 10*, 123-139.

Use hanging indentation. | Do not number the list or subdivide it into sections (e.g., books, articles, or websites).

Multiple authors are listed in the order in which they appear on the publication. |

How to Use This Table

Find the category of your source (e.g., journal article). Follow the basic model and see the examples for variations. Closely follow the style of capitalization, italicization, and punctuation.

How to Cite Online Sources (in order of preference)

DOI: If a Digital Object Identifier is available, use it instead of retrieval information. It looks like this: doi:10.1111/j.1467-6419.2009.00609.x

Stable internet address: If there is no DOI, but you found the source at a "stable" internet address, such as http://www.jstor.org/stable/25064490, include the address, but no retrieval date.

Changeable internet address: If the internet address is subject to change (i.e., does not include the word "stable"), include both the address and your retrieval date, like this: Retrieved October 24, 2005, from http://www.oecd.org/dataoecd.pdf

BOOK	Author, A. B. (Year). *Book title.* City: Publisher.
Authored book	Krugman, P. R., & Obstfeld, M. (2006). *International economics: Theory and policy* (7th ed.). Boston: Pearson-Addison Wesley.
Edited book (chapters written by different authors) *See also* book chapter	Migdal, J. S., Kohli, A., & Shue, V. (Eds.). (1994). *State power and social forces: Domination and transformation in the Third World.* Cambridge: Cambridge University Press.
JOURNAL ARTICLE	Author, A. B. (Year). Article title. *Title of Journal, vol*(no), page#-page#.
Journal article (print only)	Calvo, G., Leiderman, L., & Reinhart, C. (1996). Inflows of capital to developing countries in the 1990s. *Journal of Economic Perspectives, 10,* 123-139.
Journal article (print and online)	Linares, P., & Labardiera, X. (1999). Energy efficiency: Economics and policy. *Journal of Economic Surveys, 24*(3), 573–592.
Journal article (online only)	MacLachlan, P. (2004). Post office politics in Japan: The postmasters, iron triangles, and the limits of reform. *Journal of Japanese Studies, 30,* 281-313. http://www.jstor.org/stable/25064490
THESIS or DISSERTATION	Author, A. B. (Year). *Title.* (Unpublished master's thesis). School, location.
Thesis	Angelova, A. N. (2004). *Data pruning.* (Unpublished master's thesis). California Institute of Technology, Pasadena, CA.
Dissertation	Young, R. F. (2007). *Crossing boundaries in urban ecology: Pathways to sustainable cities.* (Unpublished doctoral dissertation). Cornell University, Ithaca, NY.
BOOK CHAPTER	Author, A. B. (Year). Chapter title. In X. Y. Editor (Ed.), *Title of book* (pp. page#-page#). City: Publisher.
Book chapter (in an edited book)	Shue, V. (1994). State power and social organization in China. In J. S. Migdal, A. Kohli, & V. Shue (Eds.), *State power and social forces: Domination and transformation in the Third World* (pp. 65-88). Cambridge: Cambridge University Press.
Encyclopedia entry (print, with author)	Pittau, J. (1983). Meiji constitution. In *Kodansha encyclopedia of Japan* (Vol. 2, pp. 1-3). Tokyo: Kodansha.
Encyclopedia entry (online, no author)	Ethnology. (2005, July). In *The Columbia encyclopedia* (6th ed.). New York: Columbia University Press. Retrieved November 21, 2005, from http://www.bartleby.com/65/et/ethnolog.html

CONFERENCE PAPER	Author, A. B. (Year, Month Day). *Paper title.* Paper presented at the Conference Title, Place of Conference. Retrieved Month Day, Year, from http://...
Conference paper	Pasadilla, G. O., & Milo, M. (2005, June 27). *Effect of liberalization on banking competition.* Paper presented at the Conference on Policies to Strengthen Productivity in the Philippines, Manila, Philippines. Retrieved August 23, 2006, from http://siteresources.worldbank.org/ INTPHILIPPINES/Resources/Pasadilla.pdf
RESEARCH REPORT, WORKING PAPER, TECHNICAL PAPER	Author, A. B. (Year, Month). *Title of paper* (Series Name, Report No. #). Retrieved Month Day, Year, from http://...
Put series name and report number (if any) in parentheses immediately after the title and before the period.	Organization for Economic Cooperation and Development. (2001). *Trends in international migration: Continuous reporting system on migration* (Annual Report, 2001). Retrieved October 24, 2005, from http:// www.oecd.org/dataoecd/23/41/2508596.pdf Ministry of Foreign Affairs of Japan. (2004, March). *2003 annual evaluation report on Japan's economic cooperation.* Retrieved September 21, 2006, from http://www.mofa.go.jp/policy/oda/evaluation/2003/ Maki, D. (2005, October). *FDI flows to Asia* (IMF Working Paper 07/199). Washington, DC: IMF. Retrieved October 30, 2005, from http://www.imf.org/external/pubs Cowan, K., & Gregorio, J. D. (2005). *International borrowing, capital controls and the exchange rate: Lessons from Chile* (NBER Working Paper 11382). Retrieved January 30, 2006, from http://www.nber.org/papers/w11382

GOVERNMENT DOCUMENT

Executive directive	Executive Order 34/2006. *Code of Federal Regulations*, sec. 586. (2006).
Legislation	Local Government Code of the Philippines. (1991). Retrieved August 23, 2006 from http://www.dilg.gov.ph/ LocalGovernmentCode.aspx#b2t1c2
Government publication	Royal Government of Bhutan. Department of Revenue and Customs. (1998). *Bhutan tax manual, 1998.* Thimphu: Royal Government of Bhutan.

DATA or MATERIAL from WEBSITES

| Published data | World Bank. (2002). *Governance indicators: 1996-2002.* Retrieved July 21, 2004, from http://www.worldbank.org/wbi/governance/govdata2002

Commission on Higher Education. (2008). *CHED statistical bulletin 2007-2008.* Retrieved May 27, 2009, from http://www.ched.gov.ph, updated January 30, 2009. |

Unpublished data, updated frequently	National Bureau of Statistics. (n.d.). [Yearly statistics]. Retrieved July 23, 2006, from http://www.nbs.gov/stat, updated June 30, 2006. *If no title is given, describe the data in brackets.*
Material from an organizational or institutional website	Bank for International Settlements. (n.d.). Banking services for central banks. Retrieved September 21, 2006, from http://www.bis.org/banking/index.htm

UNPUBLISHED RAW DATA

Raw data collected by you or obtained from an organization or a researcher	National Bureau of Statistics of Japan. (2006). [Sources of local revenue]. Unpublished raw data.

COMPUTER SOFTWARE

	Miller, M. E. (1993). The Interactive Tester (Version 4.0). [Computer software]. Westminster, CA: Psytek Services.

NEWS or PRESS RELEASE

Print	Harbinus, A. (2006, April 1). China's exchange rate: Gently towards the heavens. *The Economist,* pp. 59-60.
Online	Stewart, I. (2004, December 18). Book fuels mistrust of meritocracy. *South China Morning Post.* Retrieved June 10, 2005, from http://www.singapore-window.org/sw00/001218sc.htm
No author	Book fuels mistrust of meritocracy. (2004, December 18). *South China Morning Post*, p. A12.
Press release (online)	World Health Organization. (2005, October 21). Safe water remains top priority in Pakistan. Retrieved November 4, 2005, from http://www.who.int/en/

NON-ENGLISH WORK

Original title with your translation	Utomo, H. (2005, August 1). Pendidikan asar untuk rakyat miskin [Primary education for poor people]. *Kompas*, p. 34.
Translated title only	Utomo, H. (2005, August 1). Primary education for poor people (in Indonesian). *Kompas*, p. 34.

Chicago Style Guide: Notes and Bibliography

Part 1. Basic Principles

Citations are indicated in the text by a superscript note reference that refers the reader to the numbered source note.

Note references usually appear at the end of the sentence.

Many theoretical and empirical studies have found connections between financial development and economic growth. Schumpeter contended that well-functioning banks spur technological innovation, thereby promoting economic growth.[1] King and Levine used cross-country regression analysis with data on 80 countries to determine whether higher levels of financial development are positively associated with economic growth.[2] They concluded that there is an important link, agreeing with Schumpeter's notion that "the banker...authorizes people, in the name of society as it were, to...[innovate]."[3] The cross-country regression approach has been criticized as ignoring large differences between countries and their development, yielding unreliable results due to the instability of long-term series data, and being insufficient for explaining the direction of causality.[4] In an effort to avoid these shortcomings, many economists have recently opted instead to use time series regression to examine the relationship between financial development and economic growth. Whereas Rajan and Zingales, using this approach, found that "financial development has a substantial supportive influence on the rate of economic growth,"[5] others have identified a two-way causal relationship.[6]

The first citation (F) for each work includes author's name (conventional order), title of work, and full publication details.

Subsequent citations use the short form (S).

Ibid. (not italicized) refers to the single work cited in the immediately preceding note.

If you include a quotation, give the page number.

Works by different authors are separated by a semicolon.

---

[1] Joseph A. Schumpeter, *The Theory of Economic Development: An Inquiry Into Profits, Capital, Credit, Interest, and the Business Cycle* (Cambridge, MA: Harvard University Press, 1911).

[2] Robert G. King and Ross Levine, "Finance and Growth: Schumpeter Might be Right," *The Quarterly Journal of Economics* 108, no. 3 (1993).

[3] Schumpeter, *Theory of Economic Development*, 74.

[4] Raghuram G. Rajan and Luigi Zingales, "Financial Dependence and Growth," *The American Economic Review* 88, no. 3 (1998).

[5] Ibid., 584.

[6] Valerie R. Bencivenga and Bruce D. Smith, "Financial Intermediation and Endogenous Growth," *The Review of Economic Studies* 58, no. 2 (1998); Keith Blackburn and Victor T. Y. Hung, "A Theory of Growth: Financial Development and Trade," *Economica* 65, no. 257 (1998).

The bibliography lists all cited works (exceptions noted below) in alphabetical order. It gives the same information as the first citation, but it is formatted differently.

Alphabetize by author's family name.

List multiple authors in the order in which they appear in the publication.

Use hanging indentation

Bencivenga, Valerie R., and Bruce D. Smith. "Financial Intermediation and Endogenous Growth." *The Review of Economic Studies* 58, no. 2 (1998): 195-209.

Blackburn, Keith, and Victor T. Y. Hung. "A Theory of Growth: Financial Development and Trade." *Economica* 65, no. 257 (1998): 107-124.

King, Robert G., and Ross Levine. "Finance and Growth: Schumpeter Might be Right." *The Quarterly Journal of Economics* 108, no. 3 (1993): 717-737.

Rajan, Raghuram G., and Luigi Zingales. "Financial Dependence and Growth." *The American Economic Review* 88, no. 3 (1998): 559-586.

Schumpeter, Joseph A. *The Theory of Economic Development: An Inquiry Into Profits, Capital, Credit, Interest, and the Business Cycle*. Cambridge, MA: Harvard University Press, 1934.

Do not number the list or subdivide it into sub-sections (e.g., books, articles, websites).

Part 2. Specific Content

Type of Work	(F)	First citation (full information)
	(S)	Subsequent citations (short form)
	(B)	Bibliography entry (full information)

BOOK (Author variations shown here apply to all types of work)

Authored book	(F)	[1] Elizabeth J. Remick, *Building Local States: China during the Republican and Post-Mao Periods* (Cambridge, MA: Harvard University Press, 2004), 85.
		[2] Remick, *Building Local States*, 31.
	(S)	Remick, Elizabeth J. *Building Local States: China during the Republican and Post-Mao Periods*. Cambridge, MA: Harvard University Press, 2004.
	(B)	
Edited book *To cite one chapter, see* **book chapter** *below.*	(F)	[3] Bjørn Lomborg, ed., *Global Crises, Global Solutions* (Cambridge: Cambridge University Press, 2004), 422.
	(S)	[4] Lomborg, *Global Crises*, 385.
	(B)	Lomborg, Bjørn, ed. *Global Crises, Global Solutions*. Cambridge: Cambridge University Press, 2004.
2 authors or editors	(F)	[5] Peter J. Katzenstein and Yutaka Tsujinaka, *Defending the Japanese State* (Ithaca, NY: Cornell University East Asia Program, 1991), 129.
	(S)	[6] Katzenstein and Tsujinaka, *Defending the Japanese State*, 136.
	(B)	Katzenstein, Peter J., and Yutaka Tsujinaka. *Defending the Japanese State*. Ithaca, NY: Cornell University East Asia Program, 1991.
3 authors or editors	(F)	[7] Kartik C. Roy, Clement A. Tisdell, and Hans C. Blomqvist, eds., *Economic Development and Women* (Westport, CT: Praeger Publishers, 1999), 55.
		[8] Roy, Tisdell, and Blomqvist, *Economic Development and Women*, 80.
	(S)	Roy, Kartik C., Clement A. Tisdell, and Hans C. Blomqvist, eds. *Economic Development and Women*. Westport, CT: Praeger Publishers, 1999.
	(B)	
4 or more authors or editors	(F)	[9] Cynthia C. Cook et al., eds., ...
	(S)	[10] Cook et al., ...
	(B)	Cook, Cynthia C., Tyrrell Duncan, Somchai Jitsuchon, Anil Sharma, and Wu Guobao, eds. ...
Institution as author	(F)	[11] United Nations Conference on Trade and Development, *Controlling Carbon Dioxide Emissions: The Tradeable Permit System* (Geneva: UNCTAD, 1995), 24.
	(S)	[12] UNCTAD, *Controlling Carbon Dioxide Emissions*, 26.
	(B)	United Nations Conference on Trade and Development. *Controlling Carbon Dioxide Emissions: The Tradeable Permit System*. Geneva: UNCTAD, 1995.

JOURNAL ARTICLE, BOOK CHAPTER, CONFERENCE PAPER

Journal article (accessed in print)	(F) (S) (B)	[15] Lisa Claypool, "Zhang Jian and China's First Museum," *The Journal of Asian Studies* 64, no. 3 (2005): 575. [16] Claypool, "Zhang Jian," 580. Claypool, Lisa. "Zhang Jian and China's First Museum." *The Journal of Asian Studies* 64, no. 3 (2005): 567-604.
Journal article (accessed online)	(F) (S) (B)	[17] Eugene F. Provenzo, Jr. "Time Exposure," *Educational Studies* 34, no. 2 (2003): 266, doi: 10.1080/ 00131946.2012.668481 [18] Provenzo, "Time Exposure," 268. Provenzo, Eugene F. "Time Exposure." *Educational Studies* 34, no. 2 (2003): 250-75. http://search.epnet.com. doi: 10.1080/ 00131946.2012.668481
Journal article (electronic only)	(F) (S) (B)	[19] Supang Chantavanich, "Recent Research on Human Trafficking," *Kyoto Review of Southeast Asia* 4 (2003), http://kyotoreview.cseas. kyoto-u.ac.jp/issue/issue3/index.html (accessed March 8, 2006). [20] Chantavanich, "Recent Research on Human Trafficking." Chantavanich, Supang. "Recent Research on Human Trafficking." *Kyoto Review of Southeast Asia* 4 (2003). http://kyotoreview.cseas.kyoto-u.ac.jp/issue/issue3/index.html (accessed March 8, 2006).
Book chapter	(F) (S) (B)	[21] Jane Richardson, "Women in the Japanese Workplace," in *Economic Development and Women*, ed. Kartik C. Roy, Clement A. Tisdell, and Hans C. Blomqvist (Westport, CT: Praeger Publishers, 1999). [22] Richardson and Riethmuller, "Women," 93. Richardson, Jane. "Women in the Japanese Workplace." In *Economic Development and Women*, edited by Kartik C. Roy, Clement A. Tisdell, and Hans C. Blomqvist, 79-96. Westport, CT: Praeger Publishers, 1999.
Conference paper	(F) (S) (B)	[23] Gloria O. Pasadilla, and Melani Milo, "Effect of Liberalization on Banking Competition" (Paper presented at the conference on Policies to Strengthen Productivity in the Philippines, Manila, Philippines, June 27, 2005), http://siteresources.worldbank.org/INTPHILIPPINES /Resources/Pasadilla.pdf (accessed August 23, 2006). [24] Pasadilla and Milo, "Effect of Liberalization." Pasadilla, Gloria O., and Melani Milo. "Effect of Liberalization on Banking Competition." Paper presented at the conference on Policies to Strengthen Productivity in the Philippines, Manila, Philippines, June 27, 2005. http://siteresources.worldbank.org /INTPHILIPPINES/Resources/Pasadilla.pdf (accessed August 23, 2006).
Encyclopedia entry (print)	(F) (S) (B)	[25] *Kodansha Encyclopedia of Japan*, 1st ed., s.v. "Meiji constitution." [26] *Kodansha Encyclopedia of Japan*, s.v. "Meiji constitution." [No entry]
Encyclopedia entry (online)	(F) (S) (B)	[27] *Columbia Encyclopedia*, 6th ed., s.v. "Ethnology," http://www .bartleby.com/65/et/ethnolog.html (accessed November 21, 2005). [28] *Columbia Encyclopedia*, s.v. "Ethnology." [No entry]

RESEARCH REPORT, WORKING PAPER

Research report	(F)	[29] Organization for Economic Cooperation and Development [OECD], *Trends in International Migration: Continuous Reporting System on Migration* (Annual Report, 2001), 83, http://www.oecd.org /dataoecd/23/41/ 2508596.pdf (accessed September 21, 2006).
	(S)	[30] OECD, *Trends in International Migration*, 52.
	(B)	Organization for Economic Cooperation and Development. *Trends in International Migration: Continuous Reporting System on Migration.* Annual Report, 2001. http://www.oecd.org/dataoecd /23/41/2508596.pdf (accessed September 21, 2006).
	(F)	[31] Ministry of Foreign Affairs of Japan [MOF], *2003 Annual Evaluation Report on Japan's Economic Cooperation* (March, 2004), http://www.mofa.go.jp/policy/oda/evaluation/2003/ (accessed September 21, 2006).
	(S)	[32] MOF, *2003 Annual Evaluation Report.*
	(B)	Ministry of Foreign Affairs of Japan. *2003 Annual Evaluation Report on Japan's Economic Cooperation.* http://www.mofa.go.jp/policy /oda/evaluation/2003/ (accessed September 21, 2006).
Working paper	(F)	[33] Danilyn Maki, "FDI Flows to Asia" (Working Paper 07/199, International Monetary Fund, 2005), http://www.imf.org/external /pubind.htm (accessed October 30, 2005).
	(S)	[34] Maki, "FDI Flows."
	(B)	Maki, Danilyn. "FDI Flows to Asia." Working Paper 07/199, International Monetary Fund, 2005. http://www.imf.org/external /pubind.htm (accessed October 30, 2005).
	(F)	[35] Kevin Cowan and Jose D. Gregorio, "International Borrowing, Capital Controls and the Exchange Rate: Lessons from Chile" (NBER Working Paper 11382, 2005), http://www.nber.org/papers/w11382 (accessed June 30, 2006).
	(S)	[36] Cowan and Gregorio, "International Borrowing."
	(B)	Cowan, Kevin., and Jose D. Gregorio. "International Borrowing, Capital Controls and the Exchange Rate: Lessons from Chile." NBER Working Paper 11382. NBER, 2005. http://www.nber.org /papers/w11382 (accessed June 30, 2006).

GOVERNMENT DOCUMENT

Executive directive	(F)	[37] Executive Order no. 34, *Code of Federal Regulations*, sec. 586 (2006).
	(S)	[38] Executive Order no. 34.
	(B)	[No entry]
Legislation	(F)	[39] Singapore Attorney General, *Trade Disputes Act*, chapter 331 (1985), http://statutes.agc.gov.sg/.
	(S)	[40] Singapore Attorney General, *Trade Disputes Act.*
	(B)	[No entry]
Government publication	(F)	[41] Department of Revenue and Customs, Royal Government of Bhutan, *Bhutan Tax Manual, 1998* (Thimphu: Royal Government of Bhutan, 1998), 118.
	(S)	[42] Department of Revenue and Customs, *Bhutan Tax Manual, 1998*, 145–150.
	(B)	Department of Revenue and Customs. Royal Government of Bhutan. *Bhutan Tax Manual, 1998.* Thimphu: Royal Government of Bhutan, 1998.

NEWS or PRESS RELEASE

Magazine article	(F)	[43] Andres Harbinus, "China's Exchange Rate: Gently Towards the Heavens," *The Economist,* April 1-7, 2006, 59-60.
	(S)	[44] Harbinus, "China's Exchange Rate," 59.
	(B)	[Usually no entry]
Newspaper article	(F)	[45] Ian Stewart, "Book Fuels Mistrust of Meritocracy," *South China Morning Post,* December 18, 2000, http://www.singapore-window.org/sw00/001218sc.htm (accessed October 2, 2007).
	(S)	[46] Stewart, "Book Fuels Mistrust of Meritocracy."
	(B)	[Usually no entry]
Press release	(F)	[47] World Health Organization, "Shelter and Water Remain a Top Priority in Pakistan," October 21, 2005, http://www.who.int/en/ (accessed November 4, 2005).
	(S)	[48] World Health Organization, "Shelter and Water."
	(B)	[Usually no entry]

OTHER SOURCES

Published data	(F)	[49] World Bank, "Governance Indicators: 1996-2002," http://www.worldbank.org/wbi/governance/govdata2002 (accessed July 21, 2004).
	(S)	[50] World Bank, "Governance Indicators."
	(B)	World Bank. "Governance Indicators: 1996-2002." http://www.worldbank.org/wbi/governance/govdata2002 (accessed July 21, 2004).
Unpublished data	(F)	[51] National Bureau of Statistics, unpublished yearly statistics, http://www.nbs.gov/stat (accessed July 23, 2006).
	(S)	[52] National Bureau of Statistics, unpublished yearly statistics.
	(B)	National Bureau of Statistics. Unpublished yearly statistics. http://www.nbs.gov/stat (accessed July 23, 2006).
Material from organization or institutional website	(F)	[53] Bank for International Settlements, "Banking Services for Central Banks," undated, http://www.bis.org/banking/index.htm (accessed March 21, 2006).
	(S)	[54] Bank for International Settlements, "Banking Services."
	(B)	Bank for International Settlements. "Banking Services for Central Banks." Undated. http://www.bis.org/banking/index.htm (accessed March 21, 2006).

NON-ENGLISH WORK (Provide translation of title in brackets)

Newspaper article	(F)	[55] Hadi Utomo, "Pendidikan Asar Untuk Rakyat Miskin" [Primary Education for Poor People], *Kompas,* August 1, 2005, p. 34.
	(S)	[56] Utomo, "Pendidikan Asar."
	(B)	Utomo, Hadi. "Pendidikan Asar Untuk Rakyat Miskin" [Primary Education for Poor People]. *Kompas,* August 1, 2005, p. 34.

Appendix B

Model Papers

Model Papers

This Appendix contains three papers written by graduate students as part of the graduation requirements of their programs. The students wrote these papers at the end of their one-year study while taking classes full-time. These papers represent a substantial achievement on the part of each of the students and as such, they are good models to show what can be achieved in a one-year graduate program in public policy or economics.

The first paper was written by Zongly (Lily) Hu, a Chinese student from the Public Finance program. Lily conducted an empirical regression-based study on the relationship between intellectual property rights protection and economic growth.

The second paper was written by Susan Bultitude, an Australian student from the Young Leaders Program. In her qualitative paper, Susan relied on academic literature and policy documents to trace the origins and implications of two economic bubbles—Japan's bubble economy and Australia's housing boom.

The third paper was written by Susanthi Medha Kumari, a Sri-Lankan student in Asian Economic Policy. In her quantitative paper, Medha investigated the determinants of interest margins of banks in Sri Lanka. Medha's paper was later published in the *South Asia Economic Journal* (2014, Vol. 15, pp. 265-280) and you can read the published version here. This paper is based on a proposal Medha wrote earlier in her program, which is shown in Chapter 7.

Go over each paper and analyze it for content, structure and organization, and language use. Below are some suggestions for what you could focus on in your analysis. Also, look closely at individual sections in each of the papers. What information do the authors include in each section and why? How do they organize this information?

Content

- What is the topic of the paper?
- What is the purpose of the paper?
- What are the main concepts under study? How are they defined?
- What data are used? Where do the data come from?
- What is the study's methodology? Is it appropriate for the study's purpose?
- What are the main findings? Are they in line with those of previous research (as outlined in the literature review)?
- What is the main argument of the paper? Is it warranted by the presented evidence?
- What kind of title does the paper have? Does it reflect what the paper is about?

Structure and Organization

Look at the headings of each section. How do they help you navigate the paper? In what way are the headings of the quantitative papers different from those of the qualitative paper?

How much space does the author of each paper devote to the description of the three conceptual parts that are described in Chapter 8:

- Research background
- Methodology
- Results and main arguments

Language

Use of linguistic markers. Go over each paper and highlight the various linguistic markers that the authors use. (See Chapter 1 for a review of linguistic markers.) How do these markers help the authors engage the reader, direct the reader to what is important, show proper respect for the reader, and present themselves as an authority?

Use of citations. How do the authors use in-text citations? Which arguments are supported by integral, and which ones, by nonintegral citations? What signal phrases are most common in each paper?

Use of verbs and verb tense. What verbs and verb tenses do the authors use most frequently when describing previous research? When referring to their own results? When describing the visuals? When explaining implications and providing recommendations?

Paper Sections

- **Abstract**: What information do the authors include in the abstract? How does the abstract of the qualitative paper differ from those of the quantitative papers?

- **Introduction:** How do the authors describe the problem under study and how do they indicate its importance? How do they describe a research gap? What kind of gap does each paper have? How do the authors describe the purpose of their study and its contribution?

- **Review of previous research:** Where do the authors review previous research? Do they have a separate literature review section? If not, why not? How do the authors organize previous research? What order do they impose on the material? How is the literature review in the qualitative paper different from that in the quantitative papers? What specific arguments do the authors make about previous research and how do they support their arguments? How strongly do they word their arguments? How do they summarize previous studies (i.e., in how much detail)?

- **Data and Methodology:** What specific details do the authors include in the description of the data and methodology?

- **Results and Discussion**: How do the authors present their results? How do they interpret them? How often do they refer to the visuals and for what specific purposes?

- **Conclusion**: What information do the authors include in the conclusion?

Intellectual Property Rights and Economic Growth:
An Empirical Study of Developing Countries
By Zongli Hu

Abstract

Theoretical models of economic growth predict that intellectual property rights (IPR) protection can be both harmful to and beneficial for the growth of developing countries. This paper reports on an empirical study that investigated the effect of IPR protection on economic growth in developing countries. Results show that IPR protection has no clear relationship with economic growth when all developing countries are pooled together. However, the impact of IPR on economic growth in developing countries appears to depend on a country's growth rate. When the dataset was divided into high-growth and low-growth developing countries, a positive and significant relationship between IPR protection and economic growth was found for high-growth developing countries. In contrast, there was no conclusive evidence of a relationship between IPR and economic growth in low-growth developing countries.

1. Introduction

In this century of knowledge and ideas, the topic of international property rights (IPR) protection has been attracting attention all around the world. IPR protection refers to the protection of the inventions of the human mind. This protection is thought to stimulate innovation, which in turn leads to economic growth. During recent decades, there has been a global trend towards stronger intellectual property rights protection, and this trend has recently extended from developed to developing countries (Forero-Pineda, 2006).

Because most high-tech products requiring IPR protection are outputs of advanced economies, developed countries have more incentive than developing countries to enforce stronger protection of IPR. Developed countries seek to motivate innovators and prevent free riders from other countries by protecting IPR, thus making innovation profitable.

On the other hand, developing countries often catch up with developed countries by way of imitation. Therefore, excessive protection of IPR may harm the development of domestic industries in developing countries. Moreover, the cost of IPR protection is higher for developing countries than for developed countries. Thus, many policy makers question the incentives for developing countries to protect IPR. Despite this lack of incentive in developing countries to enforce IPR protection, a milestone for IPR protection was reached with the signing of the World Trade Organization's (WTO) agreement on trade-related aspects of intellectual property rights (TRIPS), which came into force in 1995. Some developing countries became members of the TRIPS agreement and enforced stronger IPR protection. This may be because in the 21st century's global economic environment, in order to boost the economy, developing countries have to facilitate international trade and attract foreign direct investment. In many instances, this requires enforcing IPR protection. If developing countries do not comply with IPR regulations, they may be forced to stay out of global trade and may encounter economic stagnation.

Several empirical studies have been conducted regarding the relationship between IPR protection and economic growth for developed and developing countries. Gould and Gruben (1996), for example, examined the role of IPR protection for growth in open versus closed trade regimes. Their results show that the effect on growth of IPR protection is slightly stronger in relatively open economies. Regarding IPR protection and innovation, Schneider (2005) found a more significant impact of IPR protection on the innovation rate for developed countries. Similarly, Falvey, Foster, and Greenaway (2006) found a positive relationship between IPR protection and economic growth for low-income and high-income countries, but not for middle-income countries. Other studies (e.g., Chu, 2009) suggest a strong impact from IPR protection on growth in developed countries, but ambiguous results for developing countries.

In keeping with this observation, Alikhan and Mashelkar (2009) suggest that the potential economic value of IPR protection in developing countries should be fully explored, especially in scientifically advanced developing countries. However, there is a limited number of studies regarding the effect of IPR protection in developing countries, and no study has yet examined the effect of IPR protection in advanced developing countries. In this paper, I try to fill this gap by answering the question: Do the effects of IPR protection differ between high-growth and low-growth developing economies? In order to answer this question, I conducted an empirical study using an ordinary least squares regression analysis. I used a panel dataset of 89 developing countries covering a 35-year period, from 1971 to 2005.

I separated the developing countries into high-growth and low-growth countries. The results show that IPR protection has a much stronger effect on economic growth in high-growth developing countries than in low-growth developing countries. The findings suggest that when the growth rate of a developing country reaches a certain level, IPR protection may play an important role in economic growth.

In the following sections, I will first briefly introduce IPR and explain how it is related to economic growth. Then, in section 3, the methodology of this empirical study is presented. Section 4 describes the data. Section 5 shows results. In section 6, I test the robustness of my results. Finally, section 7 reports the conclusion of this paper.

2. Intellectual property rights

The World Intellectual Property Organization (WIPO) broadly defines intellectual property as the legal rights that result from intellectual activity in the industrial, scientific, literary, and artistic fields. The convention establishing the WIPO states in Article 2 that "intellectual property shall include rights relating to: literary, artistic and scientific works, performances of performing artists, phonograms, and broadcasts, inventions in all fields of human endeavor, scientific discoveries, industrial designs, trademarks, service marks, and commercial names and designations, protection against unfair competition, and all other rights resulting from intellectual activity in the industrial, scientific, literary or artistic fields" (WIPO, 2001).

2.1 Brief history of IPR

The earliest attempts to implement IPR protection date back to the late 19th century. To meet the need for a uniform legal system of intellectual property and copyright protection among different countries, the Berne Convention for the Protection of Literary and Artistic Works was adopted in 1886. It was followed by the Paris Convention for the Protection of Industrial Property, established in 1888. During the 20th century, other international treaties and conventions on IPR, such as the Patent Cooperation Treaty and the Trademark Law Treaty, were concluded. However, these treaties and conventions cover different fields of IPR. In 1995, the most comprehensive international agreement, the TRIPS agreement, came into force. The TRIPS agreement covers copyright and related rights, trademarks, geographical indications, industrial designs, patents, layout designs (topographies) of integrated circuits, and undisclosed information (WIPO, 2001).

Initiated by the developed countries, the TRIPS agreement has had a dramatic influence on the decisions of developing countries regarding IPR protection. However, the question still remains as to what costs and benefits the TRIPS agreement brings to developing countries. Matthews (2002) analyzed the beneficial effects and the costs of the TRIPS agreement for developing countries. He stated that the benefits of the TRIPS agreement for developing countries mainly include increased foreign direct investment, greater transfer of know-how and expertise, higher levels of domestic innovation, and reduced threat of bilateral trade sanctions from the U.S. due to the content of dispute settlement included in the TRIPS agreement. However, he pointed out that the costs of the TRIPS agreement for developing countries include possible restriction of access to technologies and information as a result of patent protection. Thus, whether the benefits of IPR protection outweigh the costs in developing countries remains an open question.

2.2 IPR protection and economic growth theory

While the extended Solow model with human capital of Mankiw, Romer, and Weil (1992) has, in many respects, become a benchmark in the economic growth literature, it does not provide a linkage between IPR and economic growth. Grossman and Helpman (1991) developed an endogenous growth model for the analysis of innovation and growth. They argued that innovation and growth depend on the diffusion of technology, and IPR protection plays an important role in this process. Barro and Sala-i-Martin (2003) developed a growth model to analyze technological diffusion. Their main idea is that follower countries catch up with the leaders by taking advantage of imitation, which is less costly than innovation.

Another channel through which IPR may affect economic growth is international trade. Gould and Gruben (1996) found a stronger linkage between intellectual property protection and innovation in open trade regimes, which suggests that market structure may affect the relationship between IPR, innovation, and growth. Schneider (2005) argued that imports may introduce previously unavailable innovations in the domestic market. Therefore, trade stimulates technological diffusion, which in turn enhances economic growth.

These theories and empirical results help to identify the channels through which IPR may affect economic growth. Moreover, they suggest that the effects of IPR on economic growth differ between leaders and followers (Barro & Sala-i-Martin, 1997), between the North and the South (Helpman, 1993), and between developed and developing countries (Ginarte & Park, 1997). However, no empirical study has yet investigated the effects of IPR protection on the economic growth of high-growth versus low-growth developing countries. This paper attempts to fill this empirical void.

3. Methodology

My analysis uses ordinary least squares regressions to investigate the effect of IPR protection on economic growth for 89 developing countries. The panel data used in this study consist of 7 sub-periods: 1971-1975, 1976-1980, 1981-1985, 1986-1990, 1991-1995, 1996-2000, and 2001-2005. The panel regressions were estimated using country dummies and year dummies to control for omitted variables that change over time and between countries.

The first growth equation is estimated as follows:

$$\gamma_{it} = \beta_0 + \beta_1 \text{IniGDP}_{it} + \beta_2 S^k_{it} + \beta_3 S^h_{it} + \beta_4 \text{ngd}_{it} + \beta_5 \text{Trade}_{it} + \beta_6 \text{IPR}_{it} + \varepsilon_{it} \tag{1}$$

where the dependent variable, γ, is the 5-year GDP growth rate during each sub-period. The independent variables are the determinants of economic growth: *IniGDP* is the initial real GDP per capita at the beginning of each sub-period; S^k is the investment share of GDP, and S^h is a proxy for human capital. In order to test the robustness of the results, I used two common proxies that are used in the literature for human capital: S^h_1 is enrolment rate of secondary schooling, and S^h_2 is average years of secondary schooling. The variable *ngd* is the growth rate of population plus the sum of the growth rate of technology and depreciation rate. The sum of the growth rate of technology and the depreciation rate is assumed to be 0.05 and it is common for all countries, as shown in Mankiw et al. (1992). All these independent variables are the determinants of economic growth according to the extended economic growth model with human capital (Mankiw et al., 1992). Because the literature suggests that the linkage between intellectual property protection and innovation is stronger in open trade regimes, I included the variable *Trade* to investigate the effect of IPR protection on economic growth in an open economy. *Trade* is the sum of exports and imports of goods and services measured as a share of GDP. Finally, *IPR* is the updated index of patent rights developed by Park (2008). All the variables used are in natural logs and real terms.

As stated in the introduction, pooling the developing countries together may not capture the real effect of IPR protection on economic growth for developing countries. Therefore, I analyzed the effect of IPR protection on economic growth in high-growth and low-growth developing countries. Hence, the second growth equation is estimated as follows:

$$\gamma_{it} = \beta_0 + \beta_1 \text{IniGDP}_{it} + \beta_2 S^k_{it} + \beta_3 S^h_{it} + \beta_4 \text{ ngd}_{it} + \beta_5 \text{Trade}_{it} + \alpha_1 \text{IPR\_high}_{it} \ (\gamma_1' >= \lambda) \ + \alpha_2 \text{IPR\_low}_{it}$$

$$(\gamma_1' < \lambda) + \varepsilon_{it} \tag{2}$$

where the variable *IPR* is separated into *IPR_high* for high-growth developing countries and *IPR_low* for low-growth developing countries. The growth rate γ_i' is the average growth rate of all the 5-year sub periods. The benchmark estimation uses a cutoff of $\lambda = 20\%$, or 4% annual growth rate. Moreover, I tested the robustness of the results by using $\lambda = 15\%$ and $\lambda = 25\%$ (3% and 5% annual growth rate) as different cutoffs for defining high-growth and low-growth developing economies. α_1 estimates the effect of IPR on economic growth for those developing countries whose growth rates are equal to, or greater than, the cutoff value, whereas α_2 estimates the effect of IPR protection on the economic growth of those developing countries whose growth rates are below the cutoff value.

4. Data

In this paper, I included recent data that span the period from 1971 to 2005 for 89 developing countries. The list of these developing countries is provided in Appendix A. The data on the growth rate, the initial GDP, and the investment share of GDP, S^k, are from the Penn World Table, Version 6.3 (Heston, Summers, & Aten, 2009), provided by the Center for International Comparisons of Production, Income and Prices at the University of Pennsylvania. Population growth, *ngd*, and *Trade* come from the World Bank (2010). Secondary school enrolment rate, S^h_1, is taken from the United Nations Educational, Scientific and Cultural Organization (UNESCO). Average years of secondary schooling, S^h_2, is taken from Barro and Lee (2000). *IPR* is the updated index of patent rights (Park, 2008), which was extended to 2005 and includes a larger number of countries, especially high-growth developing countries such as China, Lithuania, and Ukraine. A full list of all the variables, their descriptions, and sources are shown in Appendix B. Because the variable *IPR* is very important for this study, in what follows I explain the IPR index in greater detail.

Different proxies for IPR protection have been used in empirical literature. Gould and Gruben (1996) used the index of patent protection developed by Rapp and Rozek (1990) as a proxy for IPR protection. The criterion of this index is the consistency of a country's patent laws with the standards of patents of the U.S. Chamber of Commerce Intellectual Property Task Force. However, this index has been criticized for not being sufficiently comprehensive. Recent studies (Falvey et al., 2006; Kanwar & Evenson, 2003; Schneider, 2005; Weinhold & Nair-Reichert, 2009) have used the index developed by Ginarte and Park (1997) as a proxy for IPR protection. This index was constructed for 110 countries, spans the period from 1960 to 1990, and includes five categories of patent laws. The five categories are the extent of coverage, membership in international patent agreements, provisions for loss of protection, enforcement mechanisms, and duration of protection (Ginarte & Park, 1997). However, the original index has become somewhat outdated. In order to analyze the impact of IPR protection on economic growth including in the recent period from 1990 to 2005, I used the index for IPR that was updated to 2005 by Park (2008). The updated index includes 122 countries and contains economies such as China, Russia, Tunisia, Ukraine, and Vietnam. Another advantage of the updated index is that it includes the impact of recent developments, such as the TRIPS agreement, new legislation, and revised national patent laws. According to Park (2008), the average increase in the patent rights index was the highest for the second quintile income group, which contains developing countries. The mean value of the updated index increased over time from the average value of 1.80 during the period of 1960-1990 to 3.34 in 2005. This trend reflects the influence of recent international agreements, particularly the TRIPS agreement.

5. Results

Table 1 reports the results of the three main regressions. I first estimated an open economy version of the regression shown in Table VI of Mankiw et al. (1992) in order to understand if my results are consistent with the theory outlined in their paper. I then included *IPR* in the regression to investigate the overall effect of IPR on the growth of developing economies. This regression is very similar to the one estimated in Falvey et al. (2006). Finally, I estimated the main regression, where the effect of IPR protection was separated for high-growth and low-growth developing economies.

Growth regression 0 shows the initial result without the variable *IPR*. In this regression, *IniGDP* has a negative sign and it is statistically significant, which is consistent with the theory outlined in Mankiw et al. (1992). The estimation also suggests that savings in physical capital and the openness of the economy play an important role in explaining the economic growth of developing countries. The results also show a positive sign for human capital S^h_1, although it is the opposite sign to that of population growth, *ngd*. These two variables are insignificant, which is a commonly found result in empirical studies, such as Falvey et al. (2006).

Growth regression 1 shown in column 3 is the same as the first growth equation shown in the methodology section of this paper. After the variable *IPR* is added, the result for physical capital becomes highly significant and the coefficient of human capital increases. The coefficient for IPR is positive, but very small and insignificant. This result is consistent with the results in Thompson and Rushing (1996). Similarly, Ginarte and Park (1997) found that IPR matters for developed economies but not for less developed economies, so it is not surprising that my results also show an inconclusive relationship between IPR protection and economic growth in developing economies as a whole.

Given the previous result, I used the second growth equation shown in the methodology section to answer the main question of the paper. More precisely, growth regression 2 estimated if IPR has a stronger effect on economic growth when a developing country reaches a certain level of growth. The 5-year cutoff growth rate used in this regression was 20%, or 4% annually, for the whole sample period of 1971 to 2005. I chose annual growth rate of 4% as a standard cutoff because 4% seems a reasonable annual rate for high-growth developing countries. Because it could be argued that 5% might be a better cutoff point, I also used 5% as a cutoff in the robustness checks of the results, which are described in the following section. However, there were only three countries—Botswana, China, and Lithuania—whose average annual growth rate in all the sub-periods was over 5%. Hence, I used a 4% annual growth rate in the benchmark regression, because eight countries in my dataset exceeded that threshold. Those eight countries with the average growth rate exceeding 20% during the 7 sub-periods from 1971 to 2005 were Botswana, China, Grenada, Lithuania, Malaysia, Malta, Thailand, and Ukraine. The other 81 developing countries in the sample were defined as low-growth developing countries, with an average growth rate below 20%.

Interesting, when the sample is divided into high-growth and low-growth developing countries, the results show that the coefficient of IPR for the high-growth developing countries is significant and much bigger than the coefficient of IPR for low-growth developing countries, which is not statistically significant. This result suggests that the effect of IPR on economic growth depends on the growth rate of the economy. Intuitively, this might be because the developing countries with a high growth rate may be able to afford the cost of IPR protection and take full advantage of the benefits from IPR protection through the channels of innovation or international trade.

In addition, from growth regressions 0, 1, and 2, we can see that the adjusted R^2 increases from 0.378 to 0.411. The adjusted R^2 indicates that IPR protection is an important determinant of growth, which should not be ignored. It also suggests that the independent variables *IPR_high* and *IPR_low* in growth regression 2 predict growth for developing countries better than does the variable *IPR* in growth regression 1.

6. Robustness Checks

In this section, I tested the robustness of my results to two changes: (i) use of different proxies for the variable *human capital*, and (ii) use of different cutoff growth rates. The results are reported in Table 2. Growth regression 2 from Table 1 is included again in Table 2 for comparison. Regressions 2 and 3 use 20% as a cutoff growth rate. Regressions 4 and 5 estimate the results by changing the cutoff growth rate to 15% and 25%, respectively[1]. Regressions 6, 7, and 8 show the results of regressions when I defined high-growth and low-growth developing countries by using the growth rate in the last sub-period of the sample, i.e., from 2000 to 2005, instead of the average growth rate of all the 5-year sub-periods from 1971 to 2005, as in regressions 4 and 5. The cutoff growth rate was again chosen at the levels of 15%, 20%, and 25%[2].

---

[1] Seventeen countries satisfy the criterion of $\gamma_i{}' >= \lambda$ ($\lambda=0.15$). These countries are Botswana, Bulgaria, China, Dominica, Egypt, Grenada, Indonesia, Lithuania, Malaysia, Malta, Mauritius, Sri Lanka, Swaziland, Thailand, Tunisia, Ukraine, and Vietnam. Three countries satisfy the criterion of $\gamma_i{}' >= \lambda$ ($\lambda=0.25$). These countries are Botswana, China, and Lithuania.

[2] The 27 countries that satisfy the criterion of $\gamma_i{}' >= \lambda$ ($\lambda=0.15$) are Angola, Botswana, Bulgaria, Chad, Chile, China, Grenada, Hungary, India, Iran, Liberia, Lithuania, Malaysia, Mali, Mauritius, Mozambique, Nigeria, Poland, Russia, Sri Lanka, Sudan, Tanzania, Trinidad and Tobago, Tunisia, Ukraine, Vietnam, and Zambia. The 16 countries that satisfy the criterion of $\gamma_i{}' >= \lambda$ ($\lambda=0.20$) are Chad, China, Grenada, Hungary, India, Liberia, Lithuania, Mozambique, Nigeria, Poland, Sudan, Trinidad and Tobago, Tunisia, Ukraine, Vietnam, and Zambia. The 3 countries that satisfy the criterion of $\gamma_i{}' >= \lambda$ ($\lambda=0.25$) are China, Liberia, and Lithuania.

Growth regression 3 tested the robustness of the results by replacing S^h_1, the enrolment rate of secondary schooling, which was taken from UNESCO, with S^h_2, years of schooling, which was taken from Barro and Lee (2000) as a proxy for human capital. I found that even when I used years of schooling as a proxy for human capital, the coefficients for the variables *IPR_high* and *IPR_low* were still positive and statistically significant. However, in this case, the effect of human capital on economic growth became smaller, and the coefficient decreased from 0.020 to 0.014. Furthermore, the positive effect of *ngd* became more positive and statistically significant. Since the result for *ngd* was at odds with the growth theory, I conclude that S^h_1, enrolment rate of secondary schooling, is a better proxy for human capital in these growth regressions.

As suggested by previous results, I used the variable S^h_1 in the remaining regressions. In regressions 2, 4, and 5, the coefficients of *IniGDP*, S^k, S^h_1, *ngd*, and *Trade* were quite similar. Furthermore, I found that the variable *IPR_high* was always significant at least at the 10% level and that its coefficient increased when the cutoff point was increased from 15% to 25%. In contrast, the coefficients of *IPR_low* were small and always insignificant. These results, which are consistent with the results in Table 1, once again suggest that the effect of IPR protection on economic growth is stronger when countries' growth rates are higher.

The results of regressions 6, 7, and 8 demonstrate the robustness of results when the time period chosen for the cutoff growth rate is changed. If I define high-growth and low-growth developing countries by using the growth rate of the last 5-year sub-period, the estimated coefficients still indicate that IPR protection has a positive, strong, and significant impact on growth in high-growth developing countries. In contrast, the effect of IPR on economic growth for low-growth developing countries is always insignificant. The sign of *IPR_low* even becomes negative in regression 6.

In Table 2, the adjusted R^2 ranges from 0.408 to 0.446, indicating the robustness of the fit of the model. In conclusion, these results suggest that the finding of a stronger effect of IPR protection on economic growth in high-growth developing countries is quite robust to changes in the proxies of the variables, as well as in the cutoff points for the growth rate or the time period chosen for the cutoff point.

7. Conclusion

This paper investigated the effect of IPR protection on the economic growth of developing countries by using ordinary least squares regression analysis. Because IPR protection in developing countries has been largely influenced by international agreements after the 1990s, this empirical study included the time period between 1990 and 2005. The main purpose of this paper is to address the question of whether IPR protection has a stronger effect on economic growth in high-growth developing countries than in low-growth developing countries.

The results suggest that when all the developing countries are pooled together, IPR has a slightly positive but insignificant effect on economic growth. This may be due to the fact that IPR protection has both benefits and costs for developing countries, which often rely on imitation, and the overall effect is uncertain.

However, when the sample is split into high-growth and low-growth developing countries, the results of the estimated regressions show a positive and highly significant relationship between IPR protection and economic growth for high-growth developing countries. Moreover, the effect for high-growth developing countries is much stronger than the effect for the other developing countries. One possible explanation for this result is that high-growth developing countries may be in a better position to afford the cost of IPR protection. Another explanation is that high-growth developing economies can substantially benefit from international trade and foreign direct investment, which gives them more incentive to adopt stronger intellectual property protection. It is also possible that high-growth developing countries have their own emerging innovations and industries that need to be protected by IPR regulations. Finally, the TRIPS agreement may have had some good influence on the economic growth of high-growth developing countries.

In conclusion, in the current economic globalization environment, IPR protection has become more important for developing countries. However, as stated in Lall (2002), the importance of IPR protection may vary with the level of development. Given the ambiguous results found for developing countries in the literature, this paper shows that pooling the developing countries together may not capture the real effect of IPR protection on economic growth. IPR protection may contribute more to the economic growth of high-growth developing countries than of low-growth developing countries.

Table 1. *Main Results of Growth Regressions*

Growth	0		1		2	
IniGDP	-0.311		-0.318		-0.347	
	(0.026)	***	(0.026)	***	(0.029)	***
S^k	0.070		0.080		0.081	
	(0.024)	**	(0.024)	***	(0.024)	***
S^h_1	0.010		0.024		0.020	
	(0.029)		(0.028)		(0.028)	
ngd	0.109		0.143		0.129	
	(0.076)		(0.077)	*	(0.077)	*
Trade	0.103		0.065		0.065	
	(0.033)	**	(0.034)	*	(0.034)	*
IPR			0.032			
			(0.035)			
IPR_high					0.187	
					(0.076)	***
IPR_slow					0.020	
					(0.035)	
Adjusted R^2	0.378		0.405		0.411	

Note. All regressions include country dummies and time dummies.
Standard errors are in parentheses.
  * indicates significance at 0.10 level
 ** indicates significance at 0.05 level
*** indicates significance at 0.01 level

Table 2. Growth Regressions for Testing the Robustness of Results

Growth	2	3	4	5	6	7	8
Time Period	1975-2005	1975-2005	1975-2005	1975-2005	2000-2005	2000-2005	2000-2005
Growth Rate	0.2	0.2	0.15	0.25	0.15	0.2	0.25
IniGDP	-0.347 ***	-0.352 ***	-0.360 ***	-0.330 ***	-0.355 ***	-0.329 ***	-0.323 ***
	(0.029)	(0.038)	(0.030)	(0.027)	(0.026)	(0.026)	(0.026)
S^k	0.081 ***	0.123 ***	0.088 ***	0.080 ***	0.081 ***	0.079 ***	0.083 ***
	(0.024)	(0.037)	(0.024)	(0.024)	(0.023)	(0.023)	(0.023)
S^h_1	0.020		0.022	0.017	0.023	0.023	0.020
	(0.028)		(0.028)	(0.029)	(0.027)	(0.028)	(0.028)
S^h_2		0.014					
		(0.037)					
ngd	0.129 *	0.468 ***	0.146 *	0.144 *	0.134 *	0.125 *	0.134 *
	(0.077)	(0.108)	(0.076)	(0.077)	(0.074)	(0.075)	(0.075)
Trade	0.065 *	0.079 *	0.065 *	0.069 **	0.050	0.050	0.057 *
	(0.034)	(0.044)	(0.033)	(0.034)	(0.033)	(0.033)	(0.033)
IPR_high	0.187 ***	0.251 ***	0.200 ***	0.214 *	0.271 ***	0.252 ***	0.382 ***
	(0.076)	(0.111)	(0.065)	(0.116)	(0.055)	(0.061)	(0.092)
IPR_slow	0.020	0.066	0.016	0.027	-0.003	0.004	0.013
	(0.035)	(0.046)	(0.035)	(0.035)	(0.034)	(0.035)	(0.035)
Adjusted R^2	0.411	0.430	0.417	0.408	0.446	0.430	0.428

Note. All regressions include country dummies and time dummies.
Standard errors are in parentheses.
    * indicates significance at the 0.10 level
   ** indicates significance at the 0.05 level
  *** indicates significance at the 0.01 level

References

Alikhan, S., & Mashelkar, R. (2009). *Intellectual property and competitive strategies in the 21ˢᵗ century* (2nd ed.). Alphen aan den Rijn: Kluwer Law International.

Barro, R. J., & Sala-i-Martin, X. (1997). Technological diffusion, convergence, and growth. *Journal of Economic Growth, 2,* 1-27.

Barro, R. J., & Sala-i-Martin, X. (2003). *Economic growth.* (2nd ed.). Cambridge: MIT Press.

Barro, R.J., & Lee, J. W. (2000). International data on educational attainment: Updates and implications (CID Working Paper 42). Retrieved from http://www.hks.harvard.edu/centers/cid/publications/faculty-working-papers/cid-working-paper-no.-42

Chu, A. C. (2009). *Macroeconomic effects of intellectual property rights: A survey* (MPRA Paper 17342). Retrieved from http://mpra.ub.uni-muenchen.de/17342/

Falvey, R., Foster, N., & Greenaway, D. (2006). Intellectual property rights and economic growth. *Review of Development Economics, 10*(4), 700-719.

Forero-Pineda, C. (2006). The impact of stronger intellectual property rights on science and technology in developing countries. *Research Policy, 35,* 808-824.

Ginarte, J. C., & Park, W. G. (1997). Intellectual property rights and economic growth. *Contemporary Economic Policy, 15*(3), 51-61.

Gould, D. M., & Gruben, W. C. (1996). The role of intellectual property rights in economic growth. *Journal of Development Economics, 48,* 323-350.

Grossman, G. M., & Helpman, E. (1991). *Innovation and growth in the global economy.* Cambridge: MIT Press.

Helpman, E. (1993). Innovation, imitation, and intellectual property rights. *Econometrica, 61*(6), 1247-1280.

Heston, A., Summers, R., & Aten, B. (2009). Penn World Table, Version 6.3, Center for International Comparisons of Production, Income and Prices at the University of Pennsylvania. [Database]. Retrieved from http://pwt.econ.upenn.edu/php_site/pwt63/pwt63_form.php

Kanwar, S., & Evenson, R. (2003). Does intellectual property protection spur technological change? *Oxford Economic Papers, 55*(2), 235-264.

Lall, S. (2002). Indicators of the relative importance of IPRs in developing countries. *Research Policy, 32,*1657-1680.

Mankiw, N. G., Romer, D., & Weil, D. N. (1992). A contribution to the empirics of economic growth. *The Quarterly Journal of Economics, 107*(2), 407-437.

Matthews, D. (2002). *Globalising intellectual property rights.* London: Routledge.

Park, G. P. (2008). International patent protection: 1960-2005. *Research Policy, 37,* 761-766.

Rapp, R., & Rozek, R. (1990). Benefits and costs of intellectual property protection in developing countries. *Journal of World Trade, 24*(5), 74-102.

Schneider, P. H. (2005). International trade, economic growth and intellectual property rights: A panel data study of developed and developing countries. *Journal of Development Economics, 78,* 529-547.

Thompson, M. A., & Rushing, F. W. (1996). An empirical analysis of the impact of patent protection on economic growth. *Journal of Economic Development, 21*(2), 61-79.

United Nations Educational, Scientific and Cultural Organization. (n.d.). Public reports: Education. [Data set]. Retrieved from http://stats.uis.unesco.org/unesco/ReportFolders/ReportFolders.aspx].

Weinhold, D., & Nair-Reichert, U. (2009). Innovation, inequality and intellectual property rights. *World Development, 27*(5), 889-901.

World Bank. (2010). *World development indicators: 1960-2009.* Retrieved from http://databank.worldbank.org/ddp/home.do?Step=2&id=4&DisplayAggregation=N&SdmxSupported=Y&CNO=2

World Intellectual Property Organization. (2001). *WIPO intellectual property handbook.* Geneva: WIPO.

Appendix A. *List of Developing Countries Used in the Regression Sample*

No.	Country	No.	Country	No.	Country
1	Algeria	31	Guyana	61	Papua New Guinea
2	Angola	32	Haiti	62	Paraguay
3	Argentina	33	Honduras	63	Peru
4	Bangladesh	34	Hungary	64	Philippines
5	Benin	35	India	65	Poland
6	Bolivia	36	Indonesia	66	Romania
7	Botswana	37	Iran	67	Russia
8	Brazil	38	Iraq	68	Rwanda
9	Bulgaria	39	Israel	69	Saudi Arabia
10	Burkina Faso	40	Jamaica	70	Senegal
11	Burundi	41	Jordan	71	Sierra Leone
12	Cameroon	42	Kenya	72	Somalia
13	Central African Republic	43	Liberia	73	South Africa
14	Chad	44	Lithuania	74	Sri Lanka
15	Chile	45	Madagascar	75	Sudan
16	China	46	Malawi	76	Swaziland
17	Colombia	47	Malaysia	77	Syria
18	Congo, Dem. Rep.	48	Mali	78	Tanzania
19	Congo, Republic of	49	Malta	79	Thailand
20	Costa Rica	50	Mauritania	80	Togo
21	Dominica	51	Mauritius	81	Trinidad &Tobago
22	Ecuador	52	Mexico	82	Tunisia
23	Egypt	53	Morocco	83	Uganda
24	El Salvador	54	Mozambique	84	Ukraine
25	Ethiopia	55	Nepal	85	Uruguay
26	Fiji	56	Nicaragua	86	Venezuela
27	Gabon	57	Niger	87	Vietnam
28	Ghana	58	Nigeria	88	Zambia
29	Grenada	59	Pakistan	89	Zimbabwe
30	Guatemala	60	Panama		

Appendix B. *List of Variables*

No	Variable	Description	Source
1	γ	GDP growth rate	Penn World Table, Version 6.3 (Heston, Summers, & Aten, 2009)
2	*IniGDP*	Initial GDP per capita	Penn World Table, Version 6.3 (Heston, Summers, & Aten, 2009)
3	$S^{\ast}$	Investment share of GDP	Penn World Table, Version 6.3 (Heston, Summers, & Aten, 2009)
4	S^{h}_1	Enrolment rate of secondary schooling	UNESCO
5	S^{h}_2	Average years of secondary schooling	Barro and Lee (2000)
6	*ngd*	Growth rate of population+growth rate of technology+depreciation rate	World Bank (2010)
7	*Trade*	Exports plus imports divided by GDP	World Bank (2010)
8	*IPR*	IPR index	Park (2008)

A Tale of Two Bubbles:
Lessons from Japan's Bubble Economy and Australia's
Housing Boom

By Susan Bultitude

Abstract

Asset price bubbles represent a significant threat to macroeconomic performance and financial market stability, yet their nature and policy implications are not fully understood. This paper complements the existing literature by comparing Japan's infamous 'bubble economy' and Australia's most recent housing boom. It identifies significant differences between the two episodes, including the number of markets affected and the existence of spillover effects; the extent to which the bubbles burst; and the severity of the associated macroeconomic impacts. These differences suggest that asset price bubbles are heterogeneous in nature and can be classified into a number of different categories. In particular, a bubble may be more severe if it is characterised by optimistic expectations that relate to the economy as a whole (rather than a single asset market), or if it impacts on business activities (in addition to those of households). Because of the significant variation between different episodes, the optimal policy response is likely to differ from case to case. For example, recommendations that central banks increase interest rates to offset an asset price boom may not be appropriate in all circumstances. However, there is a clear role for monetary and other authorities in managing expectations during a boom period, and for sound prudential regulation to ensure that the financial system can withstand a bust in asset prices.

1. Introduction

Asset price bubbles represent a significant threat to macroeconomic performance and financial market stability, yet their nature and policy implications are not fully understood. While asset price bubbles are not a new or recent development, the frequency and impact of major asset price fluctuations have increased in recent decades, with stock market and property bubbles becoming a distinctive feature of the economic landscape. In view of this growing threat, there is an urgent need for a better understanding of bubble phenomena, including their defining characteristics, potential economic impacts, and appropriate policy responses.

The academic literature on asset price bubbles dates from the infamous Dutch 'tulipmania' of the 17th century. It is generally accepted that the term *asset price bubble* refers to a rapid rise (boom), followed by a fall (bust), in the price of a tradeable asset, either in absolute terms or relative to the price supported by economic fundamentals (Filardo, 2004; Helbling, 2005; Simon, 2003). It is also widely recognised that asset price bubbles can weaken economic growth and contribute to financial crises (Filardo, 2004; IMF, 2003). However, there is considerable debate as to the causes and underlying characteristics of asset price bubbles, and the appropriate policy responses (Hunter et al., 2003). Another limitation of the existing literature is that it typically focuses on a single country or episode, rather than comparing two or more different bubbles (Helbling, 2003; IMF, 2003). Additionally, relatively little analysis has been undertaken to distinguish between the effects and implications of different types of asset bubbles (Carmichael et al., 2003; McKibbin, 2003).

This paper complements existing research by comparing two recent episodes of significant asset price volatility. The first of these is Japan's bubble economy of the late 1980s and early 1990s, arguably the most infamous bubble of recent economic history due to its size and devastating legacy (de Brouwer, 2003).[3] The second is Australia's housing boom of the first few years of the 21st century, which appears to have subsided without a noticeable bust.

The striking contrast between the recent economic performance of Australia and that of Japan is a valuable research topic for economic policymakers. Following the crash of its bubble economy in the early 1990s, Japan experienced more than a decade of economic stagnation, including a recession that was more severe than those of any other major industrial country since the Second World War (Bayoumi & Collyns, 2000). In contrast, over a similar period, Australia consistently outperformed the world's leading industrialised economies, despite its unprecedented boom in housing prices. In addition, while Japan's experiences provided valuable lessons for Australian policymakers at the time of the Australian housing boom (de Brouwer, 2003), there is little previous analysis directly comparing the two phenomena.

This paper identifies significant differences between the causes, behaviour, and impacts of the two periods of asset price fluctuation. The results suggest that asset price bubbles are heterogeneous in nature and effects. In particular, this paper distinguishes between different types of bubble on the basis of whether the associated optimism or unrealistic expectations are broadly or narrowly based, and the extent to which they affect the business sector. This paper also examines each country's monetary and prudential policy responses and demonstrates that certain policy recommendations put forward in response to Japan's bubble economy may not be necessary, effective, or appropriate for addressing other asset price booms.

2. Comparison of Japan's Bubble Economy and Australia's Housing Boom

2.1 Characteristics and Causes

Japan's bubble economy was characterised by a rapid and significant rise and subsequent fall in equity and property prices.[4] As depicted in Panel A of Figure 1 (Appendix A), equity prices began increasing in 1983 and grew rapidly from 1986 until the end of 1989. At that time, the Japanese share market peaked at around three times its total value in 1995. The subsequent decline in equity prices was even more rapid; within one year the share market had fallen by more than one-third relative to its peak, and by the end of 1992 it had fallen by more than half.

The rise in equity prices was followed by a rise in land prices, which was most pronounced in Japan's major cities. As indicated in Panel C of Figure 1, the growth in commercial land prices was particularly strong, with the relevant Urban Land Price Index reaching a peak of four times its 1985 value in September 1990. Residential and industrial land prices also grew strongly over this period. Since 1991, prices for all

---

[3] Some academic texts (for example, Okina et al., 2001) call this period the 'Heisei bubble' to differentiate it from previous episodes.
[4] For a more comprehensive discussion of, and additional statistics relating to, Japan's bubble economy, see Okina et al. (2001) and Fukao (2003).

categories of land have declined significantly, with the Urban Land Price Index for commercial land falling to half its peak in 1994 and to pre-1985 levels by 1998. In the case of Australia, the primary feature of the recent asset bubble was a significant increase in house prices. As Panel D of Figure 1 indicates, house prices in major Australian cities doubled in the five years from March 1999 to March 2004. Subsequently, the house price indexes for Sydney, Melbourne, and Canberra fell (by around 6 percent in Sydney but less than 1 percent in Melbourne and Canberra), while house prices in other major cities remained stable.

Unlike Japan's bubble economy, Australia's housing price boom was not accompanied by a boom in commercial or industrial property. For example, prices for commercial properties grew modestly from the mid-1990s onward, at an average annual rate of just over 4 percent (RBA, 2003a). Similarly, there was no corresponding boom in equity prices. As Panel B of Figure 1 shows, the rate of growth in Australia's share market trended downwards over the 1990s, and the share market actually fell in value over much of the housing boom period, before rebounding sharply in 2004.

The different behaviour of asset prices in the two countries reflects the different factors driving the price booms. In the case of Japan's boom, the key factors driving asset price increases were widespread optimism among businesses and consumers regarding a new era of growth and prosperity (sometimes referred to as 'bullish expectations') and aggressive credit growth following financial deregulation and monetary easing (Fukao, 2003; Okina et al., 2001). These factors were not limited to a small number of sectors, but were broadly based, prompting growth in the prices of a wide range of investment assets and spillover effects from one market to another. Moreover, once the initial asset price rise had been triggered, it became self-reinforcing. For example, the appreciation in the values of firms' and households' assets provided firms and households with greater collateral with which to borrow more funds for investment, while the appreciation in banks' balance sheets enabled the banks to increase lending. Eventually, when successive monetary tightening by the Bank of Japan increased the cost of borrowing and the expected drivers of economic growth failed to materialise, the cycle was broken, triggering a decline in asset prices (Bayoumi & Collyns, 2000; Fukao, 2003).

In contrast to Japan's bubble, Australia's house price boom was largely driven by factors specifically related to the housing market, as opposed to other asset markets or the economy as a whole.[5] The initial increase in house prices reflected the establishment of stable growth and falling unemployment, which, in combination with the low interest rate and low inflation, enabled households to service larger amounts of debt. The latter, more significant period of the price boom was driven by an unprecedented demand for investment properties, based on optimistic expectations of continued price growth and fuelled by enhanced competition in the residential mortgage market and the development of new lending products targeted at households and investors in residential property.

It is important to note that, unlike the drivers of Japan's bubble economy, these triggers were narrowly based, and the housing boom did not spillover into other markets, such as the stock market or commercial property sector. One reason for this is that general expectations about Australia's potential economic growth were well-anchored at a moderate rate of around 3-5 percent per annum, reflecting the experiences of preceding decades (including the conduct of monetary policy since the

---

A more detailed discussion of the factors underlying the housing price boom can be found in RBA (2003a) and Productivity Commission (2004).

introduction of inflation targeting) and confidence in official forecasts. This was not the case in Japan, for which double-digit growth was the norm only 15 years' prior to the bubble, and which had long been hailed as a miracle economy. Another factor is the relative recency of the dot.com crash and subsequent slump in the US and global stock markets, and the decline in commercial property prices in the early 1990s, which may have prevented optimism about the housing market from spreading to other sectors. Similarly, unlike Japan, the supply side factors fuelling credit creation were largely specific to the housing market. For example, rapid growth in the market for asset-backed securities in the late 1990s increased the liquidity value of residential mortgage lending, and the entry of mortgage brokers and non-bank lenders into the mortgage market increased competition among lenders in the mortgage sector (RBA, 2004).

In a similar vein, many of the factors triggering the easing of Australia's housing boom were specific to the housing sector. For example, record-low rental yields, an increase in supply in key geographical areas, and the introduction of a new tax on housing in Australia's largest state put downward pressure on house prices and dampened investor sentiment. In addition, the upswing in the share market in 2004 attracted investment away from the housing market, while two increases in official interest rates in late 2003 increased the cost of borrowing. More important, as the optimistic expectations driving Australia's boom were weaker and more narrowly targeted than those in Japan and as the underlying economic fundamentals remained stable, Australia's housing prices did not fall as severely.

The above analysis indicates that asset price booms may vary widely between episodes and across countries. First, it indicates that price booms may be limited to only one type of asset, as was the case in Australia, or may involve simultaneous increases in the prices of several different assets, as was the case in Japan. This observation contradicts much of the existing literature on asset price bubbles, which focuses on single asset bubbles in isolation or on spillover effects from one bubble to another asset class (IMF, 2003). Second, the comparison confirms that while asset price booms may be followed by equivalent or even greater price busts (as in Japan's case), not all booms are followed by severe price busts. This is one of the difficulties faced by policymakers in considering not only how to respond to booming asset prices, but also whether a response is required.

More substantially, the comparison suggests that the dynamics driving asset price booms also vary widely. It supports the view in much of the existing literature that bubbles may be driven by changes in economic fundamentals (as was the case early in Australia's housing boom), by irrational exuberance or optimistic expectations (a factor in both episodes), or by a combination of the two.[6] However, it also supports a conceptual and empirical distinction between a bubble economy, or a macro-bubble, in which increases in asset prices are driven by optimistic expectations (whether rational or irrational) about the economy as a whole, and a micro-bubble, such as Australia's housing boom, in which the optimistic expectations relate primarily to a single asset. This distinction, which appears to have been largely overlooked in the existing literature, may be an important indicator of a bubble's severity.

In particular, the comparison between Japan's bubble economy and Australia's housing boom suggests that if factors exist to prevent widespread optimism from arising, or exuberance in one market from spilling over into another market, the range

---

[6] The different theories on the causes of asset price bubbles are discussed in more detail in Filardo (2004) and Simon (2003).

of sectors subject to asset price bubbles and the severity of the bust period may be reduced.

2.2 Macroeconomic Consequences

Japan's asset price bubble had a significant and prolonged impact on the wider economy. As can be seen in Panel A of Figure 2 (Appendix B), Japan's Gross Domestic Product (GDP) grew substantially during the bubble period, averaging 5 percent per annum in the five fiscal years from 1986 to 1990 and peaking at 6.7 percent in fiscal year 1988. In contrast, between 1991 and 1993, following the collapse of asset prices, GDP grew at an average annual rate of only 0.8 percent. Despite a brief recovery between 1994 and 1996, GDP growth remained subdued throughout most of the 1990s.

Japan's inflation rate also rose and then fell during the bubble period, but with a lag, as illustrated in Panel A of Figure 3 (Appendix C). While inflation remained at historically moderate levels, rising from around 0 percent to a peak of 3.7 percent in early 1991, growth in the consumer price index accelerated between 1987 and 1990. Following the decline in GDP growth during the recession, inflation quickly subsided, falling to negative levels (deflation) in 1996. Inflation remained subdued at levels below or near zero during the following decade.[7]

A key factor driving this extended recession was the decline in aggregate demand as unrealistic optimism associated with the bubble subsided, and as lenders' and borrowers' balance sheets deteriorated, curtailing the creation of credit (Okina et al., 2001). More important, while changes in consumer spending contributed to the increase and subsequent decline in GDP growth, their effect was relatively minor compared with the weakening of business investment and output. As Panel C in Figure 2 (Appendix B) indicates, the contribution of household consumption to GDP growth was much less volatile than GDP growth itself, maintaining a narrow range of between 1 and 3 percentage points almost exclusively throughout the bubble period. In particular, the contribution of household consumption to GDP growth remained positive following the bust in asset prices, falling to 0.9 percentage points in 1992 and 1993 before recovering to 1.3 percentage points in 1994. Similarly, residential investment began to recover in early 1993, a number of months before there were signs of recovery in GDP or business investment (Mori et al., 2001).

In contrast, business investment and output fluctuated significantly during the bubble and post-bubble periods and were the primary drivers of GDP growth. This is illustrated in Figure 2 (Appendix B) by the similarities between the pattern of GDP growth (Panel A) and the contribution of private non-residential investment to GDP growth (Panel C). During the boom, industrial production grew at an average annual rate of 7.2 percent and business fixed investment maintained a relatively high value of 20 percent of GDP (Okina et al., 2001). During the subsequent bust, the decline in GDP growth was largely driven by a sharp fall in business fixed investment, and industrial production fell by 5.2 percent annually (Okina et al., 2001).

To date, Australia's housing boom has not been associated with GDP and expenditure fluctuations or with deflationary pressures as strongly as has Japan's bubble economy. As can be seen in Panel B of Figure 2 (Appendix B), Australia's GDP growth has been relatively stable since 1993, even throughout the period of

---

[7] There was an increase in measured inflation in 1997 due to the one-off impact of an increase in the consumption tax rate. However, underlying (or tax-adjusted) inflation remained stable throughout this period, as shown in Mori et al. (2001).

rapid growth in house prices, ranging between 2 and 5 percent per annum. Similarly, as Panel B of Figure 3 indicates, while Australia's inflation rate grew from near-zero to 2.8 percent per annum in the period before the housing boom, it remained relatively stable during the boom period, ranging between 2 and 3.5 percent per annum.

The stability of Australia's GDP reflected the relatively steady growth in its underlying components. As Panel D of Figure 2 (Appendix B) indicates, growth in household consumption, business investment, and housing investment remained relatively stable throughout the boom, varying by little more than two percentage points (after adjusting for the impact of taxation changes). This stable growth in business investment in particular is in sharp contrast to Japan's experience (Panel C). Following the boom, each component of aggregate demand weakened slightly, contributing to slower GDP growth in 2005. However, at a rate of 2.3 percent per annum, GDP growth remained robust relative to that during Japan's post-bubble recession.

A number of important conclusions can be drawn from the above analysis. Perhaps the most obvious is the observation that asset price booms are not always followed by busts, nor do they always have strong macroeconomic impacts, as Australia's experience demonstrates. Nonetheless, as indicated by Japan's experience, asset price bubbles can be associated with severe macroeconomic fluctuations and prolonged detrimental effects, including low and unstable GDP growth and deflation.

More important, the above discussion suggests that bubbles inflict more damage on macroeconomic performance through their impact on business activities such as investment and production than on household consumption and housing investment. That is, household expenditure appears to be more resilient to bubbles than are business activities. Japan experienced a combination of asset price bubbles that impacted on both the household and the business sectors; yet, whereas household consumption remained relatively stable throughout the bubble, business investment and output experienced a boom and bust similar to that affecting asset prices. This led directly to a period of strong economic growth, followed by a recession. In contrast, Australia experienced a boom in the price of housing, an asset that was of little direct relevance to the general business sector, and both business investment and household consumption—and hence GDP and inflation—remained relatively stable.

This observation supports the need for further analysis of the effects of different types of price bubbles. In relation to the work undertaken thus far, this observation accords with McKibbin's (2003) argument that asset price bubbles may have a stronger detrimental effect if they impact on the supply side of the economy, and with Zhu's (2003) argument that residential property price bubbles have fewer significant macroeconomic impacts than do commercial property price bubbles. On the other hand, this analysis suggests that comparisons between property price bubbles and equity price bubbles (see, for example, Helbling, 2003; IMF, 2003) should be interpreted with caution, as the results may differ depending on whether the property price bubbles relate exclusively to residential or commercial property, or to both. Thus, it is important that data limitations preventing commentators from separately analysing each of these markets be overcome.

2.3 Policy Settings and Responses

Commentary on the policy framework associated with Japan's bubble economy generally focuses on two aspects of economic policy: monetary policy and prudential and related financial sector regulation. In relation to monetary policy[8], the bubble began in an environment of unprecedented monetary easing and record-low interest rates of 2.25 percent, as show in Panel A of Figure 4 (Appendix D). This largely reflected Japan's efforts to generate demand and stabilize the yen following the 1985 Plaza Agreement. In the absence of high inflation and amid fears of a spillover from the US stock market crash of October 1987, interest rates remained low for the first few years of the boom, contributing to widespread expectations that interest rates would remain low indefinitely (Okina et al., 2001; Shiratsuka, 2005). It was not until May 1989 that rates were increased in order to prevent the boom from generating inflationary pressures.[9] Continued rapid growth in the economy, money supply, and asset prices, and increasing inflation prompted further monetary tightening, with interest rates reaching 6 percent in August 1990.

Following the bust in asset prices, the Bank of Japan repeatedly reduced the official discount rate from 6 percent in July of 1991 to 2.5 percent in February of 1993. When business investment and sentiment failed to recover and land prices continued to fall, the Bank further reduced interest rates to 0.5 percent in 1995. In 1997, the onset of the East Asian economic crisis as well as deflationary pressures arising from financial system instability resulted in the adoption by the Bank of its zero interest rate policy.

There is considerable debate as to the appropriateness of these policy settings and responses. In particular, some commentators argue that the Bank of Japan should have tightened monetary policy much earlier in response to the build-up of inflationary pressures (Bernanke & Gertler, 2000; Posen, 2003). Some critics even suggest that the Bank should have raised interest rates in a pre-emptive manner specifically to prick the asset-price bubble in its early stages, consistent with the general arguments put forward by Kent and Low (1997) and Borio and Lowe (2002) (see, for example, Okina et al., 2001).

In response to these criticisms, it has been argued that the dangers associated with the boom and the optimal policy responses were only discernible with the benefit of hindsight. In particular, a number of the recommendations were based on output gap forecasts, which may be especially difficult to make for an economy that is widely believed to be entering a new era of higher growth. This is because the same judgements as to the extent to which asset prices reflect economic fundamentals versus irrational exuberance also apply to output forecasts (Okina & Shiratsuka, 2002). In addition, given that the actual inflation remained low throughout the first few years of the boom and the widespread belief—even among government officials—that Japan had entered a new era of high growth potential, proposals to raise interest rates to offset inflationary pressures or burst the bubble could not be justified to the public and relevant political institutions (Okina et al., 2001; Saxonhouse & Stern, 2004).

In relation to prudential policy, a key policy setting at the onset of the boom was the recent deregulation of Japan's financial system, consistent with the general transition towards liberalised financial markets among other industrialised nations.[10] Controls on bank lending and other forms of capital raising were removed around

---

[8] For a more detailed description of Japan's monetary policy settings prior to, during, and following the bubble, see Okina et al. (2001).

[9] It should be noted that the Bank of Japan was not operating an explicit inflation-targeting framework at the time of the bubble. However, inflation was clearly an important factor in monetary policy considerations, as discussed in detail in Okina et al. (2001).

[10] For a more detailed discussion of the deregulation of the Japanese financial system, see Tsuda (1999), IMF (1998), and Kuroda (1998).

1980, which led to rapid growth in alternative capital markets and greater competitive pressures within the banking industry. As a result, Japanese banks lent aggressively, particularly to small and medium-sized enterprises and real estate ventures, often using real estate as collateral and paying little attention to projected cash flows or risks (Fukao, 2003; Katz, 1998). These lending practices, combined with a dramatic increase in corporate fundraising through securities markets, contributed to an acceleration in credit growth, as illustrated in Panel C of Figure 4 (Appendix D).

Following the asset price bust, banks' heavy exposure to falling asset prices led to a rapid increase in non-performing loans, which slowed Japan's recovery from the recession. More important, inadequate legislation and lenient banking supervision enabled financial institutions to avoid writing off their losses, initiating bankruptcy procedures, and publicly disclosing the full extent of their financial position (Fukao, 2003; Katz, 1998; Kuroda, 1998; Mori et al., 2001). As a result, many banks maintained a significant proportion of non-performing loans, while severely restricting new lending. Thus, credit growth remained subdued in the decade following the asset price bust, as illustrated in Panel C of Figure 4 (Appendix D).

As with monetary policy, these prudential policy settings have been criticised for a number of reasons. In particular, financial sector deregulation and the failure to prevent banks from undertaking excessive and risky lending and financing activities have been criticised for facilitating credit-creation and demand for assets, thus contributing to the boom (IMF, 1998). Moreover, it is now widely recognised that inadequate risk management by both banks' management and banking regulators contributed to the vulnerability of the financial sector by failing to protect banks' capital reserves or prevent excessive concentration of risks (Miwa & Ramseyer, 2003; Okina & Shiratsuka, 2002).

In contrast to Japan's experiences, Australia's monetary policy settings remained remarkably stable in the periods immediately prior to, during, and following the house price boom. As shown in Panel B of Figure 4 (Appendix D), Australia experienced only one change in official interest rates between July 1997 and November 1999, the period immediately prior to the boom. Moreover, interest rates remained within the relatively narrow band of 4.25 to 6.25 percent throughout the housing boom period, with the small increases over 2002 and 2003 reflecting favourable internal and external conditions for economic growth, rather than housing market pressures (MacFarlane, 2003).

Another important difference between the monetary policies of Australia and Japan was in the use of verbal intervention to manage expectations in the economy. Whereas the Bank of Japan was unsuccessful in communicating its concerns about the downside risks associated with the boom, the Reserve Bank of Australia repeatedly warned that the housing boom posed risks to the economic outlook and contributed to expansionary pressures, and that the rapid growth in asset prices might not be sustainable.[11] The credibility of these warnings was reinforced by Australia's well-established policies of inflation targeting and central bank's independence, policies that were not introduced in Japan until after the bubble economy. As such,

---

[11] Indeed, house prices were mentioned in virtually all of the RBA's key policy statements throughout the boom period. For example, in its August 2003 Statement on Monetary Policy (RBA, 2003b), the RBA noted that the rapid growth of credit and housing prices posed a risk to the economic outlook in that "the longer they go on, the larger will be the contractionary effect on the economy when they inevitably turn" (p. 3), and that this risk implied a tightening bias to monetary policy. Various speeches also referred to the RBA's use of moral suasion or alarm bells to persuade house purchasers, particularly investors, to thoroughly consider their investment decisions.

although the Reserve Bank of Australia did not actually increase interest rates for much of the housing boom, it exerted downward pressure on optimistic expectations and prices through its communication with the public, thus decreasing the severity of the boom and the risk of a bust.

Australia's prudential framework also differed significantly from the regulation applied in Japan during its boom. In particular, Australia had completed the transition to a liberalised financial system and had implemented international risk-management and capital adequacy standards such as the Bank of International Settlements' Basel Capital Accord. Despite this prudential framework, Australian banks (like the Japanese banks before them) adopted more aggressive lending policies and increased their exposure to real estate prices throughout the boom, This was achieved through the introduction of and rapid growth in higher-risk lending products and products targeting higher-risk customers, as well as a general increase in the amounts that banks were willing to lend in a particular set of circumstances (RBA, 2005). This contributed to strong credit growth throughout the boom period, as shown in Panel D of Figure 4 (Appendix D).

The Australian prudential regulator responded to this build-up of risks in three ways. First, it conducted comprehensive stress-testing of all banks' financial positions to assess their capacity to withstand a significant fall in housing prices. This analysis concluded that Australia's banks could withstand such a shock and were maintaining adequate capital reserves. Second, the regulator made minor changes to Australia's prudential requirements to ensure that new lending products were treated in a manner commensurate with their risks. Third, it requested that banks review their lending policies when questionable practices were identified (Laker, 2003). Nonetheless, some of these products continued to grow strongly throughout and following the boom, even when demand for credit slowed (RBA, 2005). Thus, while Australia's prudential policy framework may have protected the financial system from instability following the boom, it appears to have had little effect on the underlying build-up of inflationary pressures in the housing market.

This comparison of the policy settings in the two countries reveals some important lessons for policymakers. First, it provides further support for sound prudential and financial stability policies to ensure that the financial system continues to function in the event of an asset price bust. Inadequate risk management by Japan's financial sector and its regulators made it vulnerable to a decline in asset prices, resulting in financial instability that prolonged Japan's recovery from the asset price bust. In contrast, while Australia's financial sector was ultimately not exposed to significant declines in asset prices, Australia's lending institutions and policymakers demonstrated that the financial sector was able to withstand such a shock, largely owing to the implementation of international prudential and risk-management standards. Such reassurances arguably contributed to the economy's 'soft landing' following the housing boom.

Second, whereas Japan's lack of prudential regulation has been criticised for contributing to the bubble economy, Australia's experience demonstrates that such regulation does not necessarily prevent asset price booms. Australia's financial institutions engaged in aggressive and increasingly risky lending practices, and thus contributed to strong credit growth and housing demand, while remaining compliant with international prudential standards. Moreover, fine-tuning of the prudential framework to accommodate the new, higher-risk lending practices had little effect on their rate of adoption. Assuming that prudential policy is targeted at financial stability and depositor protection, in preference to macroeconomic outcomes, this suggests that there is a limit to the extent to which prudential policy can prevent or mitigate a credit-fuelled asset price boom. Thus, the real value of prudential policy is its ability to prevent an initial asset price bust from becoming a financial crisis and an associated credit crunch; prudential policy alone cannot prevent the emergence of a bubble.

Third, the comparison provides only mixed support for the argument made by Carmichael et al. (2003), among others, that the degree of leveraging during an asset boom has an important bearing on its macroeconomic outcomes, because of the potential for financial sector instability. Whereas the high levels of borrowing during Japan's bubble economy contributed to financial sector insolvency and negative financial accelerator effects following the bust, the unprecedented growth in household debt during Australia's housing bubble does not appear to have had any similar impacts. Thus, while high levels of leveraging may exacerbate the effects of an asset price bust, they do not necessarily result in detrimental macroeconomic outcomes. This observation suggests that authorities should focus on the appropriate prudential management of debt, rather than on the absolute levels of debt, in their policy responses to asset price bubbles.

Fourth, the comparison provides new input into the debate on the appropriate role of monetary policy in responding to an asset price bubble. Whereas many economists have argued that Japan should have raised interest rates earlier in the boom, and some suggest that, as a general rule, monetary policy should be tightened in the event of an asset price bubble, Australia's experience suggests that such responses may not always be appropriate. Australia's inflation and economic growth remained at sustainable levels throughout and following the housing boom, without aggressive monetary policy action, and despite the length and severity of the boom. Had the Reserve Bank of Australia significantly increased interest rates to lean against, or prick, the housing price boom, this may have had a detrimental impact on output and employment, and may have resulted in a stronger bust in housing prices, while yielding no discernible macroeconomic benefits. Thus, the comparison of the two experiences supports the alternative argument that there is no simple rule for determining how monetary policy should respond to a boom in asset prices.

Fifth, although actual monetary tightening may not always be an appropriate response to a boom in asset prices, it is clear from this comparison that credible verbal intervention may be of use in the management of optimistic expectations in the economy. As discussed above, the nature and extent of optimism in the economy are important determinants of the severity of the associated bubble. This suggests that policies aimed at the deflation of excessive optimism may reduce the economic impact of potential bubbles. The Reserve Bank of Australia played an active role in warning participants in the housing market that the boom could contribute to inflation, and hence to future increases in interest rates, and that the higher prices resulting from the boom might not be sustainable. This put downward pressure on prices and expectations in the economy, limiting the spillover of optimism from the housing market to other sectors, and contributed to an orderly end of the housing boom. The Bank of Japan, much less successful in communicating such messages, implicitly contributed to widespread expectations that interest rates would remain low and to general confidence in the rising asset prices.

A final observation emerging from the comparison is that the impact of an asset price bubble on monetary policy processes differs depending on the nature of the bubble. As Japan's experience arguably demonstrates, monetary policy is significantly more difficult to implement in an economy experiencing a macro-bubble, even if asset prices are not specifically targeted. This is because the output gap forecasts that are used to measure whether the current economic performance is sustainable are more difficult when the optimistic expectations relate to the general economic growth as well as individual asset prices. In contrast, Australia's micro-bubble had a limited impact on the country's monetary policy settings as the bubble related only to subsections of aggregate demand and supply and hence had relatively little effect on the output gap forecasts. Thus, the comparison suggests that monetary policy may be more difficult during macro-bubbles than during micro-bubbles.

3. Discussion and Conclusion

Overall, the comparison of Japan's bubble economy and Australia's housing boom highlights the heterogeneous nature of asset price bubbles. Japan's bubble affected a range of asset markets, involved a price bust at least as severe as the preceding boom, and distorted business investment and production. In contrast, Australia's boom was related only to one asset market, did not involve a noticeable bust, and had little impact on business activities. In light of those differences, it could be said that the macroeconomic impact of Japan's bubble economy was more severe than that of Australia's housing boom.

The differences between the two experiences have important ramifications for policymakers. Only two policy actions appear to be of general and significant value: active management of expectations by monetary and other authorities and sound prudential regulation. These are complementary policies with different beneficial effects. Managing expectations in the economy will reduce the build-up and spillover of optimism causing asset price booms and busts, and thus may reduce the frequency and severity of bubbles. However, this is arguably an imprecise and indirect policy mechanism. Prudential policy is a more concrete approach but its main effect in relation to asset price bubbles is to prevent a downturn in asset prices from becoming a more severe financial crisis and credit crunch—prudential policy is relatively ineffective in actually preventing an asset price boom.

Other policies— particularly the tightening of monetary policy to offset an asset price boom— may or may not be appropriate, depending on the balance of risks. This analysis suggests that the downside risks may be larger, and hence the justification for pre-emptive policy intervention greater, when optimism about the economy is related to a number of different assets and general expectations about economic prosperity (rather than a single asset), or when business activities are affected by the bubble. This distinction between the transmission mechanisms of different types of bubble warrants further investigation.

To date, Australia appears to have experienced an orderly exit from its housing boom, with relatively mild economic consequences. This reflects a combination of good management and good luck, and considerable credit for that success must be given to the lessons learned world-wide from Japan's experiences during its bubble economy. Japan has strengthened its economic structure to protect against asset price shocks, and is well on the path to recovery. However, the findings of this paper suggest that neither country can be completely confident of its resilience to future asset price fluctuations. The next bubble afflicting Japan or Australia could be considerably different from its predecessor. Authorities in both countries must remain alert for potential asset price misalignments and must be prepared to adapt their policymaking frameworks in response.

References

Bayoumi, T., & Collyns, C. (Eds.) (2002). *Post-bubble blues: How Japan responded to asset price collapse.* Washington, DC: International Monetary Fund.

Bernanke, B., & Gertler, M. (2000). *Monetary policy and asset price volatility* (NBER Working Paper 7559). Massachusetts, MA: National Bureau of Economic Research.

Bernanke, B., & Gertler, M. (2001). Should central banks respond to movements in asset prices? *American Economic Review, 91*(2), 253-257.

Bollard, A. (2004). *Asset prices and monetary policy* (BIS Quarterly Review, 7/2004). Basel, Switzerland: Bank for International Settlements.

Bordo, M., & Jeanne, O. (2002). Monetary policy and asset prices: Does "benign neglect" make sense? *International Finance, 5*(2), 139-164.

Borio, C., & Lowe, P. (2002). *Asset prices, financial and monetary stability: Exploring the nexus* (BIS Working Paper 114). Basel, Switzerland: Bank for International Settlements.

Carmichel, J., & Esho, N. (2003). Asset price bubbles and prudential regulation. In W. Hunter, G. Kaufman, & M. Pomerleano (Eds.), *Asset price bubbles: The implications for monetary, regulatory and international policies* (pp. 481-502). Massachusetts, MA: MIT Press.

Carmichael, J., Plender, J., & Stevens, G. (2003). Round-table/wrap-up discussion. In A. Richards & T. Robinson (Eds.), *Asset prices and monetary policy* (pp. 287-298). Sydney, Australia: Reserve Bank of Australia.

Cecchetti, S., Genberg, H., & Wadhwani, S. (2002). *Asset prices in a flexible inflation targeting framework* (NBER Working Paper 8970). Massachusetts, MA: National Bureau of Economic Research.

De Brouwer, G. (2003). It takes more than a bubble to become Japan: Discussion. In A. Richards & T. Robinson (Eds.), *Asset prices and monetary policy* (pp. 250-259). Sydney, Australia: Reserve Bank of Australia.

Filardo, A. (2004). *Monetary policy and asset price bubbles: Calibrating the monetary policy trade-offs* (BIS Working Paper 155). Basel, Switzerland: Bank for International Settlements.

Fukao, M. (2003). Japan's lost decade and weaknesses in its corporate governance structure. In R. Stern (Ed.), *Japan's economic recovery: Commercial policy, monetary policy and corporate governance* (pp. 289-328). Cheltenham, UK: Edward Elgar.

Goodhart, C. (2003). The historical pattern of economic cycles and their interaction with asset prices and financial regulation. In W. Hunter, G. Kaufman, & M. Pomerleano (Eds.), *Asset price bubbles: The implications for monetary, regulatory and international policies* (pp. 467-480). Massachusetts, MA: MIT Press.

Helbling, T. (2005). *Housing price bubbles: A tale based on housing price booms and busts* (BIS Papers 21). Basel, Switzerland: Bank for International Settlements.

Australian Government. House of Representatives Standing Committee on Economics, Finance and Public Administration. (2002, December 6). *Official Committee Hansard: Reference: Reserve Bank of Australia annual report 2001-02.* Canberra: Author.

Hunter, W., Kaufman, G., & Pomerleano, M. (2003). Overview: Asset price bubbles. In W. Hunter, G. Kaufman, & M. Pomerleano. (Eds.), *Asset price bubbles: The implications for monetary, regulatory and international policies* (pp. xiii-xxvi). Massachusetts, MA: MIT Press.

Hutchison, M., McDill, K., & Madrassy, R. (1999). Empirical determinants of banking crises: Japan's experience in international perspective. In C, Freedman (Ed.), *Why did Japan stumble? Causes and cures* (pp. 157-183). Cheltenham, UK: Edward Elgar.

International Monetary Fund. (1998). Japan's economic crisis and policy options. In *World economic outlook, October 1998: Financial turbulence and the world economy* (pp. 107-122). Washington, DC: Author.

International Monetary Fund. (2003). When bubbles burst. In *World economic outlook, April 2003: Growth and institutions* (pp. 61-94). Washington, DC: Author.

Katz, R. (1998). *The system that soured: The rise and fall of the Japanese economic miracle.* New York, NY: East Gate.

Kent, C., & Lowe, P. (1997). *Asset price bubbles and monetary policy* (RBA Research Discussion Paper 9709). Sydney, Australia: Reserve Bank of Australia.

Kroszner, R. (2003). Asset price bubbles, information and public policy. In W. Hunter, G. Kaufman, & M. Pomerleano (Eds.), *Asset price bubbles: The implications for monetary, regulatory and international policies* (pp. 3-14). Massachusetts, MA: MIT Press.

Kuroda, A. (1998). Prudential policy in Japan. In C. Freedmen (Ed.), *Japanese economic policy reconsidered* (pp. 219-245). Cheltenham, UK: Edward Elgar.

Laker, J. (2003). The resilience of housing loan portfolios: APRA's "stress test" results. (Address to the Securities Institute of Australia, 9 October 2003).

Lowe, P. (2003). Asset prices, financial imbalances and monetary policy: Are inflation targets enough? Discussion. In A. Richards & T. Robinson (Eds.), *Asset prices and monetary policy* (pp. 97-99). Sydney, Australia: Reserve Bank of Australia.

Macfarlane, I. (2003). Statement to parliamentary committee. *RBA Bulletin*, 9-12. Sydney, Australia: Reserve Bank of Australia.

McKibbin, W. (2003). Asset prices, financial imbalances and monetary policy: Are inflation targets enough? Discussion. In A. Richards & T. Robinson (Eds.), *Asset prices and monetary policy* (pp. 100-107). Sydney, Australia: Reserve Bank of Australia.

Miwa, Y., & Ramseyer, J. M. (2003). Japan's lost decade and corporate structure: Comment. In R. M. Stern (Ed.), *Japan's economic recovery: Commercial policy, monetary policy and corporate governance* (pp. 335-340). Cheltenham, UK, Edward Elgar.

Mori, N., Shiratsuka, S., & Taguchi, H. (2001). Policy responses to the post-bubble adjustments in Japan: A tentative review. *Monetary and Economic Studies*, *19*(S1), 53-112.

Okina, K., Shirakawa, M., & Shiratsuka, S. (2001). The asset price bubble and monetary policy: Japan's experience in the late 1980s and the lessons. *Monetary and Economic Studies*, *19*(S1), 395-450.

Okina, K., & Shiratsuka, S. (2002). Asset price bubbles, price stability, and monetary policy: Japan's experience. *Monetary and Economic Studies*, *20*(3), 35-76.

Okina, K., & Shiratsuka, S. (2004). Asset price fluctuations, structural adjustments, and sustained economic growth: Lessons from Japan's experience since the late 1980s. *Monetary and Economic Studies*, *22*(S1), 143-177.

Posen, A. (2003). It takes more than a bubble to become Japan. In A. Richards & T. Robinson (Eds.), *Asset prices and monetary policy* (pp. 203-249). Sydney, Australia: Reserve Bank of Australia.

Australian Government. Productivity Commission. (2004). *First home ownership* (Report No. 28). Melbourne, Australia: Author.

Reserve Bank of Australia (2003a). *Submission to the Productivity Commission inquiry on first home ownership* (RBA Occasional Paper No 16). Sydney, Australia: Author.

Reserve Bank of Australia (2003b). Statement on monetary policy. *Reserve Bank of Australia Bulletin August 2003*, 1-56. Sydney, Australia: Author.

Reserve Bank of Australia (2004). *Financial stability review March 2004*. Sydney, Australia: Author.

Reserve Bank of Australia (2005). *Financial stability review September 2005*. Sydney, Australia: Author.

Sato, K. (1999). *The transformation of the Japanese economy*. New York, NY: East Gate.

Saxonhouse, G., & Stern, R. (2004). *Japan's lost decade: Origins, consequences and prospects for recovery*. Massachusetts, MA: Blackwell.

Shiratsuka, S. (2005). *The asset price bubble in Japan in the 1980s: Lessons for financial and macroeconomic stability* (BIS Papers 21). Basel, Switzerland: Bank for International Settlements.

Shiratsuka, S. (2000). *Asset prices, financial stability, and monetary policy: Based on Japan's experience of the asset price bubble* (IMES Discussion Paper No 2000-E-34). Tokyo, Japan: Institute for Monetary and Economic Studies.

Simon, J. (2003). Three Australian asset price bubbles. In A. Richards & T. Robinson (Eds.) *Asset prices and monetary policy* (pp. 8-41). Sydney, Australia: Reserve Bank of Australia.

Tsuda, K. (1999). Japanese banks in deregulation and the economic bubble. In K. Sato (Ed.), *The transformation of the Japanese economy* (pp. 267-290). New York, NY: East Gate.

Tsuru, K. (2001). *The choice of lending patterns by Japanese banks during the 1980s and 1990s: The causes and consequences of a real estate lending boom* (IMES Discussion Paper No 2001-E-8). Tokyo, Japan: Institute for Monetary and Economic Studies.

Trichet, J-C. (2005). *Asset price bubbles and monetary policy* (BIS Quarterly Review 44/2005). Basel, Switzerland: Bank for International Settlements.

Yoshitomi, M. (1999). Why has the Japanese economy been stumbling for so long? In C. Freedman (Ed.), *Why did Japan stumble? Causes and cures*. Cheltenham, UK: Edward Elgar.

Zhu, H. (2005). *The importance of property markets for monetary policy and financial stability* (BIS Papers 21). Basel, Switzerland: Bank for International Settlements.

Appendix A. Asset Price Movements in Japan and Australia

Figure 1: Asset price movements in Japan and Australia

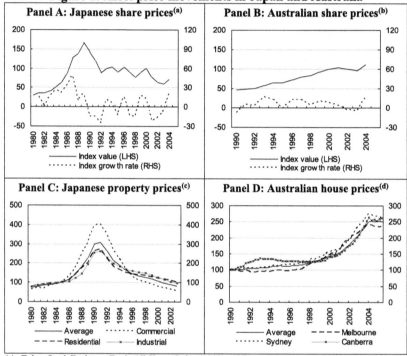

(a) Tokyo Stock Exchange Topix All Shares Index (2000 = 100).
(b) Standard and Poor's Australian Stock Exchange 200 Index (2000 = 100).
(c) Indexes of urban land prices in major Japanese cities (1985 = 100).
(d) Indexes of prices of established homes in major Australian cities (1989 = 100).
Source: OECD Main Economic Indicators; Japanese Real Estate Institute, *Index of Urban Land Prices by Use*; Australian Bureau of Statistics, *Price Index of Established Homes* (Cat No 6416.0).

Appendix B. Output and Demand Growth in Japan and Australia

Figure 2: Output and demand growth in Japan[(a)] and Australia[(b)]

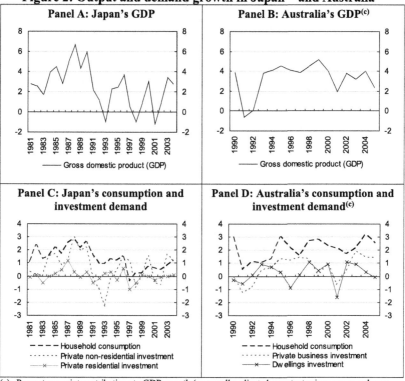

(a) Percentage-point contributions to GDP growth (seasonally adjusted, constant prices, measured over the fiscal year from 1 April to 31 March).

(b) Percentage-point contributions to GDP growth (chain volume measures, measured over the fiscal year from 1 July to 30 June).

(c) The Australian Government introduced a goods and services tax at the beginning of the 2001 fiscal year. This resulted in the bringing-forward of some expenditure from 2001 into 2000, increasing GDP in 2000 and decreasing it in 2001.

Source: Cabinet Office, Government of Japan, *Quarterly Estimates of GDP;* Australian Bureau of Statistics, *Australian System of National Accounts* (Cat. No. 5204.0).

Appendix C. Inflation in Japan and Australia

Figure 3: Inflation in Japan and Australia

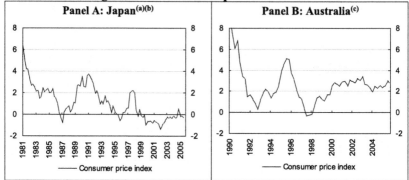

(a) Year-ended percentage change in consumer price index (all items).
(b) The increase in inflation in 1997 reflects an increase in consumption tax from April 1997.
(c) Year-ended percentage change in consumer price index (all items) (adjusted for impact of changes in consumption tax that took effect in June 2000).

Source: OECD Main Economic Indicators; Australian Bureau of Statistics, *Consumer Price Index* (Cat No 6401.0); Reserve Bank of Australia.

Appendix D. Interest Rates and Credit Growth in Japan and Australia

Figure 4: Interest rates and credit growth in Japan and Australia

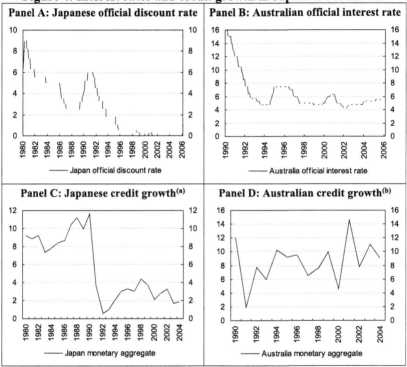

| Panel A: Japanese official discount rate | Panel B: Australian official interest rate |
| Panel C: Japanese credit growth[a] | Panel D: Australian credit growth[b] |

(a) Year-ended percentage change in M2+CDs, seasonally adjusted.
(b) Year-ended percentage change in M3, seasonally adjusted. Data for 2000 and 2001 reflect the
     bringing-forward of some activity ahead of the introduction of a goods and services tax at the
     beginning of the 2001 fiscal year.
Source: Bank of Japan; Reserve Bank of Australia; OECD Main Economic Indicators.

Determinants of Interest Margins of Banks in Sri Lanka

By S.M. Susanthi Medha Kumari

Abstract

Net interest margin (NIM) is an indicator of the level of efficiency of financial intermediation by banks. This study analyses the determinants of NIMs of domestic banks of Sri Lanka for the period of January 2002 to March 2011 based on the model developed by Ho and Saunders and its extensions using panel regression. Sri Lankan banks are inward looking in setting NIMs as operating costs, credit risk, risk aversion, non-interest income and capital adequacy requirements are determinants. Market competition, other regulations on banks, risk arising from the volatility of market prices and macroeconomic variables do not have a significant impact on the determination of NIMs.

Introduction

Financial intermediation by banks plays a vital role in economic growth by channeling savings for investments, working capital of businesses and consumption. Net interest margin (NIM), which refers to the difference between lending and deposit rates in terms of average assets of banks, is the main indicator of the level of efficiency of financial intermediation by banks.

It is expected that banks set interest rates based on policy rates decided by the central bank and the yield curve of risk-free securities. However, when setting interest rates, financial institutions create a gap between deposit and lending rates to compensate for costs, risks undertaken, regulatory requirements and to respond to competitors' interest rate changes. The deposit and loan rates set thus by financial institutions are not wholly responsive to policy rate changes or the changes in the yield curve of risk-free securities. Therefore, the gap between deposit and lending rates created by financial institutions to compensate for operational and regulatory costs, credit and market risks undertaken, and to take advantage of imperfect competition in the industry, reflects frictions in financial markets for monetary policy transmission. Furthermore, larger gaps can affect economic activities if lending rates are kept high, leading to a reduction in credit obtained by the private sector. This warrants the investigation of determinants of interest margins.

Having recognized the importance of identifying determinants of NIMs, researchers have analysed interest margins against various bank-specific, industry-specific and macroeconomic variables for various countries, regions and time periods. Determinants identified include market power (Valverde & Fernandez, 2006), volatility of market interest rates, capital adequacy requirements and segmentation in the industry (Saunders & Schumacher, 2000), operating costs, reserve requirements and uncertainty in the macroeconomic environment (Brock & Suarez, 2000), and the extent of bank risk aversion and the inflation rate (Aboagye et al., 2008). Many such researchers have employed the model for explaining and analysing NIMs developed by Ho and Saunders (1981) while extending it to incorporate more explanatory factors (Aboagye et al., 2008; Allen, 1988; Valverde & Fernandez, 2007).

Sri Lanka's financial system is largely dominated by banks. Sri Lanka experienced a substantial level of financial deepening in the recent years and envisages that growth in the credit stock will help accelerate economic growth. The yearly NIM of the banking industry fluctuated between 4.1 per cent and 4.6 per cent from 2005 to 2010 and stood at 4.6 per cent in December 2010. By considering the NIM of Sri Lankan banks as high compared to some other developed and emerging market economies, the Central Bank of Sri Lanka (CBSL) conducted moral suasion for banks to reduce NIMs in the past several years (Central Bank of Sri Lanka, 2006, 2012). It was also experienced lately that when policy rates were reduced, banks were prompt to lower deposit rates only, thus widening the interest margin. Future consolidation in the banking industry may also affect the NIM of the banking industry.

The determinants of the NIM revealed by previous researchers indicate that factors influencing NIMs are highly contextual and vary with the characteristics of the economy, banking industry and management practices. Development issues specific to developing economies affect the NIMs in such economies (Chirwa & Mlachila, 2004). Therefore, to formulate policy action for maintaining healthy NIMs, and to understand the nature of financial market frictions prevalent, determinants specific to the country and time period have to be investigated.

Despite the importance placed on the NIM by the financial sector policy in Sri Lanka during the period from 2005 to 2012, no research analysed factors determining NIMs of banks in Sri Lanka using econometric techniques while taking into account the specific characteristics of the Sri Lankan banking industry. The Ho and Saunders (1981) model is a comprehensive model that encompasses bank-specific, industry-related and macroeconomic variables that have been used to study NIMs of many other developed and developing countries. Therefore, this research purports to identify the determinants of NIMs of banks in Sri Lanka for the period from January 2002 to March 2011, using the Ho and Saunders model and its extensions.

As of 31 March 2011, the Sri Lankan banking industry consisted of 32 banks of which 23 are Licensed Commercial Banks (LCBs) that were authorized to maintain demand deposits and transact in foreign currency. The rest were Licensed Specialized Banks (LSBs) that included savings and development banks. Eleven of the 23 LCBs were domestic banks, while the rest were branches of foreign banks. The share of domestic LCBs out of total assets of the banking system was 71 per cent as of December 2010. Only domestic LCBs will be considered in this study. Foreign banks will not be included in the analysis as they do not actively engage in retail banking or the local currency loan and deposit markets. LSBs will not be included in the analysis as they operate in specific niche markets and account for a small share of the assets of the banking system.

The CBSL, under its co-objective of financial system stability, regulates and supervises banks. During the period under concern, the banking system remained safe and sound, resilient to global and domestic shocks. The private sector and foreign banks were encouraged to actively compete in the industry and no credit ceilings or interest ceilings were imposed. The major regulations included capital adequacy, minimum liquid asset ratio, classification and provisioning for bad loans, limits on large exposures, share ownership and corporate governance. All regulations were similarly applicable to the government-owned, private sector and foreign banks.

The rest of the article is organized as follows. The second section presents a literature review. Empirical specifications are presented in the third section. Results are discussed in the fourth section, while conclusions are drawn in the fifth section.

Literature Review

Significance of the Net Interest Margin
Generally, a high NIM is perceived as detriment to the economy because it indicates

high intermediation costs leading to high social costs. Bank failures also result in negative social externalities. A high NIM is a result of either low deposit rates, causing low fund flow to the banking system and high fund flow to other savings instruments, or high lending rates causing low investments (Aboagye et al., 2008). From a bank's point of view, the NIM is the main determinant of the profit of a bank. A bank should generate sufficient profits to build its capital base to absorb various risks. Banks in countries with less developed equity markets rely more on building capital through the NIM (Chirwa & Mlachila, 2004; Saunders & Schumacher, 2000).

An appropriate level of the NIM needs to be maintained to ensure the stability of individual banks and the financial system and achieve economic growth.

Models for Analysing Factors that Determine the Interest Margin

Different approaches to identify determinants of NIMs have been used in previous research studies. In a seminal study on the determinants of NIMs, Ho and Saunders (1981) develop a model which is widely referred to as the dealership approach. In order to analyse the determinants of bank margins, the hedging hypothesis, which views the bank as attempting to match maturities of assets and liabilities to avoid reinvestment risk, is integrated to the objective function of a bank, which is maximization of the expected utility of profit. It is assumed that the bank is risk-averse. The discount or premium on lending and deposit rates leading to the creation of an interest margin is set in such a manner that the expected utility of wealth is maximized. This model posits that even under perfect competition, 'transactions uncertainty' generated by an asynchronous deposit supply and loan demand compels banks to maintain an interest margin. Because of the asynchronous deposit supply and loan demand, the bank is compelled to lend and borrow in the money market which leads to the bank's interest rate risk (risk arising from fluctuations in money market interest rates). The part of the NIM which arises due to transaction uncertainty is named the 'pure spread' and accounts for the monopoly rent element in the bank margin (or degree of market competition), risk aversion of the bank management, size of transactions and variance in deposit and loan rates. The NIM consists of the pure spread and a further mark-up for regulatory requirements and other imperfections such as the payment of implicit interest (non-interest income and expenses of banks), opportunity cost of holding non-remunerated reserve requirements and default risk of loans.

The dealership model developed by Ho and Saunders has been used and extended by other research. Allen (1988) extended the model to take into account heterogeneity of loan products. Lerner (as cited in Aboagye et al., 2008) included production costs of intermediation. McShane and Sharpe (1985) replaced interest rate risk on credit and deposits with uncertainties in the money market. Angbazo (1997) extended the model by including credit risk and its interaction with interest rate risk, and analysed whether risk effects are heterogeneous across banks of different sizes. Valverde and Fernandez (2007) analyzed the relationship between NIM and specialization of banking activities by using a multi-output model for different types of products as banks' non-interest income has increased due to non-traditional banking activities. Maudos and Guevara (2004) found that banks' operating costs is a determinant of the NIM and if excluded from the theoretical explanation, can result in omitted variable bias. Maudos and Guevara (2004) also introduced direct measures of market power, calculated using concentration indices and Lerner indices, to capture the degree of competition.

Other models to identify determinants of the NIM include the banking firm micro-model approach (Wong, 1997; Zarruk, 1989). Under this model, the banking firm is viewed in a static setting in which demand and supply of deposits and loans simultaneously clear both markets.

Determinants of Interest Margins

By virtue of the Ho and Saunders model, determinants of the NIM have been widely analysed in terms of bank-specific factors, industry-related factors and macroeconomic factors (Aboagye et al., 2008; Saunders & Schumacher, 2000).

Bank-specific Factors

Bank-specific factors include operating costs, level of operations, risks undertaken, off-balance sheet exposure and non-interest income. Operating cost of banks is a significant factor that affects the level of NIMs (Aboagye et al., 2008; Angbazo, 1997; Brock & Suarez, 2000; Maudos & Guevara, 2004) as banks need to compensate for costs through interest earnings.

The level of operations as measured through capital expenditure, total assets, size of credit and deposit operations, and the level of technology have also been revealed to affect NIMs by increasing costs. (Aboagye et al., 2008; Angbazo, 1997; Maudos & Guevara, 2004). Higher level of operations also results in greater losses from interest rate risk and credit risk, for a given level of market and credit risk assumed by the bank which should be covered by the NIM (Maudos & Guevara, 2004).

Angbazo (1997) argues that the effect of credit risk and interest rate risk on NIMs depends on the size and type of operations of the bank and has found that in large banks the NIM is affected more by credit risk than by interest rate risk. This outcome is attributed to large banks undertaking more hedging contracts and having more short-term assets in their portfolios.

The level of NIM is also affected by liquidity risk, credit risk, and interest rate risk of the bank (Aboagye et al., 2008; Angbazo, 1997; Brock & Suarez, 2000). Brock and Suarez (2000) reveal a negative relationship between non-performing assets (indicating credit risk) and NIM. The reason is attributed to the reduction of the NIM when non-performing assets increase compared to loan loss reserves, or reduction of lending rates to attract more borrowers and reduce defaults. However, Maudos and Guevara (2004) find a positive relationship between credit risk and NIM. Absolute risk-aversion by banks, too, affects the level of NIMs (Angbazo, 1997; Maudos & Guevara, 2004).

Angbazo (1997) highlights the importance of off-balance-sheet exposure as a determinant of NIMs and finds that off-balance-sheet activities allow banks to engage in non-traditional activities and diversified margin generation.

Saunders and Schumacher (2000) found that implicit interest income such as fees and commissions affect NIMs. Product diversification can reduce NIMs through cross elasticities among a bank's products (Allen, 1988). By using a multi-output model that incorporates broader definitions of NIM, Valverde and Fernandez (2007) find that market power of a bank, and consequently its total revenue and NIM, are influenced by the extent of diversification into non-traditional banking products. However, diversification gains can also be offset by the bank being exposed to a greater range of volatile activities (Stiroh & Rumble, 2006, as cited in Valverde & Fernandez, 2007).

Industry-related Factors

Industry characteristics, including the nature and extent of competition among banks and regulatory requirements, affect the level of NIMs. The extent of competition can be inferred by a bank's capacity to set prices above marginal cost and the market share of the bank (Aboagye et al., 2008; Maudos & Guevara, 2004). Saunders and Schumacher (2000) contend that the more segmented and restricted a market is, the higher the monopoly power of banks and the higher the NIM would be. Greater competition in the banking industry reduces the NIM and promotes greater efficiency (Aboagye et al., 2008; Maudos & Guevara, 2004; McShane & Sharpe, 1985). However, in respect of the European banking industry in the 1990s, Maudos and Guevara (2004) find that the NIM decreased with the relaxation of competitive conditions because the effect on the NIM was counteracted by reductions in interest rate risk, credit risk, and operating costs.

Non-interest-bearing reserve requirements imposed by monetary authorities is a main regulatory requirement that increases the opportunity cost of funds leading to increases in the NIM (Angbazo, 1997; Brock & Suarez, 2000; Maudos & Guevara, 2004). Capital to asset requirements, liquid fund reserve requirements, and other prudential regulations also adversely impact the NIM (Aboagye et al., 2008; Angbazo, 1997; Saunders & Schumacher, 2000).

Macroeconomic Factors

Apart from bank-specific and industry-specific factors, macroeconomic variables are considered by banks when setting interest rates. Volatility of money market interest rates is a key factor affecting NIMs (Aboagye et al., 2008; Ho & Saunders, 1981; Maudos & Guevara, 2004; Saunders & Schumacher, 2000). Angbazo (1997) finds that less liquid credit market conditions result in a low NIM because of credit rationing in which loan rates are less responsive to market interest rates.

GDP growth rate (Brock & Suarez, 2000) and the business cycle (Jayaratne & Strahan, 1997) affect NIMs as high GDP growth increases the net worth of firms, reducing credit risk and thereby the lending rates. The business cycle together with regulatory trends can explain the differences in NIMs across countries and regions (Jayaratne & Strahan, 1997). Expected inflation and actual inflation also have an influence on NIMs (Aboagye et al., 2008; Chirwa & Mlachila, 2004). Similarly, uncertainty in the macroeconomic environment, too, affects NIMs (Brock & Suarez, 2000).

Factors Relating to Developing Countries

In light of the determinants of NIM in developing countries revealed by various research, Chirwa and Mlachila (2004) propose a number of reasons why persistently high NIMs are common in developing countries despite financial liberalization and structural reform programs undertaken. These include financial sector reforms not significantly altering the structure in which banks operate, high liquidity reserve requirements due to non-existence of deposit insurance schemes, removal of credit controls leading to moral hazard and increased amount of risky loans in bank portfolios, high non-financial costs on physical capital and employment, large capital to assets ratios, macroeconomic instability including high and volatile inflation and instability in the policy environment.

Therefore, to formulate effective policy action to maintain healthy NIMs, determinants specific to the country/region have to be analysed against structural characteristics of that country/region.

Empirical Specification

The interest margin can be gauged from financial statements of banks using various ratios. The most commonly used measure is the difference between interest earnings and interest expenses in terms of average assets, which will be used in this study as well. As opposed to the interest rate spread (which is the difference between the average lending rate and the average borrowing rate), the NIM is affected by changes in the interest rates as well as changes in the denominator, that is, amounts of assets and liabilities. The NIM reflects a bank's business model, or the amounts and types of assets and liabilities it chooses to hold. Therefore, the NIM is a better measure of efficiency of financial intermediation than the interest rate spread.

To decompose determinants of NIMs into bank-specific, industry-related and macroeconomic factors as per the Ho and Saunders (1981) dealership model, a single-step approach or a two-step approach can be utilized. Under the two-step approach, as conducted by Ho and Saunders (1981), Saunders and Schumacher (2000), and Brock and Suarez (2000), first the explanatory variables that are not explicitly introduced into the model are controlled for, to obtain an estimate of the pure margin. In the second step, the validity of the theoretical model is tested by examining the empirical relationship between the pure spread and variables included in the theoretical model. On the other hand, some researchers have used a single-step approach by including variables of the theoretical model as well as imperfections that reflect exogenous variables in the same regression (Angbazo, 1997; Maudos & Guevara, 2004; McShane & Sharpe, 1985).

This research follows the one-step regression approach similar to the methodology followed by Angbazo (1997), Maudos and Guevara (2004), and McShane and Sharpe (1985). A one-step regression is preferred as the objective is to identify factors affecting interest margins of banks in Sri Lanka out of both factors included in the theoretical model as well as imperfections which are not included in the theoretical model but acknowledged to be present by other researchers. A one-step regression is preferred also due to the lack of time series data for a considerably long period of time.

The NIM is hypothesized to vary with bank-specific variables, industry-related variables and macroeconomic variables as follows:

$$NIM_{it} = \{x_{it}, y_{it}, z_t, e_t\}$$

where x represents the bank-specific variables for each bank at each time period, y represents the industry-related variables for each bank for each time period, and z represents the macroeconomic variables for each time period.

The 11 domestic LCBs of Sri Lanka will be taken into account. Quarterly data from 2002 quarter 1 to 2011 quarter 1 obtained from published financial statements of the banks are analysed.

The variables used and their expected coefficient signs are given in Table 1. The variables, their measures and expected coefficient sings, except volatility in the exchange rate, were selected from past research mentioned in the second section and are the variables and measures commonly used by other researchers who used the Ho and Saunders model. This study additionally tests exchange rate volatility as an explanatory variable, as the banks under concern held a significant share (10–15 per cent) of assets and liabilities in foreign currency in the period under concern and hence were subject to considerable exchange rate risk.

Table 1. Variables Considered in the Study

Variable	Proxy Used	Expected Coefficient Sign	Rationale for the Expected Coefficient Sign
Net interest margin (NIM)	(Interest income– Interest expenses)/ Average assets		Dependent variable.
Operating cost (OC/TA)	Operating cost/Total assets	Positive	Banks increase the NIM to compensate for higher costs.
Scale of operations (TA)	Change in total assets (in LKR billions)	Negative	Banks can pass on to customers the benefits of cost savings from large- scale operations.
Extent of risk aversion (E/TA)	Equity and reserves/ Total assets	Positive	A more risk-averse bank will have more equity capital in its balance sheet and therefore will widen the NIM to earn high returns for equity holders.
Credit risk (NPA)	Non-performing loans/Total gross loans	Positive	To compensate for higher risk, a bank will charge a higher margin.
Management quality (OC/REV)	Operating expenses/ Revenue	Positive	Banks increase the NIM to compensate for higher cost per unit of revenue.
Concentration in the banking industry (HHI)	Herfindahl–Hirschman index (Sum of squares of assets of the bank/Assets of the industry)	Positive	A higher HHI index indicates higher concentration in the industry, in which case the NIM will be wider.
Capital adequacy requirements (CAR)	Statutory Total Capital Adequacy Ratio calculated according to Basel I (before 01 January 2008) and Basel II (after 01 January 2008), which is eligible capital/risk- weighted assets	Positive	A higher capital adequacy ratio constrains lending by the bank. Banks will compensate for the reduced interest income by widening the NIM.
Opportunity cost of non-interest earning reserves maintained at the central bank (CB/TA)	Balance in the account maintained at the Central Bank/ Total assets	Positive	The higher the non- interest earning reserves, the wider the NIM will be, in order to compensate for the reduced interest income that could have been earned with the funds in the reserve account.

Table 1. Variables Considered in the Study—cont'd.

Variable	Proxy Used	Expected Coefficient Sign	Rationale for the Expected Coefficient Sign
Implicit interest received (Fee/TA)	Fees and commissions received/Total assets	Negative	Increase in non-interest income such as fees and commissions will enable banks to narrow the NIM.
Volatility in the money market interest rates (CM)	Quarterly standard deviations of daily call money rates (interbank overnight uncollateralized)	Positive	The higher the volatility in the market interest rates, the higher the market risk of the bank and the greater the NIM.
Volatility in the exchange rate (USD)	Quarterly standard deviations of daily exchange rates between the USD and the LKR	Positive	The higher the volatility in the exchange rates, the higher the market risk of the bank and the greater the NIM.
Inflation (INF)	Point-to-point change in the Colombo Consumers Price Index (2002 = 100)	Positive	Higher inflation indicates greater uncertainty in the macro environment, which will induce banks to widen the NIM.
GDP growth rate (GDP)	Real GDP growth rate of Sri Lanka	Cannot be determined	The relationship between NIMs and GDP depends on the correlation between prices, costs and the business cycle (Carbo et al., 2003, as cited in Valverde & Fernandez, 2007).

Source: Compiled by the author based on past studies.

The variables in the model are of the characteristics given in Table 2 when all the banks are considered together. The model is estimated using fixed effects least squared panel regression. For each of the 11 banks, dummy variables were assigned to capture the importance of differences among banks in their individual characteristics such as their business models and management. A fixed effects least squared regression estimate revealed that all yearly time dummies are significant at the 1 per cent significance level. Therefore, yearly time dummy variables were included in the panel regressions.

With the assumption that time-invariant characteristics of the individual banks are unique to each bank, a fixed effects panel regression is preferred. However, the Hausman test indicates that individual bank errors are in fact correlated with the regressors. Therefore, the results obtained under fixed effects least squares panel regression, random effects panel regression, and ordinary least squares are reported in Table 3.

Table 2. Descriptive Statistics of Variables

Variable	Mean	Standard Deviation
NIM	3.67	1.45
OC/TA	3.94	2.50
FEE/TA	1.05	0.41
TA	4.71	20.5
E/TA	6.46	5.09
NPA	11.41	7.82
SLAR	25.59	6.46
OC/REV	33.41	24.58
HHI	0.013	0.025
CAR	11.04	6.87
CB/TA	4.34	1.56
CM	1.17	1.44
USD	0.56	0.49
INF	10.74	5.88
GDP	6.00	1.83

Source: Author's calculations.

Table 3. Results of the Regression Analysis

Variable	Ordinary Least Squares		Random Effects		Fixed Effects	
	Coefficient	Standard Error	Coefficient	Standard Error	Coefficient	Standard Error
OC/TA	0.118	0.048**	0.241	0.054***	0.118	0.048**
FEE/TA	−0.638	0.168***	−0.082	0.157	−0.638	0.168***
TA	0.000	0.000	0.000	0.000	0.000	0.000
E/TA	0.035	0.019*	0.041	0.020**	0.0353	0.019*
NPA	0.022	0.009**	0.041	0.008***	0.0225	0.009**
SLAR	0.016	0.010	0.019	0.011*	0.016	0.010
OC/REV	−0.037	0.005***	−0.045	0.005***	−0.037	0.005
HHI	0.211	3.751	−2.970	2.640	0.211	3.751
CAR	0.024	0.014*	0.024	0.014*	0.024	0.014*
CB/TA	0.020	0.054	−0.029	0.042	0.020	0.054
CM	−0.075	0.096	−0.086	0.117	−0.075	0.096

Continued

Table 3. Results of the Regression Analysis—cont'd.

Variable	Ordinary Least Squares		Random Effects		Fixed Effects	
	Coefficient	Standard Error	Coefficient	Standard Error	Coefficient	Standard Error
USD	−0.117	0.113	−0.109	0.137	−0.117	0.113
INF	−0.026	0.018	−0.025	0.022	−0.026	0.018
GDP	0.020	0.054	0.029	0.065	0.020	0.054
Time 2003	0.470	0.223**	0.256	0.262	0.470	0.223**
Time 2004	0.801	0.222***	0.083	0.264***	0.801	0.222***
Time 2005	0.607	0.224***	0.612	0.267***	0.607	0.224***
Time 2006	1.368	0.276***	1.490	0.329***	1.368	0.276***
Time 2007	1.165	0.504**	0.151	1.208**	1.165	0.504**
Time 2008	0.998	0.355***	0.695	0.883**	0.998	0.355***
Time 2009	1.014	0.279***	−0.224	0.746***	1.014	0.279***
Time 2010	1.425	0.283***	0.076	1.158***	1.425	0.283***
Time 2011	0.438	0.341***	0.429	0.974***	1.438	0.341***
Cons	0.167	1.262***	2.422	0.640***	3.275	0.569***
Adjusted R squared	0.649		0.510		0.454	
F Statistic	23.71***				24.32***	
No. of observations	407		407		407	
Wald Chi2 (22)			398.18***			
Corr (u_i, X)					−0.103	
Rho			0		0.413	
F Statistic for Rho					19.35***	

Source: Author's calculations.

Notes: Coefficients significant at 1 per cent are marked with ***. Coefficients significant at 5 per cent are marked with ** and coefficients significant at 10 per cent are marked with *. OC/TA, operating cost to total assets; FEE/TA, fees and commissions received to total assets; TA, total assets; E/TA, equity to total assets; NPA, non-performing asset ratio; SLAR, statutory liquid asset ratio; OC/REV, operating cost to revenue; HHI, Herfindahl–Hershman Index; CAR, total capital adequacy ratio; CB/TA, balance in the reserve account with the central bank to total assets; CM, volatility in daily call money rates; USD, volatility in the exchange rate; INF, inflation rate; GDP, real gross domestic product growth rate.

Results and Discussion

According to the panel regressions, operating costs, credit risk, extent of risk aversion (equity to total assets ratio), implicit interest earned (fees and commissions) and capital adequacy requirements are significant in explaining NIMs of domestic Licensed Commercial Banks of Sri Lanka.

The results show that under the three methods, the variables OC/TA, NPA, ETA, FEETA and CAR are statistically significant. The overall results under the three methods indicate the robustness of the results. According to the R squared of the three results at 45 per cent to 65 per cent, a significant proportion of the variation in NIM is explained. The intra-class correlation under the random effects model is 0, and it is 41 per cent under the fixed effects model. In this model, this indicates that 41 per cent of the variance is due to differences across panels. The correlation of the errors with the regressors in the fixed effects model is weak. The OLS regression shows that the individual characteristics of banks are important for three banks in relation to bank 11.

The finding that operating costs are a determinant of NIMs of banks is consistent with the findings of Aboagye et al. (2008) for Ghana, Angbazo (1997) for the US, Brock and Suarez (2000) for Latin America, and Maudos and Guevara (2004) for Germany, UK, France, Italy and Spain. This reflects banks' efforts to set interest margins to cover operating costs.

Scale of operations, proxied by change in total assets, is not significant in explaining changes in NIMs. It was expected that the larger the operations of a bank, the more will be the ability to pass on cost savings through greater efficiency to customers. Scale of operations must be affected by the fact that the government owned domestic banks account for more than one third of the assets of the banking system during the period under concern. These banks are characterized by higher cost to income or cost to asset ratios. For these banks, expanding operations do not sufficiently translate into cost savings through efficiency.

The proxy variable for risk aversion, equity in terms of total assets, has a positive relationship with the NIM. When the perceived risk is greater, a bank will try more to compensate for the risk through greater returns. This result may also mean that banks widen NIMs to generate adequate returns for shareholders as the banks' equity funds increase.

Credit risk is a determinant of NIMs of banks in Sri Lanka as postulated in the Ho and Saunders model. Banks increase NIMs to compensate higher credit risk and probable loss of interest income. This finding agrees with the results obtained by Aboagye et al. (2008) for Ghana, Angbazo (1997) for the US, and Maudos and Guevara (2004) for Germany, France, UK, Italy and Spain but contrasts with the negative relationship revealed by Brock and Suarez (2000) for Latin America. Liquidity risk is not a significant determinant of NIMs of banks as per the fixed effects and OLS regressions.

Implicit interest earnings or fees and commissions charged by banks have an influential power on determining NIMs in Sri Lankan banks, similar to the findings of Maudos and Guevara (2004) and Saunders and Schumacher (2000) for European countries and the US. Alternative income sources such as fees and commissions allow banks to narrow the interest margins.

Industry concentration, as measured by the Herfindahl–Hirschman index is not significant in determining the NIMs. The banking industry is structured such that two government-owned banks dominate the market with more than one third of the assets of the financial system in the period under concern. These banks operate with public welfare objectives in tandem with their main objective of generating profits. Certain features of these banks such as the large market share, wide branch network, diverse product portfolios that compete with private banks in a range of market segments, enable these banks to become market leaders in interest rate setting. In fact, when interest rates charged from customers were not reduced in response to policy rate reduction of the CBSL in 2010, the government publicly requested the two large government owned banks to reduce their loan rates, in anticipation that this move would compel the private sector banks to reduce their interest rates as well. Therefore, in the Sri Lankan banking industry, the players with larger market power in fact maintain low NIMs. On the other hand, smaller banks become reluctant to reduce their NIMs, as larger players may retaliate by reducing their NIMs as well.

The capital adequacy ratio is the only significant regulatory variable in explaining NIMs according to the results of this study. The minimum total capital adequacy ratio, which is eligible capital items in terms of risk-weighted assets (calculated according to Basel II from 1 January 2008), is 10 per cent in Sri Lanka. As per the presumed rationale for the expected relationship, high capital adequacy ratios constrain lending by banks, and the reduction in earnings is compensated for by widening the NIM.

The opportunity cost of non-remunerated reserve requirements at the CBSL was reduced in 2008 and 2009 when the CBSL gradually reduced the Statutory Reserve Requirement ratio from 10 per cent of deposit liabilities to 7 per cent of deposit liabilities, injecting further liquidity into the system. Not factoring this into NIMs indicates that banks may not be fully evaluating the opportunity cost of use of funds when making pricing decisions.

This study finds that macroeconomic factors, i.e., volatility in interest rates, inflation and GDP growth rates, which are found to affect NIMs of banks in other countries, are not significant in the context of Sri Lankan domestic banks. As volatility of call money rates and exchange rates denote market risk for a bank, this result suggests that banks do not include a mark-up for market risk when setting the interest margin, although the credit risk is taken into account. Volatility of the exchange rate which was introduced into the model by this study also is not a significant explanatory factor.

Banks need to assess the opportunity cost of funds constrained by regulatory requirements such as the unremunerated reserve requirement and maintenance of liquid assets, if such opportunity costs are to be compensated through the NIM. Similarly, banks need to assess gains and losses from fluctuations in interest rates and exchange rates if market risk is to be constantly factored into pricing decisions. This result indicates that there may be deficiencies in banks' technical capabilities in making projections and factoring a diverse set of variables into pricing decisions.

The findings of this study conform to some of the reasons identified by Chirwa and Mlachila (2004) by surveying literature for persistently high NIMs in developing countries. Some of these reasons in common with other developing countries are high physical capital, high employee costs, large amounts of risky loans in bank portfolios, high credit risk in the economy, large capital to asset ratios leading to less productive use of funds and macroeconomic instability.

Conclusion

According to the results of this study, the gap between lending and deposit rates created by the domestic banking industry largely consists of operating costs borne for financial intermediation, premium for credit risk and a mark-up for the regulatory cost pertaining to minimum capital ratios. Meanwhile, implicit income in the form of fees, charges, commissions, and so on from non-traditional banking activities contributes to reducing the NIM. Banks are mostly inward looking in deciding NIMs. Industry competition, opportunity cost of funds constrained by regulatory requirements other than capital adequacy requirements, market risk arising from fluctuations in money market interest rates and exchange rates as well as other macroeconomic variables are not factored into pricing decisions.

According to the findings, revisions to banking practices can help reduce NIMs through measures for improving cost efficiency, increasing non-interest income by diversifying operations and improving technical capabilities of assessing risks and opportunity cost of funds. Inefficiencies in government-owned banks should not undermine the efficiency of the financial system.

Limitations of technical capabilities of banks, which result in market risks and opportunity costs being inadequately assessed, can have serious implications for the adoption of new international prudential regulations. Authorities need to promote appropriate tools and techniques to be used for risk analysis and product pricing.

On the other hand, structural issues in the financial system present rigidities and impediments for effective financial intermediation. The effect of market competition on the NIM is undermined by the fact that banks with larger market share and market power are government-owned banks with social welfare objectives. The competitive pressure exerted on private banks by the government-owned banks results in NIMs of private banks being less affected by the variables in the Ho and Saunders model that are rationally expected to be the determinants of NIMs in a market economy. Consolidation among private banks will not help to reduce NIMs of the industry if the government-owned banks maintain their market power. However, if consolidation results in equalization of market power, greater competition and reduction of industry NIMs can be expected.

With regard to the macro-economy, volatility in interest rates and exchange rates remained high throughout the period under concern. Due to the significance of credit risk and risk aversion by banks, reduction of credit risk in the economy and a general climate of financial stability can contribute to reducing NIMs.

Monetary policy needs to take into account that banks create a gap between lending and deposit rates because of operational costs, compensation for risk, compensation for regulatory cost and as a result of imperfect competition. Reponses of the lending rates and deposit rates to policy rates vary when financial market frictions are present.

Acknowledgements

The author is grateful to the anonymous referee of the journal for interesting comments. The usual disclaimers apply. All views expressed in this article are those of the author and do not reflect the official stance of any organization she is affiliated with.

References

Aboagye, A.Q.Q., Akoena, S.K., Antwi-Asare, T.O. & Gockel, A.F. (2008). Explaining interest rate spreads in Ghana. *African Development Review, 20*(3), 378–399.

Allen, L. (1988). The determinants of bank interest margins: A note. *Journal of Financial and Quantitative Analysis, 23*(2), 231–235.

Angbazo, L. (1997). Commercial bank net interest margins, default risk, interest rate risk, and off balance sheet banking. *Journal of Banking & Finance, 21*(1), 55–87.

Brock, P.L. & Suarez, L.R. (2000). Understanding the behavior of bank spreads in Latin America. *Journal of Development Economics, 63*(1), 113–134.

Central Bank of Sri Lanka (2006). *Annual report 2006.* Colombo, Sri Lanka: Central Bank of Sri Lanka.

——— (2012, December 12). Governor, Cabraal enumerates 21 point plan for bankers. Retrieved 15 December 2012, from http://www.cbsl.gov.lk/htm/english/02_prs/prs. html

Chirwa, E.W. & Mlachila, M. (2004). Financial reforms and interest rate spreads in the commercial banking system in Malawi. *IMF Staff Papers, 51*(1), 96–122.

Ho, T.S.Y. & Saunders, A. (1981). The determinants of bank interest margins: Theory and empirical evidence. *Journal of Financial and Quantitative Analysis, 16*(4), 581–600.

Jayaratne, T. & Strahan, P.E. (1997). The benefits of branching deregulation. *Federal Reserve Bank of New York—Research Paper Series, 3*(4), 13–29.

Maudos, J. & Guevara, J.F. (2004). Factors explaining the interest margin in the banking sectors of the European Union. *Journal of Banking & Finance, 28*(9), 2259–2281.

McShane, R.W. & Sharpe, I.G. (1985). A time series/cross section analysis of the determinants of Australian trading bank loan/deposit interest margins: 1962–1981. *Journal of Banking and Finance, 9*(1), 115–136.

Saunders, A. & Schumacher, L. (2000). The determinants of bank interest margins: An international study. *Journal of International Money and Finance, 19*(6), 813–832.

Valverde, S.C. & Fernandez, F.R. (2007). The determinants of bank margins in European banking. *Journal of Banking & Finance, 31*(7), 2043–2063.

Wong, K.P. (1997). On the determinants of bank interest margins under credit and interest rate risks. *Journal of Banking & Finance, 21*(2), 251–271.

Zarruk, E.R. (1989). Bank spread with uncertain deposit level and risk aversion. *Journal of Banking & Finance, 13*(6), 797–810.

Appendix C

Data Sources

Institute of Developing Economies: Japan External Trade Organization (IDE-JETRO)
Social research on political, economic, and societal issues in developing economies.
http://www.ide.go.jp/English/Data/index.html

World Bank Data
Online database focusing on developing economies.
http://data.worldbank.org/

World Bank Group
Evaluation of regulations that promote and limit business activities in 190+ countries, economies, and selected cities at the subnational level.
http://www.doingbusiness.org/

Taylor & Francis Group
Database of a variety of academic journals.
http://www.tandfonline.com/

Organization for Economic Co-operation and Development (OECD)
Reports and macroeconomic and financial data on OECD member countries as well as on short- and long-term development projects.
http://www.oecd.org/

Asian Development Bank (ADB)
Economic data on developing countries in Asia.
http://www.adb.org/data/main

International Statistical Institute's National Statistics Offices
Contact information for, and links to, countries' statistical offices.
http://www.isi-web.org/index.php/resources/national-statistical-offices

United Nations Statistical Division
Database of all official UN statistics consolidated by country, indicator and theme.
https://unstats.un.org/home/

Food and Agriculture Organization of the United Nations
Database containing statistics showing the relationship between agriculture and the environment, economy, food security, and trade.
http://www.fao.org/economic/ess/en/#.VLyeINKUeSo

International Atomic Energy Agency (IAEA)
Reports and databases on international nuclear energy use.
http://www.iaea.org/

International Labour Organization (ILO)
Statistics and databases on modern labor trends.
http://www.ilo.org/global/statistics-and-databases/lang–en/index.htm

International Monetary Fund (IMF)
Database organized by country and containing information concerning various aspects of economic health.
http://www.imf.org/en/Data

United Nations Educational, Scientific and Cultural Organization (UNESCO) Institute for Statistics
Statistics on education, science and technology, culture, and communication for more than 200 countries and territories.
http://www.uis.unesco.org

United Nations Industrial Development Organization (UNIDO)
Database of major indicators of industrial performance by country.
http://www.unido.org/

International Telecommunication Union (ITU)
Statistics on the evolution of the telecommunications sector.
http://www.itu.int/en/Pages/default.aspx

World Health Organization (WHO)
Health statistics by country.
http://www.who.int/gho/database/en

United Nations World Tourism Organization (UNWTO)
Largest online collection of publications and statistics on international tourism.
http://www2.unwto.org/content/data

World Trade Organization (WTO)
Database focusing on economic research and data.
https://www.wto.org/english/res_e/res_e.htm

United Nations Statistical Institute for Asia and the Pacific (UNSIAP)
Statistics on population, labor, and gender for Asia and the Pacific.
http://www.unsiap.or.jp/

Office of the United Nations High Commissioner for Refugees (UNHCR)
Statistics on at-risk populations.
http://www.unhcr.org/data.html

United Nations Children's Fund (UNICEF)
Data on the status of children and women around the world.
https://data.unicef.org/

United Nations Conference on Trade and Development (UNCTAD)
Data on areas of finance, technology, investment, and sustainable development.
http://unctad.org/en/Pages/Statistics.aspx

United Nations Human Settlements Programme (UN-Habitat)
Data on the social and environmental factors affecting 741 urban areas in 220 countries.
urbandata.unhabitat.org

United Nations Office on Drugs and Crime (UNODC)
Reports and data on the illicit drug trade, human trafficking, and transnational crime.
http://www.unodc.org/

United Nations Population Fund (UNFPA)
Publications and data on population matters, gender and sexual and reproductive health.
http://www.unfpa.org/

United Nations Economic Commission for Africa (UNECA or ECA)
Indicators and economic statistics for Africa.
http://ecastats.uneca.org/data

United Nations Economic Commission for Europe (UNECE or ECE)
Economic and population data for Europe, including statistics on gender, health and mortality, globalization indicators, transportation, and forest health.
http://w3.unece.org/pxweb/en

Eurostat
A variety of statistical data on Europe organized by theme (e.g., economy and finance, population and social conditions, and science and technology).
http://ec.europa.eu/eurostat/data/database

United Nations Economic Commission for Latin America and the Caribbean (UNECLAC)
Statistical information on Latin America and the Caribbean.
https://www.cepal.org/en/datos-y-estadisticas

United Nations Economic and Social Commission for Asia and the Pacific (UNESCAP or ESCAP)
Demographic, migratory, educational, health, and gender statistics for Asia and the Pacific.
http://www.unescap.org/stat/data

United Nations Economic and Social Commission for Western Asia (UNESCWA)
Demographic, social, economic, environmental, and gender statistics for Western Asia.
https://www.unescwa.org/our-work/statistics

Open Data for Africa
Data sets, presented by country, for most of the African continent.
http://dataportal.opendataforafrica.org/

European Bank for Reconstruction and Development (EBRD)
Macroeconomic data and growth forecasts for Europe.
http://www.ebrd.com/what-we-do/economic-research-and-data/data.html

Inter-American Development Bank (IADB or IDB or BID)
Information graphics as well as raw data and economic indicators for the
Americas.
https://data.iadb.org

Bank for International Settlements
Data on the financial system, including securities, derivatives, and exchange
markets.
http://www.bis.org/index.htm

European Central Bank (ECB)
Data pertaining to the European banking and financial system.
http://www.ecb.europa.eu/home/html/index.en.html

World Legal Information Institute (World LII)
Catalog of legal materials organized by country that includes statutes,
judicial opinions, and other materials from legal regimes around
the world.
http://www.worldlii.org/

Macro Economy Meter (MecoMeter)
Data from a variety of sources presented in visual and easy-to-understand
formats.
www.mecometer.com

Evidence for Policy and Practice Information and Coordinating Centre
(EPPI Centre)
Health-based statistical data.
https://eppi.ioe.ac.uk/cms/Default.aspx?tabid=185

Central Intelligence Agency (CIA)
General demographic and geographic data on every country in the world.
https://www.cia.gov/library/publications/the-world-factbook/

United States Census Bureau
General and population statistics and foreign trade data on goods and
services imported and exported from the United States.
https://www.census.gov

Bureau of Economic Analysis
Major US macroeconomic indicators and regional and state data.
https://www.bea.gov

Bureau of Labor Statistics
Data related to employment and prices (e.g., Consumer Price Index).
https://www.bls.gov

The Federal Reserve
Various financial data including exchange rates, interest rates, bank assets,
household assets, and corporate debt.
https://www.federalreserve.gov

Inter-University Consortium for Political and Social Research (ICPSR)
Data collections in education, aging, criminal justice, substance abuse,
terrorism, and other fields.
https://www.icpsr.umich.edu/icpsrweb/

World Economic Outlook Database
Macroeconomic data (e.g., data on national accounts, inflation, unemployment rates, balance of payments, fiscal indicators, trade, and commodity
prices for country groups and individual countries).
https://www.imf.org/external/pubs/ft/weo/2017/02/weodata/index.aspx

Appendix D

Journals in Economics and Public Policy

	Name	Impact Factor	Areas	Publisher	Details
1	Quarterly Journal of Economics	6.662 (2016)	**Broad range of issues in various areas of economics** (e.g., microeconomics, macroeconomics, monetary economics, finance, healthcare, education, welfare, inequality)	Oxford Academic	**From the journal's website:** *The Quarterly Journal of Economics* is the oldest professional journal of economics in the English language. Edited at Harvard University's Department of Economics, it covers all aspects of the field. This is one of the top journals in economics, and it has one of the lowest acceptance rates—around 3%.
2	Journal of Finance	6.043	**All major areas of financial research** (e.g., corporate governance, risk management, international finance, trading, financial structures, capital markets, investment)	American Economic Association	**From the journal's website:** *The Journal of Finance* publishes leading research across all the major fields of financial research. It is the most widely cited academic journal on finance. Each issue of the journal reaches over 8000 academics, finance professionals, libraries, and government and financial institutions around the world. Published six times a year, the journal is the official publication of The American Finance Association, the premier academic organization devoted to the study and promotion of knowledge about financial economics.

3	American Economic Review*	4.73 (2015)	**Various topics in general-interest economics** (e.g., macroeconomics, microeconomics, comparative, reform, development, international economics)	American Economic Association	**From the journal's website:** The *American Economic Review* is a general-interest economics journal. Established in 1911, the AER is among the nation's oldest and most respected scholarly journals in the economics profession and is celebrating over 100 years of publishing. The journal publishes 11 issues containing articles on a broad range of topics.
					This is one of the top journals in economics, and it has a very low acceptance rate—around 8%.
4	Review of Economic Studies	4.030 (2016)	**Broad range of issues in various areas of economics** (e.g., microeconomics, macroeconomics, monetary economics, financial economics, health, education, welfare, labor, demographic economics)	Review of Economic Studies	**From the journal's website:** The *Review* is published quarterly by The Review of Economic Studies Ltd, whose objective is to encourage research in theoretical and applied economics, especially by young economists. *The Review of Economic Studies* is essential reading for economists. It is one of the core economics journals, consistently ranking among the top five titles.

Continued

	Name	Impact Factor	Areas	Publisher	Details
5	American Economic Journal: Macroeconomics*	3.58 (2015)	**Macroeconomics** (e.g., growth, trade, finance, inflation macroeconomic policies, monetary policies, income inequality, productivity)	American Economic Association	**From the journal's website:** *American Economic Journal: Macroeconomics* focuses on studies of aggregate fluctuations and growth, and the role of policy in that context. Such studies often borrow from and interact with research in other fields, such as monetary theory, industrial organization, finance, labor economics, political economy, public finance, international economics, and development economics. To the extent that they make a contribution to macroeconomics, papers in these fields are also welcome.
6	Review of International Political Economy	3.452 (2016)	**Broad range of issues in political economy** (e.g., comparative economics, international trade, finance, production, consumption, global governance, regulation)	Taylor & Francis Online	**From the journal's website:** The *Review of International Political Economy (RIPE)* has successfully established itself as a leading international journal dedicated to the systematic exploration of the international political economy from a plurality of perspectives. The journal encourages a global and interdisciplinary approach across issues and fields of inquiry. It seeks to act as a point of convergence for political economists, international relations scholars, geographers, and sociologists, and is committed to the publication of work that explores such issues as international trade and finance, production and consumption, and global governance and regulation,

in conjunction with issues of culture, identity, gender, and ecology. The journal eschews monolithic perspectives and seeks innovative work that is both pluralist in its orientation and engages with the broad literatures of IPE.

| 7 | Econometrica | 3.379 | **Broad range of issues in various areas of economics** (e.g., asset demand, trade, globalization, labor, wages, redistribution, inequality, monetary policy) | Wiley | *From the journal's website: Econometrica* publishes original articles in all branches of economics—theoretical and empirical, abstract and applied, providing wide-ranging coverage across the subject area. It promotes studies that aim at the unification of the theoretical-quantitative and the empirical-quantitative approach to economic problems and that are penetrated by constructive and rigorous thinking. We strongly encourage recent PhD graduates to submit their work to *Econometrica*. Our policy is to take into account the fact that recent graduates are less experienced in the process of writing and submitting papers. | This is one of the top journals in economics and it has a very low acceptance rate—around 8%. |

Continued

	Name	Impact Factor	Areas	Publisher	Details
8	Journal of Political Economy	3.923 (2016)	**Broad range of issues in political economy** (e.g., labor, trade, finance, monetary economics, comparative/reform economics, development and fiscal policies, wealth inequality)	University of Chicago Press	**From the journal's website:** One of the oldest and most prestigious journals in economics, the *Journal of Political Economy (JPE)* has since 1892 presented significant research and scholarship in economic theory and practice. The journal aims to publish highly selective, widely cited articles of current relevance that will have a long-term impact on economics research. JPE's analytical, interpretive, and empirical studies in a number of areas—including monetary theory, fiscal policy, labor economics, development, micro- and macroeconomic theory, international trade and finance, industrial organization, and social economics—are essential reading for all economists wishing to keep up with substantive new research in the discipline. This is one of the top journals in the field and it has a very low acceptance rate—around 5%.

9	Journal of Economic Literature*	3.01 (2015)	**Reviews of economic literature on a wide range of topics** (e.g., economic interdependence, social justice, housing, capitalism, immigration economics, economic theories, poverty)	American Economic Association	**From the journal's website:** The *Journal of Economic Literature (JEL)*, first published in 1969, is designed to help economists keep abreast of the vast flow of literature. JEL issues contain commissioned, peer-reviewed survey and review articles, book reviews, an annotated bibliography of new books classified by subject matter, and an annual index of dissertations in North American universities.
10	Economic Policy	2.844 (2016)	**All areas of economics focusing on policy debate** (e.g., exchange rate, fiscal policy, gender gap, health policy, trade, labor market, immigration policy, effect of sanctions, financial crises)	Oxford Academic	**From the journal's website:** *Economic Policy* provides timely and authoritative analyses of the choices confronting policymakers. The subject matter ranges from the study of how individual markets can and should work to the broadest interactions in the world economy. *Economic Policy* is at the forefront of economic policy debate. Since its inception, *Economic Policy* has published some of the most cited studies anywhere in the world—on financial crises, deregulation, unions, the euro, and other pressing international topics.

Continued

	Name	Impact Factor	Areas	Publisher	Details
11	Economic Journal	2.608	**Broad range of issues in economics and finance** (e.g., finance & banking, health care, welfare, infant mortality, labor, wages & income inequality, risk assessment, regulation, market structures)	Wiley	**From the journal's website:** The *Economic Journal* is the Royal Economic Society's flagship title and is one of the founding journals of modern economics. Over the past 125 years the journal has provided a platform for high quality and imaginative economic research, earning a worldwide reputation for excellence as a general journal publishing papers in all fields of economics for a broad international readership. It is invaluable to anyone with an active interest in economic issues and is a key source for professional economists in higher education, business, government and the financial sector who want to keep abreast of current thinking in economics.

| 12 | Journal of Public Policy | 1.778 (2016) | **Topics that cut across disciplines and political, economic, and social issues** (e.g., environmental issues, international political economy, regulatory policy and European Union processes, environment, government policies, financial crises, institutions) | Cambridge University Press | **From the journal's website:** The *Journal of Public Policy* applies social science theories and concepts to significant political, economic, and social issues and to the ways in which public policies are made. Its articles deal with topics of concern to public policy scholars in America, Europe, Japan, and other advanced industrial nations. The journal often publishes articles that cut across disciplines, such as environmental issues, international political economy, regulatory policy, and European Union processes. Its peer reviewers come from up to a dozen social science disciplines and countries across three continents, thus ensuring both analytic rigor and accuracy in reference to national and policy context. |
| 13 | New Political Economy | 1.667 (2016) | **Various topics in political economy across different disciplines** (e.g., economic competition, business interest groups, regional integration, global production networks, global financial crises, governance) | Taylor & Francis Online | **From the journal's website:** *New Political Economy* aims to create a forum for work which combines the breadth of vision which characterized the classical political economy of the 19th century with the analytical advances of 20th century social science. It seeks to represent the terrain of political economy scholarship across different disciplines, emphasizing original and innovative work which explores new approaches and methodologies, and addresses core debates and issues of historical and contemporary relevance. |

Continued

	Name	Impact Factor	Areas	Publisher	Details
14	American Economic Journal: Microeconomics*	1.32 (2015)	**Microeconomics** (e.g., industrial organization, international trade, political economy, and finance, procurement, elections, patents, auctions, firm level dynamics, risk management)	American Economic Association	**From the journal's website:** *American Economic Journal: Microeconomics* publishes papers focusing on microeconomic theory; industrial organization; and the microeconomic aspects of international trade, political economy, and finance. The journal publishes theoretical work as well as both empirical and experimental work with a theoretical framework.
15	Journal of Asian Economics*	1.30 (2015)	**All aspects of Asian economies** (e.g., exchange rate, FDI, trade policies, economic inequality, tax reforms, development of manufacturing, state-owned enterprises, productivity, foreign and domestic economic policy)	Elsevier	**From the journal's website:** The *Journal of Asian Economics* was founded in 1990 by the American Committee on Asian Economic Studies (ACAES) as a forum for research on all aspects of the economies of Asia. The Journal serves the ACAES mission to promote economic research on Asia and facilitate engagement between American and Asian economists. The editors invite submissions that illuminate the distinctive features of economies in

#	Journal		Topics	Publisher	Description
					Asia with respect to their institutional characteristics, their development paths, their policy experiences, or their international engagements. The focus on a geographical region lends itself to empirical analysis, though theoretical pieces will also be considered. Work that places Asian economies in comparative perspective is welcome.
16	International Studies Review	1.259 (2016)	**Diverse topics in economics, politics, and the law** (e.g., security studies, international regimes, trade and finance, comparative studies, development studies, international law)	Oxford Academic	**From the journal's website:** The *International Studies Review* (ISR) is a journal of the International Studies Association. It provides a window on current trends and research in international studies worldwide. Published four times a year, ISR is intended to help (a) scholars engage in the kind of dialogue and debate that will shape the field of international studies in the future; (b) graduate and undergraduate students understand major issues in international studies and identify promising opportunities for research; and (c) educators keep up with new ideas and research.

Continued

	Name	Impact Factor	Areas	Publisher	Details
17	Social Policy and Administration	1.239	**A wide range of issues in economics and sociology** (e.g., government, administration, social policy, welfare and governance, income redistribution, social insurance, unemployment)	Wiley	**From the journal's website:** *Social Policy & Administration* is the longest established journal in its field. Whilst remaining faithful to its tradition in academic excellence, the journal also seeks to engender debate about topical and controversial issues. Typical numbers contain papers clustered around a theme. The journal is international in scope. Quality contributions are received from scholars world-wide and cover social policy issues not only in Europe but also in the United States, Canada, Australia, and Asia Pacific.

| 18 | Development Policy Review | 0.7 | **Development issues** (e.g., agriculture, globalization, inequality and social exclusion, poverty-reduction strategies, property rights, industrial policy, aid effectiveness, governance) | Wiley | **From the journal's website:** *Development Policy Review* is a refereed journal that focuses on the links between research and policy in international development. The editors welcome original contributions on any aspect of development policy from all social science disciplines. Papers that are interdisciplinary and address contemporary policy questions are particularly welcome. We also consider proposals for special issues that explore a compelling theme from a range of institutional and/or geographical perspectives. All submissions should both draw on the relevant research literature and debates and be of broad policy relevance. While meeting the prevailing standards of disciplinary rigor, submissions must also be accessible in terms of their content, focus, and methodological approach. |

Continued

	Name	Impact Factor	Areas	Publisher	Details
19	International Finance	0.636	**Macroeconomics and finance** (e.g., corporate finance, exchange rates, financial markets, monetary policy and transition economies, banking, international labor, external debt, global inflation)	Wiley	**From the journal's website:** *International Finance* is a highly selective ISI-accredited journal featuring literate and policy-relevant analysis in macroeconomics and finance. The journal's readership extends well beyond academia into national treasuries and corporate treasuries, central banks and investment banks, and major international economic organizations.
20	Applied Economics	0.648 (2016)	**Broad range of issues in economics** (e.g., exchange rate, fiscal policy, globalization, growth, inflation, productivity, wages, foreign direct investment, economic policy, trade liberalization, labor, unemployment)	Taylor & Francis Online	**From the journal's website:** *Applied Economics* is a peer-reviewed journal encouraging the application of economic analysis to specific problems in both the public and private sectors. It particularly fosters quantitative and empirical studies, the results of which are of use in the practical field, and thus helps to bring economic theory nearer to reality. Contributions which make use of the methods of mathematics, statistics and operations research will be welcomed, provided the conclusions are factual and properly explained.

| 21 | Asian Survey | 0.323 | **Politics, economics, and foreign relations** (a broad spectrum of current Asia-related issues including diplomacy, disarmament, missile defense, military, modernization, ethnicity, ethnic violence, economic nationalism, general elections, global capitalism) | University of California Press | **From the journal's website:** The only academic journal of its kind produced in the United States, *Asian Survey* provides a comprehensive retrospective of contemporary international relations within South, Southeast, and East Asian nations. As the Asian community's matrix of activities becomes increasingly complex, it is essential to have a sourcebook for sound analysis of current events, governmental policies, socioeconomic development, and financial institutions. In *Asian Survey* you will find that sourcebook. *Asian Survey* consistently publishes articles by leading American and foreign scholars, whose views supplement and contest meanings disseminated by the media. |

Note. Information about the impact factor for the journals shown with an asterisk comes from Research Gate (researchgate.net); for all the other journals, the impact factor was taken from each journal's website. Information about acceptance rates comes from a study by Card and DellaVigna (2013); a version of this paper is available at http://voxeu.org/article/nine-facts-about-top-journals-economics

Corpus Details

The present book is based on a qualitative analysis of a large corpus of published and unpublished works representing various areas and sub-areas of economics and public policy. The corpus was constructed using three types of sources: academic journals, working papers, and student papers. The original number of papers examined for potential inclusion in the corpus exceeded 1000; however, many papers were excluded because they were too technical or not well-written. Below I briefly describe the procedures I followed.

The journals were chosen to represent a wide range of areas in economics and public policy, cover a relatively long time period, and be international in scope. A list of 62 journals was created, which included both disciplinary and interdisciplinary journals as well as those that publish a mix of academic and policy-related papers. Each journal was then examined for quality and scope and eight journals were excluded at this stage because they were deemed to be too technical, too broad in coverage, or too local in scope. The final corpus included 54 journals, from each of which I chose between two and eight articles.

The working papers included in the corpus came from GRIPS Discussion Papers, a series of papers on a wide range of policy-related issues published by the National Graduate Institute for Policy Studies (GRIPS). Papers in this series were chosen because they cover a wide range of policy-related international topics, are written by an international faculty, and are freely available on GRIPS' website; 46 working papers were included in this corpus.

The student papers included in the corpus are research proposals and research papers written by master's students at GRIPS who were enrolled in the following programs: Public Policy; Macroeconomic Policy; Asian Economic Policy; Public Finance; Transition Economy; and Economics, Planning and Policy. Thirty student papers were included in this corpus.

Three types of papers were included in the corpus: empirical quantitative papers (60%), empirical qualitative papers (30%), and nonempirical papers (10%) including argumentative papers, theoretical papers, and literature reviews. The papers were selected purposively according to the following criteria:

- Relevant to public policy

- Written on topics that are readily understandable

- Covering a wide range of areas in economics and public policy

- Representing a 30-year time period, with at least half of the papers written in the past 10 years

Additionally, I solicited high-quality papers from colleagues working in various areas of economics and public policy and obtained a total of 92 such papers. The final corpus included 443 papers.

JOURNALS INCLUDED IN THE CORPUS

1. Administration and Society
2. American Economic Journal: Macroeconomics
3. American Economic Review
4. American Journal of Sociology
5. American Political Science Review
6. American Review of Public Administration
7. Annual Review of Political Science
8. Applied Economics
9. Asian Survey
10. Contemporary Policy Issues
11. Development Policy Review
12. Econometrica
13. Economic Development and Cultural Change
14. Economic Inquiry
15. Economic Journal
16. Economic Policy
17. Economics Letters
18. European Economic Review
19. European Journal of International Relations
20. European Journal of Political Economy
21. Evaluation and Program Planning
22. International Finance
23. International Review of Economics and Finance
24. International Studies Review
25. Journal of Asian Economics
26. Journal of Corporate Finance
27. Journal of Development Economics
28. Journal of Economic Education
29. Journal of Economic Literature
30. Journal of Economic Perspectives
31. Journal of Finance
32. Journal of Higher Education
33. Journal of Human Resources
34. Journal of Political Economy
35. Journal of Public Administration Research and Theory
36. Journal of Public Economics
37. Journal of Public Policy
38. Local Government Studies
39. New Political Economy
40. Policy and Politics
41. Policy Studies Journal
42. Public Administration
43. Public Administration Review
44. Public Money and Management
45. Public Policy and Administration
46. Quarterly Journal of Economics
47. Review of Economic Studies
48. Review of Economics and Statistics
49. Review of International Political Economy
50. Social Policy and Administration
51. Social Problems
52. Sociology of Education
53. South Asia Economic Journal
54. Theory and Public Administration Review

References

I use three types of references in this book. References for academic writing and research are those to sources I cite throughout the book to show the origin of ideas, support my own claims, or suggest further reading. References to published studies are those to journal articles, working papers, and books from which I have taken examples to demonstrate my points. References to student papers are those to research proposals and research papers written by graduate students in various programs in public policy and economics at the National Graduate Institute for Policy Studies, where I teach.

REFERENCES FOR ACADEMIC WRITING AND RESEARCH

American Psychological Association, 2010. Publication manual of the American Psychological Association, sixth ed. American Psychological Association, Washington, DC.

Babbie, E., 1998. The Practice of Social Research, eighth ed. Wadsworth Publishing Company, Belmont, CA.

Backhouse, R., Dudley-Evans, T., Henderson, W., 1993. Exploring the language and rhetoric of economics. In: Henderson, W., Dudley-Evans, T., Backhouse, R. (Eds.), Economics and Language. Routledge, London, pp. 1–20.

Ballard, B., Clanchy, J., 1991. Assessment by misconception: cultural influences and intellectual traditions. In: Hamp-Lyons, L. (Ed.), Assessing Second Language Writing in Academic Contexts. Ablex Publishing Corporation, Norwood, NJ, pp. 19–35.

Bereiter, C., Scardamalia, M., 1987. The Psychology of Written Composition. Lawrence Erlbaum Associates, Hillsdale, NJ.

Card, D., DellaVigna, S., 2013. Nine facts about top journals in economics. J. Econ. Lit. 51 (1), 144–161.

Creswell, J.W., 2003. Research Design: Qualitative, Quantitative, and Mixed Methods Approaches, second ed. Sage Publications, Thousand Oaks, CA.

Creswell, J.W., 2014. Qualitative Inquiry and Research Design: Choosing Among Five Approaches, third ed. Sage Publications, Thousand Oaks, CA.

Denzin, N.K., Lincoln, Y.S. (Eds.), 2005. The SAGE Handbook of Qualitative Research. third ed. Sage Publications, Thousand Oaks, CA.

Diederich, P.B., 1974. Measuring Growth in English. NCTE, Urbana, IL.

Evans, G.R., 1997. Economic Models. (Chapter 1). Retrieved from, http://pages.hmc.edu/evans/chap1.pdf. Accessed 6 October 2017.

Feak, C.B., Swales, J.M., 2009. Telling a Research Story: Writing a Literature Review. The University of Michigan Press, Ann Arbor, MI.

Firestone, W.A., 1987. Meaning in method: the rhetoric of quantitative and qualitative research. Educ. Res. 16 (7), 16–21.

Firestone, W.A., Rossman, G.B., 1986. Exploring organizational approaches to dissemination and training. Knowl. Creat. Diffus. Util. 7 (3), 303–330.

Firestone, W.A., Wilson, B., 1986. Management and Organizational Outcomes: The Effects of Approach and Environment on Schools. Research for Better Schools, Philadelphia, PA.

Gilovich, T., 1991. How We Know What Isn't So: The Fallibility of Human Reason in Everyday Life. Free Press, New York, NY.

Greenlaw, S.A., 2009. Doing Economics: A Guide to Understanding and Carrying out Economic Research. South-Western Cengage Learning, Mason, OH.

Hyland, K., 1998. Hedging in Scientific Research Articles. John Benjamins Publishing Company, Amsterdam.

Hyland, K., 2004. Disciplinary Discourses: Social Interactions in Academic Writing. University of Michigan Press, Ann Arbor, MI.

Hyland, K., 2005. Metadiscourse. Continuum, London.

Hyland, H., 2008. Myth 4: make your academic writing assertive and certain. In: Reid, J. (Ed.), Writing Myths. The University of Michigan Press, Ann Arbor, MI, pp. 70–89.

Hyland, K., 2009. Academic Discourse: English in a Global Context. Continuum, London.

Hyland, K., Bondi, M. (Eds.), 2006. Academic Discourse Across Disciplines. Peter Lang, Bern.

Irvin, L.L., 2010. What is "academic" writing? In: Lowe, C., Zemliansky, P. (Eds.), Writing Spaces: Readings on Writing. In: vol. 1. Parlor Press, West Lafayette, IN, pp. 3–17.

Jacobsen, B., 2014. Some research and writing tips (Part 1: Research). Retrieved from, https://papers.ssrn.com/sol3/papers.cfm?abstract_id=2541366. Accessed 5 July 2017.

Johns, A.M., 1990. L1 composition theories: implications for developing theories of L2 composition. In: Kroll, B. (Ed.), Second Language Writing: Research Insights for the Classroom. Cambridge University Press, Cambridge, pp. 24–36.

Kahneman, D., 2011. Thinking, Fast and Slow. Farrar, Straus and Giroux, New York, NY.

Kraft, M.E., Furlong, S.R., 2015. Public Policy: Politics, Analysis, and Alternatives, fifth ed. Sage CQ Press, Thousand Oaks, CA.

Lim, T.C., 2006. Doing Comparative Politics: An Introduction to Approaches and Issues. Lynne Reinner Publishers, Boulder, CO.

McCloskey, D.N., 2000. Economical Writing, second ed. Waveland Press, Long Grove, IL.

Meloy, J.M., 2002. Writing the Qualitative Dissertation: Understanding by Doing, second ed. Psychology Press, New York, NY.

Merriam, S.B., 1998. Qualitative Research and Case Study Applications in Education, second ed. Jossey-Bass, San Francisco, CA.

Monroe, A.D., 2000. Essentials of Political Research. Westview Press, Boulder.

Morçöl, G., Ivanova, N.P., 2010. Methods taught in public policy programs: are quantitative methods still prevalent? J. Public Aff. Educ. 16 (2), 255–277.

Neugeboren, R., 2005. The Student's Guide to Writing Economics. Routledge, New York, NY.

Neuman, W.L., 2004. Basics of Social Research: Qualitative and Quantitative Approaches. Pearson Education Inc., Boston, MA.

Nilsen, P., 2015. Making sense of implementation theories, models and frameworks. Implement. Sci. 10 (53), 1–13.

Paltridge, B., 2001. Genre and the Language Learning Classroom. University of Michigan Press, Ann Arbor, MI.

Paltridge, B., 2004. Academic writing. Lang. Teach. 37 (2), 87–105.

Pfleiderer, P., 2014. Chameleons: The Misuse of Theoretical Models in Finance and Economics (Working Paper No. 3020). Stanford University, Stanford, CA. Retrieved from, https://www.gsb.stanford.edu/faculty-research/working-papers/chameleons-misuse-theoretical-models-finance-economics. Accessed 6 October 2017.

Piore, M.J., 1979. Qualitative research techniques in economics. Adm. Sci. Q. 24 (4), 560–569.

Piore, M.J., 2006. Qualitative research: does it fit in economics. Eur. Manag. Rev. 3, 17–23.

Putt, A.D., Springer, J.F., 1989. Policy Research: Concepts, Methods, and Applications. Prentice Hall, Englewood Cliffs, NJ.

Radin, B., 2000. Beyond Machiavelli: Policy Analysis Comes of Age. Georgetown University Press, Washington, DC.

Reid, J., 2001. Advanced EAP writing and curriculum design: what do we need to know? In: Silva, T., Matsuda, P.K. (Eds.), On Second Language Writing. Routledge, London, pp. 143–160.

Rudestam, K.E., Newton, R.R., 2001. Surviving your Dissertation: A Comprehensive Guide to Content and Process, second ed. Sage Publications, Thousand Oaks, CA.

Sandelowski, M., 1993. Theory unmasked: the uses and guises of theory in qualitative research. Res. Nurs. Health 16 (3), 213–218.

Shaw, P., 2006. Relations between text and mathematics across disciplines. In: Hyland, K., Bondi, M. (Eds.), Academic Discourse Across Disciplines. Peter Lang, Bern, pp. 103–122.

Shih, M., 1986. Content-based approaches to teaching academic writing. TESOL Q. 20 (4), 617–648.

Smith, J.K., 1983. Quantitative versus qualitative research: an attempt to clarify the issue. Educ. Res. 12 (3), 6–13.

Sonobe, T., Otsuka, K., 2014. Cluster-Based Industrial Development: KAIZEN Management for MSE Growth in Developing Countries. Palgrave Macmillan, Basingstoke, New York.

Stokey, E., Zeckhauser, R., 1978. A Primer for Policy Analysis. W.W. Norton & Company, New York, NY.

Swales, J.M., Feak, C.B., 2012. Academic Writing for Graduate Students: Essential Tasks and Skills, third ed. The University of Michigan Press, Ann Arbor, MI.

Tabachnick, B.G., Fidell, L.S., 2013. Using Multivariate Statistics, sixth ed. Pearson Education, Boston, MA.

The University of Chicago Press, 2003. The Chicago Manual of Style: The Essential Guide for Writers, Editors, and Publishers, 15th ed. The University of Chicago Press, Chicago, IL.

Thomson, W., 2011. A Guide for the Young Economist, second ed. The MIT Press, Cambridge, MA.

PUBLISHED STUDIES

Abowd, J.M., Corbel, P., Kramarz, F., 1999. The entry and exit of workers and the growth of employment: an analysis of French establishments. Rev. Econ. Stat. 81 (2), 170–187.

Adger, W.N., 2010. Climate change, human well-being and insecurity. New Polit. Econ. 15 (2), 275–292.

Akerlof, G.A., 1970. The market for "lemons": quality uncertainty and the market mechanism. Q. J. Econ. 84 (3), 488–500.

Allgood, S., Walstad, W.B., Siegfried, J.J., 2015. Research on teaching economics to undergraduates. J. Econ. Lit. 53 (2), 285–325.

Altmann, S., Traxler, C., 2014. Nudges at the dentist. Eur. Econ. Rev. 72, 19–38.

Amiti, M., Konings, J., 2007. Trade liberalization, intermediate inputs, and productivity: evidence from Indonesia. Am. Econ. Rev. 97 (5), 1611–1638.

Araujo, M.C., Carneiro, P., Cruz-Aguayo, Y., Schady, N., 2016. Teacher quality and learning outcomes in kindergarten. Q. J. Econ. 131 (3), 1415–1453.

Arroyo, D., 2008. The Political Economy of Successful Reform: Asian Stratagems (Working Paper No. 356). Stanford Center for International Development, Stanford, CA. Retrieved from, http://globalpoverty.stanford.edu/sites/default/files/publications/356wp.pdf. Accessed 25 May 2017.

Arts, W., Hermkens, P., Van Wijck, P., 1999. Modernisation theory, income evaluation, and the transition in Eastern Europe. Int. J. Comp. Sociol. 40 (1), 61–78.

Arum, R., LaFree, G., 2008. Educational attainment, teacher-student ratios, and the risk of adult incarceration among U.S. birth cohorts since 1910. Sociol. Educ. 81 (4), 397–421.

Atkin, D., 2016. The caloric costs of culture: evidence from Indian migrants. Am. Econ. Rev. 106 (4), 1144–1181.

Baade, R.A., Matheson, V.A., 2016. Going for the gold: the economics of the Olympics. J. Econ. Perspect. 30 (2), 201–218.

Babb, S., 2012. The Washington consensus as transnational policy paradigm: its origins, trajectory and likely successor. Rev. Int. Polit. Econ. 20 (2), 268–297.

Baccini, L., Dür, A., Elsig, M., 2015. The politics of trade agreement design: revisiting the depth–flexibility nexus. Int. Stud. Q. 59 (4), 765–775.

Baker, S.R., Bloom, N., Davis, S.J., 2016. Measuring economic policy uncertainty. Q. J. Econ. 131 (4), 1593–1636.

Beam, E.A., 2016. Do job fairs matter? Experimental evidence on the impact of job-fair attendance. J. Dev. Econ. 120, 32–40.

Beath, A., Christia, F., Egorov, G., Enikolopov, R., 2016. Electoral rules and political selection: theory and evidence from a field experiment in Afghanistan. Rev. Econ. Stud. 83 (3), 932–968.

Bertoli, S., Ticci, E., 2012. A fragile guideline to development assistance. Dev. Policy Rev. 30 (2), 211–230.

Bharadwaj, P., Loken, K.V., Neilson, C., 2013. Early life health interventions and academic achievement. Am. Econ. Rev. 103 (5), 1862–1891.

Bharadwaj, P., Giorgi, G., Hansen, D., Neilson, C.A., 2016. The gender gap in mathematics: evidence from Chile. Econ. Dev. Cult. Chang. 65 (1), 141–166.

Blattman, C., Jamison, J., Koroknay-Palicz, T., Rodrigues, K., Sheridan, M., 2016. Measuring the measurement error: a method to qualitatively validate survey data. J. Dev. Econ. 120, 99–112.

Bloom, H.S., 1987. Lessons from the Delaware dislocated worker pilot program. Eval. Rev. 11 (2), 157–177.

Bogan, V.L., Turvey, C.G., Salazar, G., 2015. The elasticity of demand for microcredit: evidence from Latin America. Dev. Policy Rev. 33 (6), 725–757.

Bognanno, M.L., 2001. Corporate tournaments. J. Labor Econ. 19 (2), 290–315.

Bonsang, E., 2007. How do middle-aged children allocate time and money transfers to their older parents in Europe? Empirica 34 (2), 171–188.

Booij, A., Leuven, E., Oosterbeek, H., 2017. Ability peer effects in university: evidence from a randomized experiment. Rev. Econ. Stud. 84, 547–578.

Borge, L., Parmer, P., Torvik, R., 2015. Local natural resource curse? J. Public Econ. 131, 101–114.

Borjas, G.J., Doran, K.B., Shen, Y., 2018. Ethnic complementarities after the opening of China: how Chinese graduate students affected the productivity of their advisors. J. Hum. Resour. 53, 1–31.

Boyne, G.A., 2004. Explaining public service performance: does management matter? Public Policy Admin. 19 (4), 100–117.

Brinton, M.C., Lee, Y., Parish, W.L., 1995. Married women's employment in rapidly industrializing societies: examples from East Asia. Am. J. Sociol. 100 (5), 1099–1130.

Broz, J.L., Frieden, J.A., 2001. The political economy of international monetary relations. Annu. Rev. Polit. Sci. 4, 317–343.

Byun, K., Kim, M., 2011. Shifting patterns of the government's policies for the internationalization of Korean higher education. J. Stud. Int. Educ. 15 (5), 467–486.

Cardenas, J., 2003. Real wealth and experimental cooperation: experiments in the field lab. J. Dev. Econ. 70, 263–289.

Cardoso, E., 1993. Private investment in Latin America. Econ. Dev. Cult. Chang. 41 (4), 833–848.

Charles, K.K., Hurst, E., 2003. The correlation of wealth across generations. J. Polit. Econ. 111 (6), 1155–1182.

Chen, P., Chien, M., Lee, C., 2011. Dynamic modeling of regional house price diffusion in Taiwan. J. Hous. Econ. 20, 315–332.

Chen, J., Leung, W.S., Evans, K.P., 2016. Are employee-friendly workplaces conducive to innovation? J. Corp. Finan. 40, 61–79.

Coffman, K.B., 2014. Evidence on self-stereotyping and the contribution of ideas. Q. J. Econ. 129 (4), 1625–1660.

Cohen, W.M., Levinthal, D.A., 1989. Innovation and learning: the two faces of R&D. Econ. J. 99 (397), 569–596.

Cohen, N., Mizrahi, S., Yuval, F., 2012. Black-market medicine and public opinion towards the welfare state: evidence from Israel. Soc. Policy Adm. 46 (7), 727–747.

Conner, T.W., Rabovsky, T.M., 2011. Accountability, affordability, access: a review of the recent trends in higher education policy research. Policy Stud. J. 39 (S1), 93–112.

Cuyvers, L., Soeng, R., Plasmans, J., Van Den Bulcke, D., 2011. Determinants of foreign direct investment in Cambodia. J. Asian Econ. 22 (3), 222–234.

D'Ippoliti, C., Roncaglia, A., 2015, January 4. In: Heterodox economics and the history of economic thought.Paper Presented at the Allied Social Science Associations Program in Boston, Massachusetts, United States of America.

D'Addio, A.C., Eriksson, T., Frijters, P., 2007. An analysis of the determinants of job satisfaction when individuals' baseline satisfaction levels may differ. Appl. Econ. 39 (19), 2413–2423.

De Bonis, R., Stacchini, M., 2013. Does government debt affect bank credit? Int. Finance 16 (3), 289–310.

de Coulon, A., Wolff, F., 2010. Location intentions of immigrants at retirement: stay/return or go 'back and forth'? Appl. Econ. 42 (26), 3319–3333.

de Grauwe, P., 2002. Challenges for monetary policy in Euroland. J. Common Mark. Stud. 40 (4), 693–718.

Dixon, J., 2009. What causes civil wars? Integrating quantitative research findings. Int. Stud. Rev. 11, 707–735.

Dorey, E., Roberts, V., Maddison, R., Meagher-Lundberg, P., Dixon, R., Mhurchu, C.N., 2009. Children and television watching: a qualitative study of New Zealand parents' perceptions and views. Child: Care Health Dev. 36 (3), 414–420.

Doroodian, K., 1993. Macroeconomic performance and adjustment under policies commonly supported by the International Monetary Fund. Econ. Dev. Cult. Chang. 41 (4), 849–864.

Draper, P., 2010. Rethinking the (European) Foundations of Sub-Saharan African Regional Economic Integration: A Political Economy Essay. OECD Working Paper No. 293.

Dreher, A., Fischer, J.A.V., 2011. Does government decentralization reduce domestic terror? An empirical test. Econ. Lett. 111 (3), 223–225.

Dube, A., Kaplan, E., Naidu, S., 2011. Coups, corporations, and classified information. Q. J. Econ. 126 (3), 1375–1409.

Duflo, E., 2012. Women empowerment and economic development. J. Econ. Lit. 50 (4), 1051–1079.

Enamorado, T., López-Calva, L.F., Rodríguez-Castelán, C., Winkler, H., 2016. Income inequality and violent crime: evidence from Mexico's drug war. J. Dev. Econ. 120, 128–143.

Engström, P., Hagen, J., 2017. Income underreporting among the self-employed: a permanent income approach. Eur. Econ. Rev. 92, 92–109.

Fafchamps, M., 2000. Ethnicity and credit in African manufacturing. J. Dev. Econ. 61 (1), 205–235.

Fama, E.F., French, K.R., 2008. Dissecting anomalies. J. Financ. 63 (4), 1653–1678.

Feldman, M., Hadjimichael, T., Lanahan, L., Kemeny, T., 2016. The logic of economic development: a definition and model for investment. Environ. Plan. C: Gov. Policy 34 (1), 5–21.

Ferguson, N., Schularick, M., 2007. 'Chimerica' and the global asset market boom. Int. Finance 10 (3), 215–239.

Fey, C.F., Denison, D.R., 2003. Organizational culture and effectiveness: can American theory be applied in Russia? Org. Sci. 14 (6), 686–706.

Fischer, P.J., Breakey, W.R., 1991. The epidemiology of alcohol, drug, and mental disorders among homeless persons. Am. Psychol. 46 (11), 1115–1128.

Fourcade, M., Ollion, E., Algan, Y., 2015. The superiority of economists. J. Econ. Perspect. 29 (1), 89–114.

Franzoni, J.M., Sánchez-Ancochea, D., 2014. The double challenge of market and social incorporation: progress and bottlenecks in Latin America. Dev. Policy Rev. 32 (3), 275–298.

Freese, J., 2009. Secondary analysis of large social surveys. In: Hargittai, E. (Ed.), Research Confidential: Solutions to Problems Most Social Scientists Pretend They Never Have. The University of Michigan Press, Ann Arbor, MI, pp. 238–261.

Friedman, H., 1988. Money and the stock market. J. Polit. Econ. 96 (2), 221–245.

Frydman, R., Gray, C., Hessel, M., Rapaczynski, A., 1999. When does privatization work? The impact of private ownership on corporate performance in the transition economies. Q. J. Econ. 114 (4), 1153–1191.

Gaddah, M., Munro, A., 2011. The Rich or the Poor: Who Gains From Public Education Spending in Ghana? (GRIPS Discussion Paper 11–12). National Graduate Institute for Policy Studies, Tokyo. Retrieved from, http://www.grips.ac.jp/r-center/wp-content/uploads/11-12.pdf. Accessed 30 June 2017.

Gelber, A., Isen, A., Kessler, J.B., 2015. The Effects of Youth Employment: Evidence From New York City Summer Youth Employment Program Lotteries (IRLE Working Paper 101-15). February. Institute for Research on Labor Development, California. Retrieved from, http://www.irle.berkeley.edu/files/2015/The-Effects-of-Youth-Employment.pdf. Accessed 25 May 2017.

Ghosh, A., 2017. How does banking sector globalization affect economic growth? Int. Rev. Econ. Financ. 48, 83–97.

Glover, D., Pallais, A., Pariente, W., 2017. Discrimination as a self-fulfilling prophecy: evidence from French grocery stores. Q. J. Econ. 132 (3), 1219–1260.

Goldstein, M., Lardy, N., 2006. China's exchange rate policy dilemma. Asian Curr. Matt. 96 (2), 422–426.

Griebeler, M.C., 2017. Friendship and in-class academic dishonesty. Econ. Lett. 150, 1–3.

Hafer, R.W., 2017. New estimates on the relationship between IQ, economic growth and welfare. Intelligence 61, 92–101.

Hamstead, M.P., Quinn, M.S., 2005. Sustainable community development and ecological economics: theoretical convergence and practical implications. Local Environ. Int. J. Justice Sustain. 10 (2), 141–158.

Hijzen, A., Martins, P.S., Schank, T., Upward, R., 2013. Foreign-owned firms around the world: a comparative analysis of wages and employment at the micro-level. Eur. Econ. Rev. 60, 170–188.

Horowitz, S., 2004. Reversing globalization: trade policy consequences of World War I. Eur. J. Int. Relat. 10 (1), 33–59.

Hossler, D., Vesper, N., 1993. An exploratory study of the factors associated with parental saving for postsecondary education. J. Higher Educ. 64 (2), 140–165.

Hryckiewicz, A., Kowalewski, O., 2011. Why do foreign banks withdraw from other countries? Int. Finance 14 (1), 67–102.

Hsu, J.W., 2016. Aging and strategic learning: the impact of spousal incentives on financial literacy. J. Hum. Resour. 51 (4), 1036–1067.

Irvine, A., 2011. Fit for work? The influence of sick pay and job flexibility on sickness absence and implications for presenteeism. Soc. Policy Adm. 45 (7), 752–769.

Iyer, S., 2016. The new economics of religion. J. Econ. Lit. 54 (2), 395–441.

Izuhara, M., Forrest, R., 2013. 'Active families': familization, housing and welfare across generations in East Asia. Soc. Policy Adm. 47 (5), 520–541.

Kalil, A., Mogstad, M., Rege, M., Votruba, M.E., 2016. Father presence and the intergenerational transmission of educational attainment. J. Hum. Resour. 51 (4), 869–899.

Kanemoto, Y., 2012. Cost-Benefit Analysis in Monopolistic Competition Models of Urban Agglomeration (GRIPS Discussion Paper 12-04). National Graduate Institute for Policy Studies, Tokyo. Retrieved from, http://www.grips.ac.jp/r-center/wp-content/uploads/12-04.pdf. Accessed 30 June 2017.

Kangasniemi, M., Kauhanen, A., 2013. Performance-related pay and gender wage differences. Appl. Econ. 45 (36), 5131–5143.

Kentor, J., 2001. The long term effects of globalization on income inequality, population growth, and economic development. Soc. Probl. 48 (4), 435–455.

Kikkawa, A., Otsuka, K., 2016. The Changing Landscape of International Migration: Evidence From Rural Households in Bangladesh, 2000–2014 (GRIPS Discussion Paper 16–13). National Graduate Institute for Policy Studies, Tokyo. Retrieved from, https://grips.repo.nii.ac.jp/?action=repository_action_common_download&item_id=1513&item_no=1&attribute_id=20&file_no=1. Accessed 30 June 2017.

Knell, M., Stix, H., 2006. Three decades of money demand studies: differences and similarities. Appl. Econ. 38, 805–818.

Kooy, M., Wild, L., Mason, N., 2015. Doing things differently: can water supply, sanitation, and hygiene services support peace- and state-building processes? Dev. Policy Rev. 33 (4), 433–456.

Kurul, Z., 2017. Nonlinear relationship between institutional factors and FDI flows: dynamic panel threshold analysis. Int. Rev. Econ. Financ. 48, 148–160.

Lago-Peñas, I., Lago-Peñas, S., 2010. The determinants of tax morale in comparative perspective: evidence from European countries. Eur. J. Polit. Econ. 26 (4), 441–453.

Lake, D.A., 1993. Leadership, hegemony, and the international economy: naked emperor or tattered monarch with potential? Int. Stud. Q. 37, 459–489.

Lee, J.J., 2016. Will China's rise be peaceful? A social psychological perspective. Asian Secur. 12 (1), 29–52.

Liberati, P., 2007. Trade openness, capital openness and government size. J. Public Policy 27 (2), 215–247.

Lloyd-Sherlock, P., 2010. Stroke in developing countries: epidemiology, impact and policy implications. Dev. Policy Rev. 28 (6), 693–709.

Mano, Y., Yamano, T., Suzuki, A., Matsumoto, T., 2010. Local and Personal Networks in Employment and the Development of Labor Markets: Evidence From the Cut Flower Industry in Ethiopia (GRIPS Discussion Paper 10-29). National Graduate Institute for Policy Studies, Tokyo. Retrieved from, www.grips.ac.jp/r-center/wp-content/uploads/10-29.pdf. Accessed 30 June 2017.

Manski, C.F., 2011. Genes, eyeglasses, and social policy. J. Econ. Perspect. 25 (4), 83–94.

Matsumoto, T., Yamano, T., 2010. The Impacts of Fertilizer Credit on Crop Production and Income in Ethiopia (GRIPS Discussion Paper 10-23). National Graduate Institute for Policy Studies, Tokyo. Retrieved from, http://www.grips.ac.jp/r-center/wp-content/uploads/10-23.pdf. Accessed 30 June 2017.

McDevitt, R.C., 2014. "A" business by any other name: firm name choice as a signal of firm quality. J. Polit. Econ. 122 (4), 909–944.

McKenzie, R.B., 1971. An exploratory study of the economic understanding of elementary school teachers. J. Econ. Educ. 3 (1), 26–31.

Meng, C., Gonzalez, R.L., 2016. Credit Booms in Developing Countries: Are They Different From Those in Advanced and Emerging Market Countries? (GRIPS Discussion Paper 15-22). National Graduate Institute for Policy Studies, Tokyo. Retrieved from, https://grips.repo.nii.ac.jp/?action=repository_uri&item_id=1332&file. Accessed 30 June 2017.

Minford, P., 2008. Why the United Kingdom should not join the Eurozone. Int. Finance 11 (3), 283–295.

Munro, A., Tanaka, Y., 2014. Risky Rotten Kids: An Experiment on Risk Attitudes Amongst Adolescents in Rural Uganda (GRIPS Discussion Paper 14-01). National Graduate Institute for Policy Studies, Tokyo. Retrieved from, http://www.grips.ac.jp/r-center/wp-content/uploads/14-01.pdf. Accessed 30 June 2017.

Nakajima, K., Okamoto, R., 2014. Measuring the Sorting Effect of Migration on Spatial Wage Disparities (GRIPS Discussion Paper 14-19). National Graduate Institute for Policy Studies, Tokyo. Retrieved from, http://www.grips.ac.jp/r-center/wp-content/uploads/14-19.pdf. Accessed 30 June 2017.

Nakajima, R., Tanaka, R., 2012. Estimating the Effects of Pronatal Policies on Residential Choice and Fertility (GRIPS Discussion Paper 12-06). National Graduate Institute for Policy Studies, Tokyo. Retrieved from, http://www.grips.ac.jp/r-center/wp-content/uploads/12-06.pdf. Accessed 30 June 2017.

Narayan, S., Narayan, P.K., Mishra, S., 2010. Investigating the relationship between health and economic growth: Empirical evidence from a panel of 5 Asian countries. J. Asian Econ. 21 (4), 404–411.

Nicoletti, G., Oliveira-Martins, J., 1993. Global effects of the European carbon tax. In: Carraro, C., Siniscalco, D. (Eds.), The European Carbon Tax: An Economic Assessment. Springer, Dordrecht, pp. 15–48.

Niels, G., Kate, A., 2006. Antidumping policy in developing countries: safety valve or obstacle to free trade? Eur. J. Polit. Econ. 22 (3), 618–638.

Nishimura, M., Yamano, T., 2008. School Choice Between Public and Private Primary Schools Under the Free Primary Education Policy in Rural Kenya (GRIPS Discussion Paper 08-02). National Graduate Institute for Policy Studies, Tokyo. Retrieved from, www.grips.ac.jp/r-center/wp-content/uploads/08-02.pdf. Accessed 5 July 2017.

Pfau, W.D., 2008. Emerging Market Pension Funds and International Diversification (GRIPS Discussion Paper 08-10). National Graduate Institute for Policy Studies, Tokyo. Retrieved from, www.grips.ac.jp/r-center/wp-content/uploads/08-10.pdf. Accessed 5 July 2017.

Pfau, W.D., Long, G.H., 2008. Gender and Remittance Flows in Vietnam During Economic Transformation (GRIPS Discussion Paper 08-06). National Graduate Institute for Policy Studies, Tokyo. Retrieved from, www.grips.ac.jp/r-center/wp-content/uploads/08-06-new.pdf. Accessed 5 July 2017.

Pudney, S., 2010. Drugs policy: what should we do about cannabis? Econ. Policy 25 (61), 165–211.

Rand, J., Tarp, F., 2012. Firm-level corruption in Vietnam. Econ. Dev. Cult. Chang. 60 (3), 571–595.

Reyes, J.W., 2015. Lead exposure and behavior: effects on antisocial and risky behavior among children and adolescents. Econ. Inq. 53 (3), 1580–1605.

Roberts, A., 2009. The politics of healthcare reform in postcommunist Europe: the importance of access. J. Public Policy 29 (3), 305–325.

Rodgers, H.R., Payne, L., 2007. Child poverty in the American states: the impact of welfare reform, economics, and demographics. Policy Stud. J. 35 (1), 1–21.

Rossi, P.H., Wright, J.D., Fisher, G.A., Willis, G., 1987. The urban homeless: estimating composition and size. Science 235, 1336–1341.

Roubini, N., 2007. Why China should abandon its dollar peg. Int. Finance 10 (1), 71–89.

Schmitz, H., Tuan, D.A., Hang, P.T.T., McCulloch, N., 2012. Who Drives Economic Reform in Vietnam's Provinces? (Research Report No. 76). Institute of Development Studies, Brighton, United Kingdom. Retrieved from, http://www.ids.ac.uk/files/dmfile/Rr76.pdf. Accessed 3 March 2017.

Schmitz, H., Tuan, D.A., Hang, P.T.T., McCulloch, N., 2015. Drivers of economic reform in Vietnam's provinces. Dev. Policy Rev. 33 (2), 175–193.

Shepherd, A., 2011. Tackling Chronic Poverty: The Policy Implications of Research on Chronic Poverty and Poverty Dynamics. Chronic Poverty Research Centre, Manchester. Retrieved from, http://www.chronicpoverty.org/uploads/publication_files/Tackling%20chronic%20poverty%20webcopy.pdf. Accessed 17 March 2017.

Siegfried, J.J., Round, D.K., 2001. International trends in economics degrees during the 1990s. J. Econ. Educ. 32 (3), 203–218.

Sigall, H., Ostrove, N., 1975. Beautiful but dangerous: effects of offender attractiveness and nature of the crime on juridic judgement. J. Pers. Soc. Psychol. 31 (3), 410–414.

Simmons, B.A., Elkins, Z., 2004. The globalization of liberalization: policy diffusion in the international political economy. Am. Polit. Sci. Rev. 98 (1), 171–189.

Sonobe, T., Otsuka, K., 2014. Cluster-Based Industrial Development: KAIZEN Management for MSE Growth in Developing Countries. Palgrave Macmillan, Basingstoke and New York.

Sudsawasd, S., 2010. An empirical assessment of the relationship between competition policy and investment. J. Asian Econ. 21 (5), 466–475.

Susanthi Medha Kumari, S.M., 2014. Determinants of interest margins of banks in Sri Lanka. South Asia Econ. J. 15 (2), 265–280.

Suzuki, A., Nam, V.H., Sonobe, T., 2013. Willingness to Pay for Managerial Training: A Case From the Knitwear Industry in Northern Vietnam (GRIPS Discussion Paper 13-08). National Graduate Institute for Policy Studies, Tokyo. Retrieved from, www.grips.ac.jp/r-center/wp-content/uploads/13-08.pdf. Accessed 5 July 2017.

Swinnen, J., 2011. The right price of food. Dev. Policy Rev. 29 (6), 667–688.

Tanaka, T., Hosoe, N., 2011. What Drove the Crop Price Hikes in the Food Crisis? (GRIPS Discussion Paper 11-16). National Graduate Institute for Policy Studies, Tokyo. Retrieved from, www.grips.ac.jp/r-center/wp-content/uploads/11-16.pdf. Accessed 30 June 2017.

Tepe, M., Vanhuysse, P., 2009. Are aging OECD welfare states on the path to gerontocracy? Evidence from 18 democracies, 1980–2002. J. Public Policy 29 (1), 1–28.

The Economist, 2017. Mediocre academic researchers should be wary of globalization. The Economist. Retrieved from, http://www.economist.com/news/science-and-technology/21715639-effects-foreign-competition-professors-mathematics-mediocre-academic. Accessed 16 March 2017.

Thompson, S.J., Pollio, D.E., Eyrich, K., Bradbury, E., North, C.S., 2004. Successfully exiting homelessness: experiences of formerly homeless mentally ill individuals. Eval. Program Plan. 27, 423–431.

Thorbecke, W., 2015. China-US trade: a global outlier. J. Asian Econ. 40, 47–58.

Tsui, L., 1998. The effects of gender, education, and personal skills self-confidence on income in business management. Sex Roles 38, 363–373.

Vandewater, E.A., Park, S., Huang, X., Wartella, E.A., 2005. "No, you can't watch that": parental rules and young children's media use. Am. Behav. Sci. 48 (5), 608–623.

Vedia-Jerez, D.H., Chasco, C., 2016. Long-run determinants of economic growth in South America. J. Appl. Econ. 19 (1), 169–192.

Voith, R., 1991. The long-run elasticity of demand for commuter rail transportation. J. Urban Econ. 30 (3), 360–372.

Waldron, S., Brown, C., Komarek, A.M., 2014. The Chinese cashmere industry: a global value chain analysis. Dev. Policy Rev. 32 (5), 589–610.

Winston, C., 1993. Economic deregulation: days of reckoning for microeconomists. J. Econ. Lit. 31 (3), 1263–1289.

Xing, Y., 2016. Rising Wages, Yuan Appreciation and China's Processing Exports (GRIPS Discussion Paper 16-01). National Graduate Institute for Policy Studies, Tokyo. Retrieved from, https://dx.doi.org/10.24545/00001355 (30 June 2017).

Yamano, T., Arai, A., 2010a. Fertilizer Policies, Price, and Application in East Africa (GRIPS Discussion Paper 10-24). National Graduate Institute for Policy Studies, Tokyo. Retrieved from, www.grips.ac.jp/r-center/wp-content/uploads/10-24.pdf. Accessed 30 June 2017.

Yamano, T., Arai, A., 2010b. The Maize Farm-Market Price Spread in Kenya and Uganda (GRIPS Discussion Paper 10-25). National Graduate Institute for Policy Studies, Tokyo. Retrieved from, www.grips.ac.jp/r-center/wp-content/uploads/10-25.pdf. Accessed 30 June 2017.

Yamano, T., Kijima, Y., 2010. Market Access, Soil Fertility, and Income in East Africa (GRIPS Discussion Paper 10-22). National Graduate Institute for Policy Studies, Tokyo. Retrieved from, www.grips.ac.jp/r-center/wp-content/uploads/10-22.pdf. Accessed 30 June 2017.

Young, D.R., 1999. Complimentary, supplementary, or adversarial? A theoretical and historical examination of nonprofit-government relations in the United Sates. In: Boris, E.T., Steuerle, C.E. (Eds.), Nonprofits & Government: Collaboration and Conflict. Urban Institute Press, Washington, DC, pp. 31–67.

Zhang, J., 2017. The evolution of China's one-child policy and its effects on family outcomes. J. Econ. Perspect. 31 (1), 141–160.

Zlotnick, C., Robertson, M.J., Lahiff, M., 1999. Getting off the streets: economic resources and residential exits from homelessness. J. Community Psychol. 27 (2), 209–224.

STUDENT PAPERS

Ahamadzie, P., 2016. The impact of the single window facility on customs revenue in Africa.

An, R., 2006. The convergence study of the Chinese economy.

Arreaga, R.R.V., 2015. What is the effect of tax rates on tax evasion in Ecuador?

Artami, R.J., 2017. The asymmetric effects of oil price changes on the economic activities in Indonesia.

Bultitude, S., 2006. A tale of two bubbles: Lessons from Japan's bubble economy and Australia's housing boom.

Butler, L., 2008. Finding a compromise: law, diplomacy, and whaling in the Southern Ocean.

Gakuya, W., 2015. The impact of intellectual property rights on economic growth of developing countries in the post-TRIPS era: the case of Sub-Saharan Africa.

Hu, Z., 2010. Intellectual property rights and economic growth: An empirical study of developing countries.

Ibrahim, M., 2014. An empirical study of the impact of customs corruption on the efficiency of customs.

Irianti, E.F., 2014. The impact of fiscal decentralization on human development.

Li, X., 2017. A tug of war: the rationale behind Japan's engagement in UN peace operations.

Majoni, B., 2015. Test of Okun's Law for 10 southern African countries.

Maparara, I.T., 2016. Government expenditure and economic growth: a case of SADC countries.

Montgomery, J., 2017. Foreign versus domestic education: does place of education matter for Australian immigrants?

Mshindo, F.D., 2017. The nexus between electronic filing and VAT collection in Africa.

Otoo, N.M., 2013. Intellectual property rights protection and foreign direct investment in Sub-Saharan Africa (SSA) countries.

Pandeya, G., 2014. Citizen participation in local government: does participation contribute to improve its performance? The case of Nepal.

Pandeya, G., 2015. Does citizen participation improve local planning? An empirical analysis of stakeholders' perceptions in Nepal.

Rahmahapianti, D., 2014. The effect of basic infrastructure development on poverty reduction in Indonesia.

Rashfa, M., 2012. Determinants of inflation in the Maldives: an empirical analysis of the short-run dynamics.

Roque, A.L., 2006. Increasing deposit insurance: Increasing bank moral hazard?

Soberanis, T.I., 2015. The effects of tariff rates on skill intensity.

Sue, L.S., 2011. The impact of trade liberalization on economic growth in Fiji.

Susanthi Medha Kumari, S.M., 2010. Determinants of interest margins of banks in Sri Lanka.

Takeda, T., 2012. Estimating holding costs of foreign currency reserves for advanced economies—taking Japan as an example.

Yuniarti, I., 2012. The motives for conversion to organic farming: the case of organic rice farmers in Yogyakarta, Indonesia.

Zhang, J., 2010. Fiscal decentralization and regional economic growth in China.

Zuhuree, I., 2014. Impact of foreign aid on economic growth in small island developing states: relevance of economic policy and aid uncertainty.

Index

Note: Page numbers followed by *f* indicate figures, *t* indicate tables, and *b* indicate boxes.

Printed in the United States
By Bookmasters